LINDLEY J. STILES

Professor of Education for Interdisciplinary Studies

Northwestern University

ADVISORY EDITOR TO DODD, MEAD & COMPANY

INTRODUCTION TO
MEASUREMENT AND EVALUATION

INTRODUCTION TO MEASUREMENT AND EVALUATION

John A. Green

Dean of Education
Central Washington State College

DODD, MEAD & COMPANY

New York   1970

To Tay

Editor's Introduction

Pressures for educational progress place a high priority on measurement and evaluation of student learning and educational procedures. Whether the emphasis is on expanding the numerical involvement of students, extending the reach of educational services by earlier beginnings with children or continuing contacts with adults, designing programs for the culturally disadvantaged, or pressing for pinnacles of quality for highly talented students, the need is to know what is being accomplished. The concern is one of widespread interest—among laymen as well as with teachers, supervisors, administrators, educational officers at state and national levels as well as with specialists in measurement and evaluation.

Interests in assessment of learning-gains assume pluralistic dimensions. Parents and teachers want accurate knowledge about the progress of individual students in comparison to classmates and to age groups generally. Communities desire information concerning the quality of their schools, their strengths and weaknesses, in the context of state and national standards. Continuing questioning relates to the relevance of educational directions and emphases to life in an increasingly complex scientific and technological society that is inescapably related to human concerns on a world-wide front. Added queries probe to know how efficient educational institutions are—in the conservation and extension of intellectual resources as well as with respect to cost-productivity matters. In a broader sense, everyone is interested in the comparative success of the system of schooling in the United States with other national programs of education. Whatever the approach, the focus is on measurement and evaluation as a process of producing evidence by which educational effectiveness may be judged.

A frequent weakness in schools and in teacher education programs has, perhaps, been too little emphasis on measurement and evaluation. The tendency has been to concentrate on promoting learning with results more or less taken for granted. Competent teachers, of course, as well as able supervisors and administrators have tried to learn how to measure outcomes. They have had little help, however, from pre- or in-service training programs or from the literature in the field. Schools of Education have shied away from emphases on measurement and evaluation in courses designed for educational practitioners. Such work has been reserved as preparation for specialists, most of whom have gone into research assignments. As a consequence, books in the field have tended to be highly technical, beyond the grasp and outside of the professional concerns of teachers, supervisors and administrators who deal with the practical day-to-day problems of learning and educational improvement. The result has been a cycle of neglect that now begs to be broken.

A first step in bringing knowledge about measurement and evaluation to those who need and can use it most is the production of resource material of general interest and utility. Such is the key contribution of this book.

Introduction to Measurement and Evaluation deals with the real and practical problems of assessing educational progress. It aims to help the prospective teacher as well as teachers, supervisors and administrators in service to advance their knowledge and techniques for determining and judging the amount and quality of learning as well as the impact of educational programs. Its objective is to take measurement and evaluation out of the realms of the theoretical and restrictive specialization and make it the province of all members of the education profession.

Readers of this book will find it a refreshing contrast with many treatises on the subject. It is packed with ideas and illustrations that are relevant to learning and teaching as they really exist. Its broad coverage includes help with measuring physical development, personality traits and interests, the social climate for learning, reflective thinking and problem solving, learning performance and reports to parents as well as the more usual techniques and emphases found in books on this subject. Its organization is so programmed that the progress from one level of insight to another is natural and developmental, easily within the capacities of all preparing for or engaged in educational work. Above all, this book is well written. Its author, Dr. John A. Green, has given his impressive scholarship a style of presentation that is readable, intellectually stimulating, yet often subtly profound in the depth of treatment attained. The final product is that rare achievement in professional literature—a text and resource book that teaches in an area in which the demand for knowledge is of highest priority.

LINDLEY J. STILES

Preface

Recent criticisms of the relevance of education, coupled with growing lay resistance to various types of pupil measurement and evaluation, highlight the need for thoroughgoing reassessments of education programs and skillful, sensitive evaluations of pupils. Resistance to measurement of aptitudes and personality on the grounds of invasion of personal privacy; persistent questioning of the validity of all current measures of intelligence; general suspicion of academic grades and most forms of educational measurement and evaluation—all have some validity when viewed in the context of current testing programs. It is obvious that testing programs cannot be justified unless they are used to improve the educational program and to provide valid indices of pupil progress and achievement. The use of invalid instruments by inept test administrators to collect data to be stored in computers or school vaults will not achieve these aims. Yet too few teachers and counselors really possess professional level skills and insights in the important area of measurement and evaluation.

Neither the professional psychologist nor the professional teacher quarrels with the need for measurement and evaluation. Indeed, it is due to their efforts that we have available such a wide range of highly refined measurement instruments and techniques. It is a major purpose of this text to help provide teachers and counselors in training and in service a background of skills and insights which will enable them to select and to apply these instruments and techniques as validly and reliably as possible. Incompetence and ineptness in this field are untenable and may indeed subvert the entire measurement program.

In this book every effort has been made to cover the essential areas using a relatively nontechnical approach with as many practical examples and suggestions as the ingenuity of the author would permit. Following the premise that significant information need not be difficult to acquire or to understand, the author has attempted to keep the book as interesting and well organized as possible. The four parts included are: Part I, the theoretical background requisite to the field; Part II, assessing the prerequisites to learning; Part III, evaluating pupil growth and change; and Part IV, assessing the educational program.

No book is written without the aid and encouragement of others. The counsel and patience of my wife, reviewers, and editors were both valuable and appreciated.

JOHN A. GREEN

Contents

Figures

Tables

INTRODUCTION TO
MEASUREMENT AND EVALUATION

Part I

THEORY AND DEVELOPMENT
OF MEASUREMENT
AND EVALUATION

In twentieth-century America the "good life" has been achieved by the common man in a wealth and fullness that were not dreamed possible a century ago. In part, at least, this achievement has been due to the recognition our citizens have given to the value of universal public education. Nevertheless we have little room for complacency since the quality of our education needs improvement. In the task of improvement, better educational measurement and evaluation can make significant contributions. The nation's future is there to read in the eager eyes of forty million school youngsters, and measurement has much to offer in helping the intuitive teacher fathom the depths behind those millions of eager eyes. An important aim of this book is to develop understandings, insights, and skills which will aid the classroom teacher in selecting or constructing appropriate measurement and evaluation devices. Thus, while the book presents a comprehensive survey of measurement and evaluation instruments and techniques, the procedures and instruments which are most adaptable to the classroom situation are emphasized. A further aim is to help the teacher to construct or select appropriate instruments for the measurement of his important classroom objectives.

Part I of the book contains three chapters which deal with the theory and development of educational measurement and evaluation. The first of these concerns social and educational importance of measurement and evaluation; the second, development of educational measurement and evaluation; and the third, theoretical background for measurement.

Chapter 1

SOCIAL AND EDUCATIONAL SIGNIFICANCE OF MEASUREMENT AND EVALUATION

INTRODUCTION

Man's progress rests squarely on a pedestal of accurate measurement. Numerous facets of measurement are so intertwined in his daily life that he rarely pauses to appreciate their significance. Yet a more frustrating existence can hardly be imagined than one in which there were no firm, accurate answers to the questions: What time? How much? What size? How fast? What price?

The urgent necessity to provide meaningful answers to such questions prompted early man to improvise measuring techniques. He learned to measure distance with his foot, with his hand, or by his pace. He estimated time by the height of the sun or the length of his shadow. These methods, although crude, provided readily understandable measures and were used for the same important reasons as modern techniques: (1) the need to summarize data and (2) the need to objectify measurement.

Measurement has always been plagued with two types of error: (1) error inherent in the measuring instruments and (2) error in the application of the instruments. Through history, measurement instruments have been vastly improved, and the human error has been reduced. However, although neither source of error has been eliminated, the level of refinement in measurement is a good yardstick for judging a nation's scientific and cultural progress. In the ancient world, those nations which possessed advanced mathematics showed the greatest progress. The Egyptians and the Greeks are noteworthy examples, and some of their mathematical and measurement concepts are still useful today. Modern society is characterized by great diversity in cultural and technological advancement, ranging from primitive societies in which crude measurement is used to societies in which cultural-scientific progress greatly exceeds that ever before attained by human beings. In these advanced societies a great variety of refined measurement instruments are used, not only in science but also in the social sciences and education.

DISTINCTION BETWEEN MEASUREMENT AND EVALUATION

In the foregoing discussion the term "measurement" has been used frequently, but little has been said of evaluation. The terms measurement and evaluation are often incorrectly used as synonyms in spite of the fact that they are distinctly different processes. Actually the two are, in a sense, the inseparable sides of a coin which are used in a working partnership—the one routine and objective, the other intellectual and subjective. Measurements are rarely made without predetermined purpose or without some evaluation of the results.

Any time a decision is made concerning the uses to which measurements will be put, some evaluation is necessary. *Measurement* is concerned with the application of an instrument or instruments to collect data for some specific purpose. *Evaluation* is the process of subjective appraisal with specific purposes or aims in mind. Most often this appraisal is based on the data or information which has been collected through the measurement process. It is possible, however, to make an evaluation on the basis of very meager data and information, even though such an evaluation would probably be invalid. Evaluation is the more comprehensive of the two terms: it may involve measurement; it always requires personal judgment and thus is subjective. It is the basis on which decision for change may be made. In contrast, measurement always tends to be as objective as the accuracy of the instrument and the skill of the person will permit it to be.

In the educational program evaluation is an essential step in the total process which includes planning, instruction, measurement, evaluation, and possible instructional change based on the evaluation. In order for the data to have relevance and importance, it is necessary first to plan the objectives for the measurement, then to measure, then to analyze and evaluate the data, and finally to apply the results in educational changes. Though the process appears to be relatively easy in this oversimplified outline, it is both complex and difficult, requiring considerable training and insight.

FUNCTIONS OF MEASUREMENT AND EVALUATION

Measurement and evaluation are tools with numerous educational and social functions. Among the most important of these functions are (1) determining human variability, (2) judging pupil progress, (3) aiding educational decision-making, (4) serving as a common medium for communicating data and information, and (5) facilitating the whole realm of social and scientific progress.

The last of these categories, though important, is not the focus of this book and will be given no other consideration than the brief allusion to its significance earlier in this chapter. The other four categories, however, are of direct concern throughout the book and are subjected to preliminary scrutiny in the following pages.

HUMAN VARIABILITY

A pertinent question prerequisite to measurement of human characteristics is "What is the nature of variability?" Both the way in which this question is answered and the significance attributed to human difference have far-reaching implications in education and society. When individual differences are viewed as unimportant compared to similarities, as some in the world would contend, then rigid social conformity and inflexible education are the logical consequence. But when differences are viewed as the unique essence of the individual, as in this country, then we must seek precise means of defining those differences and measuring their range; for society values them and education must cater to them.

Observation leads us to believe that all living things are characterized by variability. It was the striking fact of external difference that first led teachers, philosophers, and psychologists to speculate that human personality and intellectual traits might parallel physical appearance. Man's long-term concern with the problem of human differences is evident in writings of such well-known philosophers as Plato, whose ideal society in *The Republic* was shaped to fit the intellectual and physical differences of man. The Roman rhetorician Quintilian suggested as early as the first century that mind varies even as the body form does. Lombroso, an Italian army doctor, attempted to relate physical appearance and criminal tendencies. More recently W. H. Sheldon devoted considerable time to research aimed at identifying the specific body types and attempting to determine whether certain personality and intellectual traits consistently accompany these body types. After summarizing the previous works of about thirty investigators and making detailed measurements of 4,000 white subjects, Sheldon concluded that three pronounced body types stood out and that each was accompanied by characteristic personality traits.[1] While Sheldon's theory parallels the physique-personality stereotypes of the layman—e.g., the "jolly fat man"—it has gained little support among psychologists, however.

The problem of measurement would be much simpler if it were possible to take external measurements and predict from them the more abstract intellectual and personality characteristics, but there is insufficient evidence to justify such a conclusion.

Sex differences. The one notable exception to the above generalization is that of the sex-linked differences, which are either socially conditioned or hereditarily determined. The male is obviously stronger than the female, and the measurable intelligence of the two sexes also shows several significant differences. First, the male shows a greater range of variability on intelligence tests than the female. There are more males in the extremely low and extremely high categories than females, although the average for both sexes is the same. Second, when the scores on specific sections of such tests are analyzed, it is apparent that females score higher in verbal memory sections, while males perform significantly better on mathematical and spatial sections. One immediate educational implication of these measured differences is readily discernible in the general scholastic superiority of girls over boys throughout the elementary grades, a fact which directly reflects their verbal superiority plus their more rapid maturation. In the primary grades the majority of the top group in reading is invariably comprised of girls, although the most outstanding reader may be a boy. While some of these differences would seem to be a result of environmental conditioning, the difference in verbal facility appears to be innate since it is evident at ages as young as one year.[2]

Characteristics of variability. In résumé, democratic societies characteristically value variability of individual differences; and such a view certainly poses a difficult educational task, demanding more attention to

[1] Further discussion of the characteristics of the different body types and their related personality traits can be found in W. H. Sheldon, *Varieties of Human Physique* (New York: Harper & Brothers, Publishers, 1940), and in W. H. Sheldon, *Varieties of Temperament* (New York: Harper & Brothers, 1942).

[2] Frieda Keifer Merry and Ralph Vickers Merry, *The First Two Decades of Life* (New York: Harper & Brothers, 1958), pp. 219–220.

the measurement process than that required in a society which stresses conformity. Identification of the magnitude and scope of human differences requires careful measurement; however, the general nature of variability can be summarized in several principles. First, *variability is universal among animals; and the range of variability increases with the complexity of the animal.* Thus man possesses the greatest number of identifiable characteristics and the greatest range of differences within specific characteristics.

Second, *variability is continuous within the range established by the minimum and maximum cases.* For example, the height of a large number of people would vary continuously from that of the shortest person to that of the tallest.

Third, *a large group of variable cases will cluster around an average or central tendency.* To portray these three characteristics of variability we have developed the mathematical concept of the normal distribution curve. Thus it is often assumed that human variability on any measurable characteristic falls into the exact pattern of a normal curve if the entire population is measured, and measurement of an extensive random sample of the population should give a reasonable facsimile of this distribution. This concept has been substantially confirmed in the instances when large groups have been measured, as in large-scale intelligence and achievement testing.

The significance of human variability has prompted this preliminary discussion; and because of its particular pertinence to learning, three chapters in Part II follow up the discussion and survey the best measurement instruments available for assessing intellectual attributes, personality constructs, and physical characteristics.

MEASUREMENT AND DECISION-MAKING

Measurement is a significant tool in the process of educational decision-making. Information obtained through measurement plays a varying role in decisions on such important questions as: Who shall go to college? What curricular changes are needed in a secondary school? What ability group will the child be placed in? Which is the best high school? Grade school? College? Who should be awarded a scholarship?

In fact, it would be difficult to think of a decision affecting a child's education in which measurement results fail to play some part. Over the years the focus of educational measurement has shifted from a preoccupation with test form and an almost exclusive focus upon classroom learning, to the realm of educational decision-making. Measurement has become the basis for curricular change, for evaluating school programs, and for determining each child's educational future.

There are those who deplore such total dependence upon measurement on the grounds that it dehumanizes and makes routine vital educational decisions which greatly change children's lives and that it causes us to overlook important, intangible factors. While these arguments do point up some important areas of concern, the fact is that measurement *is* the basis for decisions on such questions as those posed above; and rather than decline in importance, measurement will assume even greater weight in the future—not only because the instruments are improving, but also because of the sheer number of pupils enrolled. Broadscale testing is the practical means through which sufficient information can be objectively and efficiently collected to provide the basis for individualizing the educational program. If we fail to measure pupils' achievement and personal characteristics comprehensively and frequently, the same educational decisions must still be made but with the handicap of insufficient information. It seems obvious, then, that a de-emphasis on measurement would be educational folly. The only logical alternative is to continue to seek ways to improve measurement techniques and instruments so that they will provide even more valid and comprehensive information about pupils.

Coupled with this alternative is the urgent necessity that educators become more proficient in measurement theory and practice, for they are the prime educational decision-makers. Test makers and guidance workers merely provide the instruments and expert advice; they do not, and should not, make the educational decisions.

Much of the discussion in this book touches directly or indirectly upon the relationship between measurement and evaluation and the use of measurement in educational decisions. Chapters 15 and 16 particularly relate to this topic.

LANGUAGE OF MEASUREMENT

Mathematics is the common language of measurement. Several scales and basic measurement symbols have been devised for identifying and measuring human differences, and while the technical consideration of statistics is reserved for Chapter 3, this preliminary discussion of scales and symbols is prerequisite background to the immediate following chapter. Stevens [3] gives four scale classifications: *nominal, ordinal, interval,* and *ratio.* Each of these scales commonly utilizes certain symbols. Three of these symbols will be discussed: (1) symbols that classify or describe, (2) symbols that indicate rank or order, and (3) symbols that indicate a scale position.

Nominal scales. In the nominal scale a number is used as a class or category label. Model numbers of cars, refrigerators, radios, etc. are examples of such numbers. Each individual product within a given model classification may also carry a specific serial number. Other common examples of the use of such numbers as classifying symbols are civil service classifications, the Dewey Decimal Library Classification system, and class intervals in a frequency distribution.

Ordinal scales. In measurements using the ordinal scales, numbers are assigned on the basis of rank order. Ranking is useful in measurement when the purpose is to determine the relative quality or quantity of a given trait which objects or persons possess. For example, ranking can be used to judge the relative beauty of a group of girls; but the ranks which are assigned apply only within the group and have little relevance in any other group. Rank order is often used as a measurement technique when the trait to be measured is intangible and is judged subjectively. The percentile rank technique is a refinement of ranking by which it is possible to determine the percent of the group which lies below a person within that group. If a person's score falls at the 90th percentile, 90 percent of the group lies below that point. Rank order can be subjected to statistical measurements, including *medians, percentiles,* and *rank-order coefficients of correlation* (see Chapter 3, pp. 42, 45, 55, for full discussion of these terms).

Since rank has no standard unit on a scale, it is subject to several limitations. First, *rank symbols allow only limited comparisons* since the range of two comparative groups may differ so greatly that the highest rank in the first group may be comparable to the lowest rank in the second group. When the group is increased in number in a random way, however, this limitation diminishes.

Second, *rank symbols do not show the amount of difference between*

[3] S. S. Stevens, "Mathematics, Measurement, and Psychophysics," *Handbook of Experimental Psychology* (New York: John Wiley & Sons, 1951).

any adjacent ranks. The difference between ranks one and two may be much greater than the difference between ranks two and three.

Third, *rank symbols have limited mathematical usefulness.* The fundamental processes of addition, subtraction, multiplication, and division may not be performed with rank symbols; but the rank-type statistics mentioned above may be calculated from them.

Fourth, *rank symbols may not be converted to scale symbols,* although scale symbols may be converted to rank symbols.

Interval scales. Interval scales have equal units, but the zero point is established and is not absolute; therefore, addition of units on the scale is relative to the point at which zero is established. If zero is established ten points above absolute zero, the interval numbers of six and five would have an interval sum of eleven; but the actual sum of these numbers would be 31 since their true values would be 16 and 15 respectively. Thus any shift of the arbitrary zero point changes the significance of all numbers as well as their totalled sums. The centigrade thermometer is an example of an interval scale in which an arbitrary or assumed zero has been set at the freezing point of water. With interval scales most of the important statistical calculations are possible—e.g., *mean, standard deviation,* and *Pearson Product-Moment correlation* (see Chapter 3, pp. 53–57, for full discussion of these terms).

Ratio scales. The ratio scale is similar to the interval scale, but it has an absolute zero established at the point where none of the property represented by the scale exists. All mathematical calculations are possible and meaningful with the ratio scale. Although the interval and the ratio scales have the most numerous desirable measurement characteristics, they cannot always be used because of the nature of the thing being measured. The interval scale is most often applicable to the measurement of human characteristics in education and psychology.

CHANGING ROLE OF MEASUREMENT

During the height of the objective test movement in the 1930's a few of its avid disciples became so intrigued with the "infallibility" of the objective test that they overlooked the objectives of measurement and the ultimate uses to which measurements are put. A few also failed to recognize that some important educational outcomes are difficult or impossible to measure objectively. Such blind acceptance by some led others to reject all objective-type measurements. One positive result of this controversy was a reassessment of the importance of all types of measurement—a reassessment which has resulted in several points of agreement. First, it is generally agreed that measurement should be applied to all important educational outcomes, even though the results may be inconclusive in some areas. The second point is that the significance of measurement depends upon the worth of its purpose and the constructive use of its results. A testing program, and in fact all measurement, in a school is only as good as the use to which it is ultimately put.

Functions of measurement and evaluation in the school program. The prevalence of variability in human beings has been cited earlier as one of the important reasons for measurement. Those who are familiar with modern public education realize that the range of ability among pupils represents nearly the whole range of the total population. Virtually all children of school age are now enrolled in public elementary schools; and modern, democratic education is generally committed to the concept of providing an educational program to accommodate the vast range of their intellectual differences. Thus the task of assessing individual potential assumes increasing importance at each level of education. Furthermore, during the past several decades the pendulum of purpose in public secondary education has gradually shifted from almost total concern with college preparation to growing concern for individual development and social adjustment.

It is now evident that the tendency for youth to stay in school longer is beginning to influence college enrollments, and measurement and evaluation will be necessary adjuncts to the educational reshuffling which secondary and higher education face as a result. In college, the magnitude of this change is not only felt in the enrollment impact, but also in a gradual and subtle influence on the intellectual composition of the student body. As the intellectual variability of college enrollees increases, higher education faces some of the same problems of guidance and program planning which have concerned secondary teachers for several decades.

With current and impending expansion and diversification of educational programs, teachers are assuming a more active role in the measurement-evaluation process and in the educational decisions which affect program and pupils. This involvement is both desirable and necessary; since the teacher is the key person in the educative process, changes will be effective only if he accepts and implements them. This means that he will need specific pre-service or in-service training if he is to have the skills and insights prerequisite to effective participation in the selection, administration, and use of measurement and evaluation techniques. The extent to which the development of these skills is necessary is pointed up in the following four statements:

1. The process of measurement is secondary to that of defining objectives. The ends to be achieved must first be formulated. Then measurement procedures can be sought as tools for appraising the extent to which those ends have been achieved.
2. Much of educational and psychological measurement is, and will probably remain, at a relatively low level of precision. We must recognize this fact, using the best procedures available to us, but always treating the resulting score as a tentative hypothesis rather than as an established conclusion.
3. The more elegant procedures of formal tests and measurement must be supplemented by the cruder procedures of informal observation, anecdotal description, and rating if we are to obtain a description of the individual that is useful, complete, and comprehensive.
4. No amount of ingenuity in developing improved procedures for measuring and appraising the individual will ever eliminate the need to interpret the results from those procedures. Measurement procedures are only tools which provide the data for improved evaluations.

SUMMARY

In modern society measurement has reached the stage of development where it influences every individual and group. In fact, the variety and effectiveness of measurement techniques are useful criteria in assessing the stage of advancement which a country or area has attained. In the physical sciences measurement is concerned with quantitative aspects of natural phenomena, while in social sciences and education the focus is on variability or differences among human beings.

Measurement and evaluation serve as tools in social and educational change. In this context their most significant functions fall into five broad categories: (1) determining human variability, (2) judging pupil progress, (3) educational decision-making, (4) communicating data and information, and (5) facilitating social and scientific progress.

The language of measurement is mathematics, and the scales and symbols used include (1) the nominal scale used with classification symbols, e.g., model numbers of a car; (2) the ordinal scale used with rank-order symbols, e.g., percentile rank; (3) the interval scale used with assumed scale-position symbols, e.g., IQ scores; and (4) the ratio scale used with absolute scale-position symbols, e.g., chronological age of a person. The interval scale and the ratio scale are the two scales which are most useful because more statistical computations apply to them and because they lend themselves to more meaningful interpretation and evaluation.

Measurement and evaluation have different meanings although they are occasionally used interchangeably. Measurement refers to the collection of data about some characteristic with an instrument designed for the purpose. Evaluation is somewhat more comprehensive and may include measurement since it refers to the subjective judgment or interpretation of the quality or worth of something, often on the basis of numerous data. Evaluation may lead to conclusions and applications which ultimately change that which is evaluated. Measurement is only as important as the uses to which the results are put. In education ultimate worth of measurement is attained when the classroom teacher evaluates the results and on that basis projects the educational program best suited to his pupils.

DISCUSSION QUESTIONS AND PROBLEMS

1. Enumerate the instances in your daily life which are directly influenced by some aspect of measurement.
2. Define the terms "measurement" and "evaluation," giving specific examples which clearly indicate the distinct difference in the two processes.
3. Discuss the social and economic effects which would occur if the United States were to change to the metric system of weights and measures.
4. Make comparative lists of the advantages and disadvantages of the English system of weights and measures and the metric system.
5. Visit several primary grade classes to observe the differences between male and female pupils in educational achievement, in physical development, and in emotional maturity.
6. Identify instances in your own educational career in which decisions which vitally affected your educational future were made primarily on the basis of some type of measurement data.
7. Give examples (other than those used in the text) of the use of the nominal, ordinal, interval, and ratio scales.

SELECTED READINGS

Ahmann, J. Stanley, and Marvin D. Glock. *Evaluating Pupil Growth*. 3rd ed. Boston: Allyn and Bacon, 1967. Chapter 1 explores the role of evaluation in education. It also contains discussion of the purposes of evaluation and makes a clear distinction between measurement and evaluation.

Bradfield, James M., and H. Stewart Moredock. *Measurement and Evaluation in Education.* New York: The Macmillan Company, 1957. Chapter 1 contains an interesting discussion of various types of measurement symbols. The discussion points out some of the major advantages and disadvantages of the important measurement symbols.

Flynn, John T., and Herbert Garber. *Assessing Behavior Readings in Educational and Psychological Measurement.* Reading, Massachusetts: Addison-Wesley Publishing Company, 1967. In Chapter 1, pp. 1–6 present an overview of the contributions of measurement to man's progress.

Guilford, J. P. *Psychometric Methods.* New York: McGraw-Hill Book Company, 1954. Chapter 1 provides a simple analysis of the nature of numbers, together with an explanation of the ways in which numbers are properly used as tools of measurement.

Magnusson, David. *Test Theory.* Reading, Massachusetts: Addison-Wesley Publishing Company, 1966. Chapter 1 contains a good discussion of the ratio and interval scales and of the rationale of the normal curve.

Stanley, Julian C. *Measurement in Today's Schools.* 4th ed. New York: Prentice-Hall, 1964. Chapter 2 emphasizes the importance of measurement to science and education, stressing the dependence in science upon accurate measurement. The author also contrasts the development of measurement in the two fields.

Wrightstone, J. Wayne, Joseph Justman, and Irving Robbins. *Evaluation in Modern Education.* New York: American Book Company, 1956. Chapter 1 distinguishes between measurement and evaluation and points up some of the trends in evaluation.

Chapter 2

THE DEVELOPMENT OF
MEASUREMENT AND EVALUATION

INTRODUCTION

As with many other areas of human progress, it is possible to examine the area of measurement and evaluation and wonder why the progress has been so slow; for the things which have been accomplished seem so obvious that one wonders why they were not discovered long ago. Who, however, should know better than psychologists and educators of the limitations on mental activity prescribed by mind set? Many before Newton had observed the natural phenomenon of falling objects, but it was Newton who first had the insight to relate the phenomenon to gravitational attraction. So it is in many areas of human endeavor that progress is often capricious, frequently halting until certain keys to progress—a person, a new discovery, a peculiar set of circumstances, or some combination of all these—give it new impetus and direction. It is such key events, discoveries, and persons in the area of measurement and evaluation which this chapter will treat. In the course of the discussion it will become apparent that many of the developments in the area are recent, and, further, that there has been a continuing acceleration of development and discovery in measurement paralleling the technological and educational advance of America in the past half century.

As an aid to the reader, the development of measurement and evaluation has been divided arbitrarily into four logical categories or periods which have chronological sequence. These four periods are shown in Table I and will be discussed separately in the remainder of the chapter. The following topics are to be considered in the chapter: (1) early informal measurement approaches, (2) growth of psychological measurement and experimentation, (3) origin and development of standardized tests,

(4) development of large-scale evaluation, and (5) important persons in the measurement and evaluation movement.

EARLY INFORMAL MEASUREMENT APPROACHES

Differences classified by external characteristics. The interest of early workers in measurement was generally the result of their investigations of human variability, but they approached the problem with a different viewpoint from that of recent workers. Most of these early men believed that human differences were inherited, biological, nonalterable facts.

Table I. MOVEMENTS, PERSONS, AND EVENTS IMPORTANT IN THE DEVELOPMENT OF MEASUREMENT AND EVALUATION

Period of Development	Key Persons	New Developments
I. Early informal measurement approaches (Ancient times to 1850)		Chinese essay examination, 2200 B.C.
	Socrates	Socrates' oral examination
	Quintilian	Individual difference studies
		University of Paris oral thesis examination, 1215
		Prussian "leaving exam," 1787
	Horace Mann	Boston written school exam, 1845
II. Growth of psychological measurement and experimentation (1850 to 1930's)	Sir Francis Galton	*Hereditary Genius*, 1869
	Karl Pearson	Product-moment correlation
	Wilhelm Wundt	Experimental psychological laboratory, 1879
	Hermann Ebbinghaus	Completion test
	Alfred Binet Lewis M. Terman	Individual intelligence test
	Arthur Otis	*Army Alpha* and *Beta*
	L. L. Thurstone	Primary mental abilities
	David Wechsler	Adult individual intelligence test

Period of Development	Key Persons	New Developments
III. Origin and development of standardized tests (1900 to 1940)	J. M. Rice	*Standard Spelling Scale,* 1897
	Edward L. Thorndike	Early measurement textbook, 1904
	Harold Rugg	Early educational statistics textbook, 1917
		Stanford Achievement Battery, 1919
	E. K. Strong	Strong interest test, 1927
	Charles Spearman	Aptitude testing
IV. Development of large-scale evaluation (1930 to present)	Ralph Tyler	Eight-year study of secondary schools, 1932–1940
	Jacob Moreno	Sociometry
	Hermann Rorschach	Projective techniques
		Evaluative Criteria for secondary schools, 1939

Three interesting but divergent suggestions were those of Plato, Quintilian, and Galen. Plato, in *The Republic,* proposed the creation of three classes, with education, social, and economic responsibilities appropriate to the physical and intellectual differences of each class. Although Plato was less explicit than his successors in proposing the means for identifying important individual differences, he did suggest a sort of aptitude test to select those who were qualified for military careers.

The Roman Quintilian was more specific than Plato concerning the identification of individual differences. He suggested that the mind varied as the body form did. Concerning adaptation to individual differences in school he said: "It has generally and deservedly been accounted a great merit in a master to observe the different capacities and disposition of his pupils and to know what nature has chiefly fitted them for. For in this report, the variety is so incredible, that we meet with as many different kinds of capacities as of persons." [1]

Galen, the great Greek medical doctor, proposed an idea which is the

[1] Luella Cole, *A History of Education* (New York: Rinehart and Company, 1955), p. 50.

basis of our modern lie detector tests. He believed that mental and emotional changes could be detected by measuring physical changes. As court physician to the emperor, he attempted to determine whether he could discover the empress's lover by taking her pulse rate as she observed the suspected men.

Oral examinations. The initiation or introduction of the oral examination is commonly attributed to Socrates. Indeed, Socrates was proficient in utilizing oral questioning to force the student to define his problem and to see the limitations of his thinking, to theorize and to hypothesize as a basis for testing his thinking. In this sense the Socratic method is a forerunner for the scientific method of thinking and thus a contributing factor to the modern measurement and evaluation movement. Actually, however, Socrates' method was primarily a teaching method; such oral questioning is used extensively by teachers today and was undoubtedly used by numerous teachers before Socrates. The major contribution of Socrates was refining and improving the effectiveness of the technique.

Perhaps the earliest formal use of the oral examination in education was the oral thesis examination which was introduced at the University of Paris in 1215. "To win the master's degree, the student usually was required to prepare a thesis and defend it against disputants in much the same manner that a journeyman presented his masterpiece to the guild members as proof of his qualification to become a master workman." [2]

This oral thesis theoretically offered colleagues and teachers an opportunity to judge the candidate's competence as he defended and discussed it. However, it was reputed occasionally to assume more of a Bacchanalian purpose than a measurement function. The candidate provided the refreshments, and his success sometimes depended more on the amount and quality of the wine than on the quality of his performance.

In spite of these occasional abuses, the oral thesis has stood the test of time; and it is still used as the last measurement hurdle for master's and doctoral candidates. Despite the adoption of the oral thesis, general use of oral examinations in regular college classrooms was slow in coming. It was not until 1702 that they were adopted at Cambridge University, and they were introduced shortly thereafter in the Latin grammar and elementary schools.

Early written measurement. Probably the first written examinations

[2] R. Freeman Butts, *A Cultural History of Western Education* (New York: McGraw-Hill Book Company, 1955), p. 60.

were those used by the Chinese about 2200 B.C. These were civil service examinations which were difficult, essay-type examinations based on philosophy, with little direct relationship to the civil service position for which the examinees were competing.

The written examination in education is of comparatively recent origin. In 1787 Frederick William II of Prussia established a state ministry of education and required a "leaving examination" [3] which the secondary school student had to pass before he could enter the university. These examinations in Prussia applied only at the secondary level of education and apparently did not spread to other educational levels or other countries. In fact, in early nineteenth-century American common schools, examinations were still oral. Students were drilled in the fundamentals; and the trustees or the school committee traditionally visited the school near the end of the year to quiz the students to determine their ability to read, spell, repeat arithmetic rules, and locate towns on the map. Spelling bees and reading contests were frequent, and the better students were challenged with arithmetic puzzles such as the following:

> EXAMPLE: Fifteen Christians and 15 Turks bound at sea in one ship in a terrible storm, and the pilot declaring a necessity of casting one-half of these persons into the sea, that the rest might be saved, they all agreed that the persons to be cast away should be set out by lot in this manner, viz., the 30 persons should be placed in a round form like a ring and then, beginning to count at one of the passengers and proceeding regularly every ninth person should be cast into the sea until of the 30 persons there remained only 15. The question is, how these 30 persons ought to be placed that the lot might infallibly fall upon the 15 Turks, and not upon any of the 15 Christians. [4]

In 1845 in Boston the visiting school committee under the leadership of Horace Mann made out a series of written examinations on the various subjects which were being taught in the nineteen grammar and writing schools. These examinations were given to pupils in the highest class of each of the nineteen schools, and they appear to be the earliest written examinations used in elementary schools of this country. Horace Mann, who was Secretary of the Massachusetts State Board of Education and editor of the *Common School Journal* at the time, was a strong advocate of the written examination and did much to promote its adoption

[3] Butts, p. 276.
[4] Ellwood P. Cubberley, *Public Education in the United States* (Boston: Houghton Mifflin Company, 1934), p. 331.

in other schools throughout the country. Mann attributed these written examinations with many of the characteristics which are commonly attributed to our better written examinations today.[5]

It is interesting to note that these same examinations were given to all eighth graders in the Boston schools following World War I in order to compare the results with the scores of the original pupils. The children in 1919 excelled the 1845 predecessors by a considerable degree in all areas except arithmetic problem solving. Another examination given in Springfield, Massachusetts, in 1846, and a retest in 1906 gave results similar to those in Boston.[6]

GROWTH OF PSYCHOLOGICAL EXPERIMENTATION AND MEASUREMENT

Until about the middle of the nineteenth century, psychology did not exist as a science, and philosophy rather than psychology was the key to insight into human behavior. Through astute observation and keen insight, such men as Bacon, Descartes, Rousseau, and Herbart in philosophy and Comenius, Pestalozzi, and Froebel in education, had shed some light on individual differences, modes of human learning, and human behavior. But their theories had been subjected to very little testing or experimentation.

Psychological origins. Testing and experimentation using theories of early philosophers and educators were to wait on several developments in England and Germany. In fact, the possibility of subjecting such phenomena as individual differences to numerical description was first postulated by an astronomer instead of a psychologist; and his idea came about as a result of an accident.[7] Friedrich W. Bessel, an astronomer in the Greenwich Astronomical Observatory in 1816, became intrigued with an incident in the records concerning the dismissal of an assistant in 1796 for inaccurate time reporting on the transit of stars across a hairline in the telescope. The assistant invariably recorded the time approximately one second slower than did his master. In following up this problem Bessel discovered that there was considerable individual variation among his colleagues in the time lapse between visual stimulation and

---

[5] For a further look at Mann's views see Horace Mann, *Common School Journal,* VIII (October 1, 1845), 19.

[6] Cubberley, p. 332.

[7] Leona E. Tyler, *The Psychology of Human Differences,* 3rd ed. (New York: Appleton-Century-Crofts, 1968), p. 8.

physical reaction. He called this the personal equation. Later psychologists called it reaction time.

Following this discovery was a series of events which triggered the development of experimental psychology as a science. The first of these was the publication of Sir Charles Darwin's *Origin of the Species* in 1859. Another Englishman, Sir Francis Galton, was interested in Darwin's work; and a decade later, in 1869, he published the book *Hereditary Genius*. This book was a milestone in the measurement movement, for it was the beginning of an interest which led Galton to investigate the possibility of using mathematics in human measurement. Galton became interested in the work of Lambert Quetelet, a Belgian mathematician, who had applied the mathematical theory of probability to human measurements. As a result of this interest, Galton and a contemporary, Karl Pearson, began to develop the statistical tools which permit the objective manipulation of data. Pearson developed the Pearson Product-Moment Correlation method, which has become so useful in prediction and in checking reliability and validity of standardized tests.[8] These men gave modern psychologists a major advantage over early investigators since they provided a quantitative language for describing human traits, a language which was easily understood and could be checked and verified.

In Germany during the time when Galton and Pearson were working, several scientists were interested in the fields of psychology. Among the most notable were Wilhelm Wundt and Hermann Ebbinghaus. Wundt established the first experimental psychological laboratory in 1879, just one decade after Galton's *Hereditary Genius* and two decades after Darwin's *Origin of the Species*.[9] This laboratory attracted numerous graduate students from other countries. Among those students was a young man, James McKeen Cattell, who later became a pioneer in the American mental-testing movement. One of Cattell's students, Edward L. Thorndike, was a major contributor in educational psychology and in the achievement test movement.

Ebbinghaus, a contemporary of Wundt's, developed the completion test and experimented with test forms which were later adapted to the mental testing movement.

[8] See p. 54 for further discussion of this concept.

[9] For further discussion of the history of experimental psychology see Frank N. Freeman, *Mental Tests: Their History, Principles and Applications* (Boston: Houghton Mifflin Company, 1939).

Measuring intelligence. During the same period two Frenchmen, Alfred Binet and Theophile Simon, became interested in measuring the intelligence of insane and feeble-minded children in order to classify them for further treatment. The outcome of their investigation was the first individual intelligence scale. This scale was published after fifteen years of work in 1905 and revised by Binet in 1908 and 1911. Binet changed the approach of psychologists to the measurement of intelligence when he suggested that complex mental abilities could be broken down into more specific measurable abilities. In his 1908 revision of the scale he introduced the concept of *mental age,* thus providing a numerical basis for comparing the intellectual status of children.

Binet died in 1911, but a number of American scientists became interested in his work and made further revisions of his test. Henry Goddard revised the test in 1911; Fred Kuhlmann followed with a revision in 1912; and Lewis M. Terman and John L. Childs's revision came in 1913. Terman, however, did considerably more work with the test than the others and in 1916 published the first edition of the *Stanford-Binet Intelligence Scale,* a test which was to become one of the most widely used in America. Terman also made several fundamental assumptions regarding intelligence and intelligence testing which were to influence American educators for the next several decades. He suggested that (1) intelligence quotient or IQ was not changeable and (2) IQ measured innate intelligence.[10] Both assumptions proved to be fallacious, but they continue to influence the thinking of laymen and some teachers.

Terman's IQ concept was an adaptation of mental quotient which was first used by William Stern in Germany.[11] MQ and IQ provide a basis for comparing intelligence of all age groups, that basis being rate of mental development. For example, a ten-year-old with a mental age of twelve years would have an MQ of 1.2; and his score is simply converted to IQ by multiplying it by 100, for an IQ score of 120. For this child the rate of mental growth is 1.2 years for each year of change in chronological age. Therefore, at 5 years of age his mental age was 6, at 10 it is 12, and at 15 it will be 18 if he continues to have the same rate of mental development.

Over the years the *Stanford-Binet Scale* has been acclaimed as the

[10] Lewis M. Terman, *The Measurement of Intelligence* (Boston: Houghton Mifflin Company, 1916), p. 68.

[11] $IQ = \dfrac{\text{Mental Age}}{\text{Chronological Age}} \times 100$. IQ is discussed extensively in Chapter 5.

most valid instrument for measuring intelligence. Two revisions of the scale have kept it current. The 1936 revision included two forms, the L and the M. These tests were less verbally oriented than the earlier scale and provided mental-age norms for persons ranging in age from two to 22 years and 11 months. The latest revision was made in 1960.

The need to measure the intelligence of a great number of soldiers during World War I provided the impetus for the development of group tests. Individual intelligence tests were obviously impractical for this purpose, yet some objective measure was desirable as a basis for subsequent training and placement of soldiers. Consequently, a group of five psychologists directed by Robert M. Yerkes was commissioned to develop a group test. Using material provided by Arthur Otis, this group developed the *Army Alpha,* a written group test of intelligence, and the *Army Beta,* an individual nonverbal test. Over 1,700,000 armed forces personnel were given the *Army Alpha.* Following the war the *Army Alpha* was adapted as the *National Intelligence Test* and sold over a half million copies during the first year.[12]

Since World War I numerous excellent group intelligence tests have been published for school use. Most of these tests have followed the same general theory as the early tests; however, three men took exception to this general theory. The first of these men was Charles Spearman, who suggested that intelligence could not be considered a totality as Binet had contended but consisted, instead, of a general factor and many specific factors, or the G-factor and the S-factors. This line of reasoning was important in stimulating the development of aptitude tests, some of which are incorrectly called specific intelligence tests.

The second related exception was the theory that intelligence consists of a group of factors, neither general nor specific, called primary mental abilities. L. L. Thurstone, using the statistical technique of factorial analysis, isolated out what appear to be discrete mental abilities. Following the multiple factor theory Thurstone developed the Chicago *Tests of Primary Mental Abilities,* designed to give a profile of these abilities in addition to a general IQ score.

The third exception is David Wechsler's individual intelligence test, designed primarily to measure adult intelligence. Wechsler's theory of intelligence, presented in his book *Measurement of Adult Intelligence,*[13]

[12] Ellwood P. Cubberley, *op. cit.* (above, n. 4), pp. 699–700.
[13] David Wechsler, *Measurement of Adult Intelligence* (Baltimore, Maryland: Williams and Wilkins Co., 1939).

differed from that of Terman in that Wechsler suggested that intelligence normally did not reach its peak until the middle thirties, leveling off through the middle forties with little decline until about sixty, after which it dropped somewhat more sharply. Furthermore, Wechsler adopted the deviation IQ used by Otis instead of the quotient IQ of Terman.[14] As a result of his work Wechsler published the *Wechsler-Bellevue Intelligence Scale* in 1939 and subsequently revised the scale in 1955.

The age range of the Wechsler tests was increased in 1949 by the publication of the *Wechsler Intelligence Scale for Children.* This test was designed for children between the ages of five and fifteen years and had the same kind of IQ calculation and subtest arrangement as the adult form.

ORIGIN AND DEVELOPMENT OF STANDARDIZED TESTS

Achievement testing. The standardized test is a twentieth century development, although several men were working on its development just before the turn of the century. It is apparent from the preceding discussion that some standardization was introduced into early intelligence tests and, further, that intelligence testing in schools antedated the development of other forms of testing, although achievement testing was a quick successor.

Pioneering phrase of achievement testing to 1915. At the time of the American Civil War there was one pioneer worker in achievement testing, a man whose work was little publicized or accepted by other educators. He was George Fisher, an Englishman, whose "scale books" were used in the Greenwich Hospital School in 1864 to measure pupil achievement in school subjects.[15] As is sometimes the case with pioneering efforts, Fisher's work was largely unheeded; and the achievement testing movement waited until a more opportune time for its inception. That time came in 1897, when J. M. Rice startled American educators with claims, backed by his test results, that spelling was being taught ineffectively in the schools. Although the majority of educators denied Rice's

---

[14] These two methods of calculating IQ are discussed at some length in Chapter 5.

[15] Harry A. Greene, Albert N. Jorgensen, and J. Raymond Gerberich, *Measurement and Evaluation in the Secondary School* (New York: Longmans, Green, and Company, 1954), p. 23.

claims, several saw merit in the standard testing procedures which he had used. As a result several more achievement tests or scales were devised in the next few years.[16]

Rice had introduced an idea which was fostered by Edward L. Thorndike, the man who can correctly be called the father of the achievement testing movement. Thorndike made a major contribution in 1904 when he published the first comprehensive book in the field, *Mental and Social Measurement.* In this book he proposed several of the principles which are still used in constructing standardized tests. Among these principles were (1) test items should be scaled according to difficulty, (2) tests should be objectively scored, and (3) tests should have statistical norms. Thorndike gave further impetus to the field by publishing the 1909 *Scale for Handwriting of Children* and by encouraging students to do further work in the field. During this period there were several new tests which helped turn the tide of schoolmen in favor of the movement. These tests included C. W. Stone's 1908 edition of a standardized achievement test in arithmetic, the arithmetic scales by Courtes in 1910, and the *Composition Scale* by Ayres in 1912.

Two factors at this time probably influenced schools to enter upon the "testing boom" period of the 1920's and 1930's. These were (1) the growing evidence concerning the unreliability of school marks as an indication of pupil achievement and (2) a group of city school surveys conducted between 1910 and 1917 in which standardized tests were used to measure pupil achievement.

Achievement testing, World War I through the 1930's. A book published by Harold Rugg in 1917, *Statistical Methods Applied in Education,* was the first of a series of texts which helped test makers refine their testing instruments. A significant development in 1919 was the publication of the first achievement test battery, the *Stanford Achievement Battery.* Although achievement tests changed very little after the publication of this battery, numerous test publishing companies were established, and standardized tests were developed in all fields. An idea of the rapid expansion in the field can be gained from Hildreth's bibliography of mental tests and rating scales. Hildreth listed 3500 titles in 1933, 4279

[16] Further discussion of the early development of achievement testing is discussed in Leonard P. Ayres, "History and Present Status of Educational Measurements," *Seventeenth Yearbook of the National Society for the Study of Education,* Part II (Bloomington, Illinois: Public School Publishing Company, 1918), pp. 9–15.

titles in 1939, and 5294 titles in 1945.[17] During this period teachers increased their use of informal objective tests as well as standardized tests.

Personality, aptitude, interest, and attitude tests. In spite of man's long-term interest in personality and the factors which contribute to favorable personality development, his major gains before the twentieth century were directed largely at understanding and treating deviant personality types. It was not until World War I that the first personality inventory was actually constructed, the *Woodworth Personal Data Sheet*. This was a questionnaire type of instrument which was designed to identify bad military risks. In spite of its weaknesses, the instrument was successful enough that it motivated other psychologists to publish numerous tests and inventories during the 1920's and 1930's. Several of these instruments, such as the *Bernreuter Personality Inventory*, were designed to measure a number of aspects of personality, with an aim toward understanding the normal person as well as the deviate. Others, such as the *Mooney Problem Checklist*, were designed to identify problems of young children in order that those problems might be corrected before they deteriorated to the point where major therapy would be necessary. During the latter part of this period some psychologists turned to more subjective techniques, such as the *Rorschach Test*, the *Thematic Apperception Tests*, and after 1939 numerous other projective techniques.[18] However, the extensive training required for use and interpretation of these techniques precluded their use by teachers.

Concurrent with these developments, aptitude testing was refined. *Aptitude* and *intelligence* are sometimes used interchangeably in the literature; but it should be noted that aptitude usually refers to a specific innate or developed ability which a person has, e.g., mechanical aptitude. On the other hand, intelligence is a general intellectual capacity which might include numerous specific factors. In view of this relatedness of the two terms, it is not surprising that two men interested primarily in the nature of intelligence, Charles Spearman and L. L. Thurstone, should stimulate the development of aptitude tests. The multifactor test of intelligence developed by Thurstone is, in fact, sometimes classified as an aptitude battery. Actually the distinction between aptitude batteries and intelligence tests is not clear-cut. The scholastic aptitude tests which are

---

[17] Gertrude H. Hildreth, *A Bibliography of Mental Tests and Rating Scales* (New York: Psychological Corporation, 1933; 2nd ed., 1939; supplement to 2nd ed., 1945).
[18] See Chapter 7 for further consideration of personality and interest inventories.

used to predict pupils' future school success are basically verbal-quantitative intelligence tests, and some authors classify traditional intelligence tests as scholastic tests. During this period numerous tests, such as the *Seashore Music Aptitude Test* (1919, revised 1939), and batteries, such as the *Differential Aptitude Tests* (1947), were introduced and used in schools.

During the same time that aptitude tests were being developed and refined, several men were working to devise instruments for measuring interests. G. Stanley Hall's free observation and questionnaire studies in 1907 caught the attention of several investigators; but no important tests were published until the 1920's. The *Strong Vocational Interest*, published in 1927, and the *Kuder Preference Record*, published in 1939, are still the most widely used in secondary schools and colleges.

Attitude measurement also began about this time. L. L. Thurstone and E. J. Chave introduced the equal-appearing-intervals technique for attitude measurement in 1929.[19] In the next decade others—notably H. H. Remmers, T. L. Kelly, and J. W. Wrightstone—devoted considerable time and research to this subject; and some progress was made, although considerable room for improvement remained.

THE DEVELOPMENT OF LARGE-SCALE EVALUATION

Reaction to objective test movement. Standardized testing was introduced in virtually all schools by the early 1930's, but it was soon apparent that the standardized test was no panacea for all the ills of education. Members of the Progressive Education Association were particularly critical of the movement, but within the Association there was no consensus regarding the importance of the standardized test. In fact, there was a fairly well defined schism between the pro-objective test element and the con element. Those in favor listened to men such as Ralph Tyler while the opponents favored William Kilpatrick. The opponents feared that education which relied only on objective measurement stressed the wrong aims, and they argued for a broader concept of education which included such goals as development of thinking processes and problem-solving abilities—goals which were inadequately measured by objective tests. Tyler and his followers began a series of investigations regarding the effectiveness of new educational practices which had been

[19] L. L. Thurstone and E. J. Chave, *The Measurement of Attitude* (Chicago: University of Chicago Press, 1929).

introduced by John Dewey, George Counts, Kilpatrick, and other educators. These investigations resulted in the sponsorship by the Progressive Education Association of the eight-year study, which was carried on in secondary schools from 1932 to 1940.[20]

Development of other tools and techniques of pupil evaluation. In spite of the fact that the arguments and investigations of objective measurement were inconclusive, they served to give educators a truer perspective of the place of standardized achievement tests in the overall educational evaluation program. The need for new tools and techniques of pupil evaluation became apparent, and some of those tools and techniques which had been used earlier were improved and reused. The emphasis, however, gradually shifted from measurement for marking or judging a pupil, to that of measurement and evaluation for obtaining information about each pupil for educational planning and guidance.

While this shift was taking place, new techniques for evaluating emotional, social, and mental aspects of the pupil evolved. Projective techniques were used for identifying emotional problems of pupils, and sociometric techniques were used to assess the social orientation of the pupil. Hermann Rorschach's inkblot projective approach was a precursor to a variety of projective techniques—including interpretation of drawing, painting, handwriting, stories, fantasies, play, and drama. Instruments which required concrete or verbal reproduction or interpretation by the subject were used in each area. For example, Lauretta Bender in 1938 adapted Max Wertheimer's work in drawing tests to produce the *Bender-Gestalt Test of Emotional Adjustment.* In this test the subject was asked to reproduce nine separate drawings. Interpretation of the results was based on observation and on subjective interpretation of the subject's (1) motivation, (2) selective attention and perception, (3) motor response, and (4) reaction to motor response.[21] Patterns of response and success norms for children of various ages were established to give a measure of objectivity to the interpretation. Typical response patterns of specific types of deviates were also identified.

Among the sociometric techniques was the sociogram, which was used to determine the attitudes of members of a group toward one another. With this technique children were asked to respond to such questions as

[20] Results reported in Chamberlain Dean, *Did They Succeed in College?* (New York: Harper and Brothers, 1942).

[21] Further discussion in Edward B. Greene, *Measurements of Human Behavior* (New York: Odyssey Press, 1952), pp. 437–480.

"Who is your best friend?" or "What two people would you like to invite to your next birthday party?" From the responses a sociogram could be drawn up as a referent for changing the group dynamics and for organizing future group activities. Jacob L. Moreno, editor of the periodical *Sociometry*, was a leader in developing sociometric techniques.[22]

Several other techniques for gathering and recording information about pupils were devised during this period. These included the case study, anecdotal records, time sampling, and cumulative records, each of which is discussed in subsequent chapters. A significant development in educational evaluation was the publication in 1939 of the *Evaluative Criteria* which has subsequently been used in the accreditation of secondary schools.

RECENT TRENDS

Educational measurement and evaluation in its short history has made tremendous advances, but much remains to be done. Some of the recent trends serve to point up the direction of progress.

1. There is a continuing increase in the variety and quality of available measurement instruments.

2. The testing program has become an essential part of the educational programs of so many schools that terms such as "IQ" have become part of the layman's vocabulary.

3. Teachers tend to view tests as one of many data-gathering devices which can be used to obtain information about pupils.

4. Information about pupils is gathered as a means of improving their programs as well as assessing their achievements.

5. The teacher is assuming the key role in the administration of tests and the decisions related to the use of test results.

6. The "cocksure" confidence of the 1920's and 1930's in standardized tests is being replaced by a critical but constructive attitude, with appropriate research in areas where there have been few answers.

SUMMARY

The development of measurement and evaluation in psychology and education is a chronicle of key persons, whose discoveries and contributions in this relatively young field have come to fruition in a repertoire of

[22] See Chapters 7 and 8 for further discussion of projective and sociometric techniques.

instruments and techniques for assessing most significant human characteristics. An index of the magnitude of development in the field is the
fact that over 100 million standardized tests are administered annually in
the schools of the United States.

Table II presents a summary chart which includes the names of men
who have made major contributions to the field of measurement and
evaluation. An examination of the chart will reveal that formal educational measurement and evaluation are less than a century old and that
the developments since World War II have been largely toward refinement of earlier instruments and techniques.

Table II. A SELECTED CHRONOLOGICAL LIST OF CONTRIBUTORS TO
MEASUREMENT AND EVALUATION IN THE NINETEENTH AND
TWENTIETH CENTURIES

Name of Contributor	Contribution	Date
Sir Francis Galton	Statistical techniques *Hereditary Genius*	1869
Wilhelm Wundt	First experimental psychological laboratory	1879
J. M. Rice	One of first standardized tests, *Standard Spelling Scale*	1897
Edward L. Thorndike	Early measurement textbook	1904
Charles Spearman	Stimulated aptitude measurement with two-factor theory of intelligence	1904
Alfred Binet	*Simon-Binet Scale*	1905
Lewis M. Terman	*Stanford-Binet Intelligence Scale*	1916
E. K. Strong	Interest inventory	1927
Ralph Tyler	Teacher-made tests	1930's
Jacob Moreno	*Who Shall Survive?* Beginning of sociometry	1934
L. L. Thurstone	*Primary Mental Abilities*	1938
Hermann Rorschach	*Rorschach Test*	1939
Henry Murray	*Thematic Apperception Test*	1943
David Wechsler	*Wechsler Adult Intelligence Scale*	1955

The development of measurement and evaluation can be broken into
four overlapping periods: (1) early informal measurement approaches
(ancient times to 1850); (2) growth of psychological measurement and
experimentation (1850 to 1940); (3) origin and development of standardized tests (1900 to 1940); and (4) development of large-scale evaluation (1930 to present). In reviewing these periods it is evident that most
of the developments have come during the twentieth century; and,

rather than to stabilize, the field continues to grow both in scope and number of innovations.

DISCUSSION QUESTIONS AND PROBLEMS

1. Compare examples of early and current group intelligence or achievement tests. How do they differ? What specific improvements have been made?
2. Summarize and contrast two concepts of intelligence which have been widely accepted during the twentieth century.
3. In view of the most recent concepts of intelligence, what justification is there for classifying typical group intelligence tests as scholastic aptitude tests?
4. How does the test performance of culturally-deprived and minority-group children compare to that of white, middle-class children? What is the best explanation for the difference?
5. Discuss the impact and consequences of recent public criticisms of the widespread use of intelligence and personality examinations in schools on the grounds that they constitute an invasion of the individual's privacy.
6. Examine the pro's and con's of Francis Keppel's proposal for national assessment of education. Does the present status of achievement testing warrant such assessment?
7. What are the notable trends in the development and use of measurement and evaluation in psychology and education? List trends other than those already noted in this chapter.

SELECTED READINGS

Anastasi, Anne. *Individual Differences*. New York: John Wiley & Sons, 1965. In Chapters 2 and 3 of this book of readings there is a series of articles by such pioneers in intelligence assessment as Sir Francis Galton, Alfred Binet, and Charles Spearman.

Cubberley, Ellwood P. *Public Education in the United States*. Boston: Houghton Mifflin Company, 1934. Pages 688–704 contain a general treatment of the beginning of the scientific movement in education, with particular emphasis on the impact of the testing movement.

Freeman, Frank N. *Mental Tests: Their History, Principles and Applications*. Rev. ed. Boston: Houghton Mifflin Company, 1939. In Chapters 1 and 2 the author traces the historical development of mental tests.

Freeman, Frank S. *Theory and Practice of Psychological Testing*. 3rd ed. New York: Holt, Rinehart and Winston, 1962. Briefly outlines the history of testing, emphasizing mental testing.

Gerberich, J. Raymond, Harry A. Green, and Albert N. Jorgensen. *Measurement and Evaluation in the Modern School*. New York: David McKay Company, 1962. Chapter 2 includes a brief review of the development of measurement in the Western world and an introductory look at the common types of mental and educational tests.

Noll, Victor H. *Introduction to Educational Measurement.* 2nd ed. Boston: Houghton Mifflin Company, 1965. Chapter 2 presents a chronological review of the development of educational measurement, highlighting the notable innovations and the outstanding leaders.

Stanley, Julian C. *Measurement in Today's Schools.* 4th ed. Englewood Cliffs, New Jersey: Prentice-Hall, 1964. Chapter 2 presents an excellent historical review of the development of measurement.

Stodola, Quentin and Kalmer Stordahl. *Basic Educational Tests and Measurement.* Chicago, Illinois: Science Research Associates, 1967. History and current trends in testing are concisely reviewed in Chapter 9. An interesting aspect of this text is the self-check test items presented in each chapter.

Thorndike, Robert L. and Elizabeth Hagen. *Measurement and Evaluation in Psychology and Education.* 2nd ed. New York: John Wiley & Sons, 1961. Chapter 2 gives an overview of measurement methods, together with an historical account of their development.

Chapter 3

STATISTICAL INTERPRETATION OF THE MEASUREMENT PROGRAM

INTRODUCTION

There are perhaps more misconceptions concerning the term "statistics" than any other term in the testing field. The uninitiated hold statistics in awe, and even some bright students approach the task of learning to understand and use statistics with an almost impregnable mental block of fear and distaste. Yet, many view the statistical analysis as an ultimate authority, and the phrase "statistics show" when liberally strewn throughout a paper or report blankets it with an authentic scholarly aura before which even the bravest critics may withdraw in frustrated silence. While statistics do not lie, they are occasionally used by liars to misrepresent the data. If for no other reason than to protect himself from the hazard of uncritical acceptance of the conclusions of such research findings, the teacher must develop a rudimentary understanding of statistics.

Actually statistics is a mathematical tool which greatly simplifies the task of summarizing and interpreting quantitative data. Without this aid, the teacher can neither intelligently evaluate "research" nor effectively interpret the results of his own classroom measurement. Furthermore, descriptive statistics is well within the intellectual capacity of the average teacher and requires the understanding and use of concepts no more difficult than elementary arithmetic and beginning algebra.

The task set in this chapter is to explain only those essential statistics which are required to summarize, interpret, and report the kinds of measurement data which have been discussed in various sections of this book. While this limited coverage is adequate for the typical teacher's measurement purposes, it is hoped that it will also arouse sufficient interest among a majority of the readers that they will undertake a more comprehensive study of the field.

SUMMARIZING DATA

Raw test scores or descriptive data have little meaning unless they are arranged in some order and translated into derived scores which give a common basis for comparison against other groups of scores or data. When a teacher gives a test to a class, the two most important facts which he needs to describe pupils' performance are (1) the average or *central tendency* and (2) the range of *variability* of the scores. Both of these can be quickly calculated from a simple list of the scores without arranging them in rank order.

Untabulated data. Three important measures of central tendency are (1) the *mean* or arithmetic average, (2) the *median* or midpoint, and (3) the *mode* or most frequently appearing score. Of the three the mean is used most often by teachers. With untabulated data the mean is calculated simply by totalling the scores and dividing by the number. Thus, the pupil who earns the five scores 95, 90, 85, 85, and 80 would have a mean score of 87 (435 ÷ 5 = 87). The mean gives a good measure of the central tendency of a distribution, provided there are no markedly deviant scores. The mean actually indicates the balanced center of the distribution and will move significantly in the direction of a single deviant score as in example A below:

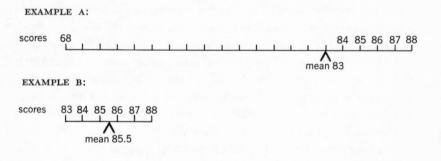

EXAMPLE A:

scores   68   84 85 86 87 88
                                                    mean 83

EXAMPLE B:

scores   83 84 85 86 87 88
                mean 85.5

On the other hand, when the scores are continuous as in example B, the mean is the actual midpoint in the distribution. One need but recall his childhood days when he played on a seesaw to understand this principle. On the seesaw one small child could readily balance two heavier children if he sat far enough out on the end, and they sat close to the middle; thus it is that the one deviant score assumes significant weight in a distribution. When the mean is used to average pupils' grades, the unfortunate child who fails to turn in one assignment is heavily penalized, even though all the rest of his grades are high.

In contrast the *median* is not influenced by a single deviant score since it is always the midpoint of the distribution, and may be located in a small group of scores simply by counting up from the bottom of a list of ranked scores to locate the point which separates the bottom and top halves. For an even number of scores it will fall *between* the two middle scores, and for an odd number it *is* the middle score. Thus, in both examples A and B above the median is 85.5. Therefore, if the teacher wishes to negate the influence of one or two atypical scores, he should use the median, not the mean, as the measure of central tendency.

The variability of untabulated data can be roughly ascertained by calculating range, that is by subtracting the lowest from the highest score and adding one. Thus, if the lowest score is 55 and the highest 85, the range would be 31 ($[85 - 55] + 1 = 31$) or started another way, the exact upper limit of the top score, 85.5, minus the exact lower limit of the bottom score, 54.5. (Scores are actually represented by continuous numbers so that the exact limits of 85 range from 84.5 to 85.5.) A test score may fall anywhere within these limits but in practice the score is rounded to the midpoint, in this case 85. Thus, the range actually represents the distance between the exact limits of the high and low scores ($85.5 - 54.4 = 31$). While range gives the total variability of a distribution, it depends upon two scores—the highest and the lowest—either of which may be quite uncharacteristic of the rest of the scores. For example, it would be possible to have a class in which the lowest IQ was 80 and the highest 140, with all other scores falling between 90 and 110. The range would be large; but, with the exception of the two pupils, the class would be quite homogeneous. For this reason other more reliable measures of variability are used with tabulated data.

Frequency distribution. When the number of scores to be summarized is large, they are most easily handled by tabulation in a frequency distribution. The frequency distribution permits calculation shortcuts in locating the mean and measures of variability, and it simplifies what would otherwise be a tedious task when the number of scores is large. Tabulation of scores in a frequency distribution can best be explained by using the series of scores obtained by 60 pupils on a high school science test. These raw scores are shown below:

118	92	82	71
114	91	82	70
112	90	81	69
110	90	80	68
109	89	80	66
107	88	78	65
106	87	77	64
104	86	76	63
100	85	76	62
99	85	75	60
98	85	75	57
97	84	74	55
96	84	74	53
95	83	73	50
94	83	72	45

The scores are tabulated in a frequency distribution in Table III. This distribution is based on a class interval of 5 (*class interval* is the number used to group scores in a distribution table for ease of handling), and there are 15 intervals in which the scores are tabulated. Two suggestions will help the teacher determine the proper class interval. First, *for most score distributions 2, 3, or 5 is an acceptable class interval.* Either 3 or 5 should be used whenever possible because with the odd-number class interval, each interval in the frequency distribution has a whole-number midpoint. (The interval 45–49 has a midpoint of 47, etc.) Second, *there should be about 15 intervals in the distribution*, although it is permissible to have 10 to 20 intervals. A method of selecting the proper class interval is first to determine the range—in the case of the raw scores given above, 74—then to divide the range by 15 to find which of the acceptable class intervals is best. In our example, 5 is selected since $74 \div 15 = 4.9$ or 5.

Graphic summary. As one looks at the tabulations in Table III, it is apparent that their profile is actually the profile of the scores if the curve were plotted on a graph. However, for the graphic summary to be more easily perceived it must be set in another format. The two graphic presentations of educational data which are most frequently used are (1) the

Table III. FREQUENCY DISTRIBUTION SHOWING THE
RAW SCORES EARNED BY 60 HIGH SCHOOL PUPILS
ON A 120-ITEM SCIENCE TEST

Intervals	Tabulations	Frequencies
115–119	|	1
110–114	|||	3
105–109	|||	3
100–104	||	2
95–99	⊬⊬	5
90–94	⊬⊬	5
85–89	⊬⊬ ||	7
80–84	⊬⊬ ||||	9
75–79	⊬⊬ |	6
70–74	⊬⊬ |	6
65–69	||||	4
60–64	||||	4
55–59	||	2
50–54	||	2
45–49	|	1
		N = 60

frequency polygon, or line graph, and (2) the *histogram,* or bar graph. The frequency polygon is used when there are two or more sets of data to be compared and which can be set to the same scale on a single page. With two sets of data, each set can be plotted in a different color for easy identification and comparison.

When the histogram is used, only one set of data can be plotted on a single page. However, the histogram is the better instrument to use when the data are to be presented to a large group of people, since the bars are clearly visible when a line graph would not be.

In constructing these two graphs the following suggestions should be followed:

1. Use graph paper with 10 or 20 squares per inch.
2. Draw the base line, or X-axis, approximately 5 inches long and lay it off in equal intervals.
3. Label the base line to designate each class interval in the frequency distribution. (Use midpoints for the frequency polygons and exact interval limits for the histogram.)
4. Include one interval above and one below those in the distribution if the frequency polygon is to be plotted.

5. Draw the verticle, or Y-axis, so that it is approximately ⅔ to ¾ as long as the X-axis, and lay it off in equal intervals.
6. Label the units of the Y-axis from zero to the greatest score frequency included in any one interval of the frequency.
7. Plot the score frequency in each interval.

Figures 3.1 and 3.2 show a frequency polygon and a histogram plotted from the frequency distribution of the 60 scores in Table III. It should

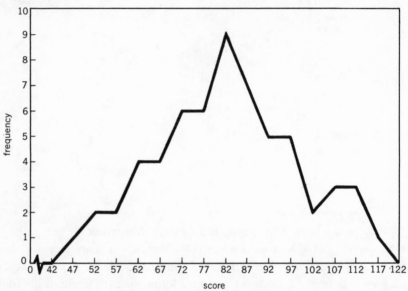

Figure 3.1. FREQUENCY POLYGON PLOTTED FROM SCIENCE TEST SCORES OF 60 HIGH SCHOOL PUPILS

be noted in the figure that the X-axis is broken from zero to the first interval to indicate the fact that the intervening intervals from zero to 42 were left out. The extra interval at the top and the bottom of the frequency polygon is necessary so that the graph can be brought down to the baseline at each end. It is customary to label the histogram with the lower limits of each interval and plot the exact lower limit slightly below the labeling as shown; however, it is also acceptable to label the midpoints with numbers centered beneath each bar.

INTERPRETING DATA

The frequency distribution which is used in plotting a graphic summary of test scores is also used in the calculation of the various measures

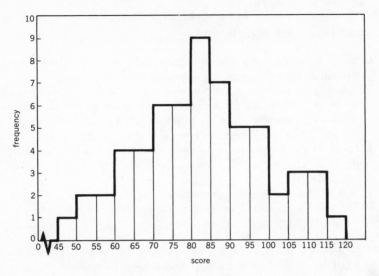

Figure 3.2. HISTOGRAM PLOTTED FROM SCIENCE TEST SCORES OF 60 HIGH SCHOOL PUPILS

of central tendency and variability. From the distribution of scores, the easiest measure of central tendency to obtain—although the least reliable —is the mode. Since the mode is simply the score which occurs most frequently in a frequency distribution it is the midpoint of the interval which contains the largest number of scores.

Mean and standard deviation. In calculating the mean of a distribution of scores the teacher selects an assumed mean or arbitrary reference point and calculates the correction which must be added or subtracted to give the correct mean. The formula used in the calculation is:

$$\text{Mean} = M' + \left[i \left(\frac{\Sigma fd}{N} \right) \right]$$

In which:

M' = assumed mean
i = class interval of the distribution
f = number of scores in each interval
d = deviation from assumed mean
N = total number of scores in the distribution
Σ = sum of

Using this formula a mean of 82.4 is obtained for the 60 test scores in

Table III. The calculation of the mean, as illustrated in Table IV, may be summarized in the following five steps:

1. Tabulate the data in a frequency table and enter the number of cases in each interval in the frequency (f) column.
2. Select as an assumed mean the midpoint of the interval which appears likely to contain the correct mean; then enter in the deviation (d) column the number of class intervals which each interval deviates above $(+)$ or below $(-)$ the interval of the assumed mean.
3. Multiply the frequency or number of cases in each interval by the deviation of the interval, entering the product in the frequency-deviation (fd) column.
4. Sum up the fd column algebraically.
5. Enter the figures thus obtained in the formula and complete the indicated computations for the mean.

Although the midpoint of any interval may be used as the assumed mean, it is best to select the interval which appears likely to contain the true mean, since a close estimate leads to a small correction and a consequent decrease in the size of the numbers to be manipulated—a factor which reduces calculation errors.

The mean and standard deviation are used together and are calculated from the same frequency distribution. Standard deviation is the most reliable measure of variability. In the normal curve, one standard deviation below the mean and one above it mark off approximately sixty-eight percent of the cases. When the method previously described is used to calculate the mean, it requires but one additional column in the table to obtain standard deviation. This is the fd^2 column, which is obtained by multiplying the d (deviation) for each interval times its fd (frequency-deviation). After the fd^2 column is summed up, the computation for standard deviation may be completed as illustrated in Table IV.

The formula used for this computation is:

$$\sigma = i \sqrt{\frac{\Sigma fd^2}{N} - \left(\frac{\Sigma fd}{N}\right)^2}$$

In which:

σ = standard deviation
i = class interval
Σfd^2 = sum of the fd^2 column
N = number of cases
Σfd = sum of the fd column

Table IV. CALCULATION OF MEAN AND STANDARD
DEVIATION OF 60 PUPILS' SCIENCE TEST SCORES

	f	d	fd	fd^2
115–119	1	+7	7	49
110–114	3	+6	18	108
105–109	3	+5	15	75
100–104	2	+4	8	32
95–99	5	+3	15	45
90–94	5	+2	10	20
85–89	7	+1	7	7
80–84	9	0	0	0
75–79	6	−1	−6	6
70–74	6	−2	−12	24
65–69	4	−3	−12	36
60–64	4	−4	−16	64
55–59	2	−5	−10	50
50–54	2	−6	−12	72
45–49	1	−7	−7	49

$$N = 60 \qquad \Sigma fd = +5 \qquad \Sigma fd^2 = 637$$

Calculation of Mean

Formula for Mean

$$\text{Mean} = 82 + \left[5 \left(\frac{5}{60} \right) \right]$$

$$\text{Mean} = M' + \left[i \left(\frac{\Sigma fd}{N} \right) \right]$$

Mean $= 82 + 5\,(.08)$

Mean $= 82 + .4 \quad$ or $\quad 82.4$

Calculation of
    Standard Deviation

Formula for
    Standard Deviation

$$\sigma = 5 \sqrt{\frac{637}{60} - \left(\frac{5}{60} \right)^2}$$

$$\sigma ^* = i \sqrt{\frac{\Sigma fd^2}{N} - \left(\frac{\Sigma fd}{N} \right)^2}$$

$\sigma = 5 \sqrt{10.62 - (.08)^2}$

$\sigma = 5 \sqrt{10.61}$

$\sigma = 5 \times 3.26 \quad$ or $\quad 16.3$

  * The standard deviation is represented by various symbols
(s, SD, and σ). σ is used throughout our discussion.

The standard deviation is the most reliable measure of variability and
has additional application as the basis of standard scores and curve grading.

Teachers in many school systems now have access to calculating machines with which they can quickly compute both mean and standard deviation from untabulated data.[1] In that case the formulae are:

$$\text{Mean} = \frac{\Sigma X}{N}$$

and

$$\sigma \quad = \sqrt{\frac{\Sigma x^2}{N}}$$

In which:

X = score
N = number of scores
x^2 = squared score deviations from the mean

Median and Q. Median and Q (semi-interquartile range—see section immediately following) are the appropriate measures of central tendency and variability when the distribution of scores is badly skewed or when —as is often the case with standardized tests—scores are reported in terms of percentile rank.

The median is readily obtained from the frequency distribution of tabulated scores. For the 60 pupils' science test scores in Table V the median is 82.17. The steps in this calculation are:

1. Divide the total number of scores by 2 or take 50 percent of the total to determine how many scores lie above and below the median $(60 \div 2 = 30)$.
2. Beginning with the bottom interval accumulate the scores until the median interval is reached. In the example in Table V there are 25 scores below the median interval.
3. Subtract the accumulated total from the number required to reach the median $(30 - 25 = 5)$.
4. Determine the required proportion of the median interval by multiplying class interval times scores needed divided by scores in the median interval $(5 \times 5/9 = 2.67)$.
5. To the exact lower limit of the median interval, add the results of the calculation in step 4. Thus, median $= 79.5 + 2.67$, or 82.17.

The median is actually the 50th percentile; and all other percentiles are calculated in the same manner as that indicated above; however, in step 1 the proportion of the total scores needed is designated by the percentile sought (e.g., 75 percent of total for 75th percentile, etc.).

[1] In schools with access to a computer, the mean and standard deviation are routinely calculated as tests are machine scored.

Table V. CALCULATION OF MEDIAN AND
QUARTILES OF THE TEST SCORES EARNED BY
60 PUPILS ON A HIGH SCHOOL SCIENCE TEST

Class Intervals	Frequency
115–119	1
110–104	3
105–109	3
100–104	2
95–99	5
90–94	5
85–89	7
80–84	9
75–79	6 ↑ f_{cum} (mdn.) $= 25$
70–74	6
65–69	4 ↑
60–64	4 f_{cum} (Q_1) $= 13$
55–59	2
50–54	2
45–49	1

$$N = 60$$

Calculation of Median

$$\text{Median} = 79.5 + \left(\frac{\frac{60}{2} - 25}{9} \times 5 \right)$$

$$= 79.5 + \left(\frac{5}{9} \times 5 \right)$$

$$= 79.5 + 2.67, \quad \text{or} \quad 82.17 \quad \text{(Median)}$$

Calculation of Q_1

$$Q_1 = 69.5 + \left(\frac{15 - 13}{6} \times 5 \right)$$

$$= 69.5 + \left(\frac{2}{6} \times 5 \right)$$

$$= 69.5 + 1.67, \quad \text{or} \quad 72.17 \quad (Q_1)$$

Semi-interquartile range. Q, or as it is properly termed "semi-interquartile range," is one-half the distance between the first and the third quartiles of the distribution. Q can be found with the following formula:

$$Q = \frac{Q_3 - Q_1}{2}$$

In which:

$$Q_3 = 75^{\text{th}} \text{ percentile}$$
$$Q_1 = 25^{\text{th}} \text{ percentile}$$

Thus with the groups of scores in Table III:

$$Q = \frac{93.5 - 72.17}{2} \text{ or } Q = 10.67$$

Relationships: central tendency and variability. The group of science test scores with which we have worked in this section of the chapter constitutes a fairly symmetrical, although not a normal, curve. As a result the mean (82.4) and median (82.17) for all practical purposes fall at the same point. In practice both would be rounded to the whole number of 82. If the distribution were unsymmetrical and skewed positively or negatively as in the accompanying examples, there would be a significant difference between the two.

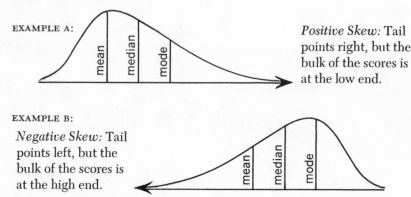

EXAMPLE A:

mean median mode

Positive Skew: Tail points right, but the bulk of the scores is at the low end.

EXAMPLE B:

Negative Skew: Tail points left, but the bulk of the scores is at the high end.

mean median mode

In example A the class performed poorly on the test so the mode is low; but because a few pupils got high scores, the mean is pulled up past the middle of the curve. However, the median which divides the area of the curve in half falls between the mode and the mean. In example B, the reverse relationship is true: the group performed well and the mode is high, the mean low, and the median in the middle.

As the standard deviation and Q for the science test scores are compared, it is evident that Q (10.67) is about two-thirds of the standard deviation (16.3). This is not a fixed proportional relationship but changes as the nature of the curve changes. Q is less reliable than standard deviation since it depends entirely upon the distance between the 25th and the 75th percentiles (Q_1 and Q_3); whereas the standard deviation reflects the influence of each score in the distribution. Standard deviation is widely accepted as the best measure of dispersion and is used to divide off the baseline of a curve in a manner somewhat analogous to the inches on a ruler. This use of standard deviation and the relationship between standard deviation and various types of test scores is shown in Figure 3.3. For the normal curve, the percent of cases which falls in the area marked off by each standard deviation range has been calculated and is indicated on the figure. The middle two deviations in the curve contain 68+ percent of all the cases. Although these same percentages do not hold for other distributions, they give an approximation of the percentages for a symmetrical curve such as that plotted for the science test in Figure 3.1.

Derived scores. In the previous discussion we have introduced the statistics necessary to translate raw scores into several types of derived scores which permit various tests and measures of performance to be compared. The derived scores most frequently used in standarized tests are:

1. Grade equivalents
2. Percentiles
3. Standard scores

1. *Grade equivalents.* Grade equivalents used with elementary school achievement batteries are simply established by determining the mean or median performance of the pupils used in the normative sample and assigning the appropriate grade equivalent. Thus, if the test is administered to a sample of fifth-grade pupils, their mean performance becomes the fifth grade equivalent. The main advantage of such scores is that elementary teachers can readily understand them. However, these scores are not directly comparable to other derived scores, nor can they be subjected to further statistical analyses.

2. *Percentiles.* When raw scores are reported as percentile equivalents, they indicate the percent of pupils who fell below each score—e.g., a pupil whose score falls at the 75th percentile excels 75 percent of those who took the test. Percentiles are commonly used for standarized achievement tests and are also easily calculated for teacher-made tests.

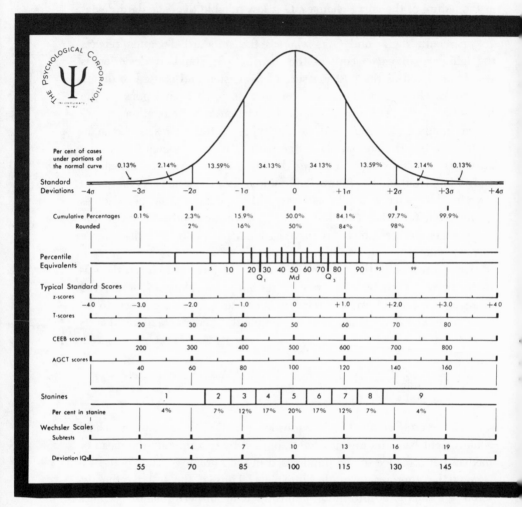

Figure 3.3. NORMAL CURVE RELATIONSHIPS BETWEEN STANDARD DEVIATIONS AND SEVERAL TYPES OF DERIVED SCORES

From *Test Service Bulletin No. 48* (New York: The Psychological Corporation, January 1955). Reprinted by permission of the publisher.

Figure 3.3 depicts the percentile scale, its relation to the normal distribution curve and to various standard scores. It should be noted in this figure that the distance on the curve between the 10th and 90th percentiles is relatively small, covering slightly less than 2.5 standard deviations of middle portion of the curve. However, the upper and lower 10 percent of the cases are spread out covering approximately 5.5 deviations in the remaining portions at either end. Thus, slight changes in performance in the middle of the curve make gross changes in rank, whereas similar performance changes at the extremes result in imperceptible changes in rank. For example, an improvement of 5 points in raw score could change a pupil's percentile rank from the 50th to the 60th percentile but would make little or no change in his rank if he were at the 95th percentile.

On teacher-made tests, the percentile ranks can be determined from the frequency distribution by calculating the percentile rank for the midpoint or upper limit of each interval. This method is demonstrated in Table VI. If the teacher wishes to use the test results to establish norms against which other groups taking the test can be compared, he may plot the results from the table on a cumulative frequency, or *ogive,* curve. This curve is plotted by consecutively accumulating the scores which lie below each interval and plotting these progressively higher points until the total number is reached. From the ogive the percentile of any pupil's score can be read directly. For example, the pupil who receives a raw score of 82 falls at the 55th percentile in the test plotted on the ogive in Figure 3.4.

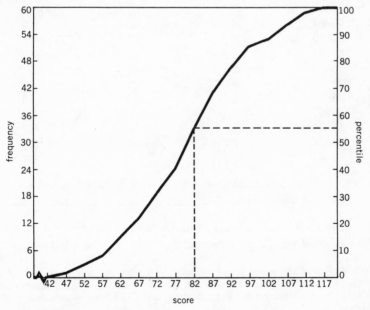

Figure 3.4. OGIVE OF SCIENCE TEST SCORES EARNED BY 60 HIGH SCHOOL PUPILS, SHOWING METHOD OF LOCATING PERCENTILE RANK OF A PUPIL'S SCORE

3. *Standard scores.* There are numerous types of standard scores, but all are based on mean and standard deviation. Examples of scores based on standard deviation include: (1) z-scores, (2) T-scores, (3) stanines, and (4) deviation IQ.[2] Reference again to Figure 3.3 shows that all except stanines measure off the same area under the normal curve between each major division, although each uses a different mean and standard deviation. T-scores with a mean of 50 and standard deviation of 10 compare to deviation IQ's with a mean of 100 and standard deviation of 15; therefore, T-scores of 50 and 60 are comparable to deviation IQ's of 100 and 115, and 34 percent of the cases lie between these two points.

Table VI. CUMULATIVE FREQUENCY AND PERCENTILES AT THE UPPER LIMITS OF EACH INTERVAL FOR THE DISTRIBUTION OF 60 HIGH SCHOOL PUPILS' SCIENCE TEST SCORES

	Frequencies	*Cumulative Frequencies*	*Percentiles*
115–119	1	60	100.0
110–114	3	59	98.3
105–109	3	56	93.3
100–104	2	53	88.3
95–99	5	51	85.0
90–94	5	46	76.7
85–89	7	41	68.3
80–84	9	34	56.7
75–79	6	25	41.3
70–74	6	19	31.3
65–69	4	13	21.3
60–64	4	9	15.0
55–59	2	5	8.3
50–54	2	3	5.0
45–49	1	1	1.7
	N = 60	$\dfrac{\text{Cum. f}}{\text{N}} =$ Percentile	

It is important that the teacher understand the comparability between various types of standard scores and that they see the relationship on the

[2] While all four scores are based on standard deviation, each is marked off differently on the curve: (1) one z-score unit per deviation; (2) ten T-score units per deviation; (3) two stanine units per deviation; and (4) fifteen or sixteen IQ units per deviation.

normal curve between standard scores and percentiles. The area $\pm 1\sigma$ from the mean contains 68+ percent of the cases and includes the scores which lie between the 16th and the 84th percentiles. The percent of cases in each of the remaining deviation units should be memorized; the following information is particularly essential:

Deviation from the mean	−2	−1	0	+1	+2
Percentile equivalent	2	16	50	84	98

As was noted earlier, *stanines,* while based on standard deviation, use a different method of dividing the curve than other standard scores. With stanines the curve is divided into nine segments. Stanines 2 through 8 cover the range on the curve from −1.75 to +1.75; each unit covers ½ standard deviation, and the 5th stanine is centered on the mean. The first stanine covers the area below −1.75, the ninth stanine, the area above +1.75. Although the stanine system would be useful in grading and assigning course marks, it has not been widely used—probably primarily because teachers lack understanding of the scores and do not know how to convert raw scores to stanines.[3]

PREDICTION

It is often useful in education to predict future performance as the basis for helping students reach decisions concerning their future educational and vocational plans. Obviously their past educational performance gives some indication of their possibilities of success in the future; but the seriousness of these decisions demands that those who counsel students must provide those students with information which will help them make their decisions regarding the future on more than a guessing basis. Predicting the future with a crystal ball is an interesting parlor game, but it leaves much to be desired as a means of deciding one's future—particularly when there are several statistical procedures which can measurably improve predictions.

In the school setting, test scores and course marks are two measures of student performance which are often used as the basis for predicting future progress. Certainly a major purpose of testing is that of prediction. Thus, it is appropriate that some consideration be given to several of the statistical techniques through which information gained in testing can be

[3] A simple method of converting raw scores to stanines for class groups of 20 to 40 pupils is shown in Robert L. Ebel, *Measuring Educational Achievement* (Englewood Cliffs, New Jersey: Prentice-Hall, 1965), pp. 260–262.

used as the basis for predictions. Among these are (1) expectancy tables, (2) regression lines, and (3) correlation.

Table VII. AN EXPECTANCY TABLE SHOWING THE RELATIONSHIP BETWEEN 30 STUDENTS' HIGH SCHOOL ACHIEVEMENT TEST SCORES AND THEIR COLLEGE GRADE-POINT AVERAGES

High School Achievement Test Scores	*College Grade-Point Averages*			
	High	*Average*	*Fail*	*Total N*
High	4	3	1	8
Average	3	9	3	15
Low	0	3	4	7
Total	7	15	8	30

Expectancy tables. The scores which students make on tests can be used to develop expectancy tables from which future achievement or performance can be predicted. The expectancy table is constructed by taking two sets of student measurements and summarizing them in a table so that the students' performance on the first measure can be conveniently compared to their performance on the second measure. For example, in Table VII a comparison is made between the scores earned by 30 high school students on a standardized achievement test and their subsequent grade-point averages as college students. In this case the achievement test is our *predictor measure* and the grade-point averages the *assessment measure*. For convenience the scores have been categorized as "high," "average," and "low" and grade-point averages as "high," "average," and "fail." However, if we wished more categories we could use actual percentile or standard scores and grade-point levels such as 3.00 (*B*), etc. In the table, of the eight students who received high achievement test scores, four subsequently earned high college grade-point averages; three, an average grade-point; and one, a failing grade-point. Thus if we assume this group to be typical of a larger group of high school students, we can use the expectancy table to predict the performance of the larger group. Specifically, we can then predict that a student who gets a high achievement test score will have about four chances out of eight or a 50-50 chance of earning a high college grade-point, three chances out of eight of earning an average grade-point, and one chance out of eight of failing. We could also say that the student who gets a low achievement test score would have about four chances out of seven of failing in college.

Since the expectancy table is a representation of the performance of a sample of the larger group, and the table is used to predict the performance of members of the large group, it is important to remember that the sample must be typical or representative of the larger group if the predictions are to be accurate.

Scattergram. The scattergram is another method of depicting a *bivariate* relationship (a relationship between two such variables as test scores and grade-point averages). A scattergram of the data in Table VII is shown in Figure 3.5. The scattergram gives a visual picture of the

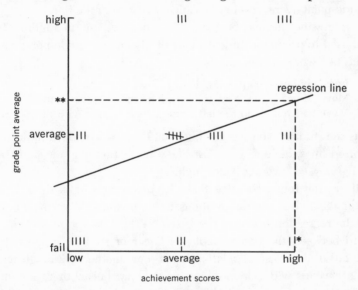

Figure 3.5. SCATTERGRAM OF PUPILS' ACHIEVEMENT TEST SCORES AND COLLEGE GRADE-POINT AVERAGES ILLUSTRATING USE OF REGRESSION LINE FOR PREDICTION

* Pupil's achievement test score
** Pupil's predicted college grade-point average

closeness of the relationship between the two variables which have been plotted. If there were a perfect relationship between the two variables, all tallies would fall on a straight line rising diagonally from left to right if positive, and from right to left if negative. As the relationship declines, the dispersion from the straight line increases.

In our example with achievement test scores and grade-point averages, it is apparent that a strong, though far from perfect, relationship exists. Earlier we determined from the expectancy table the chances of a student with a high test score of receiving "high," "average," and "failing" college grade-point averages. It is often more practical to determine more specifically what the student's most likely grade-point average would be. A line of best fit or a regression line can help us make this determination. This line could be roughly approximated by drawing a freehand straight line through the tallies in such a way that it is as close as possible to each one. Statistically the line can be placed by the least-squares method [4] or by computing the correlation between the independent variable—in this case our test scores, and the dependent variable, our grade-point averages—to determine the slope of the line.

The regression line has been drawn in our example in Figure 3.5 and can be used to predict a student's most likely college grade-point average from his test score as follows:

1. Locate his score on the base line or X-axis.
2. Move vertically to the intersect point on the regression line.
3. Move horizontally to the left to the intersect point with the Y-axis.

Thus the student who scored "high" on the test would, as indicated by the dotted lines, have as his most likely prediction a grade point about halfway between "average" and "high."

In using the regression line to make predictions, it is desirable that both the X- and Y-axis distributions be approximately normal. Furthermore, the regression procedure is based on the assumption that the relationship between the two variables is linear or straight line—that they rise or fall in a consistent relationship to one another. Although most of the relationships with which educators deal are linear, there are curvilinear relationships for which this procedure is inappropriate. For example, we expect a person's speed and accuracy in a skill such as typing to improve with practice; but there is a point beyond which practice leads to no gain. Thus the number of hours of practice and skill improvement would not have a linear relationship.

It is also assumed in the regression procedure that the scores are *homoscedastic,* which means that for each value of X the corresponding spread or variability of Y scores remains approximately equal.

[4] See J. P. Guilford, *Psychometric Methods* (New York: McGraw-Hill Book Company, 1954), pp. 63–66.

Correlation. The index for determining the relationship between two variables is the coefficient of correlation. As the term correlation implies, it indicates the "co-relationship" or common variance which two variables share.

Correlation varies in magnitude from an index of no relationship or 0.00, to ±1.00, an index of perfect relationship. The higher the index, the better the chances become of predicting an unknown score from a correlated known score. For example, it is unlikely that there exists any significant relationship between darkness of hair measured on a numerical index and intelligence as indicated by IQ. Thus if one were known, the other could not be predicted. In contrast there is normally a high relationship, +.90 to +.95, between the scores earned by a pupil on a good achievement test and the scores which he would earn on a readministration of the same test a month later. In the latter case, the correlation is high enough that a pupil's score on the second test could be predicted within close limits from his score on the first test.

If the correlation is negative or inverse, it is still just as useful in prediction as a positive correlation, since it is the magnitude—not the direction—that is important. When the correlation is positive, the two variables move in the same direction; and when negative, in opposite directions. Therefore, in the positive correlation, as one score rises the other also rises (↑↑); and in the negative correlation, as one rises the other declines (↑↓). While correlation shows the extent of relationship, it does not, as some mistakenly infer, explain the cause. Nor does it indicate that the variation in one causes the variation in the other, for the change in one or both may be caused by another factor or factors. For example, physical coordination and intelligence have a low, positive correlation, but it is unlikely that one causes the other.

Since correlation ranges on a scale from 0.00 to ±1.00, it is sometimes mistakenly interpreted as a percentage relationship. The fallacy in this line of reasoning is best explained with the aid of a scattergram to indicate the extent of common variance for sample coefficients of correlation. The scattergram is a convenient method of tabulating two sets of data on one sheet by cross tabulating with one tally for each individual's pair of scores. Thus, the vertical position of a tally on the scattergram is determined by the individual's first score and the horizontal position of the tally is determined by his second score. The three scattergrams of hypothetical scores in Figure 3.6 have respective coefficients of correlation of

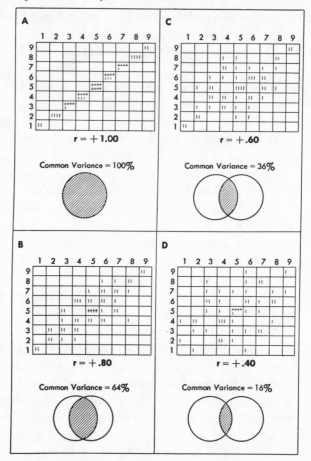

Figure 3.6. REPRESENTATIVE SCATTERGRAMS, WITH CORRESPONDING CORRELATIONS AND INDICES OF COMMON VARIANCE

(All scattergrams are based on N's of 50)

From Robert H. Bauernfeind, *Building a School Testing Program* (Boston: Houghton Mifflin Company, 1963), p. 64. Reprinted by permission of the publisher.

$+1.00$, $+.80$ and $-.60$. The common variance for a correlation of 1.00 is 100% since all the tallies are in a straight line. The percentage relationship, however, drops quickly as the correlation declines, decreasing as a square of the correlation; thus .80 has a 64% common variance, and $\pm.60$ a 36% relationship ($.80 \times .80 = 64\%$ and $.60 \times .60 = 36\%$).

The Pearson Product-Moment Coefficient of Correlation is calculated from the scattergram, and the method of computation is explained in the standard statistics texts. However, as an increasing number of schools gain access to computers, it becomes much simpler to make the computation from untabulated data with the aid of the computer. If the scores have been converted to stanines the simple procedure discussed by Bauernfeind [5] may be used. For teacher-made tests of achievement in typical class groups, the rank difference method of calculating correlation gives a quick, accurate estimate and is quite adequate for classroom use. The formula for this calculation is:

$$\text{rho} = 1 - \frac{6\Sigma D^2}{N(N^2 - 1)}$$

In which:

rho = rank difference correlation
D = difference in rank between sets of scores
N = number of scores in each of the two sets

The procedure is illustrated in Table VIII. The calculation is simple, requiring only about fifteen minutes for a typical class. The steps which should be followed are:

1. Rank the pupils' scores on the first test from the highest to lowest, taking care to keep pupils' scores on the two tests on the same line in adjacent columns. Ranks for the first set of scores are entered in the R^1 column.
2. Assign a rank order to the second set of scores, entering the ranks in the R^2 column. When several pupils receive the same score, the tie scores are assigned the mean rank of the preceding and following scores. For example, with scores 90, 89, 89, 88 in the science test $\dfrac{5 + 8}{2} = 6.5$, and both scores of 89 receive a rank of 6.5.
3. Subtract the difference between the ranks of each pupil's scores and enter the result in the D column.
4. Square these differences and enter the products in the D^2 column.
5. Enter the results in the formula and perform the required calculations.

Scores on the two tests in Table VIII are closely related with a correlation of $+.95$.

Correlation and prediction. An important use of correlation is in prediction. If the correlation (r) between two variables, such as two sets of test scores, is known, the scores can be converted to z-scores; and it is

[5] Robert H. Bauernfeind, *Building a School Testing Program* (Boston: Houghton Mifflin Company, 1963), pp. 72–76.

possible to predict the z_y score (assessment score) from the z_x score (predictor score). The formula for this prediction is:

$$z_y = rz_x$$

In which:

z_y = the assessment score
r = the coefficient of correlation
z_x = the predictor score

Table VIII. CALCULATION OF THE RANK DIFFERENCE FOR TWO SETS OF TEST SCORES

Pupil	Science Test	Math Test	Rank[1]	Rank[2]	D	D[2]
A	98	96	1	3	2	4
B	97	97	2	2	0	0
C	96	94	3	4	1	1
D	94	98	4	1	3	9
E	90	89	5	7	2	4
F	89	90	6.5	5	1.5	2.25
G	89	88	6.5	9	2.5	6.25
H	88	87	8	10	2	4
I	87	89	10	7	3	9
J	87	89	10	7	3	9
K	87	86	10	11	1	1
L	85	84	12	14	2	4
M	80	85	13	12.5	.5	.25
N	79	85	14	12.5	1.5	2.25
O	78	83	15	15	0	0
P	77	82	16	16	0	0
Q	76	80	17	17	0	0
R	75	65	18	20	2	4
S	70	78	19	18	1	1
T	65	75	20	19	1	1
	N = 20					$\Sigma D^2 = 62.00$

$$\text{rho} = 1 - \frac{6\Sigma D^2}{N(N^2 - 1)}$$

$$\text{rho} = 1 - \frac{6(62)}{20(400 - 1)}$$

$$\text{rho} = 1 - \frac{372}{7980}$$

$$\text{rho} = 1 - .05, \quad \text{or} \quad + .95$$

For example, if a pupil earned a z-score of $+2$ on an English achievement test, and if there were a correlation of $+.50$ between the English test scores and the mathematics test scores, the pupil's z-score could be predicted to be $+1$ on the mathematics test ($z_y = .50 \times 2$, or $z_y = +1$). If the correlation were .75, the pupil's mathematics score would be 1.5— that is, $z_y = .75 \times 2$, or $z_y = 1.5$. In each case above it is to be noted that the predicted score regresses toward or moves closer to the mean, the amount of regression—that is, the slope of the regression line—being determined by the magnitude of the correlation.

Actually the scores which are predicted above are the most likely scores which the student would obtain in the two instances, but in reality the prediction may be in error. Therefore, the *standard error of estimate* is used to determine the accuracy of the prediction. The formula for this statistic is:

$$\sigma_{est} = \sigma_y \sqrt{1 - r^2}$$

In which:

σ_{est} (standard error of estimate) = a measure of expected dispersion of scores around the predicted score

σ_y = the standard deviation of the assessment scores

r^2 = the squared coefficient of correlation of predictor and asment scores

Let us now insert known values into the formula to see how it may be applied. With a correlation coefficient between predictor and assessment tests of $+.84$ and a standard deviation of 15, the standard error of estimate would be:

$$\sigma_{est} = 15 \sqrt{1 - .84}$$
$$\sigma_{est} = 15 \sqrt{.16} \quad \text{or} \quad 15 \times .4 = 6. \quad \text{score points}$$

Thus if the assessment test were an intelligence test on which the student's IQ had been predicted to be 120, the chances are about two out of three that he actually will score between 114 and 126 and about 96 out of 100 that he will score between 108 and 132. Since the errors are assumed to be normally distributed around the predicted score, the standard error of estimate, as in the example in Figure 3.7, is used much as in standard deviation to establish levels of confidence in the prediction.

As one examines the formula, it is apparent that at least two factors in-

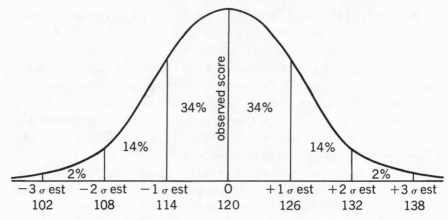

Figure 3.7. AN ILLUSTRATION OF THE USE OF STANDARD ERROR OF ESTIMATE TO ESTABLISH LEVELS OF CONFIDENCE IN LOCATING THE TRUE SCORE

fluence the size of the standard error of estimate. These are the size of the standard deviation of assessment scores and the strength of the correlation between predictor and assessment tests. When the standard deviation is small and the correlation high, the error in prediction will be small. With a perfect correlation (± 1.00), there is in fact no error in prediction.

SUMMARY

Statistics is a mathematical tool which facilitates the summarization and interpretation of measurement data. The first step in analyzing a large group of raw scores is to tabulate them in a frequency distribution. Calculation of the required statistical measures is much easier from the frequency distribution than from untabulated data, and graphic summaries can also be plotted directly from the distribution.

There are two essential items of information concerning a group of test scores which the teacher must have before he can make a meaningful interpretation of them. These are (1) the central tendency and (2) the variability. The measures of central tendency commonly used are the *mean,* the *median,* and the *mode.* The mode, which is simply the most frequently occurring score, is the easiest to obtain, but the least reliable. The mean, or arithmetic average, is used most often and is probably the best measure, despite the fact that it is heavily influenced by atypical scores. The median is the midpoint in a distribution of scores and is most useful when the curve is skewed so that most of the scores fall at the high or low end.

A crude measure of variability is the *range,* but the most reliable measure is *standard deviation.* Standard deviation and mean used together have a variety of applications, including (1) application in curve grading and (2) conversion of raw test scores to several kinds of standard scores.

Raw test scores have little meaning unless they are converted into some type of derived score which permits comparisons between several sets of scores to be made. Grade norms, percentiles, and standard scores are the derived scores used in most standardized achievement tests. Grade norms are most easily understood but are appropriate only for the elementary grades. Percentiles are most widely used for educational tests; however, a disadvantage of these scores is that they represent unequal performance units since slight performance changes in the middle of the curve result in gross changes in percentile rank, while gross changes in performance at the extremes have little effect on percentile rank. For this reason many test publishers report scores in both percentiles and standard scores—z-scores, T-scores, stanines—leaving the choice of score to the test user.

In addition to possessing a workable knowledge of the statistical measures required to interpret a group of scores, the teacher also needs an understanding of at least two other statistical concepts: (1) the *standard error of estimate,* which can help him interpret individual pupils' test scores properly, and (2) the *coefficient of correlation,* which is used to predict future performance and to establish the reliability and validity of standardized tests. Although a command of the statistical concepts outlined in this review certainly would not qualify the teacher as a statistician, it should be adequate to permit him to make a good summary and interpretation of his testing data and to equip him to read the technical test manuals with understanding.

DISCUSSION QUESTIONS AND PROBLEMS

1. Read the technical manual of a standardized achievement test and critically evaluate it. Pay particular attention to the ways in which test reliability and validity were established and are reported.
2. Obtain a set of test scores and calculate the mean and standard deviation.

3. Make an item analysis of a test which has been given in class. Use the analysis as a basis for discussion and refinement of test items.
4. Which measure of central tendency would be best to use in describing
   a. the average man,
   b. average income of Americans,
   c. a series of time trials by a race driver over a measured course?
5. Discuss the relative merits of the use of mean or median for grade averages.
6. Convert T-scores of 40 and 65 into z-scores, percentiles, and CEEB scores, using Figure 3.3 as your guide.

SELECTED READINGS

Amos, Jimmy R., Foster Lloyd Brown and Oscar G. Mink. *Statistical Concepts*. New York: Harper & Row, 1965. This simple, programmed text covers the statistical concepts which are essential for those who teach.

Davis, Frederick B. *Educational Measurements and Their Interpretation*. Belmont, California: Wadsworth Publishing Company, 1964. The appendices are particularly helpful since they contain explanations and examples of the calculation of such indices as standard error.

Garrett, Henry E. *Statistics in Psychology and Education*. 5th ed. New York: Longmans, Green and Company, 1958. A standard, widely used text which first appeared in 1926, and has been periodically updated to include new material.

Guilford, J. P. *Fundamental Statistics in Psychology and Education*. 4th ed. New York: McGraw-Hill Book Company, 1965. An excellent basic reference on statistical concepts and processes. Includes an introduction to factor theory.

Lyman, Howard B. *Test Scores and What They Mean*. Englewood Cliffs, New Jersey: Prentice-Hall, 1963. A brief and easily understood consideration of the concepts required for score interpretation.

Magnusson, David. *Test Theory*. Reading, Massachusetts: Addison-Wesley Publishing Company, 1966. This excellent book contains discussion, with many appropriate examples, of the statistics applicable to testing. Of particular interest are Chapters 3, 11, and 12.

Manuel, Herschel T. *Elementary Statistics for Teachers*. New York: American Book Company, 1962. A beginning study of statistics for students who need only basic concepts and skills. It is a convenient reference for self-help.

Stodola, Quentin and Kalmer Stordahl. *Basic Educational Tests and Measurement*. Chicago, Illinois: Science Research Associates, 1967. In Chapters 4 and 5 of this text there are excellent, easily understood discussions of basic statistical concepts.

Wallis, W. Allen and Harry V. Roberts. *The Nature of Statistics*. New York: Collier Books, 1962. An entertaining and informative book which contains an excellent discussion of the misuse and the correct use of statistics.

Chapter 4

THEORETICAL BACKGROUND
FOR MEASUREMENT

INTRODUCTION

American school children are the most tested and testwise children in the world. Each year in thousands of classrooms they listen to the instructions to press firmly on the marking pencil, to mark carefully between the lines, and to keep the answer sheets free of stray marks or smudges so that the machine scoring will be accurate. On their responses to the approximately 100,000,000 such tests administered annually hinges their educational future. They are grouped, counseled, and channeled into vocational or academic curricula on the basis of their test results. Yet in spite of this broad-scale use of tests, the test-sophistication of pupils and teachers is frequently superficial. Both groups are familiar with the test instrument, with the routine of testing, and with the types of derived scores which are commonly used; but few teachers have a real insight into the meaning of the scores or the strengths and weaknesses of the instruments. Thus the scores are often taken on faith as the unchangeable, irrefutable authority for a routinized process of pupil classifications which is made without more than cursory evaluation of the tests or the validity of the test scores. Unfortunately, too often after they have been used for these routine purposes, the tests are filed in the vault and are subsequently forgotten by most of the teaching staff. Under such circumstances the high outlay of finances and time for the testing program is difficult to justify.

The teaching staff must understand the testing program if it is to make an intelligent selection of tests and then evaluate the testing results as a basis for instructional and curricular changes. As was noted in an earlier chapter, measurement is generally the objective use of some instrument to obtain the data which one desires; however, it is the more important, but subjective, evaluation which leads to subsequent action in the form of program revision, etc. When teachers fail in their evaluation responsibility, the important decisions which affect their instruction—selection of the test program, revision of the curriculum, individualization of instruction—may be made by the administrator and the guidance personnel. Or, worse yet, these decisions may be made in other school systems, which set the pattern for the "followers."

PROBLEM AREAS IN MEASUREMENT

In schools we are interested in two categories of pupil behavior: to use Cronbach's classification [1] we want to determine what is *typical behavior* for a given group of pupils and what is the *maximum performance* for each group of pupils. Thus our measurement instruments fall roughly into these two categories. Personality and interest tests are examples of typical behavior tests which give us information about pupils which can be compared against the normal or typical behavior in their age group or in occupations which they may enter. On the other hand, we use maximum performance instruments such as achievement and intelligence tests to help us set reasonable academic standards, to pace the instruction to the pupils' capacities, and to help us make curriculum scope and sequence judgments.

Two other problems which constantly confront educators are those of *grouping* pupils for instructional purposes and of *predicting* their future success from their current classroom performance. The practice of grouping pupils in classes according to their chronological age is a tentative solution to the first problem. The difficulty with this practice is the fact that children of the same age do not perform alike, that slow, older pupils approximate average younger pupils in intellectual ability, whereas younger, bright pupils can easily match the intellectual performance of older, normal children. Consequently, educators have gradually moved toward such other practices as remedial programs, acceleration, enrichment, and homogeneous ability grouping—all of which have placed a premium on tests as the grouping criterion. While none of the current solutions to this problem of grouping pupils is wholly satisfactory, there may be others which will ensure better attention to the individual child's needs while still guaranteeing the quality of education which our mod-

[1] Lee J. Cronbach, *Essentials of Psychological Testing*, 2nd ed. (New York: Harper & Row, 1960), p. 29.

ern, competitive society demands. Certainly the development of better measurement instruments as well as better evaluations of the measurement from our current instruments will continue to influence the grouping process.

The problem of prediction is even more difficult than that of grouping, but it is a problem which must be faced in schools if we are to educate children in the rapidly changing world of today for a vastly different world tomorrow. To prepare children now for successful future performance, we must make accurate predictions and plan an educational program which will enhance the child's chances of success in that future.

Unfortunately, the types of measurement currently used are often ill suited for successful prediction. For example, heavy reliance is placed upon paper-and-pencil tests of cognitive knowledge and comprehension to predict pupils' psycho-motor performance and problem-solving ability. Unfortunately, some pupils who do well on paper-and-pencil tests—particularly those which stress memory—often fail to apply that knowledge when faced with performance tasks or practical problems. Furthermore, we infer (often wrongly), measure indirectly, or fail to measure at all a number of the important learning outcomes or human traits which we value in education. For example, we measure ability or learning, from which we infer intellectual capacity; but the ratio between learned ability and innate capacity is not the same for the culturally deprived and the average middle-class child. Thus we habitually underestimate the intelligence of lower-class or minority-group children. We measure performance indirectly or in simulated situations even in such obvious performance areas as industrial arts and physical education, where teachers may go so far as to stress knowledge tests rather than the more important skill tests. We often make no attempt to measure the pupils' attitudes—attitudes toward the field of study, toward the school, toward other pupils; yet it is these important attitudes which determine how much of the pupils' learning is retained and applied. Unfavorable attitudes fostered by inept teaching may persuade the child to avoid the field in the future and to forget as quickly as possible what he has learned in his unpleasant classroom experience.

QUALITIES OF GOOD MEASUREMENT

The phenomenal growth in the number and variety of measurement instruments and techniques in recent years has not been an unmixed blessing, for it has meant that the teacher is confronted with a hodge-podge of possibilities so numerous as to make intelligent choice of the best available instrument or technique a difficult and frequently haphazard task. Good measurement does not occur by chance. If the best results are to be obtained, the best instrument for the purpose must be selected and then skillfully used. Measurement goes awry when the wrong instrument is selected or when the proper instrument is unskillfully used.

Table IX illustrates the working partnership between instrument and process which characterizes good measurement. Clearly the instrument selected should be that which possesses the highest degree of three important qualities: (1) validity, (2) reliability, and (3) usability. Validity, as we shall see, is inseparable from purpose of measurement; reliability depends upon the elimination of errors in instrument and process; and usability determines the level of skill required in applying the instrument. The remainder of the chapter is devoted to a discussion of these necessary qualities of the instrument and the measuring process.

VALIDITY OF INSTRUMENT

Concepts of validity. Validity is unquestionably the most important of the three qualities of a measurement instrument. Validity has customarily been used to refer to the extent to which an instrument measures that which its user intends to measure.[2] According to this concept, validity is determined by comparing "what the instrument measures" against "what it ought to measure." For example, a statistical comparison is made of the measurements against some outside criterion which is presumed to be valid; or expert opinion is used to judge the degree to which what it *does* measure corresponds with what it *ought* to measure. Since with many types of measurements there is no convenient, acceptable outside criterion against which to compare, validation even of some of the "better standardized tests" has been by expert judgment—a method which obviously demands infallibility from fallible human judges.

Elaborating on the concept of validity, the American Educational Research Association [3] suggested a classification consisting of four types of validity: (1) content, (2) construct, (3) concurrent, and (4) predictive.

[2] See E. F. Linquist, *A First Course in Statistics* (Boston: Houghton Mifflin Company, 1942), p. 213.

[3] American Educational Research Association, *Technical Recommendations for Achievement Tests* (Washington, D. C.: American Educational Research Association, 1955), p. 16.

Table IX. QUALITIES OF GOOD MEASUREMENT

Qualities of Instrument	Qualities of Process
1. Validity Provides intended measure. Permits predictability of specified pupil behavior.	Clear statement of purpose Suitable choice of instrument. Clear concept of limitations of instrument.
2. Reliability Consistency of result. Free of inherent error.	Elimination of errors Minimum error in administration, scoring, and interpretation.
3. Usability Good format. Ease of administration, scoring, and interpretation.	Skillful application of instrument Required level of skill dependent upon usability.

Although this has been a reasonably satisfactory classification of the types of validity and has been generally accepted for the past decade, there have been both criticisms of the classification and suggestions for additional types. An example of the latter is Ebel's [4] classification cited below:

Direct	*Derived*
Validity by Definition	Empirical Validity
Content Validity	Concurrent Validity
Curricular Validity	Predictive Validity
Intrinsic Validity	Factorial Validity
Face Validity	Construct Validity

In this classification the direct types are established by examining the instrument and the decisions of the test maker, while the derived are validated against an outside criterion. While the list appears to proliferate the concepts, sorting them into two categories according to method of establishment is actually a step in the right direction. Validity is certainly definable as a general concept, but it may also be defined specifically in relation to the many different measuring instruments and the purposes for which they are used.

Cattell in criticizing current concepts of validity suggests that a better

[4] Robert L. Ebel, *Measuring Educational Achievement* (Englewood Cliffs, N. J.: Prentice-Hall, 1965), p. 381.

definition of the term is "the capacity of a test to predict some specified behavioral measure (or set of measures) other than itself."[5] His proposed analysis for validity is according to:

1. The degree of abstraction of the referent criterion, i.e., ranging from concrete to conceptual as from a concrete job skill to an intellectual construct.
2. The degree of naturalness of the criterion, i.e., ranging from natural to artifactual or correlation with behavior at the natural end of the scale and with other tests at the opposite extreme.
3. The degree of directness of validation, ranging from direct to indirect or circumstantial.[6]

In elaborating on the third type of analysis Cattell says:

In the simplest sense the validity of Test x as a good measure of Criterion X might seem sufficiently evidenced by the magnitude of its direct correlation with X. But in a deeper philosophical sense it depends also on x behaving toward "the not-X" universe in the same way as X does. Even at a simple statistical level it is evident that two (or more) tests might show exactly the same correlation with X and yet correlate in very different patterns from each other with the not-X variables. These differences affect the degree and kind of error which will follow when x is allowed to stand for X.[7]

In spite of the fact that current concepts of validity are being questioned and more sophisticated statistical analyses will largely replace present approaches, much of the current literature and test manuals are based on the 1955 AERA types of validity noted earlier. Each of the four types is briefly discussed therefore in the subsequent pages.

1. *Content validity.* Content validity is sometimes confused with "face validity" although actually the two are different concepts. Face validity refers to the relevant appearance of the instrument—i.e., does it appear to measure what it is intended to? Content validity, on the other hand, refers to the extent to which a test includes a representative sample of the universe of content and objectives for the course or subject field which is being measured. In achievement tests the basic concern is with content validity. Authors of standardized achievement tests are faced with the problem of constructing tests which have high validity for a large number of pupils in all areas of the country. The achievement test

[5] Raymond B. Cattell, "Validity and Reliability: A Proposed More Basic Set of Concepts," *Journal of Educational Psychology*, LV, No. 1 (February 1964), 2.
[6] Cattell, p. 2; for extended discussion see remainder of article.
[7] *Ibid.*

must be designed to fit as nearly as possible each teacher's instructional objectives and content. But the American school system is characterized by considerable diversity in curricular offerings, textbooks, and courses of study. Even children in adjoining school districts may study quite different content in any specific course. Furthermore, since the instructional objectives of teachers differ, they may teach approximately the same course content but with different emphasis dictated by the goal which they have in mind. Thus the standardized achievement test rarely, or ever, coincides with a specific teacher's concept of the course content and objectives; and insofar as the test and course fail to coincide the test lacks content validity.

In many cases a skillful teacher's carefully constructed test will have higher content validity for measuring the achievement of pupils in his course than the standardized test, but the standardized test has the advantage of providing a national norm against which each teacher can compare his class. On the other hand, during recent years increased state control and supervision of local schools and district consolidation, with enlarged school administration units, have acted together to alleviate the diversity in course offerings and content which was prevalent earlier. The increased impact of improved transportation and communication has also had a leavening influence in helping ensure minimum curricular consistency within the schools. Many educational changes still take place in the schools; but new developments are quickly reported and, when successful, are rapidly adopted in other school districts.

An achievement test may be selected by the teacher on casual examination because it appears to cover what it should. Face validity is desirable, but the teacher should also be certain that the test measures his behavioral objectives.[8] Information on standardization and norms along with a careful item tabulation of content are extremely useful in helping the teacher make the best selection. In the selection process there is no good substitute for a careful item by item examination of the test. To determine whether the test content parallels the course, the teacher should read through the achievement test, and, if time permits, tabulate the items under each main topic and instructional objective in his course.

2. *Construct validity.* The term "construct" refers to the human trait or characteristic which is to be measured. This may be an intellectual factor

[8] It should be noted that Raymond B. Cattell, p. 9, suggests that face validity is unnecessary and that content validity, without other evidence, is relatively unimportant.

such as mechanical aptitude, musical aptitude, and numerical aptitude; or it may be a personality trait such as dominance, introversion, and insecurity.

The *construct validity* of a measurement instrument reflects its effectiveness in assessing the personality traits or intellectual factors which have been selected for measurement. There is, however, another aspect to construct validity which is embodied in the question: Do the constructs selected for measurement give a representative picture of personality or intellect? Thus, an instrument may be invalid if the wrong constructs are selected, even though those selected are carefully measured. In both intelligence and personality testing construct selection, as well as the theory underlying the constructs, will appreciably influence test results. When intelligence is defined as a general ability to verbalize abstractions and is measured as such, the results will differ from measurements based on the theory that intelligence should be defined as a series of specific factors, such as memory and verbal fluency.

In personality assessment, selection is a particularly serious problem because literally hundred of constructs could be selected for measurement; but since it is practical to measure only a limited number on a single test, those selected must be of major importance if they are to give a valid picture of personality. The two problems, then, in establishing high construct validity for a test are (1) proper selection of constructs and (2) correct measurement of the constructs selected.

Construct validity is generally determined by one of two methods: (1) correlation of the test results with those of a known or acceptable instrument and (2) expert opinion. Both of these approaches are open to serious criticism, which places their results in jeopardy. If there is an acceptable instrument with high validity, then the correlation approach is useful; however such highly valid instruments are not available in some test areas, such as personality. When the test results on a poor instrument show high statistical correlation with those on a new but equally poor instrument, little has been achieved in proving validity. When expert opinion is consulted, the possibility always exists that the opinion of what is important may be fallacious. Since expert opinion in psychology and education frequently differs, the "expert" opinion of the classroom teacher is also always an important consideration in determining validity. The classroom teacher has specific aims in mind, aims which relate directly to validity of any measurement.

3. *Concurrent validity.* A test has high concurrent validity when the

test results show a close relationship to the actual concurrent behavior of the pupils. For example, the pupils who receive high scores in an American government test should also show evidence of understanding democratic society by the manner in which they behave in the school and community. Helping pupils become good citizens of our democracy is an important goal in the American government course; and when those pupils who achieve the highest scores are also the best citizens, the test is apparently high in concurrent validity. Tests frequently emphasize knowledge and understanding which teachers expect to be utilized in specific types of performance and behavior. If the knowledge gained does not modify the pupil's behavior to desirable patterns and the test is designed to measure only that knowledge, then the concurrent validity is low.

Concurrent validity of a test is easier to determine than predictive validity because present behavior can be observed, but follow-up is required to establish predictive validity. It is relatively easy to determine whether pupils who score well on an English grammer test speak and write correctly but more difficult to ascertain whether they will continue to do so.

4. *Predictive validity.* Tests which are used to determine future status or behavior of people must have high predictive validity. Increasing reliance is being placed on test scores or evaluative techniques for predicting the future success of pupils in higher levels of education or in future jobs. During these years when college enrollment overflows existing facilities, the test score and the grade-point average are almost universally used as selective devices for college admission. Nationwide testing programs, such as the *National Merit Scholarship Examination,* are being relied on to identify the nation's most able prospective college students. Years of experience with such testing programs have given educators confidence in their predictive validity. In fact, most of the good standardized intelligence and achievement tests give a reliable indication of pupils' future success in school; and it has become possible to identify as early as the lower elementary grades those who are apt to drop out of school as well as those who are good risks to complete college or higher levels. It is probably even more important, however, that society have efficient tools for identifying its future leaders, creative inventors, and so on, and at the other end of the scale, its problem cases—the misfits, the criminals, and the mentally disturbed.

Despite the relative success of test makers in devising tools to predict future success of individuals in school, accuracy in predicting success in the broader spectrum of adult society has been much more limited. Test scores, college grade-point average, civil service examinations, and job interviews—although they are relied on heavily—are still highly fallible in selecting the best teachers, political leaders, scientists, and doctors. In achieving high-level predictive validity in such cases it seems apparent that the combination of several instruments and techniques is necessary, and the refinement of current approaches as well as the addition of new ones will probably improve the predictive validity. Also several instruments which taken singly may have low predictive validity give an improved validity when used in combination.

Determining validity. The method of determining validity varies according to the measurement purpose and the type of test used. The methods can be classified as (1) curricular and (2) empirical or statistical. Content validity, which is important for achievement tests, is determined by the curricular or expert opinion approach. With this approach, subject-matter experts examine the test to judge how closely the test content conforms to the course content for which it is designed. The content of standardized tests is also compared to that of the major textbooks in the field. A teacher may also compare the test against his own course outline to assess the thoroughness of coverage. Thus the content validity of an achievement test is a matter of personal judgment; and a test which is valid for a course such as biology in one school may have poor validity for a biology course in another school if the two teachers concerned have different concepts of the course content and objectives.

Construct validity depends upon the selection of appropriate constructs for measurement together with adequate measurement of those which are selected. Statistical tools, such as factorial analysis, may be used in selecting the constructs; but expert opinion is generally used to assess the adequacy of measurement.

Both concurrent and predictive validity rely on the empirical approach, which uses an outside criterion for comparison. For instance, results on an aptitude test may be statistically compared to grade-point average, to scores on another test of the same aptitude, or to the relative success of the test subjects in the field covered by the test. When new group tests of intelligence are constructed, they are often administered to a group of pupils; and the results are statistically correlated with the scores which the same group receive on a well known test, such as the

Stanford-Binet Intelligence Scale. The assumption in this case is that the Stanford-Binet test is a valid measure of intelligence; consequently a new test which correlates highly with it is also valid. This approach is a good one, provided that there is a valid outside criterion against which to make a comparison; but when the outside criterion lacks validity, the method has little worth.

RELIABILITY OF INSTRUMENT

The second important quality of measuring instruments is reliability. Reliability refers to consistency; a reliable test is one on which pupils get approximately the same scores in repeated testings. Insofar as the pupils' scores vary from one test administration to another the reliability decreases. A test which is highly valid or measures exactly what the user wishes to measure would also undoubtedly be reliable since it should continue to get such results. High validity of an instrument as a rule is also accompanied by high reliability. The reverse relationship is not true, however, since an instrument may be reliable but lack validity. For example, an achievement test in mathematics could be very reliable but lack validity because it fails to measure important mathematical concepts.

Teachers are generally aware of the variation in pupils' test scores from year to year and of the effect on pupils' scores of such factors as health, emotion, and testing environment. While most teachers recognize the importance of these factors, few attempt to estimate the magnitude of their effects on test scores.

Systematic and unsystematic variation. Even though a measuring instrument is highly reliable, there are a number of factors which induce variation in test scores. These are classified under two categories: (1) systematic and (2) unsystematic. The systematic factors are those which produce orderly changes. Learning and growth cause pupils to receive higher scores on subsequent tests; while fatigue, forgetting, or aging cause lower scores. The systematic factors may result in a trend with definite increments of learning or definite units of loss. Unsystematic factors are those which produce random changes in test scores. Variation in attention, emotional factors, and test environmental conditions are unsystematic factors which randomly affect obtained test scores.

The score which a pupil obtains on a test is not likely to be his true score. The magnitude of difference between the obtained score and the true score can be largely accounted for by the unsystematic factors which are operative in each individual case. Although the true score is actually that which one would achieve under ideal conditions with an excellent testing instrument, in practice the true score is assumed to be the average score which a pupil would receive through repeated testings with the same or parallel test forms.

A hypothetical model which serves to illustrate the relationship between systematic factors, unsystematic factors, and average or true score appears in Figure 4.1. This model shows a pupil's status in typing speed

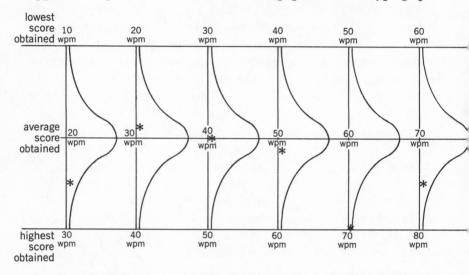

Figure 4.1. HYPOTHETICAL DISTRIBUTIONS OF THE SCORES OBTAINED BY A PUPIL ON A SERIES OF TYPING-SPEED TESTS ADMINISTERED AT THE END OF EACH MONTH OF A SIX-MONTH PERIOD

* = First score obtained at each test period

at the end of each month of a six-month period. The scores which he obtained on the six tests administered at the end of each period were 25 words per minute, 28 w/m, 40 w/m, 52 w/m, 70 w/m, and 75 w/m. The irregular changes in this hypothetical model, however, are not indicative of the steady increase in speed which was actually achieved. If the pupil had been given a series of tests at the end of each month, the range between lowest obtained score and highest obtained score each time would have been 20 words per minute, and the distribution approximately a normal curve. Thus the range of scores obtained in each test period can

accounted for by *unsystematic factors,* the average speed is the true
core, and the change in average score each period is the result of sys-
ematic factors—primarily the gain resulting from practice. Obviously a
single speed test administered at the end of each period gives an unreliable estimate of the pupil's true speed. Similarly a single score on a standardized test is fallible insofar as systematic and unsystematic factors are
operative.

Cattell has suggested that test consistency is a better term than reliability and that the three distinct forms of consistency are *reliability, homogeneity,* and *transferability.*[9] He defines test consistency as:

. . . the extent to which a test continues to measure the same psychological
concept despite such changes as inevitably and normally occur in a test, its
administration, and the populations to which it is administered.[10]

Therefore, he proposes that test consistency be evaluated statistically in
the three senses related to the above definition. These are:

1. Across occasions in reference to reliability. In this instance the agreement of scores on the same test applied to the same people on different
   occasions, or the test-retest performance, is checked.
2. Across tests in reference to homogeneity. This is the agreement of
   scores on subsets or portions of a test administered to the same people
   on the same occasion—a concept related to that which we have called
   the *internal consistency* of the test.
3. Across people in reference to transferability. This is the agreement of
   score meaning of the same test applied to different people in different
   sub-cultures.[11]

Establishing reliability. Two statistics are used to indicate the relative
reliability of a measurement. These are (1) the reliability coefficient,[12]
and (2) the standard error of measurement. The reliability coefficient
gives an index of the extent to which scores on a test can be used to predict those on a parallel test. The standard error is an index of the extent
to which individuals' scores vary over a number of parallel or alternate-
form tests.

The reliability coefficient, although affected by pupil maturation and
other factors, is most directly related to the reliability inherent in the

[9] Raymond B. Cattell, *op. cit.* (above, n. 5), p. 9.
[10] Cattell, p. 11.
[11] Cattell, p. 10.
[12] See Chapter 3, p. 54, for further discussion of the coefficient of correlation upon
which this statistic is based.

measuring instrument. Before the reliability coefficient can be
two sets of scores must be obtained from the same group of p.
methods used in obtaining these scores are (1) the test-retest
(2) the alternate-forms method, and (3) the split-half method.

1. *Test-retest method.* With the test-retest method a test is given
group of pupils, and after a suitable lapse of time—normally a month
more—the test is readministered. The two sets of scores are then statis
cally correlated to determine how consistent the scores are. If the score.
remain stable and pupils retain the same rank in the group, high reliability is present; but marked changes in score appreciably lower the reliability. With the test-retest method, reliability is reported as the *coefficient
of stability;* and a coefficient of .90 or higher is desirable.

A problem of this approach relates to the errors of measurement in the
two testings. If—as is apt to be the case—there are errors of measurement in the first set of obtained scores as well as errors in the second set,
differences between the two sets represent both error differences and real
differences resulting from changed pupil performance. By way of illustration, it is possible that pupil A's score on the first testing is in error by
being lower than his true score, while on the second testing the score is
in error by being higher than his true score. A number of such errors in
pupils' sets of scores would appreciably lower the coefficient, since it is
unlikely that for most pupils the flow of errors from the first to the second testing would be in the same direction, i.e., high first test and high
second test. Rather, the error dispersion among sets of scores would more
likely be random.

Another problem with this method is that haphazard, unpredictable
pupil changes may occur in the interim between the first and the second
testing, with consequent lowering of the reliability coefficient. For example, while several pupils could become highly motivated and show considerable learning progress, others could lose interest and actually retro-
gress.

2. *Alternate-form method.* The alternate-form method requires the use
of two parallel tests of the same difficulty level, each of which stress the
same objectives and cover the same content. In checking reliability of
the alternate forms, both tests are administered to the same group within
a short time span to avoid the problem of intervening pupil change
which besets the test-retest method. The two sets of scores are then cor-

related to determine reliability and reported as the *coefficient of equivalence*. The correlation in this instance is an index of how nearly equivalent the parallel tests are, with high correlation indicating a close relationship between the two tests. This method requires the construction of at least two tests, and the reliability coefficient obtained is usually slightly lower than either the test-retest or the split-half method. However, for the teacher, the value of having nearly equivalent test forms partially compensates for the lower reliability since he has a second form to administer as a recheck on those who did poorly or who may have missed the first testing.

3. *Split-half method.* When the split-half method is used, the one test which is administered to the group is essentially split into two tests by obtaining two sets of scores for each pupil—one his score on all odd-numbered test items, the other his score on all even-numbered test items. The correlation between these two sets of scores, called the *coefficient of internal consistency,* is an index of the relationship between the two parts of the test. Lengthening any test tends to increase its reliability. Therefore, since splitting a test into two shorter tests reduces the reliability, the Spearman-Brown Formula is used to estimate the reliability of the entire test. The formula is:

$$r_{xx} = \frac{2r_{oe}}{1 + r_{oe}}$$

In which:

r_{xx} = coefficient of internal consistency of the total test

r_{oe} = coefficient of correlation between the odd-half scores and the even-half scores

This is a convenient method for estimating test reliability, and it is often used for standardized tests.

The person examining a test needs to know that if a test manual states that the Spearman-Brown formula was used to calculate reliability, the split-half method was used, and a higher coefficient of reliability should be expected than from the alternate-form method. The Spearman-Brown reliability coefficient equivalents of the alternate-form coefficients are given in Table X. In each instance there is a significantly higher correlation with the single-test method.

Table X. COMPARISON OF RELIABILITY COEFFICIENTS OBTAINED FROM EQUIVALENT FORMS AND FROM FRACTIONS OF A SINGLE TEST

Test	Alternate Forms	Single Test
Otis Quick-Scoring Intelligence Test—Beta	.84	.90
Pintner-Durost Intelligence Test		
Scale 1. Picture Content	.78	.92
Scale 2. Reading Content	.92	.97
Essential High School Content Battery		
Mathematics	.88	.92
Science	.75	.85
Social Studies	.85	.89
English	.86	.90

Robert L. Thorndike and Elizabeth Hagen, *Measurement and Evaluation in Psychology and Education*, 2nd ed. (New York: John Wiley & Sons, 1961), p. 189. Reprinted by permission of the publisher.

Another method of estimating reliability from one testing is the Kuder-Richardson technique.[13] Their Formula 20 is:

$$r = \frac{k}{k-1}\left[1 - \frac{\Sigma pq}{\sigma^2}\right]$$

In which:

$k =$ number of items on the test

$p =$ number of correct responses to one item

$q =$ number of incorrect responses to the item

$\sigma =$ variance of scores on the test

Use of this formula requires that the number of correct and incorrect responses be determined for each test item. In the event that the items throughout the test are approximately equal in difficulty, the Kuder-Richardson Formula 21 may be used without the item analysis required by Formula 20 (above). Most frequently, however, item difficulty varies and use of Formula 21 would consequently give an underestimate of reliability.

Factors affecting reliability. Several controllable factors operate to in-

[13] G. F. Kuder and M. W. Richardson, "The Theory of the Estimation of Test Reliability," *Psychometrika*, II (September 1937), 151–160.

crease or decrease the reliability of a measuring instrument. First, *the longer the measuring instrument the more reliable it is*. This principle holds as long as the items added are at least as good as those already included and is applicable until the instrument becomes excessively long. A test which is too long may actually appear to lose reliability because some respondents become too tired or poorly motivated to complete it. Short teacher-made objective tests are extremely unreliable unless several sets of scores are accumulated to give a single composite score.

Standardized test batteries designed to test several subject fields and grade levels in the elementary school often sacrifice some reliability in the individual tests in the interest of keeping the total battery short enough to be administered conveniently to young children. Composite tests, such as the S.R.A. *Primary Mental Abilities* test, also have short sub-tests, so the reliability of these sub-tests is low compared to the relatively high reliability for the entire test.

Second, *test scores are more reliable when the range of the group tested is quite variable*. When the group is homogeneous, numerous, slight, individual shifts in score can significantly change the rank of group members in a second testing; while such small changes have negligible effects within a highly heterogeneous group.

Third, *the age range of the group tested affects reliability*. Standardized achievement and intelligence tests are generally designed to test several grade levels. In the first years of school the most reliable test is that designed for a specific grade or age level because the changes in skills and maturity are so rapid that tasks completely beyond the capability of the pupils at the beginning of the year are readily completed six months later. At the upper grades, however, changes are not so rapid; and a test for several grades or ages is more feasible. Tests designed for too broad an age span may have lower reliability and validity than they would have for a more limited age span.

Fourth, *the conditions under which the test is administered affect reliability*. If a test is given by the teacher and an alternate form is administered by the school guidance supervisor, the correlation between the two sets of scores could drop. Changed environment, improper use of the test manual, or poor light, ventilation, and heat can all affect the reliability by increasing the error of the respondents.

Fifth, *objectivity of scoring increases reliability*. When personal judgment or opinion is a factor in scoring, as in the case with the essay examination, scores tend to be unreliable. Even the objective test may become unreliable if the method of scoring encourages error. Error in scoring objective tests is reduced when punch-out stencils, carbon scoring, or machine scoring are used.

Standard error. The *standard error of measurement,* which gives an estimate of the error in measurements, also gives an indication of the reliability of an individual pupil's *obtained score* by establishing the limits within which his *true score* is most likely to fall.

To illustrate the way in which standard error is used to determine these limits, let us assume that pupil A's raw score on an English achievement test is 57 and the standard error is calculated to be 4 score points (see Figure 4.2). Then by using standard error to measure off the normal probability curve, as illustrated in Figure 4.2, we can conclude

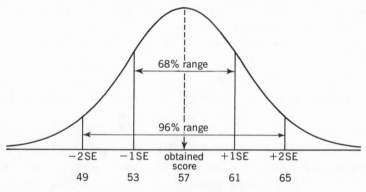

Figure 4.2. USE OF STANDARD ERROR TO DETERMINE THE SCORE LIMITS WITHIN WHICH A PUPIL'S TRUE SCORE IS LIKELY TO FALL

that there are about 68 out of 100 chances that this pupil's true score lies within one SE± of his obtained score, establishing the range in which his true score should fall 96 out of 100 times. Thus, with reasonable assurance, we could conclude that his true score falls somewhere within the limits between 49 and 65. We could not, however, pinpoint the exact location of that true score.

Although, as in the illustration above, it is common practice to use the obtained or observed score as the point from which SE is used to establish the limits within which the true score is likely to lie, the practice is defensible only when the coefficient of reliability is high. Since most of the published standardized tests have a reliability coefficient of approximately +.90, with these tests the practice introduces little error in estimating the true score limits. For teacher-made tests, where the reliability coefficients may be about +.60, the practice is not defensible.

If the reliability coefficient of the test has been determined and the test scores are converted to standard scores, it is easy to determine a student's estimated true score from his observed or obtained score. When scores are converted to T-scores, the following formula is used:

$$X_{tr} = (r_{11}D_{X\,obs}) \pm 50$$

In which:

X_{tr} = the true score in T-score units

r_{11} = the reliability coefficient of the test

$D_{X\,obs}$ = the observed score deviation from the mean in T-score units

Thus if the student's observed T-score were 70 and the reliability coefficient of the test were +.90, his most likely true score would be 68, since $X_{tr} = (.90 \times 20) + 50$, or $X_{tr} = 68$. With a reliability coefficient of .60 the computed true score would be 62, since $X_{tr} (.60 \times 20) + 50$, or $X_{tr} = 62$. In this case the possible dispersion of true scores would be scattered around the computed true score as shown in Figure 4.3.

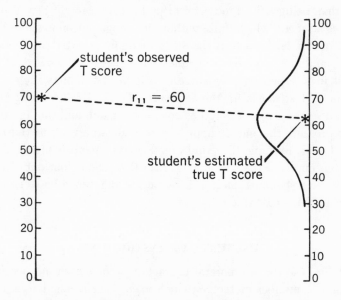

Figure 4.3. RELATIONSHIP BETWEEN STUDENT'S OBSERVED AND ESTIMATED TRUE T-SCORES SHOWING PROBABLE DISTRIBUTION WITHIN WHICH TRUE SCORE IS MOST LIKELY TO FALL

The amount of error associated with any observed score is dependent upon the standard deviation and the reliability coefficient for the set of obtained scores since both of these statistics are used in computing the standard error of measurement. The formula for standard error of measurement is:

$$SE = \sigma \sqrt{1 - r_{11}}$$

In which:

σ = standard deviation of the set of observed scores

r_{11} = reliability coefficient of the test

Thus if standard deviation is 16 score points and reliability coefficient is .91, the standard error of measurement will be 5 score points since $SE = 16 \sqrt{1 - .91}$, or $SE = 4.8$, which rounds to 5.

For the teacher-made tests it is not necessary that we calculate SE if we accept the method which Diederich[14] suggests for estimating it. He indicates that the SE for tests of 50 items is 4 raw score points and for 100 items, 5 points. The estimates of SE for various length teacher-made tests are given in Table XI.

From the foregoing discussion, it is apparent that a pupil's test score, rather than being a fixed indicator of performance, might better be considered as a score which falls within the range encompassing his true score. For standardized tests the SE is generally reported in the technical manual, and some of the companies have recently followed the range concept in interpreting pupils' scores. Figure 4.4 depicts such an interpretation of test scores for the *Sequential Tests of Educational Progress*. Here the scores are considered as covering a band, and the figure on the scale represents the pupil's approximate percentile rank in the national norms. In this example the pupil's mathematics score is higher than five out of ten pupils in the nation and lower than about four out of ten; but of his three test scores, there is a significant difference between only his science and his social studies scores.

USABILITY OF INSTRUMENT

Usability, the third important characteristic of measuring instruments, consists of a number of factors which make it convenient to administer

[14] Paul B. Diederich, *Short-Cut Statistics for Teacher-Made Tests* (Princeton, N. J.: Educational Testing Services, 1960), p. 14.

Figure 4.4. AN EXAMPLE OF THE USE OF STANDARD ERROR TO INTERPRET OBTAINED
TEST SCORES
Excerpt from STUDENT BULLETIN *showing percentile bands for one student's
scores on the Sequential Tests of Educational Progress.*

Table XI. A METHOD OF FINDING A CLOSE ESTIMATE OF THE
STANDARD ERROR OF A TEST SCORE

ESTIMATED STANDARD ERRORS OF TEST SCORES

Number of Items	*Standard Error*	*Exceptions:* Regardless of the length of test, the standard error is:
<24	2	0 when the score is zero or perfect;
24–47	3	1 when 1 or 2 points from 0 or from 100%;
48–89	4	2 when 3 to 7 points from 0 or from 100%;
90–109	5	3 when 8 to 15 points from 0 or from 100%.
110–129	6	
130–150	7	

This table may be interpreted as follows: In an objective test of
50 items, two scores out of three will lie within 4 raw-score points
(one standard error) of the "true score" these students would attain
if you continued testing with repeated random samples from the
universe of items testing the same ability, and 95% of the scores
will lie within 8 raw-score points (two standard errors) of "true
scores." The relatively few scores at the extremes will have slightly
smaller standard errors, as indicated under "Exceptions," but there
are usually not enough of these to justify separate treatment.

and use. These characteristics are (1) administrability, (2) scorability,
(3) economy, (4) proper format, and (5) comparable norms.

   1. *Administrability.* Standardized tests are frequently administered by

the classroom teacher, who may have little formal background in measurement; therefore, the instructions for administration of a test need to be followed to the letter to preserve the test standardization. The better tests contain very specific instructions for the person administering the test and for the student taking the test. Furthermore, sample exercises are provided at the beginning of the test, or sub-tests if the items change, to insure understanding and to establish desirable test psychology. Since the exact words needed to administer the test are printed in the test manuals, they should be read verbatim, and individual help should not be given students except where the instructions permit it.

The *Iowa Tests of Basic Skills* contains one of the better teacher's manuals. The manual goes into detail concerning the preparations for testing, suggesting seating arrangements, types of supplies which should be provided, time limits to be observed, way in which pupils must mark answers for machine scoring, and suggestions for preparing pupils to take the test. When pupils begin the test, they are given specific instructions concerning the method of marking the answer sheets for machine scored tests. The specific instructions for administering the vocabulary test are given in Figure 4.5.

[Begin by saying:]
"We are now ready to begin work on the first test. This is a vocabulary test like the practice test we just studied. Find the section labeled Test V, Vocabulary, on your answer sheet near the top on the front side. [Pause.] Now place your answer sheet beside page 3 of your test booklet. [Pause.] We will read the directions at the top of page 3 to remind you of what you are to do. Read them silently while I read them aloud. They say:

"In each exercise, you are to decide which one of the four words has most nearly the same meaning as the word in heavy black type above them. Then, on the answer sheet, find the row of circles numbered the same as the exercise you are working on. You are to fill in the circle on the answer sheet that has the same number as the answer you picked. The sample exercise in the box at the right has already been marked correctly on the answer sheet.

"What is the right answer to the sample exercise? [Pause for reply.] Yes, the first answer, *high*, is correct. Notice on the answer sheet that the first circle for the question numbered zero has been filled in. [Pause.]

"You will have 17 minutes for this first test. If you finish early, close your test booklet and wait quietly. Don't look at the other tests in the booklet. If you have any questions, raise your hand, and I will help you after the others have begun. Now, look at the table at the end of the directions which we just read. Notice that different grades begin at different places in the test. Find where your grade is to begin." [If grade 3 is being tested say, "Turn to page 3 and begin with exercise 1."] [Pause.] "Does everyone have the right place? [Pause.] Ready, go." [Note the *exact* time and (unless you have a stop watch) write it down in the box at the left.]

Figure 4.5. DIRECTIONS FOR ADMINISTERING THE VOCABULARY SECTION OF THE IOWA TEST OF BASIC SKILLS

From E. F. Lindquist and A. N. Hieronymus, *Iowa Test of Basic Skills* (Boston: Houghton Mifflin Co., 1956). Reprinted by permission of the publisher.

2. Scorability. The scoring of achievement tests is often done by school personnel, although most of the tests now have provisions for machine scoring. Machine scoring is feasible if the cost is low and the scoring machine is convenient to expedite scoring. When tests are machine scored, the answer sheets should be returned so that the teacher can detect any problem situations, such as an individual's misinterpretation of test directions. If there is adequate time provision in the schedule, teacher administration and scoring of tests are desirable. This permits the teacher to observe areas of consistent weakness and individual misunderstandings. It also insures his having some knowledge of the test results as a first step toward their application in the classroom. Tests have been made easier for the teacher to score by the development of carbon-[15] or stencil-[16] scoring devices.

3. Economy. Tests should be reasonably economical, although this is not always the primary consideration. An original high cost for test booklets which can be used several years with separate answer sheets may, in the long run, be more economical than cheaper booklets which cannot be reused. Likewise, cheaper cost is undesirable if considerable quality is sacrificed.

4. Format. Format of the test is also important. The test should be printed in large, clear print on good quality paper. If the booklet is to be reused with answer sheets, the quality of its physical construction should be such that it can be reused several times. In this case, also, the pages

[15] For an example of a carbon-scored test, see L. L. Thurstone and Thelma G. Thurstone, *SRA Primary Mental Abilities* (Chicago: Science Research Associates, 1963).

[16] For an example of a stencil-scored test, see Arthur S. Otis, *Otis Quick Scoring Mental Ability Tests* (New York: World Book Company, 1962).

should be arranged so that the answer sheet can be conveniently fitted into the test booklet with little possibility of error in matching booklet and answer sheet.

5. Norms. The norms on the test should be comparable to those on the other tests used in the school. Otherwise meaningful summaries or profiles of a pupil's test record are difficult to make. Many tests now have several methods of reporting scores—e.g., grade norms, percentile rank, *T*-scores, and several standard scores based on standard deviation.

MEASUREMENT PROCESS

We noted earlier that good measurement results when the best instrument is selected, then skillfully used. The general type of measurement instrument or technique selected depends upon the purpose of measurement, while the specific choice is made from among the various appropriate instruments according to their relative validity, reliability, and usability.

Need for purpose. Measurements are not needed unless there is an explicitly stated reason or purpose for these measurements. If the purpose is to measure height, a tape measure is appropriate. If the purpose is to measure recall of specific knowledge, the completion test is a suitable instrument. Thus the instrument changes as the purpose of the measurement changes. Educational measurements are often made to pinpoint strengths and weaknesses in the educational program, in which case they may result in changes in the program. Such uses of measurement data require understanding of the completeness of measurement; of the accuracy of the instrument; of the nature of the data; and of the type of derived scores used—e.g., intelligence quotient, standard scores, percentiles. The effective use of measurement data is also necessarily preceded by thoughtful evaluation and planning for subsequent action or change.

In the instructional program the purpose of measurement is to determine the extent of pupil achievement. Test data can help the teacher evaluate his teaching effectiveness, plan instructional changes, revise the course content, and review weak areas of instruction. However, tests will be of limited use to the teacher unless he has a clear statement of instructional objectives to assure selection of the proper measuring instrument and to assure identity between measurement and teaching. If teachers are to get maximum value from measurement, they must avoid three common pitfalls: (1) failure to state their objectives with consequent poor relationship between measurement and instruction; (2) failure to select instruments appropriate to their stated objectives; and (3) failure to follow measurement with careful evaluation to determine what changes in the program of instruction are needed. The common practice of using measurement merely to give a course mark is poor justification for measurement.

ERRORS IN MEASUREMENT

Since the purpose of measurement determines the choice of instrument, and consequently the completeness of measurement, selection of an inappropriate instrument will lead to faulty, incomplete measurement. However, even when the instrument or measurement approach selected is the best available for the purpose, some error will still attend the results. It is virtually impossible to avoid all error in measurement, but the error can be minimized by foresight and skill. Society relies constantly on accurate measurement, but it is puzzling that we will not tolerate inaccuracy in science and technology while too frequently ignoring the presence of error in educational measurements.

The common errors in educational measurement are of three types: (1) errors inherent in the measuring instrument, (2) errors resulting from unskilled use of the instrument, and (3) errors emanating from the subject's responses. The test which consists of items with haphazard levels of difficulty and no attempt at scaling gives inconsistent or erroneous measurement. The inexperienced tester who attempts to administer an individual test of intelligence, such as the *Standford-Binet*, would certainly get an inaccurate measurement as a result of his ineptness. And the pupil who uses little care in properly aligning the answer sheet as he responds to achievement test items would certainly contribute an increment to the error in his score.

Each of these three types of error relates to the reliability or consistency of the obtained test scores. There are, in addition, at least three other significant sources of error which must be controlled. These are (1) errors in standardization and interpretation of the test, (2) errors in scoring the test which relate to its objectivity, and (3) errors related to validity which result from incongruence between content of the test and content of the learning.

The typical teacher has difficulty in detecting errors in standardization and interpretation. However, careful perusal of the technical manual is helpful, assuming that he understands the technical report and that the standardization has been faithfully and fully reported. The mental measurement yearbooks [17] are also an excellent, unbiased source which give useful aid in evaluating the standardization of the test.

Errors in scoring are minimized in the standardized objective test as contrasted to the gross scoring error typical of the subjective essay test. However, even with the objective test the scoring key can be improperly positioned on the answer sheet, or the scorer can miscount the number of errors.

Achieving congruence between the test and the content to be measured is always a difficult problem. For example in achievement testing the time limits imposed upon the test prohibit inclusion of all the course content, with the consequence that only the most important areas can be selected for measurement and test items merely sample within these areas. When the content areas selected are poor and/or when the test item sampling within each area is too sketchy, the test fails to measure what was intended and, therefore, has low validity.

Sampling error. In testing, important decisions concerning the educational future of pupils often hinge on one test score. Common sense, however, tells us that the child may be sick or poorly motivated when the test was administered, so the score may misrepresent his true achievement or ability. If this problem does not provide sufficient argument for further testing, then certainly the existence of chance sampling errors in the test itself should present an additional reason for using the scores from several tests as the basis for judging pupils' intelligence and school achievement.

Perhaps an illustration will help the reader grasp the significant problem resulting from the chance factor in test item sampling. In a given area of subject matter which is to be tested there may be as many as 100,000 test items which could be written to measure different aspects of the content. In order to make the test usable within the normal school time limits, however, probably fewer than 100 items can be included. Thus if we were to test two pupils who hypothetically had learned exactly the same proportion of the 100,000 items, there would be little likelihood that they had learned the same items, with the result that one or the other of the pupils might well know more of the specific items which

[17] O. K. Buros, *The Sixth Mental Measurements Yearbook* (Highland Park, N. J.: The Gryphon Press, 1965).

were by chance selected for the test. One way to control these sampling errors is to teach all pupils in the classroom the same basic content. But learning extends far beyond the classroom, and each pupil's learning environment is unique and different, adding greatly to the diversity of learning.

SUMMARY

Good measurement depends upon selection of the best instrument for the purpose and skillful use of the instrument selected. The quality of a measurement instrument is determined by its relative *validity, reliability* and *usability*. Of the three characteristics validity is the most important since it indicates the degree to which the instrument measures what is intended, but validity is also the most difficult to establish. Validity is determined either through the curricular approaches—comparison to texts, judgment of experts, etc.—or through statistical approaches, such as correlation with an outside valid criterion. The four important types of validity are: (1) content validity, (2) predictive validity, (3) concurrent validity, and (4) construct validity.

Reliability, the second important characteristic, is essential to the evaluator who expects consistency of results throughout repeated use of the technique or instrument. Errors in measurement which lower reliability result from a poor instrument, faulty application of the instrument, or pupil problems leading to faulty performance. Reliability is usually established through correlation methods using the test-retest method, the alternate-forms method, or the split-half method. Of these methods the split-half method using the Spearman-Brown formula is apt to give the highest reliability coefficient and the alternate-form method the lowest; however, the unquestioned value of having equivalent forms of a test outweigh the problem of somewhat lower reliability. Since a pupil's true score and the score which he obtains on a test may vary, the statistical calculation of probable error gives further evidence of reliability by helping to set the limit of error inherent in the test scores.

The third important characteristic of evaluative instruments is usability, consisting of (1) administrability, (2) scorability, (3) economy, (4) proper format, and (5) comparable norms. Proper format is best determined by a careful examination of the actual test.

Many of the errors in educational measurement are not the fault of the test but are a result of the process—for example unskillful administration of the test, errors in scoring, poor testing environment, improper pupil motivation. These errors can be greatly reduced when teachers are adequately prepared and conscientiously carry out the measurement task.

DISCUSSION QUESTIONS AND PROBLEMS

1. Why is the validity of a test important?
2. Is it possible to have high validity in a test without high reliability?
3. Define the term "validity"; define "reliability."
4. What are the major types of measurement error?
5. Is it necessary to check the validity and reliability of teacher-made tests?
6. Using the Spearman-Brown formula, compute the reliability coefficient for a test which has been administered in class.
7. Why does the split-half technique generally give higher coefficients of reliability than either the alternate-forms or the test-retest techniques?
8. In evaluating a test, which do you consider to be most important, high validity, high reliability, or high usability?

SELECTED READINGS

Cattell, Raymond B. "Validity and Reliability: A Proposed More Basic Set of Concepts," *Journal of Educational Psychology*, LV, No. 1 (February 1964), 1–22. Criticizes the concepts of validity and reliability which have been accepted for the past several decades and proposes a different set of concepts.

Cronbach, Lee J. *Essentials of Psychological Testing*. 2nd ed. New York: Harper & Row, 1960. Validity is discussed in Chapter 5, reliability in Chapter 6. A good form for evaluating a test is shown on p. 148.

Davis, Frederick B. *Educational Measurements and Their Interpretation*. Belmont, California: Wadsworth Publishing Company, 1964. Chapter 2 deals with various types of errors in measurement and the validity of test scores.

Dick, Walter, and Richard E. Spencer. "An Application of Computer Programming to Test Analysis and Item Analysis," *Educational and Psychological Measurement*, XXV, No. 1 (1965), 211–215. This contains a good discussion of the application of the computer in test analysis.

Ebel, Robert L. *Measuring Educational Achievement*. Englewood Cliffs, N. J.: Prentice-Hall, 1965. Chapter 10 deals with the estimation and improvement of test reliability. In Chapter 12 there is a good discussion of test validity.

French, John W., and William B. Michael (Chairmen), Joint Committee of the American Psychological Association, American Educational Research Association, and National Council on Measurement Education. *Standards for Educational and Psychological Tests and Manuals*. Washington, D. C.: American Psychological Association, 1966. This excellent handbook presents general discussion of measurement standards and a specific, classified list of the standards for assessing measurement instruments. It is valuable for teachers and essential for guidance directors and test specialists.

Ghiselli, Edwin E. *Theory of Psychological Measurement*. New York: McGraw-Hill Book Company, 1964. Chapters 8 and 11 consider the concepts of reliability and validity.

Helmstadter, G. C. *Principles of Psychological Measurement*. New York: Appleton-Century-Crofts, 1964. Chapter 3 discusses reliability. Chapters 4, 5, and 6 deal with the various types of validity.

Hopkins, Kenneth D. "Extrinsic Reliability: Estimating and Attenuating Variance from Response Styles, Chance, and Other Irrelevant Sources," *Educational and Psychological Measurement*, XXIV, No. 2 (1964), 271–281. Note particularly the effects of speed and guessing on pupils' test scores.

Magnusson, David. *Test Theory*. Reading, Massachusetts: Addison-Wesley Publishing Company, 1966. Chapters 5, 6, 8, and 10 are concerned with the concepts of reliability and validity. The reader needs some statistical background to benefit from these readings.

Millman, Jason, Robert Ebel, and Carol H. Bishop. "An Analysis of Test-Wiseness," *Educational and Psychological Measurement*, XXV, No. 3 (1965), 707–726. Contains an interesting discussion of the effects of test-wiseness on pupils' scores. Principles to help avoid the problem are suggested in pp. 711–712.

Part II

ASSESSING THE
PREREQUISITES
TO LEARNING

All children come to teachers' classrooms with a background of previous learning and a willingness to learn that are the complex products of their innate potential and of their previous environment and experience. This background and this willingness are the prerequisites to learning which establish the practical baseline from which each teacher must begin his efforts if he is to achieve optimum success in promoting pupil achievement. However, herein lies the crux of the initial teaching problem; for the level of pupils with regard to these prerequisites is not readily apparent, nor can it be intuitively assessed. And although the teacher may conscientiously desire to know the pre-instructional level of each pupil, he often lacks the time and know-how to accomplish the task of accurately assessing it.

Intelligence, health and physical well-being, emotional adjustment, and interest are at the initial stages of learning, and throughout the child's educational career will continue to be, vital factors which affect his ability and willingness to learn—factors which persist like an inseparable shadow to set the pace of his educational achievement. In this section of the book we turn our attention specifically to these factors and to the most promising instruments and techniques which are available for assessing them. The concepts discussed and the measuring instruments and techniques examined are those which seem most essential to the classroom teacher, but those preparing to become school psychologists and guidance workers as well should find profitable background reading in this section.

Chapter 5

EVALUATING PUPILS' INTELLECTUAL ATTRIBUTES

INTRODUCTION

Countless times each day we hear reference to some aspect of intelligence. We hear it in the proud boast of the new father's "Look how bright my boy is; he knows me." We hear it in the schoolboy's chant, "My dad's smarter than your dad!" Again it appears in the appraisal of a businessman, "He's really a shrewd operator," and in Mama's "He's a very bright boy," and in the irate driver's "He ain't got the brains he was born with." All these comments in one way or another refer to intelligence; yet none really characterizes intelligence. Moreover, together the comments exemplify the widespread confusion concerning its nature.

Intelligence is the essential prerequisite to learning. In school those who possess a high degree of this attribute can, but may not, learn; however, those who lack it cannot learn even if they wish to. In the mass educational process it becomes easier to lose those who can but choose *not* to learn within the ranks of those who cannot, thus unnecessary social tragedies may result from cases in which pupils might have become productive members of society. The gifted school dropout, the misguided college failure, the ill-served dull child all cry out for better assessment of intelligence and for educational programs adapted to the various intellectual levels. The magnitude of the modern educational task compounds the importance of evaluating the potential of each pupil as the basis for planning an individual blueprint for his educational program. Few would argue the importance of this assertion, but many would query, "What is intelligence?" and "Can intelligence be accurately evaluated?" The modern teacher must both understand the nature of intelligence and know how to measure it if he is to fulfill the educational task which society has set him. These two problems are the concern of this chapter.

NATURE OF INTELLIGENCE

Human intelligence has many facets. The ability to communicate effectively, the ability to deal with abstractions, the ability to solve difficult problems, the ability to succeed in a group—all constitute intelligence. The first two of these have commonly been of most concern in the school, and many children fail or succeed academically on the basis of these alone without regard for the other aspects.

Concepts of intelligence. The three concepts of intelligence which underlie most current measurement instruments are: (1) Terman's verbal concept, (2) Thurstone's primary abilities concept, and (3) Spearman's S- and G-factor concept.[1] Terman believed intelligence to be the generalized ability to verbalize abstractions. This belief was exemplified in his first edition of the *Stanford-Binet Intelligence Scale* (1916), which was heavily loaded with verbal concepts. While later editions contain a greater diversity of tasks, the major emphasis is still verbal. Most of the early group intelligence tests followed this concept. This emphasis is not without justification, for the size of a person's vocabulary gives a quick and fairly reliable estimate of his intelligence and his potential for academic success.

Reading ability, which depends upon verbal intelligence, is unquestionably the most important factor in school success, in intellectual grouping of pupils, and in identifying potential school dropouts. The child who possesses quantitative intelligence but reads poorly is apt to become a school dropout, even though he may have excellent potential in the mathematical and scientific fields. Virtually all the group intelligence tests currently on the market include measures of verbal ability, although some stress it less than others.

With the development of factorial analysis as a statistical tool, it became possible to isolate the discrete elements of intelligence. Working with this approach Spearman formulated a different concept of intelligence. He suggested that intelligence was actually a complex of factors which included a general intellectual ability, similar to that which Terman suggested, and a number of specific factors (S-factors) or aptitudes correlated to but separate from the general factor (G-factor). This line

[1] See earlier discussion of these concepts in Chapter 2, pp. 22–23.

of reasoning led to the development of the *Differential Aptitude Test* for measuring such specific factors as mechanical aptitude and numerical reasoning. In accord with this concept some authorities classify typical group intelligence tests as scholastic aptitude tests, primarily because of their usefulness in predicting future school success.

Thurstone's effort toward identifying a small number of basic mental abilities culminated in the development of the *SRA Primary Mental Abilities Test*. This test measures five of these factors: (1) verbal ability, (2) reasoning, (3) mathematical ability, (4) spatial judgment, and (5) verbal fluency. The value of such a test is that it permits the pupil's score to be shown as a profile of abilities in addition to his composite IQ score. The test profiles, thus, show the specific differences between pupils with similar IQ scores. Without this information children of similar IQ's are expected to perform equally well in the various school subjects even though this may be an unjustified conclusion which can lead to undue pressure on some pupils. For instance, two children with IQ's of 130 could have reciprocal scores in the verbal and mathematics sections of the test: one high in mathematics and average in verbal, and the other high in verbal and average in mathematics.

Additional factors which have been given considerable attention in recent years are creativity and social intelligence. Since both factors have a significant bearing on adult success, continued efforts will undoubtedly be made to improve the measuring instruments of these factors.

Capacity and ability. In the foregoing discussion the term "ability" has been used frequently since "ability" refers to a measurable characteristic. The tests actually *measure* the intellectual ability from which we *infer* the innate intellectual capacity, thus "ability" and "capacity" are not synonymous terms. The difference between the two terms can be represented by a concrete example: capacity is comparable to a bucket whereas ability represents the water in the bucket. The water is usable and measurable, but the bucket-size limits the amount of water which it can contain. Thus intellectual capacity, the ultimate potential, is limited by genetic inheritance and is not directly measurable; but the ability which has been acquired can be measured and is environmentally conditioned by such factors as individual drive, home background, quality of the schooling, and interest. It is possible, then, to have children with comparable measured abilities but strikingly different capacities. The first child, with extremely high innate capacity, could have low ability as reflected in his test scores because of laziness, lack of challenge, poor environment, emotional problems, or a variety of other reasons. On the other hand the second child, with limited capacity, might show comparable ability if he had high-level interest, intense drive, and a good environment.

Unfortunately the limits of capacity cannot be inferred from the size of the pupil's head or his looks. Test scores give the best indication, but the teacher must be aware of other environmental factors before concluding that the score shows potential. The test obviously provides no pat answer to the question, "Does the pupil need further challenge?" The current status of ability is shown by intelligence test scores. The pupil with high capacity will show tremendous growth given a good combination of environment, personal adjustment, and drive; while the pupil with limited capacity will show no such change.

Unique characteristics of human intelligence. The newborn baby is among the most helpless of all newborn animals, but in his genetic pattern he has unfathomed potential for long-term learning. There is in every child a prolonged and unquenchable thirst to learn, to grow, to be adult. The multitude of "whys" which every parent must answer for his child gives ample evidence of this desire to learn. During his first years the child learns easily and continually; and by the time he enters school he has already far surpassed his nearest intellectual competitors in the animal world.

In school, for the first time, one remarkable human intellectual characteristic becomes apparent, the extreme range of variability of intellect in the human species. No other animal approaches this range of variability. Although variation in children's intelligence is most discernible as they grow older, it is quite apparent in their early development. Intellectual differences can be observed when they first make social overtures; when they first reach and grasp objects; when they begin to crawl, walk, and talk. Bright children develop early; they are well coordinated, they walk early; they talk early; and they have creative imaginations. The earliest indication of intelligence is the level of coordination, but from the age of one year the best single indication of intelligence is the size of the vocabulary. However, other specific facets of general intelligence are also discernible at an early age. The musically inclined sing tunes early; the mechanically inclined take apart and put together simple toys at an early age; the artistically inclined draw recognizable pictures when very young.

The gifted child also frequently has numerous talents and interests, which make it difficult to settle on a single vocation or field of study. He is frequently a "Jack-of-all-trades" who performs well in most areas, from athletics to Greek. Of course there are exceptions, for example, the child who performs brilliantly in the classroom but who, either because of lack of training or lack of aptitude, is "all thumbs" when attempting to work with anything mechanical.

Types of intelligence classification. The most common ways in which intelligence scores are classified are mental age, intelligence quotient, percentiles, and profiles. Mental age gives a basis for comparing the mental maturity of children. Children of the same mental age can perform similar intellectual tasks; however, their chronological ages must also be known before one can determine whether they are mentally above or below their age group. A five-year-old and a nine-year-old who both have a mental age of seven have the same mental status, but the five-year-old is bright for his age and the nine-year-old, dull.

The *intelligence quotient* as used by Terman takes the relationship between mental and chronological age to indicate the child's rate of mental development. The formula for obtaining intelligence quotient is

$$IQ = \frac{MA}{CA} \times 100.$$ Thus the child whose mental age is 12 years and chronological age is 10 has a mental quotient of 1.2 and an intelligence quotient of 120. This child has a mental growth of 1.2 years for each chronological year.

IQ is a useful means of classifying intelligence; but both teachers and parents often misconstrue its meaning as *level* of intelligence rather than *rate* of intellectual growth. This problem is alleviated by *deviation IQ*.

Deviation IQ does not show the relationship between MA and CA but indicates the position of the child's score on the normal distribution curve in terms of the standard deviation of that particular test.[2] For the *Wechsler Adult Intelligence Scale* the standard deviation is 15 IQ points and the mean, 100; thus a person whose score is one standard deviation above the mean would have an IQ of 115. The tests which utilize devia-

[2] See Figure 3.3 in Chapter 3 for a comparison between deviation IQ and other standard scores.

tion IQ give approximately the same IQ scores as quotient IQ tests for children whose scores are close to 100, but at the extreme ends of the scale deviation scores tend to fall closer to the mean than quotient scores.

Percentile rank is another method of reporting intelligence. This method is used by colleges and universities. The *American Council on Education Psychological Examination* and the *Graduate Record Examination* are examples of examinations for different college levels which use percentile rank as one method for reporting the scores. At the college level percentile rank is probably more meaningful than intelligence quotient in view of the fact that the student body is a select group comprising the upper portion of the normal distribution curve, and the percentile rank of a student's score indicates his position within that select group.

In elementary and secondary schools percentile scores are useful because they can be recorded on profile charts along with other standardized achievement and aptitude scores to give a one-page summary of the pupil's strengths and weaknesses. The parent probably also understands this type of score better than IQ.

PROBLEMS OF MEASUREMENT

Tests of intelligence and aptitude are among the most highly refined of the various types of standardized tests which are available. Historically they predate most other types of standardized tests, and more money and research effort have been spent to assure the validity and reliability of these instruments than any others, with the possible exception of achievement tests. Still we would be negligent if we failed to take account of some of the problems which still persist in this realm of measurement.

Aptitude vs. achievement. The fact that there is a high positive correlation between the scores on various group intelligence tests and those on the achievement batteries has led some to criticize the validity of the intelligence tests. The contention is that both types of tests are measuring essentially the same things and that the intelligence tests actually measure learning and not the potential for learning. There is some basis for this criticism since the amount and quality of a child's schooling, as well as the type of reading material in his home do affect the IQ score. Children from better schools and from homes in which there is a wide variety

of reading material perform better on the tests than those from less privi-
leged environments although the relative effects of their environment
and genetic background are not clearly discernible.[3]

Test makers are aware of this problem and have used considerable ingenuity in providing test problems which are not appreciably affected by
previous learning.

Culture-fair tests. Intelligence tests prepared for children in this country are not directly applicable in Europe or in Asiatic countries. The tests
are predicated on a viewpoint and cultural context peculiar to our country. In fact they are often culturally biased in favor of our middle- and
upper-class pupils—that is, the items represent a sample of verbal and
experiential content familiar to these groups but unfamiliar to culturally
deprived, foreign-born, and minority-group children. It is reasonable to
expect that a test consisting exclusively of items drawn from the verbal-
experiential background of any one of these educationally handicapped
groups with its reflected cultural bias would discriminate against pupils
in other social groups. Nevertheless, because the culturally deprived and/
or minority-group child actually does perform poorly on conventional
intelligence tests, some have come to the questionable conclusion that he
is intellectually inferior to the native-born white. For the reading-handi-
capped pupil, nonverbal performance tasks appear to give a closer estimate of intelligence than the verbal test.

As we have moved toward universal schooling and improved educational quality, with better transportation and communication to reduce
the cultural differences between subgroups in the nation, cultural bias
becomes progressively less significant than in the past. However, it cannot be ignored by those who teach in communities where there are many
minority groups or culturally deprived children.

Problems of definition. Several problems of measurement relate to the
definition and understanding of intelligence. Three problems are particularly important:

1. The lack of consensus in definition and measurement approach.
2. The tendency to restrict the measurement to school-related tasks.
3. The numerous folkloric misconcepts which persist and cloud laymen
   and educators' understanding of intelligence.

[3] For an interesting, informative discussion of the effects of environment on children's school success, see James Bryan Conant, *Slums and Suburbs* (New York:
McGraw-Hill Book Company, 1963).

The lack of consensus of definition was discussed earlier as the three currently most acceptable concepts of intelligence were reviewed. Each of these concepts has numerous adherents, and each requires a slightly different measurement approach; however, the factor concept of intelligence is the most widely accepted if the design of the majority of the newer tests is a valid gauge of acceptance. The newer instruments have widened the scope of sub-tests, placing less reliance on reading and vocabulary. Some attention is also being given to creativity and social intelligence.

Several folkloric misconcepts concerning intelligence continue to be widely held, and they often confuse both parents and teachers. Two such misconcepts will serve to illustrate this problem. First, it is often suggested that genius is akin to insanity; therefore the bright child is expected to be unusual or at least slightly maladjusted. Terman in his longitudinal study of bright children did as much as any one person to dispel this myth, for his study confirmed the commonsense logic that bright people are actually better adjusted and more adaptable to changeable circumstances than their average peers.[4] A second widely held misconcept is the belief that IQ is unchangeable. This belief arises from Terman's early allegations that IQ was stable; but subsequent research has demonstrated the changeability of IQ, particularly with culturally deprived children, whose IQ's tend to increase when their environment, motivation, and education are improved.

INDIVIDUAL TESTS OF INTELLIGENCE

Individual tests of intelligence are generally regarded as the best measures currently available; however, the fact that they must be administered by a specially trained person plus the fact that they require an hour or more with each subject makes their use impractical with a large group of children. These tests are typically reserved for use with exceptional or problem children to verify and enlarge on the information already available from the scores on the regular group tests.

The individual tests which are used most frequently are: (1) the 1937 *Stanford-Binet*, Forms L and M; (2) the 1960 *Stanford-Binet*, Form L-M; (3) the *Wechsler Adult Intelligence Scale* (*WAIS*); and (4) the *Wechsler Intelligence Scale for Children* (*WISC*). There are numerous

[4] See L. M. Terman and M. Oden, "The Significance of Deviates," *Third Yearbook National Social Studies Education* (1940), pp. 74–89.

other individual scales which are used less frequently and have not gained the reputation of those above. Some of the scales, such as the *Draw-a-Man Test* and the *Kohs' Block-Design Test,* were developed primarily for use with verbally handicapped or culturally deprived children.

Stanford-Binet Scale. The *Stanford-Binet Intelligence Scale* is designed to measure intelligence of subjects ranging from two years of age through superior adult levels. In the early age levels the tasks include the use of simple vocabulary and word combinations, form board for spatial judgment, delayed responses for memory, and identification of parts of the body for observation acuity. The tasks at the upper-age levels tend to be quite verbal in nature and include sub-tests for measuring vocabulary, reasoning, proverb meaning, ingenuity, ability to recognize essential differences, and memory. Each age level in the scale contains six tests, with the exception of level for the average adult, which contains eight. With this test it is assumed that human intellectual growth is essentially completed during the late teens, and adult subjects are compared against the nineteen-year-old scale.

The 1937 revision of the *Stanford-Binet Scale* is available in two parallel forms which were equated so that they could be used in a test-retest situation when it is desirable to check the first score which a subject obtained. The quotient IQ is used in the 1937 forms; and because the standard deviations of the scores in the various age levels differ somewhat, the IQ's at each age level are not exactly equivalent. While this inconsistency has only minor effects in the 90–110 IQ range, it does account for spurious changes at the extremes below 70 and above 130 IQ, and it has been referred to as the "wandering IQ."

The 1960 revision has dropped the quotient method of calculating IQ and adopted the deviation IQ, with a mean IQ of 100 and a standard deviation of 16 at each age level.[5] This method of reporting IQ scores permits direct comparisons of scores among the various age levels and eliminates the "wandering IQ" problem noted above. However, a correction factor must be applied if the 1960 deviation IQ scores are to be compared to earlier scores on the 1937 forms.

The *Stanford-Binet* has long enjoyed a reputation for high validity and reliability. Notable advantages of this test are:

[5] Lewis M. Terman and Maud A. Merrill, *Stanford-Binet Intelligence Scale: Manual for the Third Revision,* Form L–M (Boston: Houghton Mifflin Company, 1960), pp. 27–28.

1. It provides testing levels for the complete age range from two years through adulthood.
2. It is the recognized instrument for testing intelligence of preschool and mentally deficient subjects.
3. It is the test against which other intelligence tests are generally validated.
4. Because of its verbal emphasis, it has excellent validity for predicting the future school success of test subjects.

The test also has several disadvantages which detract from its usefulness:

1. It is not an appropriate test for foreign-born and nonwhite populations, which tend to be verbally handicapped.
2. It seems to yield spuriously high IQ's for college graduates and superior adults.
3. It does not provide a means of depicting a profile of the subject's specific abilities.

Wechsler Scales. The *Wechsler Adult Intelligence Scale* (*WAIS*), which was published in 1955, is the best individual test currently available for measuring adult intelligence. Wechsler's concept of the growth of human intelligence differs somewhat from his predecessors. He believes that intelligence continues to develop a number of years after physical growth has ceased and that the peak intellectual performance is reached during the decade between 25 and 34 years of age. The *WAIS* is a revision of the earlier *Wechsler-Bellevue Intelligence Scale* and was standardized on a nation-wide sample of 1700 adults prorated according to the 1950 U.S. Census and including proportional nonwhite representation. The norms were developed for seven age groups, 16 through 64 years of age; and norms were also established from an area sample for the 65–75 age group.

The test contains eleven sub-tests, six of which are grouped in the verbal scale and five of which comprise the performance scale. The following sub-tests are included in the full scale.

Verbal tests	*Performance tests*
Information	Digit symbol
Comprehension	Picture completion
Arithmetic	Block design
Similarities	Picture arrangement
Digit span	Object assembly
Vocabulary	

The test is designed to measure the various verbal and nonverbal primary mental abilities. For each subject it provides a profile of abilities and three separate IQ scores—verbal, performance, and full scale.

The deviation IQ concept is used with a mean of 100 and a standard deviation of 15; thus the scores are approximately equivalent to the *Binet* deviation scores, with the greatest difference at the extreme ranges. For example, the scores are equivalent at 100, but a score of 148 on the *Binet* is equivalent to 145 on the *Wechsler*.

The *Wechsler Intelligence Scale for Children* (*WISC*) is used with children 5 to 15 years of age. It has the same verbal sub-test arrangement as the *WAIS* but has a slightly different performance sub-test arrangement, deleting the digit symbol test and adding coding and mazes.

The Wechsler tests are easier to administer than the *Binet,* but they must also be administered by qualified persons. The *WAIS* and *WISC* yield considerably more information about the subject than the *Binet,* but some authorities question the scores obtained at the extreme ends of the test.

The major advantages of the Wechsler tests are:

1. The *WAIS* is generally recognized as the best test for measuring adult intelligence.
2. The systematic arrangement of sub-tests makes it possible to obtain more information from the test than that which the *Binet* yields.
3. Profile analyses of the scores indicate specific strengths and weaknesses of the subject.

The major disadvantages are:

1. The tests are difficult to administer and score.
2. The tests are not appropriate for mentally deficient children and adults.
3. Scores at the extreme ranges of the scale may be inaccurate.

GROUP INTELLIGENCE TESTS

Although good group intelligence tests are subject to more error than the good individual tests, they are much more practical for use in schools. A teacher who has minimum training in testing can administer a group test to a large number of pupils in one testing session. Directions for administration on all the good tests are simple and definite so that the examiner does nothing more than read the instructions verbatim. In fact some companies, such as the California Test Bureau, have provided tape recorded verbal instructions which may be used with the tests instead of having the instructions read by the examiner.

With group tests the scoring is also simplified so that the average teacher has no difficulty completing it. The tests usually provide one or more of the following scoring aids: (1) an answer key, (2) punch-out stencils, (3) carbon-score answer sheets, or (4) machine scoring. Machine scoring is the simplest but most expensive of the methods since it is usually done by the test publisher for a nominal fee. For hand scoring the other three methods are quite adequate, requiring only a few minutes per test. In fact, the carbon-score method requires the teacher merely to count the incorrect responses and record the pupils' correct raw scores on the answer sheet. Each test also provides convenient tables for converting the pupils' raw scores into IQ scores, and many also show the percentile rank and mental age equivalent for the various IQ scores.

The major disadvantage of the group test is that the examiner does not have personal contact with each subject and is unable to determine whether the subject actually understood the directions and put forth a maximum effort to complete the test items. Children who are ill, sleepy, or emotionally upset may perform poorly on the group test without the examiner becoming aware of their problem. In these instances such children may be unfairly classified by the uncharacteristically low scores which they receive. Group tests do, however, provide several equivalent forms of the same instrument so that an alternate form can be administered to the children whose scores appear to give an unrealistic picture of their intelligence. Also there is always the possibility of administering an individual test, such as the *Binet*, to the small number of children whose scores need further verification. Since most group tests rely heavily on reading ability, pupils with reading handicaps will perform poorly on them; and in such cases verification by individual tests is particularly desirable.

Nature of group tests. The group tests are characteristically arranged as both speed and power tests. The tests are timed, and the items are scaled in difficulty so that the pupils' ceilings of performance may be established both in terms of the rate at which they can work and in terms of the difficulty level of the items which they can complete. Certain instruments—for example, the number sub-test of *SRA Primary Mental Abilities* examination—include numerous problems of approximately equal difficulty; but too many problems are included for the pupil to complete in the time limits, and the performance ceiling is established by the pupil's speed of calculation. In this case if the pupil were given more time, he could complete all the items correctly since they are not difficult.

Most of the group tests include sections or items to measure (1) verbal concepts, (2) quantitative or numerical reasoning, (3) abstract reasoning, and (4) spatial judgment. The test items are arranged in one of two ways. The first is the spiral-omnibus method, in which items to measure each of the various abilities noted above are presented together at scaled levels of difficulty—for example, easy items to measure reasoning, verbal concepts, spatial judgment, etc.; then a repeat of the same sequence of items at increasingly difficult levels throughout the test. In this case the test is not divided into sub-tests; the student works through the entire test after receiving the preliminary instructions. Such a test provides only a total score, and the profile of abilities is not given.

The second method of presenting items is to include a series of sub-tests in which similar items are grouped together, usually in a scaled arrangement. Thus all items measuring verbal concepts would be grouped together. Tests, such as the *California Test of Mental Maturity,* which use this method are designed to give a profile of the subject's primary mental abilities in addition to his composite IQ score. They are a bit harder to administer since there are instructions which must be read preceding each sub-test, but the added information provided by the tests offsets this difficulty.

In addition to the verbal tests for the child without a serious reading handicap, there are also a number of group performance tests for children with language handicaps and reading deficiencies. These nonverbal performance tests include such tests as block designs, picture completion, and picture analogies. Such tests give a more valid estimate of intelligence for children with reading deficiencies than do the verbal forms. However, the tests are more difficult to administer since they generally require the administrator to read the instructions throughout the test. A test such as the *Kuhlmann-Anderson* includes a combination of verbal and nonverbal tasks and is a good compromise in schools in which the student body includes both verbally inclined and language handicapped children.

Group test examples. Among the most widely used of the group tests are the *Otis Self-Administering Tests of Mental Ability,* the *California*

Test of Mental Maturity, and the *Kuhlmann-Anderson Intelligence Test.*[6] The Otis and the Kuhlmann-Anderson tests have been available for many years.

Otis tests. The *Otis* was first published in 1922 and has not changed essentially in format since that time, although the items have been updated and additional alternate forms have been published. Perhaps the greatest advantage of this test is that since it requires very few instructions to the examinees, it can be administered by a classroom teacher who has had little training in testing. Furthermore, the IQ scores are easily figured since they need not be calculated but can be located directly from the chart which is provided with the test. This test has proved to be extremely reliable and has gained a wide reputation for giving a valid measure of intelligence at all except the upper levels in the range above the middle 130's. Since the ceiling of the test in the upper-age groups is 133 IQ, it does not provide a measure of the quite gifted pupil.

The Kuhlmann-Anderson scale. The *Kuhlmann-Anderson* test was first published in 1927 and, like the *Otis,* has been updated; and alternate forms have been added from time to time. By virtue of having been used for over 40 years, this test and the *Otis* have a backlog of thousands of cases upon which to base the norms. The *Kuhlmann-Anderson* scale covers the entire age range from four years mental age to adulthood. The tests progress in difficulty throughout the scale, but each test overlaps the preceding and the following test in difficulty. Tests are available for each of the eight grades and the kindergarten, with each including approximately ten sub-tests which are appropriate in difficulty for the age-grade level of the particular battery.

The tests are quite easy to administer and score; but since they are not corrected for guessing, the pupil who randomly answers the remaining items, after completing those to which he knows the answers, can improve his score.

Reliability of the test has been determined by three methods: (1) test-retest, (2) adjacent forms, and (3) split-half. The reliability coefficients determined by these three methods range from .77 to .95.

California test. The *California Short Form Test of Mental Maturity,* 1963 revision, is one of the newer group tests of intelligence. It contains seven sub-tests, the first four of which are nonlanguage, with tests five through seven comprising the language section. The language and non-

[6] See the end of this chapter for a more extensive list of group tests.

language sections each contain 60 items. The seven sub-tests are designed to measure four factors of intelligence: (1) logical reasoning, (2) numerical reasoning, (3) verbal concepts, and (4) memory. This test is based on the Thurstone primary mental abilities rationale, and the test uses the deviation IQ concept, with each age level scaled to the *Stanford Binet Intelligence Scale*, Form L-M—the mean IQ being 100 and the standard deviation 16. A sample of 38,793 cases from schools in seven geographic areas of the United States was used to scale the tests and establish the norms. The test may either be hand scored or machine scored.

A particularly desirable feature of this test is the variety of types of scores which are provided for each pupil: (1) standard score; (2) percentile ranks; (3) stanine; and (4) language, nonlanguage, and total scale IQ's. The summary sheet for each pupil provides an easy means of converting the raw scores into each of these derived scores and, in addition, provides a profile which shows the complex of the pupil's abilities. This summary sheet is shown in Figure 5.1.

Scholastic aptitude tests. Since the intelligence tests have high validity for predicting pupils' future school success, they have sometimes been classified as scholastic aptitude tests. In this book we would prefer not to accept this classification, but we should note that there are several reputable scholastic aptitude tests which are specifically designed to predict pupils' success in school. Perhaps the greatest variety of these tests is available for measuring the reading readiness of preschool children. These are essentially nonlanguage intelligence tests which attempt through picture relationships to measure the abilities essential to reading —i.e., using symbols, visual discrimination, auditory discrimination, and context clues. Arthur I. Gates and William Gray have done much work in this field and in the related one of diagnostic testing of reading skills.[7]

A number of scholastic aptitude tests are used at the high school and college level to predict pupils' success in college; and in recent years, as college enrollment has increased, they have been used extensively to help identify for admission those who would be the best college risks. These tests tend to be heavily loaded in the verbal and quantitative

[7] For further reading see Arthur I. Gates, *The Improvement of Reading: A Program of Prognostic and Remedial Methods.* (New York: Macmillan Company, 1927; 2nd ed., 1935; 3rd ed., 1947). *See also* William S. Gray, "The Major Aspects of Reading," in *Sequential Development of Reading Abilities,* Helen M. Robinson (ed.), Supplementary Educational Monographs, No. 90 (Chicago: University of Chicago Press, 1960), pp. 8–24.

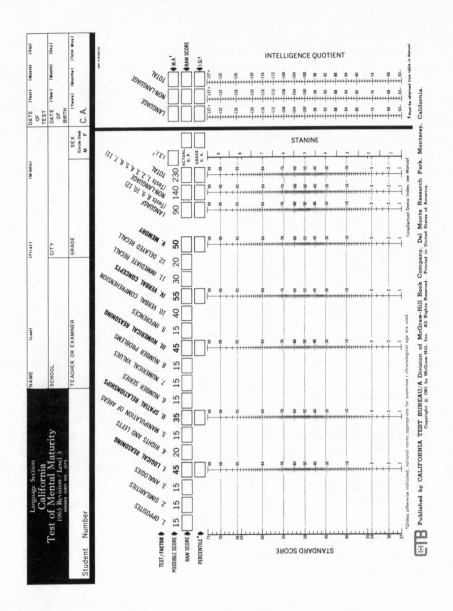

Figure 5.1. EXAMPLE OF AN IBM 1230 ANSWER SHEET AND A PROFILE SHEET FOR THE *California Short-Form Test of Mental Maturity.*

Reprinted by permission of the publisher, California Test Bureau, a Division of McGraw-Hill Book Company, Monterey, California.

areas, although some also include what are essentially achievement sub-tests in specific subject areas. Examples of the most widely used tests include (1) the *College Entrance Examination Board Scholastic Aptitude Test (SAT)*, (2) *American College Testing Program (ACT)*, (3) the *College Qualification Tests (CQT)*, (4) the *School and College Ability Tests (SCAT)*, and (5) the *National Merit Scholarship Examination*. Although it was initiated only a decade ago, the *National Merit Scholarship Examination* has become an annual, nationwide high school testing program and has gained a wide reputation as an instrument capable of identifying the most able scholars.

The tests in this program are revised annually, but pupil performance has improved over the years. This improvement may reflect improved teaching, but it probably also reflects the test sophistication of pupils as well as the tendency of some teachers to focus instruction on the content of previous test batteries.

Scholastic aptitude tests which have been widely used for preselection of college gradute students at the master's or doctoral levels include the *Ohio State Psychological Examination*, the *Miller Analogies Test*, and the *Graduate Record Examination*.

General aptitude batteries. The best known of the general aptitude batteries is the *Differential Aptitude Tests (DAT)*. This battery contains the following tests: (1) Verbal Reasoning, (2) Numerical Reasoning, (3) Abstract Reasoning, (4) Space Relations, (5) Mechanical Reasoning, (6) Clerical Speed and Accuracy, and (7) Language Usage. Each test is published in a separate booklet so that it can be administered independently. When the entire battery is used, pupils are either tested during most of an entire school day, or the test administration is broken into several sessions on consecutive days. The individual test reliability of the *DAT* is high. Numerous studies have also been made of the test validity. Correlation between the *DAT* and achievement tests is about 0.60 to 0.70, and the follow-up studies indicate that the battery has predictive validity for numerous occupational areas. The test manual reports extensive evidence which has been collected through numerous studies of *DAT* reliability and validity.

Another interesting aptitude battery is the *Flanagan Aptitude Classification Tests (FACT)*, developed in 1959. The *FACT* battery is based on extensive job classifications and measures specific job elements which have been identified as those which are important for successful performance in many occupations. An advantage over other approaches which is claimed for this battery is that the tests are based on a pragmatic rationale involving an analysis of specific behavior which determines on-the-job success or failure, whereas other tests approach measurement either from the psychological rationale of the miniature job approach or the primary mental factor approach. On the basis of the job analysis approach a list of 21 job elements was identified, and the 19-test *FACT* battery was constructed to measure all but two of these elements. The standardization sample consisted of about 11,000 high school students from different sections of the country.

The 19 tests included in the battery are:

1. Inspection	11. Ingenuity
2. Mechanics	12. Scales
3. Tables	13. Expression
4. Reasoning	14. Precision
5. Vocabulary	15. Alertness
6. Assembly	16. Coordination
7. Judgment and Comprehension	17. Patterns
8. Components	18. Coding
9. Planning	19. Memory
10. Arithmetic	

Sample items from test 6—Assembly—are shown in Figure 5.2. In spite

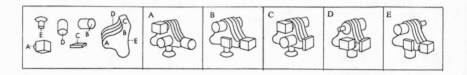

Figure 5.2. SAMPLE PROBLEM FROM THE FLANAGAN APTITUDE CLASSIFICATION TESTS

Directions: Following the picture of the parts are five assemblies of these parts. You are to select the assembly which shows how the parts will look when fitted together. Each part is marked with one or more letters which identify some particular place on the part. Letters referring to places which do not show are placed outside the part, with a dotted line pointing to the underneath side—or the place that you can't see.

of the recent origin of this test, extensive studies have been conducted to establish its reliability and validity; and the results reported in its technical manual indicate quite acceptable levels.

Thurstone's *SRA Primary Mental Abilities Test*, though used to measure intelligence, can be used also in lieu of an aptitude battery such as the *DAT* when the school has limited funds and wants a quick check on intelligence and the profile of abilities. However, since the sub-tests are short, they do not have the reliability of the *DAT* individual tests.

SPECIFIC APTITUDES AND SPECIAL FEATURES OF INTELLIGENCE

In addition to the tests of overall intellectual ability such as those discussed in this section, there are also specialized instruments designed to measure specific aptitudes and special aspects or features of intelligence. These include (1) tests of social maturity, (2) tests of creativity, (3) tests of mental alertness or flexibility, and (4) specific aptitude tests.

In recent years it has become increasingly apparent that conventional intelligence tests measure but a limited number of human intellectual abilities. It is the theory of Guilford [8] that there are 120 such abilities, of which he has tentatively identified and measured 60. Guilford's model of the structure of intellect is depicted in Figure 5.3. This approach to a more precise classification of the various specific intellectual abilities could lead to the development of new measurement instruments to give valuable information about some abilities heretofore measured incompletely or not at all.

Social intelligence. Social intelligence has been poorly measured even though it is obviously an important factor in the adult success of some whose IQ scores were not outstanding. The *Vineland Social Maturity Scales* and others similar to it give some indication of the development of this factor in children. It is quite likely that other instruments adaptable to the school situation will be developed to help in the evaluation of this important facet of intelligence.[9]

Creativity. Creativity is a special aspect of intelligence which correlates positively with general ability but which definitely relates to an individual's mental flexibility or ability to relate ideas and concepts in new

---

[8] J. P. Guilford, "Structure of Intellect," *Psychological Bulletin*, LIII (1956), 267–293.

[9] The discussion in Chapter 7 is relevant to this topic.

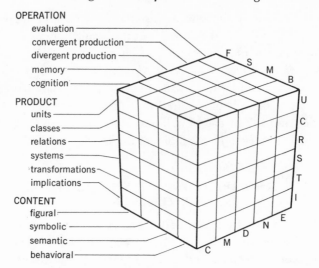

Figure 5.3. GUILFORD'S MODEL OF THE STRUCTURE OF INTELLECT

From J. P. Guilford, *The Nature of Human Intelligence* (New York: McGraw-Hill Book Company, 1967), p. 63. Reprinted by permission of the publisher.

or different patterns from those which are typical. Since it is the creative individual who makes many of the unique social contributions—particularly in aesthetic, literary, and scientific fields—many psychologists and educators have recently focused their attention on the problem of identifying this desirable trait and fostering it in the school program. Although there has been considerable investigation of creativity recently, no standardized tests have been devised, and the traditional intelligence tests have only limited predictive validity.

Torrance,[10] building on the ideas of Guilford, has developed some promising measurement instruments which are described below.

1. *Test of Imagination—Form D.* This test consists of several parts, the first of which includes four tasks (Product Improvement, Product Utilization, Unusual Uses of Tin Cans, and Circles). The second section is the Ask-and-Guess Test, consisting of three tasks.

The first four tasks are best described by the testing instructions which are quoted below:

[10] For a comprehensive report on his recent investigations and measuring instruments see E. Paul Torrance, *Rewarding Creative Behavior* (Englewood Cliffs, N. J.: Prentice-Hall, 1965). Reprinted by permission of the publisher.

Now, I am going to show you a little stuffed toy dog. On the first sheet of your test booklet, I want you to list the most interesting, clever, and unusual ways you can think of for changing the toy dog so that children would have more fun playing with it. You will have eight minutes to write down as many ideas as you can think of. (Time: Eight minutes after instructions have been completed.)

Your time is up on this part. As soon as you have finished the sentence you are writing, go ahead to Part II. List here the most interesting, clever, and unusual uses you can think of for this toy dog other than as a plaything. These may be uses of it as the toy now is or as it might be changed. For example, it could be used just as it is for a pincushion. Or, it could be made two or three feet tall, and a child could sit on it or ride it. All right, go ahead and work as rapidly as you can for the next five minutes. (Time: Five minutes after completion of instructions.)

All right, your time is up. As soon as you have finished the sentence you are writing, go ahead to Part III. List on this page the most unusual, interesting, and clever ideas you can think of for using tin cans. The cans can be of any size and shape, and you can use as many cans as you like. You will have five minutes. Go ahead. (Time: Five minutes after completion of instructions.)

Your time is up. As soon as you have finished writing the idea you are on, go ahead to Part IV. In the next ten minutes, see how many objects you can sketch which have a circle as the main part. Just use a few lines on the circles below to identify your ideas which might start: Wheel, tire, steering wheel, etc. Your lines might be either inside or outside the circle, or both inside and outside. (Demonstrate on blackboard.) If you don't think we'll be able to guess what object you have sketched, label it. All right, go ahead. (Time: Ten minutes after completion of instructions.) [11]

These four tasks are scored for fluency, flexibility, and originality. There is some subjectivity in the scoring but high interscorer reliability (generally in excess of .90) has been maintained in the studies. For example, the following coefficients of interscorer reliability were obtained, based upon sixty-four tests scored by two independent scores:

Product Improvement	Fluency	1.00
	Flexibility	.89
	Originality	.98 [12]

[11] *Torrance*, p. 268.
[12] *Torrance*, p. 271.

The Ask-and-Guess Test uses a picture from *Tom, the Piper's Son,* and requires that the pupils do the following three things:

1. Write down as many questions as they can think of which cannot be answered by looking at the picture.
2. List as many things as they can think of which might have caused or led up to the action shown in the picture.
3. List as many possibilities as they can of what might happen in the pictured situation.

This section of the test is scored only for fluency and adequacy of response.

Both reliability and validity of Form D appear to be good. The test-retest reliability coefficients reported are above .80, and validity checked against such strategies as teacher and peer nominations of creative individuals has shown significant relationships between high test scores and nominations. Alternate forms were also designed for the test—Forms EP and FP for kindergarten through third grade, and Forms EI and FI for fourth, fifth, and sixth grades.

2. *Imaginative Stories: Tests of Creative Writing.* There are two forms of the Imaginative Stories Test, Forms A and B. Each of these forms includes ten topics, and the subjects must choose one topic and in twenty minutes write the most interesting, exciting story about that topic that he can. Subjects are to concentrate on the ideas in the story rather than mechanics of grammar. The titles suggested in Form A are:

> The Dog That Doesn't Bark
> The Man Who Cries
> The Woman Who Can But Won't Talk
> The Cat That Doesn't Scratch
> Miss Jones Stopped Teaching
> The Doctor Who Became a Carpenter
> The Rooster That Doesn't Crow
> The Horse That Won't Run
> The Duck That Doesn't Quack
> The Lion That Doesn't Roar

Similar titles which involve an animal or person possessing some divergent characteristic are used in Form B. The essays are scored against six general criteria: organization, sensitivity, originality, imagination, psychological insight, and richness. Each criterion is divided into five components which are defined to aid the scorer. With a limited number of scorers high reliability has been obtained, but in general use with untrained scorers reliability would undoubtedly drop approximately to the level of typical essay tests.

3. *Personal-Social Motivation Inventory.* This inventory is somewhat akin to the personality inventories discussed in Chapter 7, but it is specifically designed to determine what motivations facilitate or hamper creative productivity. The inventory contains 189 items in the following eight scales:

> Creative Motivation
> Critical Motivation
> Intellectual Autonomy
> Quest for Certainty
> Quest for Power
> Quest for Meaning
> Quest for Social Relations
> Rejection of Social Relations

Inventiveness and ingenuity, which are basic characteristics of creative individuals, can also be measured by some standardized tests, such as the Ingenuity Test in the *Flanagan Aptitude Classification Tests Battery.* Because in recent years schools are devoting increasing attention to identifying and fostering creativity, it is likely that other good instruments will be developed to measure this trait.

Mental alertness. Mental alertness also relates to creativity, discussed above; and while the former trait is an aspect of intelligence, it is not specifically measured by the typical intelligence test. An interesting test designed specifically for this purpose is the *Thurstone Test of Mental Alertness.* This test provides information which will help the teacher or employer answer such questions as (1) how quickly will a person learn his job? (2) how able is the student or employee to learn new techniques or procedures? Four types of items are intermingled throughout the test; thus the subject has to change his mind set rapidly if he is to complete a majority of the 126 items in the 20-minute time limit. Three scores can be computed: (1) the Q-score or quantitative score, (2) the L-score or language score, and (3) the total score—a measure of general ability.

Specific aptitudes. Two areas of specific aptitude not measured on such batteries as the *DAT* are art and music. Actually one of the first aptitude tests was the *Seashore Measures of Musical Talents,* developed in 1915. This test is still used to help identify pupils who have special musical talent. The *Meier Art Judgment Test* can be used to help select those with particular talent in art.

In the field of business education two aptitude tests which have been widely used are the *Minnesota Clerical Test* and the *Detroit Clerical Aptitudes Examination.*

SUMMARY

The intelligent person has the ability to absorb experience, synthesize it with his past experiences into a meaningful whole, and utilize it in solving specific problems which confront him. Modern psychologists and teachers, though they have learned much about the essence of intellect, still search for completely satisfactory answers to the questions, "what is intelligence?" and "how can we evaluate human intelligence?" The most satisfactory hypotheses are (1) that intelligence consists of the ability to verbalize abstract concepts and (2) that intelligence consists of a number of related mental factors. Based on this second hypothesis, most recent tests of intelligence are designed to give a profile of several factors or aspects of intelligence. Recently, too, Guilford's concept of the structure of the intellect has gained wide acceptance. Guilford suggests that intelligence consists of as many as 120 separate intellectual abilities. Since conventional intelligence tests measure but a limited number of these abilities, a current practice is to classify them as scholastic aptitude tests.

Probably more attention has been devoted to attempts to assess intelligence than to any other aspect of measurement. Thus, numerous good individual and group intelligence tests are available for use by teachers and psychologists. The two best individual tests are the *Stanford-Binet Intelligence Scale* and the *Wechsler-Adult Intelligence Scale.* The Wechsler test is particularly valuable for measuring the intelligence of mature adults. A number of the better group tests are listed in the chapter-end bibliography.

The group tests have proved to be valuable instruments for grouping children in school and for predicting their future school success, but it must be noted parenthetically that the misunderstanding of tests and test data have been barriers to even more effective use of the instruments. A significant shortcoming of these instruments is their inadequacy in providing valid scores for minority groups and the culturally disadvantaged. Continued investigation of special facets of intelligence—for example, creativity—will undoubtedly add to the fund of understanding of the complex of man's intellect; but this insight has little practical value unless it is shared by the majority of the nation's teachers and used in planning educational programs suited to the intellectual competence of their school children.

DISCUSSION QUESTIONS AND PROBLEMS

1. What is the most serious limitation of current intelligence tests?
2. What criteria would you use for ability grouping in a school with many culturally handicapped and minority group children?
3. J. Stanley Ahmann and Marvin Glock classify conventional intelligence tests as scholastic aptitude tests. On what basis can this classification be justified?
4. Why does a pupil often show a change in IQ score when tested several times over a period of years? When tested with two different tests at approximately the same time?
5. There are several current theories of the nature of human intelligence. Compare and contrast two of these theories.
6. In what instances would you recommend that the individual intelligence test be used in addition to or in lieu of the group test?
7. Suggest reasons why the scores obtained by pupils on intelligence tests and tests of creativity do not show a high correlation.
8. Examine a number of group intelligence tests and select one which you would recommend for use in your school system. On what bases do you justify your choice?

REPRESENTATIVE INTELLIGENCE TESTS

Group Tests

American Council on Education Psychological Examination for High School Students. Grades 9–12. Cooperative Test Division.

California Short-Form Test of Mental Maturity. Grades kgn–1, 1–3, 4–8, 7–9, 9–13, 10–16 and adults. California Test Bureau.

California Test of Mental Maturity, 1957 Edition. Grades kgn–1, 1–3, 4–8, 7–9, 9–13, 10–16 and adults. California Test Bureau.

Cattell Culture Free Intelligence Test. Ages 4–8 and mentally defective adults, 8–13 and average adults, grades 10–16 and superior adults. Institute for Personality and Ability Testing. (Scales 2 and 3 also published, with manuals revised for school use, by Bobbs-Merrill Company.)

College Entrance Examination Board Scholastic Aptitude Test. Candidates for college entrance. Educational Testing Service.

Cooperative School and College Ability Tests. Grades 4–6, 6–8, 8–10, 10–12, 12–14. Cooperative Test Division.

Davis-Eells Test of General Intelligence or Problem Solving Ability. Grades 1–2, 3–6. Harcourt, Brace & World.

The Henmon-Nelson Tests of Mental Ability, Revised Edition. Grades 3–6, 6–9, 9–12, 13–17. Houghton Mifflin Company.

Kuhlmann-Anderson Intelligence Tests, Seventh Edition. Grades 7–9, 9–12. Personnel Press, Inc.

The Lorge-Thorndike Intelligence Tests. Grades kgn–1, 2–3, 4–6, 7–9, 10–12. Houghton Mifflin Company.

Ohio State University Psychological Test. Grades 9–16 and adults. Science Research Associates.

Otis Quick-Scoring Mental Ability Tests, New Edition. Grades 1.5–4, 4–9, 9–16. Harcourt, Brace & World.

Pintner General Ability Tests: Non-Language Series. Grades 4–9. Harcourt, Brace & World.

Pintner General Ability Tests: Verbal Series. Grades kgn–2, 2–4, 4–9, 9–2 and over. Harcourt, Brace & World.

SRA Tests of Educational Ability. Grades 4–6, 6–9, 9–12. Science Research Associates.

SRA Tests of General Ability. Grades kgn–2, 2–4, 4–6, 6–9, 9–12. Science Research Associates.

Thurstone Test of Mental Alertness, Revised Edition. Grades 9–12 and adults. Science Research Associates.

Individual Tests

Arthur Point Scale of Performance Tests. Ages 4–5 or 5.5 to superior adults. Psychological Corporation.

The Block Design Test. Mental ages 5–20; also called *Kohs' Block-Design Test.* C. H. Stoelting Company.

The Porteus Maze Test. Ages 3 and over. Psychological Corporation.

Revised Stanford-Binet Intelligence Scale, Third Revision. Ages 2 and over. Houghton Mifflin Company.

Wechsler Adult Intelligence Scale. Ages 16 and over. Psychological Corporation.

Wechsler Intelligence Scale for Children. Ages 5–15. Psychological Corporation.

SELECTED READINGS

Anastasi, Anne. *Individual Differences.* New York: John Wiley & Sons, 1965. Chapters 8 through 12 contain readings related to such problems of intellectual measurement as race difference, cultural bias, the exceptionally gifted, and creativity.

Downie, N. M. *Fundamentals of Measurement.* New York: Oxford University Press, 1958. Chapters 12 and 13. These chapters deal with both the general intelligence tests and tests of special abilities. They also include numerous illustrations of items from both intelligence and aptitude tests.

Freeman, Frank S. *Theory and Practice of Psychological Testing*. 3rd. ed. New York: Holt, Rinehart and Winston, 1962. An excellent source which gives extensive coverage of the various types of instruments. The text contains thorough analyses of both the Binet and Wechsler scales. Chapters 7, 10, 11, and 12 are of particular interest.

Garrett, Henry E. *Testing for Teachers*. 2nd ed. New York: American Book Company, 1965. Chapters 3 and 4 contain concise, understandable discussions of individual and group intelligence tests. Several of the better group tests of intelligence are described in considerable detail.

Getzels, Jacob W., and Philip W. Jackson. *Creativity and Intelligence: Explorations with Gifted Students*. New York: John Wiley & Sons, 1962. Points out inadequacy of conventional measures of intelligence.

Gowan, John Curtis, *et al. Creativity: Its Educational Implications*. New York: John Wiley & Sons, 1967. Chapter 6 is of particular interest and relevance to the topic of evaluation.

Guilford, J. P. *The Nature of Human Intelligence*. New York: McGraw-Hill Book Company, 1967. A most valuable book for those interested in delving into the theoretical basis of intelligence. Chapter 3 presents the general theory of the "structure-of-intellect" concept and its antecedents. Part II gives detailed consideration to each of the intellectual abilities.

Massialas, Byron G., and Jack Zevin. *Creative Encounters in the Classroom*. New York: John Wiley & Sons, 1967. Chapter 2 contains discussion of various ways to identify and foster creativity in a variety of subject areas.

Nunnally, Jum C., Jr. *Tests and Measurements*. New York: McGraw-Hill Book Company, 1959. The rationale of the multi-factor theory is explained in Chapter 9.

Thorndike, Robert L., and Elizabeth Hagen. *Measurement and Evaluation in Psychology and Education*. 2nd ed. New York: John Wiley & Sons, 1961. Chapters 9 and 10 contain both extensive discussion of intelligence and aptitude tests and many illustrations from the instruments.

Torrance, E. Paul. *Rewarding Creative Behavior*. Englewood Cliffs, New Jersey: Prentice-Hall, 1965. Chapter 3 provides a brief survey of the development of instruments for measuring creative thinking. Instruments used in the studies described in the book are reviewed in Appendix A.

Witty, Paul (ed.). *The Gifted Child*. Boston: D. C. Heath and Company, 1951. Chapter 2 discusses techniques and instruments for identifying gifted children. In Chapter 3 Terman and Ogden discuss Terman's study of the gifted.

The Journal of Clinical Psychology and the *Journal of Consulting Psychology* are particularly good sources for those interested in research with individual intelligence tests during the past decade.

Chapter 6

ASSESSING PUPILS'
PHYSICAL CHARACTERISTICS

INTRODUCTION

Good health and adequate physical endowment are so closely involved with the total intellectual endowment of the pupil that we frequently neglect to separate the two or even to accept the fact that energy level and good health are prerequisite to sustained high-level intellectual effort. In severe cases of health handicap the teacher cannot help but take into account the resulting achievement handicap; but most frequently it is only in obvious, severe cases that the physical well-being of the pupil is systematically evaluated in relationship to his regular academic performance. As incongruous as it may seem, we have tended to separate completely the health and physical education instruction from the academic instruction, carrying on evaluation of the physical performance of pupils in one area and academic performance in the other area with little or no cross consultation. Teachers who never fail to look up the previous intelligence and achievement scores of their pupils neither seek nor desire the scores which those same pupils make on the physical fitness tests. Certainly, however, the pupils who have neither the energy nor the strength to perform at minimum levels in physical fitness tests will also be seriously handicapped in completing the rigorous intellectual tasks which their academic teachers set for them. Those who have excellent health and adequate energy to perform their daily physical and intellectual tasks easily often take their physical endowment for granted with little recognition of its value. But the child or adult who is constantly tired and frequently ill values few personal endowments more highly than the good health which his peers ignore.

Health and physical fitness. Health and physical fitness are the two important areas related to pupils' physical welfare which need to be continually evaluated throughout the school program. These two areas are strongly related; but they are distinctly different. *Health* is a term which refers to general body welfare, including such elements as resistance to disease; nutritional balance; orderly functioning of such natural processes as elimination, temperature control, and internal chemical balance. Equilibrium of these elements is necessary to good health, while imbalance results in poor health. The type and magnitude of imbalance in any of the elements are generally identifiable and measurable. The *actual* measurement and treatment of the disturbance are generally the function of a physician, but school personnel have an important evaluation role in screening out those whose health is unsatisfactory and in alerting parents to the problems for subsequent treatment by physicians.

Physical fitness, on the other hand, refers to the capacity of the individual for sustained physical activity. Elements of physical fitness include muscular endurance, muscular flexibility, speed, balance, and cardiovascular fitness. In a sense physical fitness is a relative term since it necessarily varies according to an individual's particular physical endowment and his daily needs. However, each individual needs sufficient fitness to perform his daily tasks without undue fatigue at the end of each day. For those involved mainly in physical occupations, the muscular energy expended must be great; whereas for those whose occupations are primarily sedentary, less muscular but more intellectual energy may be expended.

It is possible for a person to be physically fit but have poor health—e.g., he might suffer from stomach ulcers. Conversely it is also possible for one to have good health without possessing a high degree of muscular or motor fitness. Fitness must be judged in terms of a given person's routine and emergency daily tasks, related to his strength and endurance to perform those tasks without overtiring himself. Nevertheless, we must not overlook the fact that health and physical fitness are generally strongly related. While measurement and correction of health difficulties are a major responsibility of the physician, evaluation and improvement of children's physical fitness are clearly the joint task of classroom and physical education teachers.

EVALUATION OF THE HEALTH STATUS

In evaluating the health status of pupils, the teacher and the physician play complementary roles. The teacher, particularly in the elementary school, has the unique advantage of being able to compare the individual child against 35–40 others in his classroom and against the hundreds of others who have been under his direction. The parent, although he is vitally concerned with his child, frequently lacks the emotional objectivity or the comparative perspective to recognize health problems or slight physical deviations which the teacher may readily note as he observes the group of 35 children. The teacher's role as a trained observer is vital in evaluating each child's health and physical fitness. The total health status of pupils can be evaluated from health histories in the cumulative school records, observations by teachers and the school nurse, dental and medical examinations, and physical fitness tests.

Health records. A vital part of each child's cumulative record folder is the health history or health record. In some states such a record is a required part of the cumulative record, and forms on which to record the information are prescribed by the state department of education. This form should provide a record of the childhood illnesses; various inoculations; medical examinations; teachers' health observations; school physical examinations, including growth records and sensory perception acuity; and physical defects. The regular cumulative record provides space for limited health information.

More frequently, however, there may be an insert form which has room for more extensive information than that permitted in the limited space of the cumulative folder. Such an insert form is that recommended by the Idaho State Department of Education. This form, shown in Figure 6.1, is divided into seven categories:

1. Medical history
2. Immunization record
3. Growth record
4. Dental examinations
5. Medical examinations
6. Teacher observations
7. Comments and recommendations

Such a record is kept by teachers, guidance personnel, and school nurses; and it should follow the child from school to school as he progresses through the grade levels or from district to district if his parents move. This instrument has major value as a summary of the data and information which school and out-of-school personnel collect about each child. Much of the information is collected through different kinds of measurement, and the cumulative record merely brings this data to-

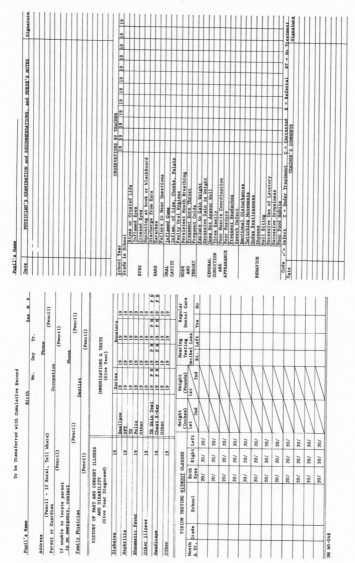

Figure 6.1 IDAHO PUPIL HEALTH RECORD

Reprinted by permission of the Idaho Department of Health, Boise, Idaho.

gether in a convenient form to facilitate evaluation of each child's status.

The value of such records obviously depends upon the care with which the information is recorded and upon the nature of the measurements themselves. However, the records are of little value, even when carefully kept, if the data consists of a hodgepodge of trivia. On the other hand, significant data haphazardly recorded also deflates the value of the record. Certainly, too, no record is any better than its ultimate use. It should be used for subsequent actions in school program improvement. Records which lie unused in the principal's vault are wasteful; they cost time to collect and yet fail to achieve the desired program improvement.

Medical and dental examinations. It is important that children have periodic medical and dental examinations. Medical examinations should be given to preschool children as they enter the first grade, then subsequently during the intermediate grades, during adolescence, and before high school graduation. Dental examinations are needed more frequently, particularly when there is evidence of some dental problem. The physically handicapped require more frequent medical examinations than do normal children, the frequency being dictated by the nature of the handicap. It is mandatory that medical examinations be required as a prerequisite to participation in intramural and interscholastic athletics. No participant should be considered eligible for competitive sports until he has undergone such an examination. These required examinations are not normally given at school unless there is a school physician. However, school officials may be able to schedule pupils' cardiovascular and dental examinations with the local physicians and dentists for a nominal fee. Most schools are too small to employ school physicians and dentists, but they can facilitate arrangements for these examinations; and in the instances when examinations are made at school, teachers or school nurses can help by recording the data.

Teacher observations. As was noted earlier in the chapter, classroom teachers have an important role to play in observing the health, growth, and development of pupils. In elementary school the teachers can give screening physical examinations, collect growth data, and note beginning health problems. Every classroom teacher should be aware of the symptoms of the common allergies and contagious and infectious diseases. Common skin diseases such as ringworm, scabies, and impetigo are easily identifiable, highly infectious, but easily treated. The teacher is negligent when he fails to identify such infections and permits them to spread throughout the classroom or the school.

The teacher should also identify for referral to physicians pupils who are low in energy level, who have slight skeletal disorders, who are habitual mouth breathers, who have persistent headaches, or who exhibit signs of persistent allergy. All of these signs of poor physical health are readily observable, and within the classroom group the child who deviates seriously is quite apparent to the discerning teacher.

Although during recent years we have come to accept the facts that body build influences posture and that all children cannot be forced into one ideal posture model, teachers are still responsible for helping the child achieve a desirable posture suitable to his body type.

Health tests. The classroom teacher also has an important role in administering and using the tests of health knowledge, attitude, and habit; and, in the elementary school, in helping to give physical examinations to pupils. In the secondary school, the health and physical education teacher often gives these examinations, but homeroom teachers can help record data and should use the results.

For most persons good health is not an accident but rather a combination of natural endowment, persistent personal attention, and healthful natural environment. Teachers can do nothing about the child's natural endowment, but they can teach and evaluate knowledge and attitudes vital to a healthy existence. As competent teachers know, knowledge about health is easily taught and measured, but it is attitudes which lead to actual application of this knowledge. Habits are the ultimate result of the combined effect of knowledge and attitude. For example, it is not difficult to teach children facts about their teeth. They will readily come to "know" what causes decay, what diet is most helpful in preserving teeth, and what kind of brushing is desirable. They can also repeat this information on a test, but the knowledge and understanding which they have acquired may but slightly change their attitudes and make no change in their diet or dental care.

The attitudes and habits which are most important are most difficult to teach and least easily measured. If changes are to be made in attitudes and habits, they must be stressed repeatedly, often dramatically; and the changes cannot be taken for granted but must be measured whenever possible.[1] Transfer from knowledge and understanding to application is often meager and needs to be assessed. The tests listed at the end of the chapter include a representative sample of published health tests which are available to aid in assessment of knowledge and attitudes.

In addition to the published tests teachers can measure knowledge and

[1] See Chapter 13 for a discussion of the measurement of attitudes.

attitudes with traditional teacher-made objective and essay tests. Other sources of information about pupil health habits include pupil opinion surveys, diaries, interviews, and observation checklists. Teachers who eat with their pupils in the school lunch program can observe the specific food preferences of individual pupils on a checklist to determine which foods are habitually accepted or rejected. Such systematic observation provides the data for an analysis of dietary deficiencies.

Physical examination. In the elementary school, annual or semiannual screening physical examinations should be given. Much of the examination and recording of data can be handled by the classroom teacher during one day set aside for the purpose. These school examinations should include measurement of height, weight, visual acuity, and hearing acuity.

Height and weight can be checked with a standard medical scale and recorded on the pupil's growth record. In evaluating growth records teachers should be aware of the fact that there is no "normal" growth pattern which all children should follow. Normal development varies for each child in terms of his specific body build. The height-weight norm charts which we have often used in the past do not take these body-build differences into account and have tended to confuse teachers and parents. The Wetzel grid,[2] which provides norms for height patterns for varying body builds and which gives a better comparison than the single-norm charts, is often used in schools today.

Visual acuity can be screened with the *Snellen Chart.* The chart should be placed at eye level twenty feet from the subjects with a minimum of ten foot-candles of light on the chart. Because this type of screening does not identify any but the nearsighted, or myopic, and the seriously astigmatic cases, the teacher must be alert to observe other visual problems as well. For example, the farsighted child may have difficulty accommodating to near vision tasks such as reading fine print. The astigmatic child may confuse uppercase letters *E* and *F* if he has severe distortion in the horizontal axis. The myopic child is a habitual squinter because by squinting he can cut out the distracting out-of-focus light waves and see more clearly at a distance. Other signs of visual problems include head tilt, frequent headache, eyelid tic, and eye muscle weakness. Any one of these symptoms may be the result of a serious problem which should be referred to the physician for diagnosis and treatment.

[2] See Carl E. Willgoose, *Evaluation in Health Education and Physical Education* (New York: McGraw-Hill Book Company, 1961), pp. 63–68.

Loss of peripheral vision can be detected by the teacher in a screening test by asking the child, with his eyes fixed straight ahead, to note when he first detects the teacher's hand as it is moved forward from each side into the visual plane. Although "tunnel vision," or lack of peripheral vision, does not too seriously handicap the child in school if his forward vision is acute, it does seriously handicap him when he begins to drive an automobile. Furthermore, such a restricted visual field may indicate progressive sight loss as a result of glaucoma, and the eyes should be weighed for tension by a physician to determine whether treatment is needed.

One other visual screening test which is important and easily administered is the *Ishihara Test* for color blindness. Many children who are color-blind do not know that they have any problem. Few females are affected, but color-blindness is common in the male; since it is a sex-linked characteristic, approximately one of each twenty males is at least partially color-blind.

Depth perception ability also varies among pupils. Although it may not be practical to examine all pupils for depth perception, certainly those who enroll in driver education courses should have such an examination. Persons who have poor depth perception are poor risks as drivers, since they have difficulty parking and are unable to judge when they have sufficient distance to pass other vehicles. Even when the state permits licensing of persons with this handicap, the driver should be aware of his deficiency so that his faulty perception can be tempered with judgment.

Hearing screening should also be part of the physical examination. Observant teachers may suspect which pupils have hearing difficulty, but examinations are needed to verify their judgment and to discover others which the teacher may not detect. The watch tick or whisper test can give a crude measure of hearing acuity and should be used if no other means of measurement is available. Larger schools should have a group audiometer available for teacher use. With the audiometer 25–30 pupils can be checked at one time. In this test situation each pupil has a set of headphones; and as he listens, he is asked to record the numbers or letters which are spoken by male and female voices at varying decibel levels. Such screening gives a measure of hearing acuity but gives poor evidence in cases of hearing loss in portions of the pitch scale.

To determine whether the child can hear well throughout the entire range of normally audible frequencies, a pure-tone audiometer is needed.

This instrument permits the transmitted frequency as well as the decibel level of sound to be varied, thus facilitating the measurement of both acuity and frequency perception. Hearing losses in the low register below 400–500 vibrations per second or in the high register above 8,000–10,000 are not seriously handicapping, but losses in the middle of the scale lead to poor perception of spoken communication and can seriously handicap the child in school as well as in his future adult life. Those who are identified as problem cases should be referred to a school audiologist or physician for further diagnosis and treatment.

Any pupil who has a physical handicap should have periodic physical examinations; provision of a special school program if the handicap is severe; and continuous evaluation to determine both his physical and his educational progress. For most effective teaching it is often necessary to segregate those with severe speech, motor, sight, and hearing handicaps into special classes. However, as soon as they achieve sufficient improvement that they can learn equally well in the regular classroom, they should be transferred out of the special class. The competition and contact with normal children are desirable, and they prepare them for a more nearly normal adjustment in adult life.

EVALUATION OF PHYSICAL FITNESS

There are numerous techniques and instruments which can be used to measure one or more of the aspects of physical fitness. Most of this measurement program will be carried out by the physical education teachers in both elementary and secondary programs as the basis for a planned health and physical education program. The data, however, should be recorded on the child's cumulative record along with the health data mentioned earlier.

Specific purposes of the physical fitness measurements are (1) to provide information about pupil needs as a basis for planning the physical education program, (2) to classify or group pupils for instruction, (3) to determine the current physical status of pupils, (4) to provide a picture of pupil progress, and (5) to provide a basis for assigning physical education course marks.

The limited coverage in this chapter does not permit a complete discussion of all the instruments and techniques available for measurement in this area, but examples are discussed for the areas of muscular strength and endurance, lung capacity, motor fitness, and cardiovascular fitness. Little consideration is given to measurement and evaluation of physique, posture, flexibility and body mechanics, motor ability, and specific motor skills. These are important factors in physical fitness, but several of them are of more concern to the physical education teacher than to the classroom teacher. Those who are interested in further inquiry in this area of measurement can consult the physical education measurement texts listed in the chapter bibliography.

Muscular strength and endurance tests. Muscular strength is an aspect of physical fitness which increases throughout the growing period of the child and achieves a peak during young adulthood. Throughout life the strength of an individual fluctuates somewhat with his general health condition and gives a fairly reliable indication of general physical fitness. This obvious attribute often becomes an exceedingly important goal to the adolescent male, who aspires to great physical strength, who often practices diligently to achieve improvement, and who glories in the display of his newfound strength for an admiring audience of his peers.

Strength depends upon the size and coordination of muscles, and muscles are developed by exercise and constant use. Those muscles which are not used tend to atrophy and degenerate into fatty tissue. Young people who exercise frequently usually have excellent muscle tone, but the decline in physical activity which often accompanies increasing age may result in loss of strength and agility.

Measuring strength as a means of determining physical fitness is not a new approach. In fact as early as the latter part of the nineteenth century Dudley A. Sargent proposed a battery of such tests; and in 1925 Frederick R. Rogers developed standard testing procedures and norms for the various elements of strength and endurance, which he included in the *Rogers Physical Fitness Index Battery*. This battery permits two types of scores to be obtained for an individual: (1) the *strength index,* which consists of the gross score obtained on six strength tests plus lung capacity, and (2) the *physical fitness index,* which is a derived score for physical fitness analogous to the intelligence quotient. The strength index is a good indicator of general athletic ability. The physical fitness index takes into account the norms for the particular age, weight, and sex of the individual. The formula for the physical fitness index is as follows:

$$\text{PFI} = \frac{\text{Individual's achieved strength index}}{\text{Normal strength index}} \times 100$$

Thus the child who achieved the mean strength index for his age, weight, and sex would have a PFI of 100. Use of the *PFI* is advantageous because it permits a numerical score which is interpretable in terms of norms and because it can be used to show subsequent gains or losses throughout the child's school career.

The tests in the *Rogers PFI Battery* include (1) *lung capacity* measured in cubic inches with a wet spirometer; (2) *grip strength* measured in pounds with a hand dynamometer, or manuometer; (3) *back lift* measured in pounds with a dynamometer; (4) *leg lift* measured in pounds with a dynamometer; (5) *pull-ups* on a chinning bar high enough that the child's feet are clear of the floor; and (6) *push-ups* on the horizontal bars for boys and from a bench for girls. The detailed instructions should be followed carefully to insure performances comparable on the standardized scale of norms.[3]

The *PFI* test can be administered to a large group of students during one day if several assistants aid in administering each test in the battery. Actual testing of individual pupils is not time consuming; and when an entire day is set aside for this purpose, class groups can be scheduled, tested, and returned to their classrooms without great loss of time. If, however, all the testing must be conducted during the regular physical education period, the tests for each group will have to be carried over several days and will result in less efficient administration and poorer pupil performance. It is important that the subjects be encouraged to perform at their maximum level, but they should not be pushed to harmful overexertion. The order of the tasks is not crucial, except that it is suggested that the push-ups and pull-ups be given last because both are endurance and strength tests; when they are administered first, cumulative fatigue affects performance in the remainder of the battery.

Several research projects have been carried out using the *PFI* as an instrument to predict various types of athletic performance. For example, McCloy [4] made slight revisions in the *PFI* and found a correlation of .77 between the strength index and a battery of four track and field events.

Another well-known test of muscular fitness is the *Kraus-Weber Tests of Minimum Muscular Fitness*, which with six tests measures strength and flexibility of important muscle groups. Although this battery was

[3] Excellent descriptions of each test along with detailed instructions for their administration are presented in H. Harrison Clarke, *Application of Measurement to Health and Physical Education*, 4th ed. (Englewood Cliffs, New Jersey: Prentice-Hall, 1967), Chapter 7.

[4] C. H. McCloy and Norma D. Young, *Tests and Measurements in Health and Physical Education*, 3rd ed. (New York: Appleton-Century-Crofts, 1954), p. 26.

designed to measure minimum muscular fitness of adults, it has also been adapted for school children. When the battery was administered to school children in this country, 57.9 percent failed the tests, with the greatest failure rates among the younger age groups. European children in contrast had 8.7 percent failure rate on one or more of the tests.[5] Older children in this country show definite increases on the strength tests but decreases on the flexibility tests.

Motor fitness and performance tests. The motor fitness or performance tests go beyond simple measurement of strength and endurance and include speed, power, agility, flexibility, and balance. These tests require a greater range of performance tasks than that required on the *PFI.*

Universities and associations of health and physical education in the various states have developed excellent motor fitness tests. Examples of these are the *New York State Physical Fitness Test,* the *California Physical Performance Test,* the *University of Maryland Motor Fitness Test,* and the *University of Florida Physical Motor Fitness Tests.*

A battery which has been widely used in schools is the *AAHPER Youth Fitness Test,* which was prepared in 1958 by the American Association of Health, Physical Education, and Recreation. This test has been administered to millions of school children in all fifty states and in numerous foreign countries. The norms for the test were established on the performances of 8,500 boys and girls throughout the United States, and pupils who achieve scores above the median of the normative group earn a fitness award emblem. This test consists of seven items: pull-ups, push-ups, 40-yard shuttle run, standing broad jump, 50-yard dash, softball throw for distance, and 600-yard run-walk. For schools in which there are swimming facilities three additional aquatic tests may be administered, but they do not figure in the regular norms because most schools lack swimming facilities.[6]

Cardiovascular tests. Cardiovascular fitness relates to cardiorespiratory and circulatory endurance, which is the ability of the heart, lungs, and circulatory system to adjust to prolonged physical activity. An individual's stamina or ability to persist in protracted physical exertion is important in many of the physical activities of life. When limited activity produces

[5] H. Harrison Clarke, *Application of Measurement to Health and Physical Education,* 4th ed. (Englewood Cliffs, N. J.: Prentice-Hall, 1967), p. 176.

[6] The required equipment and procedure for this test are described in such standard texts as Carl E. Willgoose, *Evaluation in Health Education and Physical Education* (New York: McGraw-Hill Book Company, 1961).

undue fatigue, drive and ambition are also effectively reduced. Measurement of pulse rate and blood pressure is commonly used to indicate cardiovascular fitness. Since the blood pressure tests require the use by a trained technician of the mercury sphygmomanometer and a stethoscope, the measurement of pulse rate, which requires no special equipment, is used more frequently in schools. Examples of these tests are the *Carlson Fatigue Curve Test* and the *Harvard Step Test.*

The *Carlson Fatigue Test* requires that the subject run in place as rapidly as he can for ten seconds followed by ten seconds of rest. The alternate running and resting periods are repeated ten times. During the running the number of steps is tabulated and pulse rate is recorded ten seconds after the last running period, two minutes after exercise, four minutes after exercise, and six minutes after exercise. The results are graphically recorded for each pupil, and an entire class can be tested in about ten minutes if pupils help record the scores. Improvement or changes can be shown in subsequent testings by recording the repeated test scores on the original graphs.

The *Harvard Step Test* follows a similar procedure, but substitutes a rhythmic cadence 30 steps per minute from the floor to a 20-inch-high step-up bench. For elementary school children the bench height is lowered to 14 inches. This test measures fitness for muscular work and ability to recover from exertion.

CORRECTION AND FOLLOW-UP

Use of measurements discussed in this chapter should provide sufficient data about each pupil during his school years to permit valid evaluation of both his physical education and health program together with required adjustments in the academic program. For the majority of pupils little special or individual adjustment in the school program will be required. However, it is imperative that program adjustments be made for those who deviate markedly—particularly at the low end of the scale—in physical fitness, motor performance, and cardiovascular fitness. Adjustments for the handicapped should be made with their limited physical endowment and energy in mind, and the aim of the corrective program should be to enable these children to achieve normal school progress.

Since measurement record keeping, evaluation, and program planning are intimately tied together, every effort should be made to involve the classroom teacher, who will ultimately implement the results of the measurement process in classroom instructional changes.

Record keeping. It has been recommended that teachers conduct most of the pupils' health and physical fitness measurement. Logically, then, it should also follow that the associated routine of recording data be a teacher responsibility. In the elementary school each teacher should share this responsibility with the school nurse and the physical education teacher. To facilitate the use of the records they should be duplicated and the teacher provided with a complete set to keep in her classroom, while a second set is kept in the vault of the administrative office.

At the junior high school and high school levels the homeroom teacher should help by recording measurement data. At these levels most of the measurements and examinations will be completed by others—the school nurse, the physical education teacher, the family physician. However, here also it is desirable that a duplicate set of the records be kept on file in the homeroom.

SUMMARY

Teachers and parents who are greatly concerned with the intellectual development and the educational progress of school children often fail to take into account the important effect which health and physical fitness have on school achievement. Poor health, low energy level, and sensory handicaps too frequently are overlooked as primary causes of low achievement. The onset of such problems as poor vision or subnormal hearing may be so gradual as to escape detection unless there is a systematic program of examination and constant, careful observation.

Although there is no intent in this chapter to imply that the school officials should assume the prerogatives of medical personnel, teachers have an important role in measurement and evaluation of pupils' health status and physical fitness. This program should include regular screening physical examinations; tests of health knowledge and attitudes; and measurement of physical fitness including tests of muscular strength and endurance, motor fitness, and cardiovascular fitness. The results of these examinations and tests should be recorded in the permanent cumulative record and should be evaluated as a basis for program planning and for referring problem cases to the physician.

Health and physical fitness are separate but related concepts. *Health* refers to general body welfare: resistance to disease, nutritional balance, orderly functioning of natural processes, temperature control, and internal chemical balance. Equilibrium of the elements is essential to good health, and imbalance of any element results in health deterioration. Evaluation of the health of individuals is primarily the physician's responsibility. However, knowledge of good health practices and practice of desirable health habits can and should be assessed by the teacher.

Physical fitness, on the other hand, refers to the capacity of the individual for sustained physical activity. It includes such elements as muscular endurance, muscular flexibility, speed, balance, and cardiovascular fitness. An individual's required physical fitness is relative to his physical endowment and his daily needs. Each individual needs sufficient fitness to perform his daily tasks without undue fatigue. Evaluation and improvement of children's physical fitness are the joint responsibility of the classroom and the physical education teachers. Tests such as the *Rogers PFI Battery* and the *AAHPER Youth Fitness Test* are most useful for this evaluation.

REPRESENTATIVE TESTS IN PHYSICAL EDUCATION

Health Knowledge, Attitudes, and Habits

Bridges, Frank A. *Health Knowledge Test for College Freshmen.* Rockville Center, N. Y.: Acorn Publishing Company, 1956.

Byrd, Oliver E. *Byrd Health Attitude Scale.* Stanford, Calif.: Stanford University Press, 1940.

Johns, Edward B., and Warren L. Juhnke. *Health Practice Inventory.* Stanford, Calif.: Stanford University Press, 1952.

Kilander, H. F. *Kilander Health Knowledge Test,* Forms A and B. Yonkers, N. Y.: World Book Company, 1952.

Speer, Robert K., and Samuel Smith. *Health Test: National Achievement Tests.* Rockville Center, N. Y.: Acorn Publishing Company, 1957.

Physical Fitness: Cardiovascular, Endurance, and Motor Performance

Since the tests listed below are performance tests, sources which describe their administration and use are given.

AAHPER Youth Fitness Test. AAHPER Youth Fitness Test Manual. Washington, D.C.: American Association for Health, Physical Education, and Recreation, 1958.

Carlson Fatigue Curve Test. H. C. Carlson. "Fatigue Curve Test," *Research Digest,* XVI (October 1945), 72–78.

Harvard Step Test. Lucien Brouha. "The Step Test: A Simple Method of

Measuring Physical Fitness for Muscular Work in Young Men," *The Research Quarterly,* XIV (March 1943), 31–36.

Kraus-Weber Tests. Hans Kraus and Ruth P. Hirschland. "Minimum Muscular Fitness Tests in School Children," *The Research Quarterly,* XXV (May 1954), 178–188.

Rogers Physical Fitness Index. Frederick Rand Rogers. *Physical Capacity Tests in the Administration of Physical Education.* New York: Bureau of Publications, Teachers College, Columbia University, 1925.

Schneider Test. E. C. Schneider. "A Cardiovascular Rating as a Measure of Physical Fatigue and Efficiency," *Journal of the American Medical Association,* LXXIV (May 29, 1920), 507.

Posture and Body Mechanics

New York State Physical Fitness Test. Albany, N. Y.: New York State Education Dept., 1958.

Wickens-Kiphuth Posture Test. T. Erwin Blesh, Carlton R. Meyers, and Oscar W. Kiphuth. *Photometric Photography in Posture Evaluation of Yale University Freshmen.* New Haven, Connecticut: Yale University Clerical Bureau, 1954.

Physical Achievement

Cozens Scales. Physical Scales for Boys in Secondary Schools. New York: A. S. Barnes and Company, 1936.

McCloy Achievement Scales. Charles H. McCloy, *The Measurement of Athletic Power.* New York: A. S. Barnes and Company, 1939.

Motor Intelligence

Iowa Brace Test. Charles H. McCloy. "An Analytical Study of the Stunt Type Tests as a Measure of Motor Educability," *The Research Quarterly,* VIII (October 1937), 250–265.

DISCUSSION QUESTIONS AND PROBLEMS

1. Define physical fitness. How should the standards of physical fitness differ for boys and girls, and for those who work at active occupations and those who work at sedentary ones?
2. Describe the role of the classroom teacher, of the physical education teacher, and of the physician in evaluating the child's health and physical fitness.
3. In view of the limited time and money available for the education of each child, how much attention should be given to health and physical fitness?
4. Discuss the advantages and disadvantages of employing a school physician, a school dentist, a school nurse in a public school system.
5. It is common practice to group pupils intellectually for instruction in academic subjects. Is it also desirable to group pupils on the basis of motor intelligence for instruction in physical education.

6. How much corrective instruction should the school provide for those with physical handicaps? poor coordination? poor dietary habits?
7. Administer one or more of the fitness tests to the class and discuss the results.

SELECTED READINGS

Barrow, Harold M., and Rosemary McGee. *Measurement in Physical Education.* Philadelphia: Lea & Rebiger, 1964. Part II includes a systematic analysis of the best measurement instruments for use in health and physical education. Chapter 19 includes a brief but valuable outline to be followed in constructing motor performance tests.

Clarke, H. Harrison. *Application of Measurement to Health and Physical Education.* 3rd ed. Englewood Cliffs, N. J.: Prentice-Hall, 1959. Contains numerous illustrations which should be helpful in the administration of the tests. Chapter 17 includes a consideration of the applications of measurement in the school physical education program.

Mathews, Donald P. *Measurement in Physical Education.* Philadelphia: W. B. Saunders Company, 1963. Most of the book is devoted to a detailed discussion of various instruments and techniques used in the measurement of different aspects of physical fitness and physical performance.

Meyers, Carleton R., and T. Edwin Blesh. *Measurement in Physical Education.* New York: The Ronald Press, 1962. Chapter 4 contains information on the construction of physical education tests.

Sheldon, William H. *Atlas of Men.* New York: Harper & Brothers, 1954. Illustrates photographically the variety of body types and discusses the method of somatotyping individuals.

Willgoose, Carl E. *Evaluation in Health Education and Physical Education.* McGraw-Hill Book Company, 1961. Excellent material on the numerous types of measurement in the field. Appendix A contains the scoring tables for about two dozen well-known tests.

_____ *Chapter 7* _____

EVALUATING PERSONALITY
TRAITS AND INTERESTS

INTRODUCTION

When a person is asked to describe his most familiar associates and
friends, he is apt to begin by describing their most prominent personality
traits, for instance, "She is friendly," "He is a domineering person," "She
is shy." In fact, for the closest friends and relatives this personality concept becomes so important that it is difficult for them to give a detailed,
accurate description of the person's physical appearance uncolored by
the personality concept. On the other hand, when a new acquaintance is
made, the first impression is dominantly formed from the *physical* appearance, colored somewhat by the most striking superficial personality
trait. With further acquaintance and closer association, however, this
"first impression" inevitably changes, shifting gradually to a more realistic personality *gestalt*—a changing blend of the physical-psychic traits.
Interestingly, also, one meets many of his daily associates in but one of
the many life roles which they play; thus their personalities are perceived as a single reflection from a many-faceted mirror—incomplete, a
bit distorted, but complementary to the remaining images which constitute the whole. Each person constantly plays numerous roles in life,
which reflect different personal images—e.g., a man's role as a father, as
a husband, as a member of his profession, or as a hunting partner. Obviously no single role-portrait displays the man's true personality *gestalt*,
but together they constitute the man.

In modern civilized society the roles which men play have multiplied,
and the pressures exerted upon them have increased. In the less complex
societies of the world, as in earlier American society, the pressures are
much less numerous. In such situations the individual has to learn fewer

inhibitions to participate successfully in group life, and his adaptations to society are fewer and less complex. The high incidence of mental illness in our decade is tragic testimony to the fact that many fail to adapt successfully to the stress of living in modern, competitive society. With this problem, as with many other social problems, the massive effort is focused on cure, not prevention: in this case, on the costly rehabilitation of those who have already broken under stress rather than on the more productive and much less expensive task of identification and prevention.

The school as an institution which enrolls nearly all children is ideally suited to undertake the latter task. However, teachers cannot assume psychiatric responsibilities in addition to their instructional tasks; they have neither the time nor the competence to do so. They can, however, aid in early identification of those who have serious emotional problems and in helping to rectify the minor problems of many others.

The major focus in this book is on what the child *can learn* or *has learned,* the classroom applications of measurement and evaluation; but it would be unrealistic to neglect the personality and interest factors which affect what he *will learn* and how he will participate as a citizen of society. Specific questions to be answered in this discussion are (1) What are the most important concepts of personality? (2) How can personality and social adjustment be evaluated? (3) What is the nature of interests? and (4) How can pupils' interests be assessed?

CONCEPTS OF PERSONALITY

Over the years personality development has been a genuine concern to the teachers, philosophers, psychologists, and psychiatrists who have sought to understand and assess it; channel it into acceptable patterns; and explain it to others. The avid, personal interest they have aroused in the layman is amply demonstrated by the popularity of numerous publications, ranging from the Sunday supplement personality inventories (Are You a Good Husband?) to the do-it-yourself personality improvers *à la Dale Carnegie.*

The three concepts of personality which are widely enough held as to deserve consideration here are (1) the normal-abnormal concept, (2) the traits concept, and (3) the classification concept. Of these three the majority of the theories can be classified under the last two concepts.

Normal-abnormal concept. The normal-abnormal concept to some extent underlies or is interwoven into all the theories of personality development. Normality is a term which can properly be discussed only in the context of a specific society. Whether or not an individual's behavior is normal can be judged only against the backdrop of the mores, customs, folkways, and laws of the society of which he is a member. Certain aspects of "normal behavior" in one society would certainly be considered abnormal in another. Furthermore, with a given society normality must be considered as a broad band or continuum of acceptable behavior, with the few who fall outside the limits classed as abnormal or deviant. In other words, there is a great range of individuality in behavior just as there is in other human traits, such as intelligence; and no one specific behavior pattern constitutes the acceptable norm which all must follow if they are to be considered normal.

This concept can be illustrated by an example using a specific personality construct. The construct used in this illustration is *power*, or authority, or dominance, as it may be alternately named. A person's desire to exercise power over others is reflected in his personality and ranges from a complete lack of desire to exercise power over others to a desire to exercise power over everyone. Theoretically the power constructs of a large group of individuals would be normally distributed as noted in Figure 7.1. Normality in this case would include all those individuals who fall within several standard deviations of the mean, both above and below, but would exclude as abnormal both those at the bottom end of the curve and those at the upper extreme. At the upper end of the scale there is probably a relatively narrow demarcation between such men as Hitler, who was afflicted with extreme power mania, and Churchill, whom we honor as a great leader. The great leaders are probably also motivated in their achievements by a desire for power and acclaim. While in this instance the individuals at the two extremes of the curve are readily identified as abnormal, it is in the two segments of the curve subnormal and hypernormal that a clear-cut classification of the cases as normal or abnormal is difficult. With each of the various personality constructs the real problem of screening the normal from the abnormal lies in subnormal and hypernormal extremes of the scale.

The *Bernreuter Personality Inventory*, first published in 1931, was one of the first instruments to approach the assessment of personality from the normal-abnormal concept. The construct power or dominance, used in the illustration above, is one of the six scales in the inventory. Although this instrument was used extensively for a number of years after its pub-

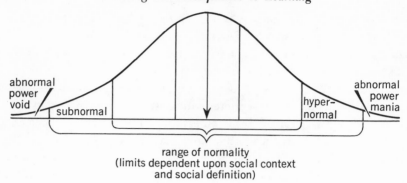

Figure 7.1. THEORETICAL DISTRIBUTION OF A LARGE GROUP OF INDIVIDUALS BASED ON THEIR POWER DESIRE

lication, the interrelationships among the scales is so high that it has questionable value in measuring the intended constructs.[1]

The *Bell Adjustment Inventory* is another example of one of the earlier inventories following the normal-abnormal rationale. Forms were provided for high school and university students and for adults, with emphasis on the assessment of home, health, social and emotional adjustment —and, in addition, vocational adjustment for adults. The purpose of this inventory was primarily that of screening or identifying the seriously maladjusted.

A more recent instrument which also uses the normal-abnormal concept is the *Edwards Personal Preference Schedule* (1954). This instrument is based upon a list of manifest psychological needs, including (1) achievement, (2) deference, (3) order, (4) exhibition, (5) autonomy, (6) affiliation, (7) intraception, (8) succorance, (9) dominance, (10) abasement, (11) nurturance, (12) change, (13) endurance, (14) heterosexuality, and (15) aggression.

Traits concept. The problem of identifying uncorrelated personality factors led Raymond B. Cattell and others to use the statistical technique of factor analysis to isolate personal constructs or traits which could be measured. The traits concept is actually an analytical approach to personality evaluation, in contrast to the organismic concept. According to the traits concept, personality consists of a series of such traits as dominance and introversion, all of which constitute personality but which can

[1] Donald E. Super, "The Bernreuter Personality Inventory," *Psychological Bulletin,* XXXIX (1942), 94–125.

be separately identified and measured. This concept is particularly useful for the teacher and psychologist since it helps delimit the problem of personality development and analysis into one which is relatively concrete and easily attacked. It is easier to agree on the nature of a trait such as dominance, then to identify and measure the extent to which an individual possesses that trait, than it is to reach a consensus concerning the total nature of personality. Unless some agreement in definition is possible among those concerned with personality development and evaluation, the evaluations will be virtually meaningless because the lack of a common base or referent prevents meaningful comparisons.

Cattell has probably done more work in identifying the specific traits than any other man. He found approximately 5500 personality trait names in the English language, which he grouped into a list of 171 traits when synonyms were eliminated. By statistical analysis Cattell then reduced these 171 traits to a list of 35, which he termed "surface" traits and which depicted the obvious behavior of individuals. From this list of 35 traits he identified a group of *source traits* which seemed to be basic, including most of the 35. The six source traits which he considered to be most important are shown in Table XII.

Two examples of instruments which follow the traits approach are the *Guilford-Zimmerman Temperament Survey* and the *Heston Personal Adjustment Inventory.* The Guilford-Zimmerman test covers ten traits: general activity, restraint, ascendance, sociability, emotional stability, objectivity, friendliness, thoughtfulness, personal relations, and masculinity. The shorter Heston test is designed to be completed in a 40- to 50-minute period; but it measures only six areas (analytical thinking, sociability, emotional stability, confidence, personal relations, and home satisfaction). It is evident from a cursory examination of these and other such inventories that there is no agreement among the authorities relative to which are the most important traits or constructs which must be measured if personality is to be validly assessed.

Proliferation of the list of traits constitutes a problem since most evaluative approaches or measurement instruments give only limited coverage when they are kept within reasonable length and time limits. For classroom use measuring instruments must fit within the typical class time modules, thirty to sixty minutes, unless they are to be divided for use in several testing sessions. This length limitation forces a choice of a limited number of the most important constructs to be measured. Those chosen,

Table XII. CATTELL'S SIX MOST IMPORTANT PERSONALITY CHARACTERISTICS

Source Trait	Chief Characteristics	
A	Cyclothymia (shy, aloof, rigid)	vs. Schizothymia (open, emotional, unsteady)
B	Intelligence	vs. Mental Defect
C	Emotionally Mature Stable Character (persevering, self-controlled)	vs. Demoralized General Emotionality (neurotic and/or delinquent)
E	Dominance-Ascendance (self-asserting, aggressive)	vs. Submissiveness (timid, unsure)
F	Surgency (uninhibited, impulsive, cheerful)	vs. Agitated Melancholic Surgency (inhibited, worried, careful)
I	Sensitive, Anxious Emotionality (tender-hearted, emotionally dependent, imaginative)	vs. Rigid, Tough Poise (cynical, logical, self-sufficient)

Adapted from Raymond B. Cattell, *Description and Measurement of Personality* (New York: Harcourt, Brace & World, Inc., 1946), pp. 475–485. Reprinted by permission of the publisher.

if they are to give a valid representation, must constitute an adequate sample of the various facets of personality. Thus validity in this type of personality measurement depends not only upon judicious selection of constructs, but also upon complete measurement of the particular constructs which are selected.

Organismic concept. While the trait adherents see personality as the cumulative product of a series of discrete, stable traits, those who accept the organismic concept conceive personality to be an adaptive, dynamic complex which must be viewed *in toto* rather than in terms of discrete elements. Thus, individual personality *exists* and *changes* in inseparable relation to other personalities within the envelope of environment to which it constantly adapts and reacts. Marked changes in the environment—residence changes, school changes, etc.—are met with immediate adaptations, as are direct, prolonged confrontations with other individuals—siblings, parents, teachers. Personality, then, is in a sense a pliable mass which maintains its essential structure and character even while consciously and subconsciously adapting and adjusting to changing circumstances and groups.

A physical, but oversimplified, parallel exists in the amoeba, which many of the readers have observed under the microscope. The amoeba can change its physical shape to move, to feed, to adapt to environmental changes in temperature and moisture. Yet it still retains the characteristic essence and physical quality of the amoeba as long as it survives. Personality in this sense, although changing, can be described concretely and evaluated.

Personal-social adjustment is a positive, dynamic process which continues throughout life; and serious maladjustment occurs only when the individual is unable over a period of time to adapt successfully to his environment and his associates.

Sigmund Freud and his follower, Alfred Adler, have profoundly influenced the development of the organismic personality concept. Freud's theory, which underlies the modern psychoanalytic approach in psychiatry, postulates that personality consists of three main components: (1) the *id*, or instinctive drives; (2) the *ego*, or rational aspect, which promulgates the individual's adjustments; and (3) the *superego*, or conscience, which relates to the conscious and subconscious moral values. In this view personal maladjustment occurs from irreconcilable conflicts between the instinctive drives of the *id* and the moral values held in the superego. The projective techniques discussed in the next section actually have their roots in Freudian psychology and are primarily useful as clinical rather than educational devices.

Personal adjustment is actually a plurality: (1) adjustment as personal equilibrium or harmonious personal integration and (2) adjustment as adaptation to one's social group. It is also important to note that adjustment is not the same as social conformity. Rather than passive conformity, it is an active process consisting of: (1) positive adaptation, (2) personal integration, and (3) correct perception of reality. In the process of achieving a satisfactory personal-social adjustment, the normal individual utilizes numerous intellectual mechanisms, any one of which when overused would result in some measure of abnormality. Such mechanisms as rationalization to explain shortcomings and fantasy to cope with the ennui and boredom of unoccupied hours are normal and acceptable modes of behavior unless they become habitual escape mechanisms.

EVALUATION OF PERSONALITY

Since there is little agreement on the definition of personality, it logically follows that there is also lack of agreement concerning the means for assessing personality. There are, in fact, numerous approaches to personality assessment, most of which closely parallel one or another of the various personality concepts. Bass and Berg [2] have classified the approaches and techniques in three categories: (1) the observation approach, (2) personality projection, and (3) self-description. This classification is accepted as the basis for discussion in the following section.

Observation. The idea underlying observation approaches is that a person's overt situational behavior depicts the nature of his underlying personality, so the nature of personality can be inferred from that overt behavior. In other words, a person's self concept, his personal-social adjustment, and his reaction to environmental pressures may be judged from his performance or behavior. In fact, the person who *behaves* as if he were personally well adjusted *is* well adjusted. This generalization is probably essentially true; although in the cases of persons who are moving toward a breakdown, the inertia of habitual "well-adjusted" behavior may be continued, in some instances almost to the brink of the moment of personal disintegration and breakdown.

When observations are used as the basis for evaluating pupils in the school situation, the brunt of the responsibility rests on the teacher. Actually no other person in the system has direct contact with as many children, and the teacher may judge each pupil against the comparative base of the remaining class members. However, the teacher is busy at many important instructional tasks; and the sheer number of pupils whom he contacts works against him, so he may fail to note pupil problems because he lacks the time to observe carefully. All evaluative methods based upon personal observation are subjective and require a judgment by the observer; however, instruments such as rating scales and checklists improve the quality of the observation by focusing the observer's attention on the most important factors and by lending an element of comparability to the evaluations of individual pupils.

For many children, particularly those unable to achieve academic success, school pressures have been a barrier to satisfactory personal-social

[2] Bernard M. Bass and Irwin A. Berg (eds.), *Objective Approaches to Personality Assessment* (Princeton, N. J.: D. Van Nostrand Company, 1959), pp. 26–37.

adjustment. In recent years as the academic pace in both elementary and secondary schools has been stepped up, this school pressure, which is often reinforced by home pressure, may push the child to unrealistic achievement levels until he reaches intolerable limits and breaks down or becomes maladjusted. Several types of mentally unhealthy behavior may indicate the onset of serious mental problems. These include (1) the "unsociable" child, who lacks friends; (2) the "model" child, who always conforms; (3) the "defensive" child, who habitually rationalizes or defends his behavior; (4) the "nervous" child, who is hyperactive and inattentive; and (5) the "emotional" child, who responds to stress with emotional outbursts. These deviant types of behavior are easily detected by the teacher; and when they persist, the child should be referred to a psychologist or psychiatrist for help.

The teacher has available a large number of instruments and techniques which are useful in gathering data, focusing observation on important factors, and evaluating pupil behavior. Notable among these are:

1. Anecdotal records
2. Checklists and rating scales
3. Interviews and questionnaires
4. Time samples
5. Case studies
6. Behavior frequency counts
7. Autobiographies
8. Sociometrics
9. *Vineland Social Maturity Scales*
10. *Syracuse Scales of Social Relations*

In the following discussion brief consideration is accorded those instruments and techniques listed above which are not discussed in other chapters.[3]

1. *Anecdotal records.* The anecdotal record is not an evaluative device. It is a means for recording observed pupil behavior in specific situations or incidents. The anecdote should be an objective, descriptive account of the pupil's behavior in the incident reported, avoiding opinion or bias. The anecdote should be filed in the pupil's cumulative folder.

Anecdotes often relate to deviant behavior or discipline problems; although examples of pupil generosity, leadership, and cooperation are also important information which should be written in anecdotal records

[3] Questionnaires, behavior frequency counts, sociometrics, and the *Syracuse Scales of Social Relations* are discussed in Chapter 8.

if a balanced picture of pupils' behavior is to be presented. When anecdotes describe only the negative aspects of behavior, they present a distorted picture of pupils' personalities to those who subsequently read
them.

2. *Checklists and rating scales.* These instruments are essentially alike
since both include a list of the traits or characteristics which are to be
observed and evaluated. The essential difference between the two is that
the rating scale requires the rater to make a more definitive assessment
than that required with the checklist. The person using a checklist merely
checks each trait or characteristic which he believes the subject possesses; but with the rating scale the extent to which the subject possesses
each trait is usually judged on a three- to five-category scale—e.g., "excellent," "very good," "good," "satisfactory," and "unsatisfactory." When
numerical values are assigned to the categories, the ratings can be quantified and handled as other numerical scores.

Neither checklists nor rating scales objectify personal evaluations as
some of their proponents allege. As long as personal judgment by the
evaluator is called for, the assessment is subjective. The major value of
these two devices is that they serve to focus the attention of the evaluator on the most pertinent aspects of behavior and thus improve the validity and reliability of evaluations.

Factors which lower the reliability of such evaluations are (1) the
tendency of some raters to over or underrate the subjects, (2) the lack of
care which some raters exercise in making ratings, (3) the lack of rater
consensus on the meaning of terms such as "superior," and (4) ambiguity of statements in the instrument.

The ratings can be improved by clear definition of such terms as "superior," careful working of the statements in the list, and the use of repeated ratings. Improved ratings result when several conscientious raters
rate the subject. The number of ratings increases reliability in the same
manner as increasing the length of a test increases test reliability. However, there is a practical limit to the number of ratings which can be
made of each individual subject.[4]

3. *Time samples.* The time sampling technique is a means for focusing
teachers' observations of pupils on specific elements of behavior. With
this technique the teacher reserves a brief time each day for a period of

[4] The use of computers has made it feasible to increase the number of raters. See
Vernon O. Tyler and Robert F. Kelly, "Method for Rapid Rating of Many People on
Many Dimensions by Many Raters Using Electronic Data Processing Equipment,"
Educational and Psychological Measurement, XXIV, No. 1 (1964), 129–135.

several weeks during which he systematically observes certain pupils. During this 10–15 minute period each specific incident involving the pupil under observation is recorded—e.g., John sharpened his pencil twice, he talked to Mary three times, he kicked Jim's chair, etc. By the end of several weeks of observation the teacher will have collected a large amount of information, which when summarized will give a fairly complete picture of that particular pupil's classroom behavior. Since both the observations and the summary and analysis take considerable teacher time, time sampling is normally limited to the few pupils who seem to have serious adjustment problems.

4. *Case studies.* The case study is a study in depth of a pupil, usually one who deviates significantly enough from the norm in behavior, intelligence, adjustment, etc., as to need some program or instructional changes to fit his unique case. In such a study all the data which bears on the case is systematically and carefully collected. Data is collected from such sources as tests, grades, opinions of previous teachers, interviews with parents, analyses of home environment, descriptions of physical characteristics, and health examinations. When the data has been summarized, a careful evaluation is made as the basis for recommendations. The time required by the case study practically limits its use to the exceptional child.

5. *Autobiographies.* Autobiographies can provide the teacher with information not easily gained by personal observation. However, since the autobiography is highly personal, the pupil may be unwilling to share personal information with his teacher, or he may lack the understanding necessary to give more than a cursory account of himself. The autobiography may be either structured around a fairly definite outline suggested by the teacher or it may be unstructured. The unstructured autobiography need not be disorganized but should follow the organization desired by the pupil to permit a wider range of information to be included. Autobiographies will probably be superficial unless pupils are given several weeks in which to plan and write them.

6. *Vineland Social Maturity Scale.* This is a published instrument used to evaluate the social competence of individuals from infancy through adulthood.

Social maturity is achieved gradually over a period of years, and progress toward maturity varies according to the individual, although there is a pattern which most children approximate. Maturity is not achieved at any given age but is rather the outcome of lifelong growth which proceeds on a continuum from helplessness in infancy, to independence in youth, to helpfulness in adulthood, and finally to dependence as senility sets in during old age.

Three major premises underlie the scale:

1. Social competence may be defined as the functional ability of the human organism for exercising personal independence and social responsibility.
2. Social maturity may be measured progressively.
3. The level of social maturity may be expressed numerically in terms of deviation from norms.[5]

The Vineland scale is designed for the American culture, and Doll points out that any scale of social competence must be considered only in relation to the culture for which it is designed. The items on the scale were developed by Doll after he had canvassed the literature which reported the experiments and observations concerning child development.

The three dimensions of social maturation measured by the scale are the changes from (1) dependence to independence, (2) irresponsibility to responsibility, and (3) incompetence to competence. Children are judged in each instance in relation to expected maturity at that age, and the items are arranged in a year-scale rather than a point-scale so that the age level of a child's maturity can be conveniently arrived at. Figure 7.2 includes sample items from the scale. To show the expected change in maturity, these sample items have been selected from three age levels —1–2, 9–10, and 18–20. In the earlier years the items deal primarily with the ability of children to help themselves in such tasks as dressing and eating, and in the later years the items show the expected progress toward total self-direction.

Separate norms are reported for boys and girls and for normal and feebleminded subjects. Most feebleminded subjects tested were over 15 years of age and thus had an advantage over the normal young children in such categories as self-help in eating. The scores of subjects on item 75, "cares for self at table," are graphically portrayed in Figure 7.3. Normal children usually achieve this ability between 8 and 10 years of age: the girls at a mean age of 8.8 years, the boys at a mean age of 9.3 years. In contrast, the older, feebleminded subjects achieved this ability at a mean social age of 6.4 years.

[5] Edgar A. Doll, *Measurement of Social Competence* (Circle Pines, Minnesota: Educational Test Bureau Division of American Guidance Services, Inc., 1953), p. 10.

VINELAND SOCIAL MATURITY SCALE*

Name .... Sex .... Grade ...... Date ....
Residence .... Descent .... Born ....
M.A. or   I.Q. or
M.G.U. .............P.A. ....Test Used ....When ....Age ....
Occupation .... Class...... Yrs. Exp. ...... Schooling ......
Father's Occupation ....Class...... Yrs. Exp. ...... Schooling ......
Mother's Occupation ....Class...... Yrs. Exp. ...... Schooling ......
Informant ....Relationship ....Recorder ....
Informant's Est. ....Basal Score ....
Remarks: Additional Pts. ....
                                         Total Score ....
                                         Age Equivalent ....
                                         Social Quotient ....

Categories**	Item	Age Levels

I — II

L	18.	Walks about room unattended
O	19.	Marks with pencil or crayon
S H E	20.	Masticates food
S H D	21.	Pulls off socks
O	22.	Transfers objects
S H G	23.	Overcomes simple obstacles
O	24.	Fetches or carries familiar objects
S H E	25.	Drinks from cup or glass unassisted
S H G	26.	Gives up baby carriage
S	27.	Plays with other children
S H E	28.	Eats with spoon
L	29.	Goes about house or yard
S H E	30.	Discriminates edible substances

IX — X

S H E	75.	Cares for self at table
S D	76.	Makes minor purchases
L	77.	Goes about home town freely

XVIII — XX

L	96.	Goes to distant points alone
S D	97.	Looks after own health
O	98.	Has a job or continues schooling
S D	99.	Goes out nights unrestricted
S D	100.	Controls own major expenditures
S D	101.	Assumes personal responsibility

**Key to categorical arrangement of items:

S H G — Self-help general   C — Communication   L — Locomotion
S H D — Self-help dressing   S D — Self-direction   O — Occupation
S H E — Self-help eating   S — Socialization

Figure 7.2. REPRESENTATIVE ITEMS FROM THE VINELAND SOCIAL MATURITY SCALE

From Edgar A. Doll, *Measurement of Social Competence* (Circle Pines, Minnesota: Educational Test Bureau Division of American Guidance Service, Inc. Copyright 1936 by the Training School, Vineland, New Jersey; 1965 by the American Guidance Service). Reprinted by permission of the publisher.

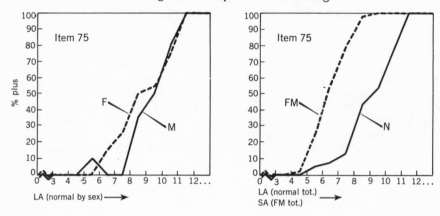

Item 75: Cares for self at table.

	Med.	Mean	SD	CR		Med.	Mean	SD	CR
M:	9.50	9.25	1.41		N :	9.25	9.03	1.61	
F:	8.50	8.80	1.75		FM:	6.33	6.40	1.12	
D:		.45		.60	D :		2.63		5.84

Figure 7.3. SUMMARY OF NORMATIVE DATA ON ONE ITEM FROM THE VINELAND SOCIAL MATURITY SCALE

From Doll, p. 110. Reprinted by permission of the American Guidance Service, Inc.

This scale is not one which the typical classroom teacher would use; however, it would be useful to teachers who were dealing with physically and intellectually handicapped children.[6]

Q-sort method. The Q-sort method offers a unique means of evaluating personality through the use of standard language, so that the evaluations from observer to observer can be compared. In the Q-sort method the judge or evaluator must use a list of 100 items to describe the person being evaluated. The items in Figure 7.4 are examples of those which are used. Each of the items is written on a separate card, and the evaluator is required to sort the 100 cards into nine piles, the number of cards in each pile being respectively 5, 8, 12, 16, 18, 16, 12, 8, and 5. The evaluative continuum ranges from the five cards at one end which are considered "most characteristic" of the subject and the eight cards which are "quite characteristic," to the eight cards at the other end of the scale which are considered to be "quite uncharacteristic" and the five cards which are considered to be "most uncharacteristic."

The Q-sort approach has several advantages over an unstructured evaluation. First, descriptions of the subject are confined to the standard, eas-

[6] For a complete discussion of the Vineland scale, see Doll.

THE CALIFORNIA Q-SET (FORM III)
Specified 9-point distribution ($N = 100$):
5, 8, 12, 16, 18, 16, 12, 8, 5

1. Is critical, skeptical, not easily impressed.
2. Is a genuinely dependable and responsible person.
3. Has a wide range of interests. (N.B. Superficially or depth of interest is irrelevant here.)
4. Is a talkative individual.
5. Behaves in a giving way toward others. (N.B. Regardless of the motivation involved.)
6. Is fastidious.
7. Favors conservative values in a variety of areas.
8. Appears to have a high degree of intellectual capacity. (N.B. Whether actualized or not.) (N.B. Originality is not necessarily assumed.)
9. Is uncomfortable with uncertainty and complexities.
10. Anxiety and tension find outlet in bodily symptoms. (N.B. If placed high, implies bodily dysfunction; if placed low, implies absence of autonomic arousal.)
11. Is protective of those close to him. (N.B. Placement of this term expresses behavior ranging from over-protection through appropriate nurturance to a laissez-faire, under-protective manner.)
12. Tends to be self-defensive.
13. Is thin-skinned; sensitive to anything that can be construed as criticism or an interpersonal slight.
14. *Genuinely* submissive; accepts domination comfortably.
15. Is skilled in social techniques of imaginative play, pretending and humor.
16. Is introspective and concerned with self as an object. (N.B. Introspectiveness *per se* does not imply insight.)
17. Behaves in a sympathetic or considerate manner.
18. Initiates humor.
19. Seeks reassurance from others.
20. Has a rapid personal tempo; behaves and acts quickly.

Figure 7.4. EXAMPLES OF ITEMS FROM THE CALIFORNIA Q-SET

From Jack Block, *The Q-Sort Method in Personality Assessment and Psychiatric Research* (Springfield, Illinois: Charles C Thomas, Publisher, 1961), p. 7. Reprinted by permission of the publisher and Dr. Block.

ily understood language of the 100 items. This decreases the amount of subjective error resulting from vocabulary misunderstanding when several evaluators use the items. It also makes it possible to get comparability between several evaluations of a single subject.

CQ-items considered as positively defining of optimal adjustment:

35. Has warmth; has the capacity for close relationships; compassionate.
 2. Is a genuinely dependable and responsible person.
60. Has insight into own motives and behavior.
26. Is productive; gets things done.
64. Is socially perceptive of a wide range of interpersonal cues.
70. *Behaves* in an ethically consistent manner; is consistent with own personal standards.
96. Values own independence and autonomy.
77. Appears straightforward, forthright, candid in dealings with others.
83. Able to see to the heart of important problems.
51. Genuinely values intellectual and cognitive matters. (N.B. Ability or achievement is not implied here.)
33. Is calm, relaxed in manner.
17. Behaves in a sympathetic or considerate manner.
 3. Has a wide range of interests. (N.B. Superficiality or depth of interest is irrelevant here.)

CQ-items considered as negatively defining of optimal adjustment:

45. Has a brittle ego-defense system; has a small reserve of integration: would be disorganized and maladaptive when under stress or trauma.
78. Feels cheated and victimized by life; self-pitying.
86. Handles anxiety and conflicts by, in effect, refusing to recognize their presence; repressive or dissociative tendencies.
22. Feels a lack of personal meaning in life.
55. Is self-defeating.
40. Is vulnerable to real or fancied threat, generally fearful.
48. Keeps people at a distance; avoids close interpersonal relationships.
68. Is basically anxious.
37. Is guileful and deceitful, manipulative, opportunistic.
36. Is subtly negativistic; tends to undermine and obstruct or sabotage.
38. Has hostility toward others. (N.B. Basic hostility is intended here; mode of expression is to be indicated by other items.)
76. Tends to project his own feelings and motivations onto others.
97. Is emotionally bland; has flattened effect.

Figure 7.5. A CQ-SET DESCRIPTION OF THE OPTIMALLY ADJUSTED PERSONALITY AS VIEWED BY CLINICAL PSYCHOLOGISTS

From Jack Block, *The Q-Sort Method in Personality Assessment and Psychiatric Research* (Springfield, Illinois: Charles C Thomas, Publisher, 1961), p. 144. Reprinted by permission of the publisher

According to Block, "the average inter-correlation among the nine definitions of optimal adjustment was .78, implying by the Spearman-Brown formula that the reliability of the composite description is .97. Individual clinicians, who on the average are equivalent to those contributing toward the consensual definition, may expect their own formulations of optimal adjustment to correlate about .87 with the composite." Block, p. 144.

Second, this approach facilitates the use of consensus evaluations of a subject wherein the final evaluation represents the composite judgment of numerous evaluators. Figure 7.5 shows a composite description of the optimally adjusted personality, using evaluations by nine clinical psychologists. Employing this same technique a single evaluator can make repeated assessments of a subject to get a more stable evaluation and to check the reliability of his assessment.

This instrument has been used in research—e.g., as a means of identifying creative people [7]—and has had considerable use in clinical psychology as an aid in identifying the problems of psychopaths.

Personality projection. The second category of evaluative techniques is *personality projection.* Unstructured or semistructured materials are used in projection (the art of externalizing or objectifying what is primarily subjective) to permit the subject a wide range of freedom in interpretation. The examiner attempts to gain an insight into the subject's self-concept from the nature of his interpretations.

The three classic media used in projection are (1) the Rorschach ink blots, (2) the Murray TAT pictures, and (3) the disjunctive or incomplete sentences. Three related media which are not strictly projective but which still contain some element of projection are: (1) drawing, (2) painting, and (3) handwriting.

1. *Rorschach techniques.* The Rorschach technique was developed in 1921 by Herman W. Rorschach and provides a means of analyzing a person's personality adjustment from his verbal responses to ten inkblots. One half of the inkblots are various shades of gray, and the remainder contain various color combinations. The inkblots are reproduced on cards, and the test is administered individually by presenting each card successively to the subject and asking him to tell what the card makes him think of. The subject normally makes several responses to each card and may take from two to ten minutes with each card. As the verbal responses are made by the subject, they are recorded by the examiner for later interpretation. This technique has proved to be a fruitful approach to the analysis of mental disorders, but is obviously not suited to classroom use since a great deal of training is needed before the examiner is qualified to administer and interpret the test.

During recent years an interesting variation of this technique, the *Standardized Objective Rorschach,* has been developed. This form of the

[7] Block, pp. 24–26.

test is objectively scored and can be administered to a group of subjects. The test is administered by projecting each inkblot successively on a screen with a slide film projector. Every subject has an answer sheet which contains numerous possible responses to each inkblot. As the inkblot is projected, the subjects are given 1½ minutes during which they must check those responses which seem most appropriate. Although this method does not provide for the free range of response of the unstructured test situation, it is more practical for group use, and it is much easier to interpret.

2. *Murray TAT*. The *Murray Thematic Apperception Test* is similar to the inkblot test, except that in this test pictures of people in indeterminate situations instead of inkblots are used on the cards. This test was developed in 1943 and consists of thirty pictures, some of which are appropriate for either sex and some of which are appropriate only for male or for female subjects.

In the testing situation twenty of the pictures are presented to the subject, and he is asked to tell what led up to the event in the picture, describe what is happening at the moment, and give the probable outcome. The subject is allowed five minutes for each card, and the test is administered in two separate sittings of fifty minutes each. As the subject tells his stories, they are stenographically or tape recorded for subsequent analysis. If the examiner is to administer and interpret the test properly, he should have clinical experience and specific training in the use of his technique.

This test, like the Rorschach, is a valuable clinical tool but is useful only in those schools in which there is a psychologist on the staff. In these schools deviant cases will be referred to the psychologist, who might choose to use this instrument as a part of the problem analysis.

3. *Sentence completion*. This type of test includes a number of provocative, incomplete sentences which the subject is asked to complete in a few words. The *Rohde-Hildreth Sentence Completion Test* includes 100 items. Greene notes the following advantages in this type of test:

1. It is suitable for administration to groups or individuals 12 years of age or older.
2. It samples a wide variety of provocative situations.
3. It has no time limits.
4. It provides material that allows fairly objective scoring methods.
5. It supplies more information than a single-word association test.

6. It keeps the subject unaware of the method of scoring or the purposes of the test.[8]

4. *Drawing, painting, and handwriting.* The *Bender-Gestalt Drawings* were adapted in 1938 by Lauretta Bender from the earlier work of Max Wertheimer. Although the drawing approach appeared to hold some promise in personality interpretation, subsequent developments have failed to fulfill the earlier promise. Nevertheless, this should not be written off as a fruitless technique; and continued investigation of the approach could lead to new insights in the field. Certainly intelligence and artistic aptitude affect both the subject's approach to drawing and the quality of his finished drawings; however, both intelligence and aptitude are intrinsic elements which affect personality. Thus, the difficulty of separating the influence of these elements from the projected personality may be no serious drawback to the approach.

Painting, although it has been little used in personality interpretation, certainly has obvious personality overtones. The artist, be he skilled or unskilled, undoubtedly projects his personality into his work. In the elementary school the aproned and paint-smeared primary child busily engaged in finger painting is a familiar sight to observers. Painting has also been used as a therapeutic measure for mentally disturbed patients.

Handwriting interpretation, or graphology, has for many years been a pseudoscience which has fallen into disrepute primarily because of its use by unprincipled charlatans to dupe an unwary public by commercial exploitation of their supposed competence in personality interpretation. Nevertheless, some serious scholars are interested in this interpretation medium, and, without further investigation, it should not be lightly dismissed as a fruitless avenue.

As one reviews the projective techniques, it is apparent that the current methods, with the exception of sentence completion, have little application in the classroom and are primarily tools of the clinical psychologist. Even among psychologists there is some disagreement concerning the value of these techniques. The lack of confidence of some clinicians in the projective techniques is noted by Bass and Berg,[9] yet they are widely used and obviously considered useful by many others.

Self description. The third category of evaluative techniques is self de-

---

[8] Edward B. Greene, *Measurement of Human Behavior* (New York: Odyssey Press, 1952), p. 532.

[9] Bernard M. Bass and Irwin A. Berg, *op. cit.* (above, n. 4), p. 30.

scription, which relies, of course, on the subject's ability to describe himself accurately. The self-description can be either unstructured, as in autobiographies, or structured, as in various inventories. The self-description approach using adjustment inventories has been widely adopted in schools, probably because of the ease of administering and interpreting the tests. The approach appears to be valid because it reflects the person's self-concept, which in turn directly influences his modes of behavior. A person who believes himself to be brave demonstrates bravery in his actions, and whether he is brave because he believes himself to be brave or vice versa is a moot point, in view of the fact that his associates will judge him by his actions.

Since the range of instruments in this category is great, the specific discussion is limited to three examples which have been widely used in education and psychology: (1) the *Minnesota Multiphasic Personality Inventory*, (2) the *Mooney Problem Check List*, and (3) the *SRA Youth Inventory*.

1. *Minnesota Multiphasic Personality Inventory.* The *MMPI* is the most carefully prepared and validated of the personality inventories, but it has a clinical rather than an educational orientation. It was constructed by S. R. Hathaway and J. C. McKinley in 1942, and more has probably been written about the various uses of this instrument than about any other in the field. It has been used in a varied range of measurement situations, from analysis of psychiatric abnormalities to screening candidates in higher education for admission to teacher preparation programs. It may be used with "normal" subjects in a group situation to identify those who have some problems which might later become serious enough to handicap or incapacitate them for certain occupations. It may also be used to help determine the nature and extent of maladjustment of neurotic or psychotic subjects by pinpointing such tendencies as paranoia, schizophrenia, and hysteria.

The original item selection was made by administering a battery of 550 items to approximately 800 clinical cases and to a group of normal adults. The items which showed the greatest discrimination between normal and abnormal subjects were retained for the published inventory. Figure 7.6 presents sample items from the inventory. Revised in 1951, it is currently available in booklet form for convenient administration and scoring.

3. I wake up fresh and rested most mornings.
8. My daily life is full of things that keep me interested.
26. I feel that it is certainly best to keep my mouth shut when I'm in trouble.
28. When someone does me a wrong I feel I should pay him back if I can, just for the principle of the thing.
32. I find it hard to keep my mind on a task or job.
33. I have had very peculiar and strange experiences.

Figure 7.6. EXAMPLES OF ITEMS FROM THE MINNESOTA MULTIPHASIC PERSONALITY INVENTORY

2. *Mooney Problem Check List.* This is not a test but rather a list of the problems of young people. Forms of the checklist are available for college, high school, and junior high school pupils. Since the pupils are asked to identify their own problems from the list, both the awareness of their problems and their willingness to reveal those problems unquestionably influence the results which are obtained. The checklist is not generally used below the seventh grade because younger pupils lack the insight to identify their most significant problems.

The checklist is particularly valuable in obtaining information from which the major individual and group problems can be identified. It can also be used to screen out problem pupils who should be referred for counseling or therapy. The information obtained from an administration of the checklist can be used in counseling interviews, in the homeroom, in group guidance, and in orientation programs.

Figure 7.7 includes a brief list of items taken from the high school checklist. The 330 items in the high school form cover a wide range of problems which are grouped in the following eleven general areas:

1. Health and physical development
2. Finances, living conditions, employment
3. Social and recreational activities
4. Social-psychological relations
5. Personal-psychological relations
6. Courtship, sex, marriage
7. Home and family
8. Morals and religion
9. Adjustment to school work
10. The future—vocational and educational
11. Curriculum and teaching procedures.

1. Being underweight
2. Being overweight
3. Not getting enough exercise
6. Needing to learn how to save money
7. Not knowing how to spend my money wisely
8. Having less money than my friends have
76. Wanting a more pleasing personality
77. Not getting along well with other people
78. Worrying how I impress people
81. Daydreaming
82. Being careless
83. Forgetting things

Figure 7.7. EXAMPLES OF ITEMS FROM THE MOONEY PROBLEM CHECK LIST

3. *STS Youth Inventory.* This inventory, published by the Scholastic Testing Service in 1967, is a revision of the 1956 *SRA Youth Inventory.* It, like the *Mooney Problem Check List,* can be used in the school situation to identify the personal problems of teen-age youth. The inventory contains 167 items and is easily administered in the school setting. Examples of items from the inventory are shown in Figure 7.8. This instrument is neither a typical personality test nor a diagnostic instrument, but rather a screening device.

Problems of self-description. Despite the widespread use of self-description inventories, several notable problems affect their validity:

1. Subjects frequently lack the personal insight required to give a correct picture of themselves.
2. Subjects occasionally fake or lie to hide undesirable aspects of their personalities.
3. It is difficult to validate the inventories since there are no well-established criteria against which they may be evaluated.

ASSESSMENT OF INTERESTS

Interest, although not strictly a specific element of personality, definitely channels persons into vocational and avocational choices, which at least indirectly affect personality by determining the roles which are assumed as one associates with colleagues in those activities. Pupil interest is of particular importance to the teacher because of its importance in motivating learning. The most effective teachers are those who are capa-

MY SCHOOL*

1. I want to learn how to read better. . . . . □ □ □ ▫
2. I wish I knew how to study better. . . . . □ □ □ ▫
3. I am a slow reader. . . . . □ □ □ ▫
4. I have trouble finding what I want in the library. . . . . □ □ □ ▫
5. I have trouble taking notes in class. . . . . □ □ □ ▫
6. I wish I knew how to prepare for tests. . . . . □ □ □ ▫
7. I wish I could be more calm when I recite in class. . . . . □ □ □ ▫
8. I have trouble keeping up with my homework. . . . . □ □ □ ▫
9. I spend more time studying than other kids do. . . . . □ □ □ ▫
10. I feel sleepy in class even when I've had enough sleep at night. . . . . □ □ □ ▫
11. I would quit school now if I could. . . . . □ □ □ ▫
12. I don't see much point in my courses. . . . . □ □ □ ▫
13. Most of my courses are dull. . . . . □ □ □ ▫
14. I would like to get some work experience while I'm still in school. . . . . . . □ □ □ ▫
15. I have trouble writing good essays. . . . . □ □ □ ▫

Figure 7.8. EXAMPLES OF ITEMS FROM THE STS YOUTH INVENTORY

(The size of the box checked by the respondent denotes his concept of the magnitude of the problem.)

From the STS Youth Inventory—Form G, published by Scholastic Testing Service, Bensenville, Illinois. Copyright 1967 by the Purdue Research Foundation. Reprinted by permission of STS.

ble of arousing and sustaining the interest of their pupils in the subjects which they are teaching. Interest, too, is an important element in the job satisfaction which adults experience. When a person lacks interest in his occupation, work becomes a frustrating drudgery, filling in the time from vacation to vacation; while the person interested in his work looks forward to each day as a stimulating challenge.

The early identification of children's occupational interests is important because the interest pattern provides a focal point for the educational choices throughout their education. Yet those familiar with children are aware of the instability of interest patterns among children, an instability which occasionally continues into adulthood. As a rule pupils' occupational interests are too unstable to permit reliable measurements before the early high school years. But since high school education is terminal for about one-half of the pupils, an assessment of interests during the first years of high school is necessary if the information is to have much use in guiding the educational choices during those last school years. It is also important to note that interest cannot be used as the sole arbiter of such choices because pupil interest and aptitude are not always correlated. The pupil interested in becoming a medical doctor must possess also the high-level aptitudes and intelligence required for success in the profession.

Interest inventories. Several obvious problems attend the development of inventories for the assessment of interests. Notable among these are (1) the large number of occupations for which people may train, (2) the instability of interest patterns during school-age years, and (3) the difference among interest patterns of men and women and adults and children.

In our complex society there are several thousands of occupations which school children will enter as adults—occupations requiring different skills, educational background, and patterns of interest. A practical compromise in coping with this problem has been adopted in such well-known inventories as the *Kuder Preference Record* and the *Strong Vocational Interest Blank*. This compromise is the practice of developing scales to assess interest patterns which relate to a limited number of representative occupations or general occupational groups. For the majority of persons who are assessed by the inventories, this is a suitable compromise; but for the few who are interested in occupations other than those represented on the scales, the inventories give invalid assessments.

But brief contact with school-age children is sufficient to acquaint one with the fluctuating nature of their interests. With the grade school child, this week's obsession may be acting; next week's, athletics; next week's, music, *ad infinitum*. While the high school pupil's interests are somewhat more stable, they fluctuate too much to provide the level of reliability and validity expected of standardized tests. Nevertheless, since it is desirable to begin preparation for a vocation in the upper secondary and beginning college years and in order to have some information available early enough to be useful in counseling pupils, an assessment of interest should be made in the early high school years.

In attempting to solve the problem of age- and sex-differences in interest patterns, the authors of the *Kuder Preference Record* have provided separate norms for men and women and for high school boys and high school girls.

1. *The Strong Vocational Interest Blank.* This inventory is the oldest of the interest inventories (first published in 1927) and is considered by

many to be the most valid and reliable of the currently available instruments. It is based on the empirical approach of analyzing the patterns of interests of successful people in the chosen occupations. Thus when the inventory is administered to a person, his responses are compared against the various profiles identified in the analysis of successful people's interests. If his pattern of responses approximates that of successful people in a specific occupation, that occupation is identified as one of those in which he has a high interest level.

An obvious problem with this approach is that there are undoubtedly some successful people in any occupation whose interests are broader than or widely divergent from those of the majority of their colleagues. If this is true of some practitioners in an occupation, it is also apt to be true of some prospective entrants into that occupation; and the Strong inventory would discourage such people from entering this field in which they might be most successful. Granted, this problem should exist in only a small number of cases, but it still cannot be overlooked.

The *SVIB* provides separate forms for men and women. The form for men provides scores on 51 different occupations and that for women provides scores on 31 occupations. The *SVIB* is not normally used below the twelfth grade; and it must be mailed in to be scored and interpreted, which results in some delay before the scores are available for use.

In 1966 the *SVIB* was revised, and the revision follows the same rationale of the original form. However, the inventory has been improved by eliminating out-of-date items and those which did not appear to discriminate among the occupations. Some new scales have been added and some eliminated, but most of the scales are still based on the groups which were analyzed during the 1930's and used as interest criterion groups for the various occupations.

2. *The Kuder Preference Record—Vocational.* The *Kuder* is the most widely used inventory in the secondary schools. It can be administered and scored by the pupil himself. Furthermore, its technical manual provides extensive information for interpreting the scores so that they may be used in occupational counseling.

The *Kuder* measures preferences in ten broad areas:

1. Outdoor	6. Artistic
2. Mechanical	7. Literary
3. Computational	8. Musical
4. Scientific	9. Social service
5. Persuasive	10. Clerical

The interest patterns in each of these broad areas have been isolated by an analysis of the interests of thousands of individuals. The items in the test are presented in a forced-choice pattern. With each group of three items the subject must select the one in which he is *most* interested and the one in which he is *least* interested. Although such forced choices are sometimes frustrating to pupils, the form has proved to be quite reliable.

The *Kuder* follows a somewhat different rationale than the *SVIB*. While the *SVIB* compares subjects against the interests in the criterion groups, the *Kuder* includes items which obviously relate to specific areas of interest, such as art, music, etc.; and the interest norms are established on the subject's age group. This introduces some problems insofar as the age group may tend to share some interest not characteristic of an older group of workers in a specific occupation. Teen-age boys, for example, tend to be interested in automobiles and athletics; and for many these interests decline during adulthood. Also, the obvious face validity of the *Kuder* items may accentuate the problem of subjects consciously biasing their scores by selecting those choices which seem related to the occupational areas in which they think they are interested. It could, however, also be argued that such biasing is unimportant because the very fact that a person believes himself to be interested in an area is important and should be reflected by a higher score in that area.

Recently a new *Kuder* inventory has been developed. This is the *Kuder Occupational Interest Inventory* (Form DD), which provides scores for a broad range of occupations. There are 79 occupational scores and 20 college-major scores given for men, and 56 occupational scores and 25 college-major scores for women. This instrument is designed for use from the eleventh grade upward, and because of the breadth of occupations and college majors covered should be valuable as a basis for counseling both those who will drop out after high school and those who continue on to higher education. It is notable also that the individual's preferences on the inventory are compared against both criterion groups in the occupations and college majors. To be included in the criterion group, members must meet certain stipulated standards of satisfaction. The instrument also includes a verification scale, which may alleviate the problem of conscious bias noted earlier in discussing the older inventory.

3. *The Minnesota Vocational Inventory.* This new instrument is of particular interest because it provides scoring keys for twenty-one semi-skilled and skilled occupations. It also can give scores for nine general

areas, such as mechanics, health services, and electronics. This inventory is particularly useful to those who work in vocational education, but it also fills an important gap for counseling students in the comprehensive secondary school since inadequate attention is typically paid to the non-college bound.

Problems of assessment. Several problems of assessment have been alluded to in the previous discussion on interest inventories; but because of the particular difficulty of valid measurement in this area of personality, some further consideration is warranted. The most significant problems are:

1. Subject biasing of results
2. Instability of interest patterns
3. Difficulty of assessing interest level
4. Difficulty of obtaining an acceptable criterion group
5. Inconsistent relationship between interest and aptitude

The problem of biasing has been discussed, but it should be added that investigation of measurement approaches which do not have the obvious face validity characteristic of several of the current instruments could provide a solution to this problem. For example, a multiple-choice word definition test in which all responses are correct but certain groups —e.g., engineers—typically select one choice, while another group selects an alternative, may offer a fruitful approach.[10]

The problem of instability of interest patterns, while not directly related to the measurement instrument, does contribute to unreliability of measurement results. To alleviate this problem, students should be encouraged to make educational and vocational decisions earlier. They can be given information concerning their prospects and helped to make vocational choices in time to plan appropriate educational programs. It would probably also be helpful to assess interest several times during the secondary school years to check the reliability of choices indicated in pupils' profiles. If interest assessment does nothing more than highlight the importance of educational and vocational decisions and begin

---

[10] For further discussion, see the unpublished Master's thesis (University of Idaho, 1962) by Charles Franklin Williamson, *An Experimental Study to Test the Hypothesis that Interests May Be Determined by Reactions to Words with Multiple Definitions,* pp. 60–62.

For another interesting approach, see Royce R. Ronning, Lawrence H. Stewart, and Walter R. Stellwagen, "An Equisection Scale of Interests: A Preliminary Approach," *Journal of Counseling Psychology,* XII, No. 2 (1965), 176–181.

to crystallize the thinking of pupils, it will have made a significant contribution.

The problem of determining the level or intensity of interest is not completely solved by the current inventories. In the *Kuder,* for example, the subject is forced to select that which he would least and most like to do from the choices given on each item; and he must respond in spite of the fact that he may dislike or like all possible choices. The frequency of choices made in an area is not necessarily the best indication of strength of interest. Scaling methods such as those used in measuring attitudes give a more definitive measure of intensity, and the method might well be adapted to interest assessment.

The problem of obtaining acceptable criterion groups against which subjects can be compared is a difficult one. In the measurement process immature pupils are often being compared against adults, whose interests are obviously more stable and quite different from those of young age groups. In the second place, it is difficult to determine a level of satisfaction which would make the members acceptable for a criterion group. Selecting persons for a criterion group because they have been highly successful in an occupation is not completely satisfactory, since success in an occupation does not necessarily guarantee high interest in that occupation. A person's success might be motivated by factors other than an extreme interest in his work. The alternative of using the same age group as that being tested as a norming or criterion group is also somewhat unsatisfactory since it gives no direct comparison with actual workers in the occupations toward which the interests are directed. Perhaps the best answer here is to use both the subject's age group and outside criterion groups as bases for comparison.

A final problem which has always plagued this area of measurement is the inconsistent relation between interest and aptitude. For a variety of reasons a young person may profess interest in some occupation for which his aptitudes do not fit him. For example, a young man may be convinced that he wishes to become a medical doctor. His conviction may have arisen from parental pressure, hero worship, friendship with a doctor, or any number of other reasons; but he may have only average intelligence and thus be obviously unfitted to enter the field. In fact, if this person persists in pursuing his interest, the consequences could be tragic and surely will be frustrating, since he almost certainly will fail and be forced to redefine his occupational objectives.

It is fortunate when a person has both strong interest in and high aptitude for a field. In this case the person is equipped with both the desire and the capability of attaining his objectives. Although interest and aptitude often lack a positive relationship, it is true that when testing results are available to be used in counseling, the counselor can help the pupil and his parents gain insight which can lead to a better vocational choice.

SUMMARY

The diversity of approaches and techniques available for evaluating personality is convincing evidence of the fact that there is no consensus among the experts either with regard to the nature of personality or the best means for evaluating it. Each of the three categories of evaluation discussed obviously has assets which make it feasible. Yet no one approach is so superior that it makes the other obsolete, and it may well be that the ultimate advantage lies with a multiple approach. It is sufficient to say that progress is being made in improving the evaluation; progress will continue to be made; and present instruments are invaluable when compared to the unreliable, invalid guess which is the alternative when available instruments are not utilized. Of course we would be negligent if we failed to note the several problems of self-description approaches, notably the problems of bias or lying and of lack of insight. But these are no more serious than the possible failure to select the most important personality constructs in the trait-list approaches.

Interest is an aspect of personality which can spark the drive and enthusiasm necessary for achievement. Developing interest in a field is often a goal of teachers, but they rarely follow up to assess the level of interest which they have stimulated.

The development of published inventories for the assessment of interests began in the 1930's with the *Strong Vocational Interest Blank*. The *SVIB* and the *Kuder Preference Record*, which is used more frequently in secondary schools, are among the best of the inventories. In 1966 the *SVIB* was updated and revised, and a recent new form of the *Kuder* has been published. Both show promise of improved assessment of vocational interests when compared to the older forms. In addition, the new *Minnesota Vocational Inventory* has been developed to measure interests in skilled and semiskilled vocations, areas not well covered in the other inventories.

Although the inventories which have been developed are reasonably valid and reliable, there are several notable problems which attend the assessment of interests. These include (1) conscious biasing of the results by the subjects; (2) instability of the interest patterns of high school pupils; (3) inadequate assessment of level of interest with current instruments; (4) difficulty of selecting acceptable criterion groups against which the subjects can be compared; and (5) the inconsistent relationship beween pupils' interests and their aptitudes. Progress is being made in solving these problems, and the currently available instruments are valuable aids in counseling, particularly when used with insight and discretion.

DISCUSSION QUESTIONS AND PROBLEMS

1. What is the major purpose of personality assessment in the schools?
2. What responsibility has the school in promoting sound mental health of pupils? What, if any, type of program would you suggest?
3. How would you use the results of an instrument such as the *Mooney Problem Check List* in the school program? At what level should it be administered?
4. Which of the personality theories is the rational basis for each of the following?
   a. *Minnesota Multiphasic Personality Inventory*
   b. *SRA. Youth Inventory*
   c. *Murray Thematic Apperception Test*
5. What problems contribute to the relative unreliability of interest inventories? How can these problems be alleviated?
6. At what age level do interest patterns tend to stabilize? In view of this and the practical necessity that tests be given during school years if they are to be used in educational guidance, when would you recommend that interest inventories be administered?
7. Are pupil interest and aptitude highly correlated? What practical problems does this pose?

SELECTED READINGS

Abt, Lawrence and Leopold Bellak (ed.). *Projective Psychology*. New York: Alfred A. Knopf, 1950. Part I. General theory of projective tests. Part II. A series of papers analyzing the nature and use of such projective techniques as the *Rorschach Protocol, TAT*, and the *Sacks Sentence Completion Tests*.

Bass, Bernard M. and Irwin A. Berg (eds.). *Objective Approaches to Personality Assessment*. Princeton, New Jersey: D. Van Nostrand Company, 1959. Chapters 1 and 2 review the historical development of personality testing and the current theories and assumptions.

Cronbach, Lee J. *Essentials of Psychological Testing.* 2nd ed. New York: Harper & Row, 1960. Chapters 14, 15 and 19 contain problems and general discussion of the measurement approaches. They also give specific consideration to the evaluative instruments and techniques.

Froehlich, Clifford P. and Kenneth B. Hoyt. *Guidance Testing.* Chicago: Science Research Associates, 1959. Chapters 11 and 12 are especially relevant. The discussion includes observational techniques, e.g., anecdotes and rating scales.

Gordon, Jesse E. *Personality and Behavior.* New York: The Macmillan Company, 1963. Good general reference on nature of personality concepts.

Greene, Edward B. *Measurements of Human Behavior.* Rev. ed. New York: The Odyssey Press, 1952. Chapters 20, 22, and 23 give a fairly detailed description of such instruments as the *Rorschach Ink-Blot Test* and the *Murray Thematic Apperception Test.*

Heiner, Harold G., et al. *A Forced-Choice Procedure for Measurement of Pupils' Attitudes Toward Major Dimensions of Work.* U. S. Office of Education Project No. ERD–257–65, Contract No. EO–5–85–109, Report No. 3. Pullman, Washington: Washington State University, 1966.

Jackson, Douglas N. and Samuel Messick. *Problems in Human Assessment.* New York: McGraw-Hill Book Company, 1967. Section E of Part 6 in this text is devoted to assessment of interests, with articles by such leading authorities as Edward K. Strong and Frederic Kuder.

Olsen, LeRoy C. *Development and Standardization of a Projective Occupational Attitudes Test.* U. S. Office of Education Project No. ERD–257–65, Contract No. OE–5–85–109, Final Report. Pullman, Washington: Washington State University, 1966. The report includes technical discussion, examples of the pictures used in the instrument, administration and scoring instructions. The instrument consists of pictures relating to ten occupational areas—the pictures designed to elicit projective attitude responses from the student.

Steward, Lawrence H. and Royce R. Ronning. *Multidimensional Analysis of an Experimental Measure of Interest.* U. S. Office of Education Cooperative Research Project No. 2209. Berkeley: University of California, 1964. Describes the development of an instrument to measure twelve interest factors. Includes the instrument and technical discussion.

Thorndike, Robert L. and Elizabeth Hagen. *Measurement and Evaluation in Psychology and Education.* 2nd ed. New York: John Wiley & Sons, 1961. Chapters 14 and 15 review a variety of inventories and projective techniques for assessing personality. Chapter 12 also includes a brief consideration of interest inventories.

_____ *Chapter 8* _____

APPRAISING THE SOCIAL
CLIMATE FOR LEARNING

INTRODUCTION

Often one hears experienced educators say that they need spend only a few minutes in a classroom or school to determine how good the educational program is. And although educational evaluation is by no means as easy as such a statement implies, it is certainly true that a short visit gives one a definite impression of the social climate for learning which prevails in the school. In the best schools there is an intangible, but nonetheless real, *esprit de corps* permeating the pupil-staff relationships, an atmosphere which communicates the feeling to all who visit that the school is a good one. At the other extreme there are also schools in which the atmosphere of frustration, lack of interest, and rowdyism is so pervasive that the casual observer is immediately aware of the poor educational program. The classroom and the school are always complex social institutions. Although learning is an individual task, within the school individual learning takes place in the theater of a social environment; therefore, a school's educational program always consists of more than the tangible elements of curriculum, facilities, and staff.

Good teachers are sensitive to the social climate within which they work, and they understand that effective teaching is more complex than the mere act of presenting the facts to be learned—that pupils will not learn unless they listen, study, and actively engage in the process. Thus establishing rapport with each pupil, motivating him to study, and building a desirable social climate for learning within the classroom are prerequisites to successful teaching. If the individuals within a class were not changeable and the group were stable, these three tasks would be relatively easy; but individuals do change, often dramatically, and the social

168

group is always fluctuating and responding to the varied circumstances which confront it. Both of these factors require the teacher to possess considerable insight, to evaluate the group and its members continually, and to exercise initiative in adapting instruction to the changes. Thus assessing and maintaining a group posture which facilitates learning is a continuous, important task of every teacher.

SOCIAL PURPOSES OF EDUCATION

Schools and the societies which nurture them are closely related in purpose and design. An educational system with purposes diametrically opposed to those of the society which supported it would either fail or quickly modify its purposes to a more harmonious pattern. It is inconceivable that a highly democratic educational system would be supported by an autocratic government or that a rigidly autocratic educational system would flourish in a democratic society, since a primary objective of state-supported educational systems is to prepare adult citizens who are philosophically compatible and intellectually competent to become productive members of the society. Pragmatically, of course, the kind of society determines the teaching approaches which are acceptable; however as long as the teaching approaches which are used remain within the bounds of acceptability to that society, they may exercise subtle reciprocal pressures toward gradual change in the society.

In a mass educational system such as ours, compulsory attendance laws require nearly all children to be in school from six to sixteen years of age or through a ten-year span of their formative years. The schools thus provide a ten-year sheltered environment, in a sense a miniature society, in which children are gradually permitted to assume the roles and status which will continue into their adult years. For many this gradual transition from family roles to broader social roles is an easy one, but some fail to achieve any satisfactory status or any acceptable social role in the group. For these few who find no satisfactory social status, there are immediate and persistent repercussions which short-circuit academic achievement as the children struggle to cope with the frustration and insecurity resulting from their social incompatibility or rejection. There are also likely to be long-term effects from this struggle, since the child who cannot achieve satisfactory social status is apt to become an adult misfit. Such misfits are at best innocuous observers on the periphery of the social groups which they contact, and at worst aggressive rebels who viciously vent their wrath on society in criminal activity.

Although the preparation of pupils for successful social roles in adult society is not stressed in the formal instruction program, as are the academic skills, the child gains experience in social living as a concomitant of group instruction. Also the extent of children's success in achieving satisfactory social status within the classroom group is directly related to the quality of the social climate which prevails as a deterrent or stimulant to other classroom learning.

ELEMENTS OF THE SOCIAL CLIMATE IN THE CLASSROOM

Teachers aware of the importance of a desirable social climate for learning may still be unaware of which aspects of group behavior are most influential in creating or destroying a harmonious social climate. Furthermore, they may be reluctant or unable to appraise the social climate satisfactorily. To help teachers achieve a modicum of success in this evaluative realm, several questions are posed for discussion in the subsequent pages: (1) What effects has the group situation on individual learning? (2) How does the nature of the group influence learning? (3) How do such factors as group competition, cooperation, leadership, and discipline affect learning? (4) What aspects of social behavior are most *important* to observe in the classroom? (5) What techniques and instruments are available to collect data as a basis for evaluation of the classroom social climate?

Social groups and individual learning. Children are keenly aware of the possible effects which their performance has on their classmates, and in the primary grades they begin to assume student roles which stabilize into a habitual cloak of student demeanor which is comfortable and easily donned throughout their remaining student career. In fact, teachers who have taught for a number of years slip easily back into this student role when attending graduate classes. And in such roles they are often reluctant to participate actively in planning the class objectives and learning activities which affect them, even though as teachers they have much experience in making such plans for pupils under their tutelage.

Most classroom groups contain several subgroups or cliques organized around several social leaders or patterned after the social status or social class of their parents, with some social mobility between the groups but a fairly rigid dichotomy between upper-class and lower-class pupils.

Children who are aware of the social class distinctions within a school are inclined to follow the adult pattern and seek to become members of the most socially desirable group, even at the expense of broken friendships among their associates in other groups to which they have given allegiance. When such cliques or social class distinctions exist in a school, they definitely interfere with learning, as many pupils direct time and energy toward achieving a desirable social status rather than studying the course work. The social configuration of the group is best portrayed by the sociogram, discussed later in this chapter under sociometric techniques.

Self-concept and nature of the group. A child's behavior is the product of the interplay between himself and his environment. His self-concept develops in the interplay of interpersonal relationships within his environmental groups—family, school, community. If he is to achieve a satisfactory personal-social adjustment, he must learn to adapt and adjust to the pressures, or "press," [1] of his environment. He must further master the role of expectations of his member groups—student role, peer group role, family role. In school a child's self-concept is built around his group status and the nature of the groups to which he belongs. For example, a bright child's concept of himself is likely to vary markedly in groups of different intellectual levels. If he is a member of a group in which the others are equally bright, he may perceive himself to be average in intellectual ability. In contrast, if he is a member of a dull group, he will be inclined to regard himself as intellectually superior since no one in the group can compete with him intellectually. Thus the bright child in the homogeneously grouped class, while he recognizes that *his group is superior intellectually,* may tend to underestimate his individual potential because the competition from his able peers prevents him from achieving the persistent academic success pattern which he would be apt to achieve in a heterogeneous or a dull group. In fact, a bright child who finds himself placed in an accelerated class with others as bright or brighter than he may experience a success-frustration pattern which leads him to develop a self-concept similar to that of a dull child who is a member of an average group. In both instances the self-concept develops in reference to the only groups with which the child is in direct competition, and he lacks a realistic concept of the total spectrum of pupils'

[1] The term "press" is used by H. A. Murry, *et al.*, in *Explorations in Personality* (New York: Oxford University Press, 1938).

intellectual ability. In some cases, particularly when children are fairly mature, candid discussion of the group level of performance and individual discussion concerning their intelligence profile with at least some of the pupils will help them to gain a more realistic intellectual self-concept.

Effects of competition and cooperation. Teachers often purposefully or inadvertently introduce the element of competition into a class as a motivating factor. The effects of this competition vary according to the maturity level and the individuals within the group. When the competition exists between groups within the class, it may stimulate the members of each group to higher achievement. On the other hand, when the competition is between members of the same social group, it may induce immediate gains in achievement; but as hostility and jealousy break down group cohesion, it may ultimately result in disintegration of the group.

While the bright pupils may regard competition as a game in which academic success and social approbation are their just rewards, the average and dull pupils generally find it a frustrating experience, a race in which they are pitted against their keener colleagues with little chance of success.

In contrast, cooperation stimulating the slow learners but providing little motivation for the bright may have reciprocal effects. However, bright pupils can be motivated by cooperation when they are given leadership status in the group. Cooperative effort in attaining common goals may also cement group bonds more permanently, while competition works to weaken group ties.

Stern suggests that the situational and individual determinants of behavior include the *alpha* press and the *common beta* press. *Alpha* press is described as those "elements in the environment which actually exist and are capable of affecting the behavior of the participating individual." Whereas a particular way of perceiving the environment *shared* by members of a functional group is called the "common beta press." [2]

Stern's four methods of assessing the effects of these determinants on behavior include analytical, empirical, synthetic, and configurational approaches. While the discussion of these four methods is beyond the scope of this work, the reader is referred to *Stern's Methods in Personality Assessment* for a complete description of their application.

[2] George G. Stern, *et al. Methods in Personality Assessment* (Glencoe, Illinois: The Glencoe Free Press, 1956), pp. 36–37.

Effects of leadership and discipline. Teachers by virtue of their positions are status leaders to whom pupils look for competence and authority. The impact of the teacher's personality, the nature of the discipline which he imposes, and the extent of his understanding of pupil behavior all have a profound influence on the learning atmosphere and social climate within his classroom. The nature of the group also decidedly influences the classroom social climate. Each class has a unique group personality, and specific groups react differently to teachers just as individuals react differently as they move from one group to another. For example, teacher-pupil conflict is invited when a middle-class teacher is assigned to a group of culturally deprived children whose defeatism he neither sympathizes with nor understands, and whose social purposes he neither shares nor condones. In such a situation the resulting antagonism between teacher and pupils frequently results in frustration for both.

The nature of discipline which the teacher attempts to maintain also directly influences the social climate in the classroom. Rigidly authoritarian discipline, while it may assure an orderly classroom, generally has two other results which relate to the quality of learning. First, it focuses the learning experience into a teacher-to-pupil experience which lacks the enriching, although sometimes disconcerting, interplay of pupil-to-pupil learning. Second, it dichotomizes the group relationship into one in which the teacher, apart from pupils, directs the learning, which is collectively accepted or rejected by pupils. While the extrinsic motivation of punishments or rewards meted out by the teacher in such an atmosphere can result in significant pupil achievement of teacher-selected goals, the incidental effects may include eroding inroads on pupils' self-concepts, their interest in the subject, and their attitude toward social discipline. Pupils can be forced to learn if the threat or reward is great enough, but total subservience to the teacher is not compatible with our society; nor does it result in a desirable social climate for learning. It is much more desirable that pupils and teacher work in partnership toward shared learning goals which both understand. A harmonious atmosphere of cooperative endeavor and mutual respect is much more conducive to the achievement of the many-faceted goals of education than the "learning from fear to avoid punishment" approach.

Since the beginning of the group dynamics movement in the 1930's, there has been increasing awareness of the concept of the *teacher as a group leader*—one who works toward increasing group motivation, stimulating participation, and generating group morale. In an atmosphere of cooperative endeavor there will be considerable interaction between members of the group, and leadership from among the pupils can be fostered and developed.

There are numerous teacher self-evaluation scales available,[3] but individuals often lack the insight or objectivity to make a highly valid self-evaluation. Therefore, together with such evaluations, there should be teacher evaluations by principals and supervisors. However, without follow-up discussions these evaluations fail to achieve their most significant purpose, since they should serve to improve instruction by helping teachers to analyze their strengths and weaknesses and to overcome their weaknesses. Without outside help the rigid disciplinarian may fail to perceive that this characteristic is a weakness in his teaching. Pupil evaluations of instruction are generally also enlightening to the teacher and can add significantly to his insight concerning the impact of his instruction.

Significant aspects of classroom group. Most classroom groups are chance associations of individuals. The child neither chose the particular group, nor was he chosen by its members. He merely happened to reside in the locality, happened to have a birthdate which decreed his grade level, and happened to be assigned by school authorities to Mr. X's classroom. Actually, then, there is nothing particularly sacred about such a group association, and there is no logical or important reason why such groups could not be purposely changed by reassigning some members to improve the quality of the classroom social climate.

Adults generally choose the groups to which they belong, but school children rarely have a choice of classroom group. The simple device of regrouping children early in the year by sociometric choice would probably alleviate the social problem but would create a major administrative problem. Thus it appears that the best compromise between rigid assignment and total reassignment is careful evaluation of each classroom group and reassignment of those few who are particularly unhappy and misassigned in their original groups. Judicious shifting of a small percent of the school's pupils can improve the classroom climate, as well as provide a better opportunity for satisfactory social adjustment to those reassigned. Aspects of the group which need to be evaluated before such reassignments include (1) the group social profile, (2) the group self-concept, (3) the group intellectual attitude, (4) the group emotional cli-

[3] See Chapter 16.

mate, (5) the group morale, and (6) the group modes of problem solving.

Actually the evaluation of all six of these factors will be based to some extent upon careful observation of the group, but there are, in addition, some other methods of assessment which should also be used. For example, the group social profile can be evaluated with the help of sociograms. These instruments help identify leaders, isolates (those who are rejected by their peers), and cliques. The social deviate, such as the persistent disciplinary problem, the child who neither respects authority nor the rights of others, is so obvious that even the most unobservant teacher will identify him. Transfer to another classroom group may help this child, and will certainly improve the learning atmosphere of the group from which he transferred, but transfer to a special classroom with a teacher specially trained to help such children may be a better answer. However, segregation of all trouble makers in one classroom is no good answer unless the teacher is well prepared to handle the social deviant.[4] Group self-concept can be partially ascertained by individual interviews with class members. In addition the use of teacher-constructed attitude scales such as those discussed in Chapter 13 can help the teacher assess self-concept, intellectual attitude, and morale. Some of the questions to be answered by observation interviews and attitude scales include these: Do pupils value group association? Do they prefer other groups? Does the group and its individual members appear to be relaxed? Anxious? Frustrated? Do the group members value learning? Social activities?

EVALUATING GROUP SOCIAL CLIMATE

Observation. As has been implied earlier in this discussion, the first and most obvious method of determining the quality and nature of the group social climate is direct observation. A teacher who has a modicum of social perception will be aware of the general level of group morale and the social climate which prevails in the classroom. However, observation, if it is to be useful in yielding more than a general impression of the class, must be planned and systematically utilized. In order to get a truly representative sample of the pupils' behavior, the teacher should not limit the observations to the classroom situation. He should also ob-

[4] For further discussion of this problem, see Herman G. Richey (ed.), *Social Deviancy Among Youth*, Sixty-fifth Yearbook of the National Society for the Study of Education (Chicago: University of Chicago Press, 1966). Chapter 12 is particularly relevant.

serve pupils in the hall, on the playground, in the library, in study halls, in the lunchroom, in club meetings, and at social events. In other words, he must seek to gain as full a picture of pupils' total behavior as possible. Care should also be taken to observe all the pupils. It is easy to become so concerned with the few who have obvious problems or who are prominent in the group that the total group climate and the remaining group members are all but overlooked. Thus it is necessary to set up a systematic record of each pupil to insure balanced observation of all. If the teacher sets aside some time each day for specifically observing pupil behavior and for taking notes on his observations, he is apt to obtain a good sample of behavior and adequate coverage of class members. In addition, he must be alert for critical incidents of behavior which occur incidentally during the day and which should be recorded for future reference.

In making observations the teacher must be careful to avoid the following common errors, which will invalidate or distort the results:

1. Bias
2. Inadequate sampling
3. Inaccuracy of reporting
4. Misinterpretation of behavior
5. Too much generalization
6. Use of subjective terms in describing behavior

Qualitative aspects, such as morale, which facilitate group performance, can be observed in terms of member satisfaction, group loyalty, enthusiasm of effort, and success as a group. In addition, several aspects of group behavior can be quantified in terms of frequency of occurrence, duration of time, and successes and errors.

For example, problem analysis of a large group, such as an entire secondary school, might well include a tabulation of the number of incidents of cheating, stealing, disciplinary infractions, and social problems —e.g., traffic infractions, premarital pregnancies, dope addictions, and delinquency cases. In smaller groups within a classroom the duration of time required to solve class-related learning problems assigned by the teacher gives a measure of relative efficiency, permitting one small group or class committee to be compared against other similar groups. In extracurricular activities the relative effectiveness of the various activity groups can be roughly ascertained from the number of successes or failures which they experience in planning and carrying out their specific purposes.

In discussion groups within the class, observations can be objectified by the use of an evaluative form such as that shown in Figure 8.1. The use of such a form provides a systematic method of evaluating and recording each member's contributions to the discussion.

The success patterns of members of a class also give a valuable indication of the quality of group motivation, morale, and atmosphere. Such an indicator is the number of leadership positions within the school held by

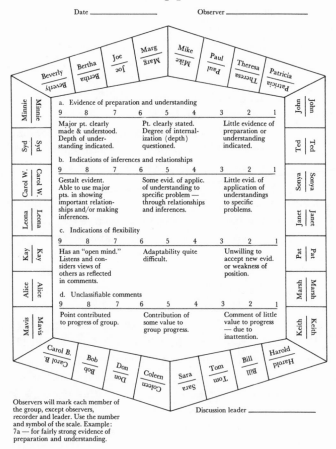

Figure 8.1. INDIVIDUAL EVALUATION FORM

From Kenneth H. Hoover, *Learning and Teaching in the Secondary School* (Boston: Allyn and Bacon, 1964), p. 245. Reprinted by permission of the publisher and the author.

members of a given class together with the number of people within the class who hold the positions. While the fact of many positions held by a few is significant information, probably indicating group domination by these few, it may also be a symptom of a poor social climate within the classroom as other potential leaders are squelched by the few most outstanding. When many individuals within the class are accorded school-wide positions of leadership, it is probably more justifiable to conclude that the social climate which fostered such leadership development was a desirable one; although special circumstances, such as homogeneous grouping which segregated most of the leaders in one classroom, could also account for the success pattern. Nevertheless, the penchant of some teacher-leaders for fostering and developing an inordinate number of school leaders within their classroom environments over a period of years cannot be overlooked as an indication that the quality of the social-personal relations within such classrooms contributes significantly to the social adjustment and success of pupils.

Informal techniques. Informal techniques which are available to supplement the information which teachers obtain through observation include (1) sociometric techniques, (2) questionnaires, and (3) attitude scales.

1. *Sociometric techniques.* The sociometric technique which has been used most often in the classroom is the classroom sociogram. The sociogram is a diagrammatic portrayal of the personal choices of pupils within a group, classroom, or school. The sociogram is not an analysis of pupil relationships, but it does portray them in a convenient form so that they can be analyzed and evaluated as the basis for subsequent action.

When this technique is used, several types of questions can be asked to indicate preferences in different types of relationships. For example, pupils might be asked to choose the two people they would like as best friends. Such a question could give an indication of the social compatibility of the group. This question would help identify the most popular, the least popular, and the subgroups or cliques within the class. It is noteworthy that with such a question the choices will be difficult for some pupils whose best-friend choices are members of another group outside the class. Also such a question is inappropriate when the group members are not well acquainted with one another.

Figure 8.2 is an example of the use of this technique to provide evi-

Figure 8.2. EXAMPLE OF THE USE OF A SOCIOGRAM TO DEPICT FRIENDSHIPS IN AN INTER-RACE SCHOOL

From Norman Nybroten (ed.), *Economy and Conditions of the Fort Hall Indian Reservation* (Moscow: University of Idaho, 1964), p. 128. Reprinted by permission.

dence of the inter-race relations between Indian and non-Indian children in the first grade. At this early grade level there was beginning to be a racial dichotomy in choices, although the Indian children made choices across the racial barrier in several instances. Other sociograms in higher grades in this school situation showed increasing cleavage between the groups, with virtually no choices across the race barrier in the upper grades.

Other relationships which can be depicted by the sociogram include leadership choices and study-mate choices. Pupils often select people other than their best friends with whom to study, since the best friend is not always the most helpful study-mate. It is also possible to identify committee groups which will work effectively together by assigning membership on the basis of the member choices which pupils make, rather than on the typical basis of topic interest. When committees are formed sociometrically and then permitted to select the topics, intercommittee jockeying can be minimized so that group time can be spent fruitfully in discussing the study topic.

The *guess-who* technique is a second sociometric approach which is used to help identify group leaders. With this approach, a number of desirable personal characteristics are listed and each pupil is asked to identify the person within the group who most nearly fits the description. When there is considerable agreement among the pupils in identifying several of the group members, these persons obviously stand out as leaders. A tabulation of the choices made by pupils gives a good current picture of the status of group leadership.

The *incomplete sentence* is a third sociometric technique. It can be used to obtain information concerning social adjustment of group members, as well as their attitude toward the class and the teacher. This technique requires that the teacher ask pupils to complete open-end sentences concerning the aspects of the group or classroom situation about which he desires information. Sentences such as the following should provoke a variety of responses and elicit considerable information concerning the group:

EXAMPLES:
My teacher_____
Homework_____
Boys are_____
I don't understand_____

Several lines should be provided after each incomplete sentence to permit pupils an extended response if they wish to make one.

The sociometric techniques give information concerning the status of the group and its members only at the time during which the information was collected. Social groups are dynamic, and even the addition or removal of one member may reorient the group structure and consequently the individual roles of the members. Thus, repeated use of these techniques is needed to identify the stable elements of the structure as well as the shifting roles and changing status of members.

Older pupils often resent the use of sociometric techniques, particularly when they are not aware of the purpose for their use. Also teachers will find that the construction of sociograms is rather time-consuming; therefore the decision to use them should be based on a clearly evident purpose, with concrete plans for improving group relationships and accomplishments as a result of their use.

2. *Questionnaires.* Questionnaires serve a worthwhile function in obtaining information related to pupils' concepts of their own status and the structure of the class group. The quality of group relations is also reflected either directly or indirectly by pupil responses to the questions which are included. Questionnaires, however—like tests, checklists, rating scales, and other measurement devices—vary considerably in quality and coverage of the areas about which information is desired. A hastily constructed questionnaire with poorly written questions and haphazard coverage of the topics may actually be misleading, eliciting only half-information, biased information, or misinformation because the respondents misunderstand or misconstrue the questions. Summarization and evaluation of the information from such a survey are frustrating and may lead to totally fallacious conclusions and recommendations.

Before questionnaires are constructed, a carefully planned outline which includes the major topics to be covered should be written. At this stage attention should be given to the relative importance and extent of coverage to be accorded each of the major areas. As the questions are written, every effort should be made to keep them clear and concise so that respondents can read them quickly with understanding and respond appropriately. Nor should the questions be worded in such a way that they force pupils to accept one of two or three limited choices in areas where numerous plausible choices are acceptable:

> EXAMPLE: The quality of social relations in this class is (better, poorer) than that in other classrooms of the school.

Such a question is too general. Several questions referring to specific aspects of the social relations referred to would be better. Additional information could also be gained in this situation by asking pupils to rate on a three-to-five point scale the quality of social relations compared to those in other classes.

EXAMPLE: Check the category which best describes the social relationships in this classroom as compared to those in other classes.

(above average   average   below average)

or

(best   better   similar   worse   worst)

Questionnaires dealing with such personal relationships as social compatibility of a group are probably answered most honestly when pupils are not required to write their names on their papers. However, this practice prevents the teacher from identifying the individual pupils who indicate personal problems which need attention.

3. *Attitude scales.* The Likert scale discussed in Chapter 13 (see p. 293) can be adapted for use in determining pupil attitude toward the class, teacher, and group colleagues. Since the Likert scores can be summarized and handled as other test scores, they can be used comparatively to give relative measures of the attitudes of several groups. For example, a teacher who is teaching several sections of freshman English could determine by the Likert technique the comparative favorableness of attitude of all sections toward the subject, teacher, or classmates.

Standardized measures. An excellent example of a standardized measure which has been used to assess the social relationships within a class is the *Syracuse Scales of Social Relations.* This instrument, currently out of print, is discussed briefly because of its unique approach. The measure, standardized on approximately 10,000 grade and high school pupils, provides normative data for social relations against which class responses can be compared in much the same manner as class achievement scores are compared against national norms.

These scales have been designed for three age levels: (1) elementary (grades 5 and 6); (2) junior high (grades 7, 8, and 9); and (3) senior high (grades 10, 11, and 12). The scales provide information about two important psychological needs of each age group:

Elementary——succorance
achievement recognition

Junior high——succorance
deference

Senior high——succorance
playmirth

At each level pupils are asked to rate their classmates as possible sources of aid in helping them solve personal problems; this psychological need is identified as *succorance*. The *playmirth* scale requires a rating of classmates as companions at a party or other recreational event. *Achievement recognition* relates to classmates as aides in helping the pupil do well in order to gain praise. *Deference* relates to classmates as persons to look up to as ideals. A pupil's ratings of his classmates is also made comparatively against the five persons in his acquaintance who range from least helpful to most helpful. The names of the persons picked as least helpful, most helpful, etc., are written in the five boxes at the top of the page as reference persons to compare against as classmates are rated.

The scales can be used in regular classrooms or in extracurricular groups where the membership does not exceed 37 pupils. Two sessions —a 30-minute and a 20-minute one—are required to administer the senior high school scales; and approximately three hours are required to score the scales. The scales provide for the following six types of scores:

1. *Individual ratings made by pupils.* Each pupil rates each of his classmates as a possible companion in a social situation designed to reflect a specific psychological need. These ratings indicate how a given pupil regards *each* of his classmates.
2. *Mid-score of ratings made.* This score provides precise information about the way a given pupil evaluates his classmates *as a group.* It is a kind of average score, indicating the rating that is most typical of a given pupil's overall evaluation of his classmates.
3. *Class average of mid-scores of ratings made.* This score indicates how all the pupils *as a group* regard their classmates. It is the mean of all the pupils' mid-scores of *ratings made.*
4. *Individual ratings received.* Each pupil receives a rating from each of his classmates. These ratings indicate how a given pupil is regarded by *each* of his classmates.
5. *Mid-score of ratings received.* This is a kind of average score and supplies information about the way a given pupil is evaluated by his classmates *as a group.*
6. *Scores relating to cliques.* These scores are combinations of individual *ratings made* and *received* and define groups of two or more members who are mutually attracted to each other for the satisfaction of a given need.[5]

The scores obviously provide a measure of the general level of the morale of the group as well as of the individual adjustment of members

[5] Eric F. Gardner and George G. Thompson, *Manual of Directions for Senior High Level—Syracuse Scales of Social Relations* (New York: World Book Company, 1959), p. 7.

of the group. From the information obtained from the scales teachers can identify those whose status might be improved by moving into other classrooms; they can also identify members of small cliques who might benefit from additional friendships.

When these scales are used over a period of years in a school, optimum social relationships can be achieved by using scale scores as a basis for reassigning some pupils to provide them the most acceptable social situation.

SUMMARY

The individual learning of a child in school is interwoven in the fabric of his classroom group. He reacts to group pressures. He interacts with group members, and his actions likewise exert influence on his colleagues and impart a unique essence to the group structure. Ideally teachers seek to build a desirable social climate for learning, a climate in which all group members find desirable roles and in which morale is high. In such a situation the desire to learn permeates the group as a self-generating spark which spreads and glows in all the class members. Occasionally, by chance, the composition of a class and the rapport between teacher and group are such that this ideal social climate for learning exists. More likely, however, no such spontaneous intergroup compatibility exists; and occasionally a class is made up of members whose incompatibility and member-to-member hostility are pervasive. Thus, persistent factors are present which constantly detract from the learning tasks and which result in innumerable discipline problems.

Such differences in the social climate of a classroom are intuitively apparent to the perceptive teacher, but more than intuition is needed to assess definitively the structure of the group and the roles and status of individual group members.

Careful, systematic observation of the pupils is a useful means for gaining information concerning their social relationships—although care must be taken to avoid such common errors as bias, inadequate sampling, and over-generalization. There are also several informal evaluation techniques which are quite useful. These include: (1) sociometric techniques, such as the sociogram; (2) questionnaires; (3) attitude scales; and (4) standardized instruments. Instruments such as the *Syracuse Scale of Social Relations* are particularly useful for collecting information from which valid evaluations of the group can be made. Measurements and subsequent evaluations are of little real worth, however, if they are not used as the basis for subsequent actions which enrich the group relations, change the roles of individuals whose influence is detrimental to the group, and improve the status of those who are constantly rejected by their classmates. With the information which measurement provides, it is often possible to improve the social climate in a classroom by judicious transfer of a few individuals to other groups with which they will be more compatible. Occasionally the information may justify transferring teachers themselves to other classes.

DISCUSSION QUESTIONS AND PROBLEMS

1. Visit an elementary school to observe the classroom and playground behavior of a group of children. From this observation, attempt to identify group leaders and those who are having trouble fitting into the group. Validate your judgment against the teacher's selections.
2. As a class project construct a rating scale to be used in evaluating the social climate for learning in an elementary or secondary classroom.
3. Construct a sociogram on the basis of the sociometric choices of the children in an elementary classroom.
4. On the basis of the above sociogram determine what, if any, reassignments should be made to achieve improved individual adjustment and an optimum social climate in the classroom.
5. Suggest ways in which the isolate can be given social status and helped to achieve group acceptance.

SELECTED READINGS

Ahmann, J. Stanley and Marvin D. Glock. *Evaluating Pupil Growth*. 3rd ed. Boston: Allyn and Bacon, 1967. Chapter 13 considers both the effects of personal-social adjustment on scholastic success and the methods of assessing adjustment.

Bruck, Max and Raymond F. Bodwin. "The Relationship Between Self-Concept and the Presence and Absence of Scholastic Underachievement," *Journal of Clinical Psychology*, XVIII (April 1962), 181–182.

Downie, N. M. *Fundamentals of Measurement*. New York: Oxford University Press, 1958. Pages 293–298 contain a brief, but useful, analysis of the use of sociometric techniques in the classroom.

Hoover, Kenneth H. *Learning and Teaching in the Secondary School*. Boston: Allyn and Bacon, 1964. Chapter 7 deals with the use of sociometric techniques; Chapter 9, with the use of group dynamics to improve the learning climate.

Moreno, Jacob. *Who Shall Survive?* Washington: Nervous and Mental Diseases Publishing Company, 1934. This is a pioneer work on sociometrics.

Schultz, William C. *FIRO: A Three-Dimensional Theory of Interpersonal Behavior.* New York: Rinehart & Company, 1958. The author elaborates the theory that each individual has three interpersonal needs: inclusion, control, and affection. Chapters 2, 4, and 10 are particularly relevant to appraising the social climate for learning; and Chapter 4 presents the measurement instrument used in the studies.

Part III

EVALUATING PUPIL GROWTH
AND CHANGE

Pupils come to school with a background prescribed by their genetic inheritance and further circumscribed by the environment in which they have been immersed during their formative preschool years. On this background schools have no influence, and teachers can do no more than assess the child's background and use the information to set the beginning point for instruction. However, from the moment the child enrolls in school, teachers seek to make changes in him—changes in attitudes, interest, knowledge, and skills. Some children adapt and change easily, others resist learning and are unable or unwilling to change. Without continuous measurement and evaluation the teacher can hazard no more than a crude guess at the impact of his instruction on each child—he can neither pace the instruction properly nor be sure of his effectiveness as a teacher.

Because of the diversity of instructional objectives, there is no one "ideal" measurement instrument which will provide a comprehensive picture of pupil achievement and change. Thus, this section of the book is broken into chapters focusing on the most important kinds of specific learnings together with the measuring instruments and techniques best fitted for measuring each. A comprehensive picture of pupil growth and change during the educational process is best attained through numerous measurement and evaluation approaches. To base judgment of educational quality and pupil progress on the "tunnel vision" provided by one test or test battery is a dangerous pitfall into which teacher and laymen alike frequently slip. The objectives of education which presumably focus the directions of pupils' educational growth and change are diverse; and those teachers who base their assessment of pupil progress on one standardized test or on one type of teacher-made test are as short-sighted as the prospective home buyer who determines the overall quality of a home solely on the basis of the quality of the plumbing.

Chapter 9

PLANNING AND CONSTRUCTING MEASUREMENT INSTRUMENTS

INTRODUCTION

Teachers who may be urgently concerned with the performance of their classes on the school's standardized achievement battery often fail to devote sufficient time and attention to their teacher-made achievement tests. Despite the value of standardized tests as normative scales of achievement, carefully planned and skillfully constructed teacher-made tests have the immeasurable advantage of being intimately related to the actual classroom instruction of that teacher. The teacher who has carefully outlined his course content and his instructional objectives has the basis from which to construct tests which duplicate instructional coverage and emphasis, a duplication rarely possible with standardized tests. This advantage of the teacher-made test, however, is not an automatic increment. The teacher who has not formulated instructional objectives or who is careless in constructing tests, besides teaching poorly, rarely gets much insight into class achievement or individual pupil progress. The sad fact is that poorly constructed tests might better not have been administered at all because they waste time on fruitless measurement while frustrating and discouraging pupils who anticipated better correlation between instruction and tests.

Teacher mastery of the principles of good test construction will not assure perfect teacher-made tests, but it will unquestionably result in improved tests and should eliminate the glaring errors so frequently present in the tests of those who do not possess this information. While this chapter is not intended to be a comprehensive manual of test construction, it does include an overview of the essential principles for planning, constructing, and evaluating the most commonly used measuring instruments.

PLANNING MEASURING INSTRUMENTS

Course evaluation plan. The competent teacher will not begin instructing a class without having planned both the outline of instructional content and the objectives which he hopes to attain. Nevertheless, while he would undoubtedly agree that evaluation of pupil learning is an essential part of instruction, it is unlikely that his planning for evaluation will consist of more than a time schedule for assignments and tests.

Measurement and evaluation in the classroom are the signposts of learning which indicate the direction, the pace, and the type of instruction necessary to achieve the goals which were set. Consequently, a thorough outline of the plan of evaluation is an essential element of the pre-teaching plan, and one which should be thought out and written just as carefully as course outlines and lesson plans. The first step in the construction of this outline is the preparation of a list of general instructional objectives and major content areas. Both of these may be taken from the course outline. However, if the objectives have not been written or are too general to lend themselves to measurement, the teacher will find *Bloom's Taxonomy of Educational Objectives*[1] the most useful resource in helping him state the objectives correctly. This step in outline construction is illustrated below for a high school world history course in which there are ten major content areas and ten general instructional objectives to be achieved.

Major Content Areas of the High School
World History Course:

1. The Ancient Roots of Civilization
2. The Greek and Roman Foundations of Western Civilization
3. The Medieval Period
4. The Renaissance and Reformation
5. The Age of Exploration
6. The Struggle for Freedom and National Unity
7. The Age of Revolutions
8. Imperialism and Great Power Rivalries
9. World Conflicts Threaten Civilization
10. East-West Confrontation and New Challenges

---

[1] See Benjamin S. Bloom, *et al.*, *Taxonomy of Educational Objectives: The Classification of Educational Goals, Handbook I: Cognitive Domain* (New York: David McKay Company, 1956).

See also David R. Krathwohl, *et al.*, *Taxonomy of Educational Objectives: The Classification of Educational Goals, Handbook II: Affective Domain* (New York: David McKay Company, 1964).

*General Instructional Objectives of the High
School World History Course:*

1. To acquire a knowledge of the chronological landmarks of history.
2. To develop an understanding of the evolution of present institutions and social customs.
3. To instill an appreciation of the American heritage.
4. To develop awareness of significant world trends.
5. To develop the ability to anticipate and cope with recurring political-social problems.
6. To encourage unbiased analyses of national-international problems.
7. To develop skill in historical research.
8. To develop skill in the use of maps, charts, and graphs.
9. To promote an interest in history.
10. To encourage active, intelligent participation as citizens of the United States and members of the world society.

A course evaluation plan based on the major content areas and general objectives listed above is presented in Table XIII. It is to be noted that while this plan is brief, it does identify the content areas and objectives of the course with the measurement instruments which are to be used. The instructional content areas are included in the outline to insure identity between instruction and measurement, but it is actually the objectives which determine the choice of measuring instrument. For example, *knowledge* in a field such as science or social studies is best measured by an objective test, *critical thinking* or problem solving by an essay or performance test, and *attitude* toward democracy by an attitude scale.

Test function. Teachers' tests are classified by function as mastery, instructional, or measurement tests. The *mastery test* is designed to measure essential skills which all pupils must master before instruction proceeds to the next step. Such a test is rarely difficult and is confined to a restricted area of the subject matter—e.g., essential grammatical rules in English or essential computational skills in arithmetic.

The *instructional test* serves primarily as an instructional rather than a measurement tool. The pop quizzes which teachers frequently give are primarily instructional since they are designed to reemphasize important points from previous lessons. The instructional test may also be one which covers a complete unit of work, in which case the test is given, scored, and returned to the pupil for discussion for maximum learning. Occasionally such tests, when they are given little grading weight, may be scored by the pupil himself. This procedure enables the pupil to iden-

Table XIII. MEASUREMENT OUTLINE FOR HIGH SCHOOL WORLD HISTORY COURSE

Content Areas

	1. Ancient	2. Greek and Roman	3. Medieval	4. Renaissance	5. Exploration	6. Nationalism	7. Revolutions	8. Imperialism	9. Conflict	10. Challenges

Instructional Objectives	*Measuring Instruments*	
1. Knowledge of historical landmarks		
2. Understanding of institutional evolution	Completion test	Multiple-choice test
3. Appreciation of American heritage		
4. Awareness of world trends		
5. Ability to handle recurring problems	Essay test	Problem-solving test
6. Analysis of national-international problems		
7. Skill in historical research	Research paper	
8. Skill in map use	Map usage test	
9. Interest in history	Interest inventory and interview	
10. National-international citizenship	Observation and attitude test	

tify and correct his own errors. Such tests can be an effective teaching device.

The *measurement test* is an achievement test with 50% difficulty level. This test is scaled in a power arrangement beginning with easy items and increasing in difficulty until a performance ceiling is reached for each pupil. The measurement test is appropriate as a semester or end-of-year examination to provide an extensive survey of pupil achievement. The test is constructed on the basis of such a test outline or table of specifications as that discussed in the following section of this chapter.

Test outlines. In addition to the overall evaluation plan for the course, specific outlines should be prepared for each test which is used. The outline for an objective test is called a test table of specifications.

An example of a table of specifications or test outline for a multiple-choice world history test is shown in Table XIV. This test is designed to measure the first two general objectives and the first four major content areas of those listed for the course in Table XIII. To facilitate measurement, the two general objectives have been broken down into more specific objectives—e.g., "knowledge of dates" and "understanding of the evolution of government."

Table XIV. TABLE OF SPECIFICATIONS FOR A MULTIPLE-CHOICE WORLD HISTORY TEST

Objectives	*Content Areas*				*Totals*
	1	*2*	*3*	*4*	
A. Knowledge of Historical Landmarks					(45)
1. Dates	3	3	4	5	15
2. Men	2	3	3	7	15
3. Events	2	4	3	6	15
B. Understanding of Institutional Evolution					(45)
1. Customs, Mores, Law	2	4	1	3	10
2. Social Institutions	3	7	2	8	20
3. Government	3	4	2	6	15
Totals	15	25	15	35	90

This outline, in addition to including the content areas and objectives which are to be measured, weights each area and objective in terms of the number of test items which will be written to measure it. The number of items which will be written to give combined measurement of each objective and content area is also indicated in the various cells of the table. For example, in Table XIII seven items will be written to measure content area 4 and objective A.2. The actual writing of items for a specific test follows the preparation of the table of specifications, although items which were written while lesson plans were being made out and items from previous tests form a pool from which some items may be drawn.

The outline for essay and oral tests need not be so detailed as that for objective tests but should include the content areas and objectives which are to be measured. For the performance test a different type of outline is required. Since this test is used to measure actual application of learning in the performance of a job, a detailed, specific job analysis should be made up to serve as the outline from which test problems may be drawn. This job analysis comprises the specific performance elements which constitute the job for which pupils are being prepared and on which they are being evaluated. Because all of these specifics cannot be included on the test, an appropriate sampling must be taken, a sampling based on the specific emphases of the course content and instructional objectives.

Team planning. Professional test makers invariably seek the help of their colleagues in planning and constructing tests which they intend to publish. In contrast, the classroom teacher, who is obviously less competent in test construction, rarely solicits the aid of his colleagues, perhaps because he views such a request as an admission of incompetence. Those who hold this view would be well advised to take a page from the book of the professionals and place the welfare of pupils above personal pride.

The team approach is particularly useful in large schools where a number of faculty are working in the same subject area and could reasonably use some common examinations. The recent introduction of team teaching in numerous elementary and secondary schools virtually assures that in those schools team planning of examinations will be correlated with team instruction. Although it takes more time for a group to plan the examination, the division of labor in writing test items will result in each individual's investing less total time on the project than would be the case with individual planning and construction. As a rule the group will also have a greater variety of item ideas than any individual within the group might think of; and the practice of subjecting both the test outline and the specific test items to critical review either by the individual members or by the group will further improve the quality of the instrument.

With the team teaching approach, it is feasible to build a large pool of test items by requiring team members to construct appropriate items to accompany each of their classroom presentations. Such items should be typed on 3″ x 5″ cards and filed for future reference. When team planning is used, one member should be designated as team leader with authority to put together and edit the final instrument.

Test length and format. Measurement instruments must normally be devised to fit within the limits of one class period—40 to 50 minutes in the secondary school and 20 to 30 minutes in the elementary school. The time which a test will take to complete is not always easy to determine beforehand; but as a general rule upper-grade and secondary pupils can complete three true-false or two multiple-choice items per minute. This rule, however, does not hold when the items are unusually long or quite difficult. By actually completing the examination himself, the instructor can get an estimate of the time which pupils will require—although pupils will work more slowly than the teacher and should be given some additional time.

The format of the examination should be such that it facilitates in every way possible both the teacher's administration and scoring and the pupils' method of response. Directions on the examination should clearly indicate the method of response desired; and, for elementary school pupils, it is helpful to include a sample item to show the correct method of response. At the upper-elementary and the secondary levels the use of machine-score answer sheets is permissible for objective tests. When such answer sheets are not used, format similar to that in the example below should be followed for true-false, multiple-choice, and matching examinations.

TRUE-FALSE EXAMINATION

Directions: In the following items cross out the T if the item is correct; cross out the F if the item is incorrect.

T   F   1. A test can be reliable without being valid. (With this format a punched-out cardboard key can be used to score the true-false examination.)

MULTIPLE-CHOICE EXAMINATION

Directions: Place the letter which identifies the correct response in the blank before each item.

_____ 1. A major weakness of essay tests is that they

     a. promote poor study habits
     b. encourage guessing
     c. are difficult to construct
     d. encourage bluffing
     e. measure only recall

MATCHING EXAMINATION

Directions: Items in column 1 are to be matched with the responses from column 2 which correctly identify them. In the blank preceding each item in column 1 place the letter of the correct response from column 2.

_____ 1. Pb	a. copper	
_____ 2. Cu	b. gold	
_____ 3. Na	c. iron	
_____ 4. Fe	d. lead	
_____ 5. Au	e. mercury	
	f. silver	
	g. sodium	
	h. tin	

The general principles which should be followed in test format are summarized in the list below.

1. The test should be long enough to be valid and reliable but short enough to be usable.
2. A measurement test should be a power test, wherein the first few items are simple enough for all pupils to answer.
3. The test should be designed in such a way that reading rate and comprehension do not unduly influence the test scores.
4. A test should generally consist of no more than two or three types of items, and all items of one type should be included in one section.
5. The test directions should be explicit so that the pupil clearly understands the method of response.
6. The test items should provide a simple method of indicating responses and of scoring the responses.
7. The test should be typed and reproduced by ditto or mimeograph.[2]

Sources for test planning. There are numerous excellent sources from which teachers may obtain other helpful suggestions relative to test planning. Among the better sources are:

[2] John A. Green, *Teacher-Made Tests* (New York: Harper & Row, 1963), pp. 17–21.

1. Bloom, Benjamin S. (ed.). *Taxonomy of Educational Objectives, Handbook I: Cognitive Domain.* New York: David McKay Company, 1956.
2. Furst, Edward J. *Constructing Evaluation Instruments.* New York: Longmans, Green and Company, 1958.
3. Gerberich, J. Raymond. *Specimen Objective Test Items.* New York: Longmans, Green and Company, 1956.
4. Green, John A. *Teacher-Made Tests.* New York: Harper & Row, 1963.
5. Krathwohl, David, *et al. Taxonomy of Educational Objectives, Handbook II: Affective Domain.* New York: David McKay Company, 1964.
6. Travers, Robert N. W. *How to Make Achievement Tests.* New York: The Odyssey Press, 1950.

CONSTRUCTING MEASUREMENT INSTRUMENTS

The planning which precedes the construction of a measurement instrument is an exceedingly important prerequisite; however, the best plan does not insure the development of a good instrument when the rules are violated in writing the test items. In the final analysis the actual construction of a test is the most important, most difficult, and most time-consuming step in all cases except the essay test. The quality of a teacher-made or informal test is really determined by composition ability, ingenuity in selecting and stating problems, and adherence to the rules of test construction. In the subsequent sections of this chapter examples of the various types of test items, together with the rules for their construction, are given to help the teacher achieve greater skill in constructing informal tests.

Objective tests. The four most frequently used objective test forms are (1) the completion or short-answer test, (2) the true-false or alternate form test, (3) the multiple-choice test, and (4) the matching test. Objective tests share the common advantages of permitting easy scoring, an extensive measurement sample, and high reliability. On the other hand, they also have in common several disadvantages which are not readily overcome. Three notable disadvantages are (1) the difficulty of preparing good objective tests, (2) the tendency to encourage pupils to guess, and (3) the difficulty of measuring such important learning outcomes as critical thinking and application of learning in problem solving.

1. *Short-answer test.* The oldest type of objective test is the completion test, which was first used by Hermann Ebbinghaus in Germany during the nineteenth century. This test form has been modified to include questions, incomplete sentences, definitions, and identification items.

Short-answer tests are most useful in measuring recall of knowledge, and their major advantage over such objective forms as the true-false and multiple-choice is that the pupil cannot guess or identify the answer but must remember it. The examples which follow show the four types of short-answer items:

1. *Question:* Who was the author of the *Grapes of Wrath?*
2. *Incomplete statement:* The (＿＿＿＿＿) amendment to the United States Constitution gave women the right to vote in national elections.
3. *Definition:* Define a prepositional phrase.
4. *Identification:* Identify the part of speech of each underlined word in the following sentence:
The dog <u>barked</u> <u>furiously</u> <u>as</u> the car <u>sped</u> <u>down</u> the highway.

For most teachers the easiest form of short-answer test to construct well is the question form. It is difficult to write incomplete sentences; they are either too easy because many clues have been left or too hard because not enough clues have been retained to indicate the single appropriate response. Questions, however, can easily be written so that only one response is appropriate.

In constructing short-answer items, it is desirable to adhere to the following rules:

First, *items should be written so that the required response is a significant, unique word or phrase.* If there is more than one plausible response, the item does not give the intended measurement, and students can justifiably argue that they should be given credit.

> FAULTY EXAMPLE: In 1215 King John signed the ＿＿＿＿＿＿.
> IMPROVED EXAMPLE: What document signed by King John in 1215 guaranteed the nobility and the clergy right to trial by their peers?
> <u>Magna Carta</u>

Obviously King John signed numerous documents during the year 1214 so that the pupil could justify as correct numerous answers which could be historically verified. The rewritten item presented as a question is specific and only one answer is correct.

Second, *the blanks should be arranged for convenient scoring,* and all blanks should be equal in length to prevent unnecessary clueing of the response. A satisfactory arrangement is to place all the blanks on the left-hand or right-hand margin so that a key can be placed beside the blanks when they are scored. (Note the examples above.) The length of the blanks is determined by the longest single response in the test.

Third, when using the incomplete statement, *undermutilation or over-mutilation should be avoided.* When too many words are removed from the statement, the pupil is unable to determine the type of response which the instructor desires. Conversely, removing too few words makes the answer too apparent.

> FAULTY EXAMPLE: The————of a simple lever is————by moving the————closer to the weight end.
>
> IMPROVED EXAMPLE: The leverage of a simple lever is <u>increased</u> by moving the <u>fulcrum</u> closer to the weight end.

Adding the one word "leverage" to the sentence gives the pupil a sufficient clue to the meaning of the item, so that he can answer it if he understands the principle involved.

Fourth, in scoring the test *one point should be allowed for each blank.* This is true even though there may be several blanks in a single statement. Since each blank is to be filled by a significant word or phrase and in each instance a single recall is required to supply the response, the items have approximately the same value.

2. *Alternate-response form.* The alternate-response form is most frequently referred to as a true-false test although there are several varieties of alternate-response items. For example, in the primary grades this type of test may consist of a series of statements or questions which are answered "yes" or "no."

> EXAMPLE:
> Yes   No   December, January, and February are the three months of the winter season.

Another variation is that in which a portion of the item is underlined, to be corrected by the pupil if the statement is false.

> EXAMPLE:
> T   F   The major function of the thyroid gland is <u>to control growth</u>.

This is a good type of item because it requires the pupil to display some understanding and also reduces the guessing factor.

A third variation of the alternate-response form is one which is similar to the multiple-choice item.

EXAMPLE: Among the major political, economic, and intellectual causes of the French Revolution was the

T F 1. despotic rule of the Bourbon kings.
T F 2. intellectual and moral degeneration of the nobility.
T F 3. decline of the nation's international prestige.
T F 4. rise of the middle class.
T F 5. inequitable system of taxation.
T F 6. widespread influence of the theories of Locke and Rousseau.

In this form a question or incomplete statement is followed by several (three to five) answers or completions. Each of these completions is to be judged true or false. Thus all of them could be true, all of them false, or any number of them true or false. Such an item is rather difficult to construct and is best adapted to fields such as literature, social studies, or science. It is useful in measuring fairly complex understandings.

The true-false test is relatively easy to construct. Unfortunately, however, it is frequently constructed without sufficient planning and care, resulting in a low quality test. A common fault of teacher-made true-false tests is that the test items are ambiguous. A teacher should examine his tests as he scores them to determine whether pupils appear to understand the items. If a number of pupils write in qualifications and/or complain about some of the items, it is apparent that these items are ambiguous. Such items should be thrown out of the test and not counted in the final score. Teachers as they construct tests should always endeavor to ask questions which are clearly and concisely stated so that all pupils readily understand the questions. Then pupil responses will be based on their knowledge of the answers and will not depend upon their ability to interpret the meaning of the questions.

Since there are only two possible responses on the true-false test, the pupil who guesses has a fifty-fifty chance of selecting the correct response to each item. Actually his chances are greater than fifty-fifty on teacher-made tests since teachers tend to include from two-thirds to three-fourths true statements in a true-false test, and pupils likewise tend to guess true more frequently than false. Thus the pupil who guesses true on every item about which he is uncertain will very likely get from two-thirds to three-fourths of these items correct.

Because guessing is such a significant factor in pupils' scores on a true-false test, a scoring formula which compensates for guessing is frequently used. This formula is $score = rights = \dfrac{wrongs}{(N-1)}$. When pupils are informed in the directions to the test that they will be penalized for guessing, some are deterred from doing so. Actually use of the correction formula is of no value unless it deters pupils from guessing. If all pupils answer all the items on the test, application of the formula does not change pupils' ranks on the test; but pupils' scores give a somewhat invalid assessment of their achievement. It is only when pupils are influenced by use of the formula to leave blank those items which they do not know that a more valid measurement of pupils' actual knowledge results. With true-false items, because of the high guessing factor, use of the formula is more necessary than with multiple-choice items. With four- or five-choice multiple-choice items, guessing becomes a relatively insignificant factor in the pupil's score, since he has only one chance out of four or five to select the correct response.

The author has found that the fairness of using the guessing correction for true-false items can be demonstrated to pupils by the following method. The pupils are asked to write numbers one to ten on a sheet of paper and write either "true" or "false" after each number, as if they had just completed a ten-item true-false test. After the pupils have written the responses, ten true-false questions are then read to them along with the correct answers to these items so that they can score the answers which they had written before the test was administered. It is not unusual for some pupils to get as many as nine items correct, and many may have more than fifty percent of the items correct. Because teachers typically include more true than false items in their tests, and pupils tend to guess true more frequently than false, the pupils' scores can be improved by making the majority of the ten items true. This procedure dramatically demonstrates to them both the significance of the element of guessing and the unreliability of a short true-false test.

Alternate-response rules. The following rules should be observed in constructing true-false items:

First, *a pattern of response should be avoided in the test.* Teachers should not consistently overload their tests with either true or false items. This error can be avoided by consciously varying the pattern so that one test has a majority of false items, another a majority of true items, another approximately an equal number of true and false items, etc.

Second, *when true-false items are constructed, each item should be written on a single 3″ x 5″ card.* If the item is written on the card first as a true statement and then written below as a false statement, either the true or false form can be selected for use in the test. When items are written on cards, they can be classified and filed for future reference.

Third, *ambiguous language should be avoided.* A statement should indicate clearly and concisely what the instructor means so that the pupil's response is based on his knowledge of the answer rather than on his failure to understand the item. In the example below, the first item is ambiguous but becomes a straightforward, understandable statement when slightly reworded.

> FAULTY EXAMPLE: Dreams occur during light sleep and usually just prior to waking.
> IMPROVED EXAMPLE: Dreams are most apt to occur during light sleep just prior to waking.

Fourth, *specific determiners should be avoided.* A word such as "never" indicates that the item is false, while the word "sometimes" generally indicates that the item is true. With such statements pupils need only pick up the word cue to answer the item correctly even when they are uninformed.

> FAULTY EXAMPLE: The midday temperature in the temperate zones of the world is *never* hotter than that in the tropic zone.

Substituting "sometimes" for "never" would make the statement true, and the pupil could answer either version on the basis of the cue word.

Fifth, *verbatim quotes from the text should be avoided.* Selecting items from the text without altering their wording encourages the student to memorize rather than understand the meaning.

Sixth, *in referring to numbers exact quantitative language is better than qualitative language.* Such qualitative words as "few," "some," and "many" have indefinite meanings, while a definite quantitative term such as "five" has the same meaning to both the instructor and the pupils.

> FAULTY EXAMPLE: During World War II the Germans exterminated a great many Jewish people.

IMPROVED EXAMPLE: During World War II the Germans exterminated 6,000,000 Jewish people.

Seventh, *the negative statement should be avoided* unless the instructor intends to measure reading ability as well as the knowledge called for by the item. Inefficient readers do poorly on negative items.

FAULTY EXAMPLE: Antibiotics have no adverse effect on nonallergic people.
IMPROVED EXAMPLE: Antibiotics have an adverse effect on allergic people.

Actually the negatives in the statement do nothing more than confuse the reader. The simple positive statement in the improved item is easily understood and can be answered on the basis of the pupil's knowledge.

Eighth, *items dealing with controversial issues should not be used unless some authority is quoted* in the statement as a resource for pupils. Without such authority pupils are forced to agree or disagree with an opinion rather than with a statement of fact.

FAULTY EXAMPLE: The deficit-spending theory of John Maynard Keynes is the economic theory which should be followed in the United States.
IMPROVED EXAMPLE: Conservative Republicans believe that John Maynard Keynes's deficit-spending theory should be followed in U. S. spending.

Ninth, *items should be entirely true or basically false*. They should not be false as a result of some trivial detail or an unimportant phrase which is included in the statement.

FAULTY EXAMPLE: Two independent clauses connected by a conjunction should be punctuated with a comma, semicolon or colon placed before the conjunction.

This is a trick statement which becomes false when the one word "colon" is included, otherwise it would be a straightforward true statement.

3. *Multiple-choice form.* The most versatile of the objective test items is the multiple-choice form. It is useful for measuring complex understandings as well as the simple information which pupils possess. Although the multiple-choice test is difficult to construct well, it can be refined and made into a scaled measurement test with reliability and validity approaching that of standardized achievement tests.

The multiple-choice item consists of two parts: (1) the premise or problem; and (2) the choices, which include both the correct response and the distractors. The premise may be presented as an incomplete statement or as a question. Most inexperienced item writers find that they write better items when they use the question form. A desirable format for multiple-choice items is as follows:

_____1. Which measure of central tendency should be used to describe the typical man in the United States?

    a. Median   d. Mode
    b. Mean   e. Average
    c. 50th percentile

Although it takes less space to place the choices consecutively in line with the premise, listing the choices below the premise makes it easier for the pupil to read them.

The difficulty of multiple-choice items depends upon the homogeneity of the alternatives. As the choices become more homogeneous, the item becomes more difficult.

HETEROGENEOUS EXAMPLE	HOMOGENEOUS EXAMPLE
Select the word which means the same as "essential."	Select the best synonym for the word "essential."
a. absolute	a. inherent
b. indispensable	b. necessary
c. complete	c. indispensable
d. basic	d. requisite

Variations of the multiple-choice form include (1) items in which several choices are correct, (2) items in which all the choices are correct but the pupil must select the best answer, and (3) items in which only one choice is correct. Teachers use the one-correct-choice type most frequently. The other two forms are most difficult to construct, and pupils who are accustomed to selecting only one correct response dislike the multiple-correct item. Good students may be annoyed by the prospect of overlooking some of the correct responses, and poor students are frustrated by the prospect of guessing several times on each item.

Probably the most frequent error teachers make in writing a multiple-choice item is failure to include a complete problem in the premise statement.

EXAMPLE: The formula for water is

    a. NaCl   d. H_2O_2
    b. H_2O e. O_2
    c. H_2SO_4

In this example no problem or question is actually posed in the premise. Using the same choices, the item could be improved by asking the question: "What is the formula for water?" Teachers inexperienced in test construction should probably adhere almost exclusively to the question form for multiple-choice items, at least until they have gained enough facility to utilize the incomplete statement correctly.

Some of the rules which apply to the construction of alternate-response items are also pertinent for multiple-choice items. Those which apply are listed below:

1. Quote authority when dealing with controversial issues.
2. Avoid negatively stated items.
3. Avoid verbatim quotes from the text.
4. Avoid statements which are unnecessarily long and ambiguous.
5. Avoid the use of specific determiners which provide cues to the correct response.
6. Vary the pattern of response by changing the position of the correct choice.

In writing multiple-choice items, it is common practice to place the correct response in the first position then reassign the position of the correct response for each item in the test on the basis of a random table of numbers. In addition to the rules listed above there are several others which apply specifically to multiple-choice items:

First, *all choices in each item should be grammatically consistent.*

EXAMPLE: In cooking the best method of measuring one-half cup of shortening is to

    a. Melt the shortening before measuring it.
    b. Cool the shortening before measuring it.
    c. Press the shortening into the cup to eliminate airholes.
    d. Place the shortening in a cup one-half full of water.
    e. Use a one-half cup measure.

In the above item, although the choices differ slightly in structure, each begins with the infinitive form of the verb.

Second, *as many words of the item as possible should be included in the premise* so that they are not repeated in the choices.

FAULTY EXAMPLE: A common type of deciduous tree is

    a. the pine   d. the fir
    b. the spruce   e. the elm
    c. the hemlock

If the word "the" had been included in the premise above, it would not have had to be repeated five times in the choices. Teachers often commit this kind of error in constructing multiple-choice items.

Third, *a minimum of four choices should be included in each item.* Actually, five choices would be better; but on teacher-made tests it is often difficult to write a good fifth choice for many of the items. In this case four choices is a good compromise. When fewer than four choices are used, the item becomes little better than a true-false item, although considerably more difficult to construct.

Fourth, *the choices should be as brief as possible,* with the correct response neither significantly longer nor shorter than the other choices.

Fifth, *each item should contain an independent problem,* and it should not provide clues which help pupils answer other items in the test. In many cases several items on a multiple-choice test are so closely related that the pupil can answer some items on the basis of clues from previous items.

EXAMPLES:

    1. The Third Crusade took place during the period between

        a. 1096–1099
        b. 1147–1149
        c. 1189–1192
        d. 1211–1215
        e. 1232–1235

    2. Following Saladin's recapture of Jerusalem, the Third Crusade was led by

        a. Louis VII
        b. Conrad III
        c. Frederick Barbarossa
        d. Philip
        e. Richard

The answer to the first item is subtly cued by the second item because the astute student may remember that Saladin reconquered Jerusalem in 1187 and thus fix the time of the Third Crusade as 1189–1192.

4. *Matching form.* The matching test is best for measuring recognition or recall of information. Matching exercises consist of two sets of items to be matched on the basis indicated in the directions. The matching exercise is referred to as a matching set.

The bases on which items may be matched are almost unlimited—men and books, dates and events, rules and definitions, etc. This form is particularly valuable in subject fields in which a great variety of facts must be learned. It is relatively easy to construct, easy to score, highly reliable, and quite valid when restricted to the measurement of factual recall. Rules for the construction of matching sets include the following:

First, *all items within the set should be kept homogeneous.* In other words, all items within the set should refer to the same group or class—men, books, events, etc.

FAULTY EXAMPLE: From the right-hand column select the place-names which match each of the phrases on the left.

———Mountainous state	a. California
———Potato-growing state	b. New York
	c. Atlanta
———Heavily populated state	d. Baltimore
———Oil-producing state	e. Texas
	f. Colorado
———Seaport city	g. Idaho
———Manufacturing city	h. Kansas
	i. Washington

IMPROVED EXAMPLE: Each city on the left is the capital of one of the states on the right. Place the letter of the state on the line before its capital city.

———Denver	a. Wisconsin
———Sacramento	b. Minnesota
	c. Colorado
———Helena	d. Kansas
———Lincoln	e. California
	f. Montana
———Madison	g. Nebraska
	h. Ohio

In the faulty example both states and cities are included in the set, thus greatly improving the pupil's guessing chances.

Second, *more choices than items to be matched should be included in the matching set.* This prevents the pupils from crossing out their responses and getting the last item correct by a process of elimination. It is also acceptable practice to construct the set so that the choices may be used more than once, thus eliminating the guessing problem without including extra choices.

Third, *each matching set should include from five to fifteen matching items.*

Fourth, *the items in the set should be arranged so that the pupil can readily locate the answers* and so that they are convenient for the teacher to score. When dates are used, a chronological arrangement facilitates pupil response, and an alphabetical or logical arrangement is often appropriate with other types of responses.

Fifth, *all elements of the matching set should be included on one page.* When the matching set extends to a second page, pupils are required to leaf back and forth between the two pages to locate the correct response for many of the items.

Sixth, *in the scoring, one point should be allowed for each item in the set.*

EVALUATION OF OBJECTIVE TESTS

An advantage of objective tests is that they can be refined and the items reused. A well-constructed objective test in which the items have been carefully refined can become extremely reliable and valid. In fact if the test is constructed so that it is closely related to the teacher's objectives and instructional content, it is likely to be more valid for his purposes than the standardized achievement tests. This statement applies, however, only when the teacher has taken the time to make out a good test outline or table of specifications in which he has listed his important objectives and instructional topics and has then written items to measure those elements. In evaluating the quality of a test it is good practice to go back and compare the items against the original outline to determine content validity. It is also helpful to have one's colleagues read through the test to spot ambiguous items or unnecessarily difficult or awkward wording. Pupils who have taken the test may also have some useful suggestions concerning the ambiguity of some items. Pupils often write in comments after items which they have difficulty understanding. It is wise to consider discarding or revising those items on which numerous pupils wrote comments.

Item analysis. A most important step in the evaluation of objective tests is the item analysis. The item analysis gives a check on the internal validity of the test through a comparison of pupils' performance on each test item against their total test scores. Such an analysis consists of a determination of the percent of pupils in the high test group and the percent in the low group who answered each item correctly. Thus, it provides information on the difficulty level of each item and on the ability of each item to discriminate between good and poor pupils. Items on which a higher percent of good pupils than poor pupils answer correctly show positive discrimination. Negative discrimination occurs when the poor pupils answer an item correctly more often than the good pupils. Items which show negative discrimination are normally discarded.

Because item analysis requires considerable time, it should not be done for tests that are carelessly prepared or for tests which appear to be too easy, too difficult, or weak in discrimination. Also, for best results there should be at least 100 test papers from which to select the item analysis papers. The following simple procedure gives adequate evidence for determining quality and difficulty of items:

1. Select the top 20 to 30 percent and the bottom 20 to 30 percent of the papers.
2. Work with one group at a time, and arrange the papers on a large table so that they overlap with only the response column of each paper visible.
3. Count the number of correct responses on each item, convert to percents, and enter on the record sheet. For example, if 16 out of 20 pupils answered correctly, 80 percent should be entered on the record sheet for that item.
4. After the correct responses on all items have been counted for both high and low groups, the power of the item can be determined from the percent in both groups who responded correctly. Thus, when 28 of the 40 pupils have answered an item correctly, the ease index is 70 percent ($28 \div 40 = 70 \%$). Or to put it another way, the difficulty level is 30 percent since 30 percent failed the item.
5. Calculate item discrimination with the following formula:

$$D = \frac{U - L}{N}$$

$U =$ number of pupils in upper group answering item correctly
$L =$ number of pupils in lower group answering item correctly
$N =$ number of pupils in each group
The discrimination index ranges from $+ 1.00$ to $- 1.00$, but only items which show positive indices should be retained. A discrimination index above $+ 0.40$ is desirable.

Actually the fifth step need not be done for all items since it is generally easy from the record sheet to quickly identify a number of items which will be discarded without further calculation. However, for those items which seem to be promising, this is an important calculation. Items to be discarded include those which are answered correctly by all pupils and those showing negative discrimination. A few of the very easy items may be retained for future use to be placed at the beginning of a test as a means of establishing a desirable test psychology for pupils who fear objective tests.

The item analysis for multiple-choice tests should include a record of the number of pupils selecting each item choice. This permits the teacher to judge the plausibility of the distractors. Items showing good discrimination but having one or more weak distractors can be salvaged for future use by rewriting the weak distractors.

After the item analysis is completed, the statistical information for each item should be recorded on the card on which the item was written; then the item can be filed for future use.

ESSAY EXAMINATIONS

Essay examinations have some unique advantages not possessed by other test forms. Teachers today often overlook the value of this venerable test form and use only objective measurement. Overuse of any one test form is rarely justified. Teaching objectives in most fields are too diverse to permit such sketchy measurement.

It is, of course, these objectives which dictate the choice of examination form. The essay examination is best adapted for measuring the ability of pupils to express themselves verbally, their ability to organize information, the scope and depth of their knowledge, the range of their imagination, and the extent of creativity. These types of learning are important and are difficult to measure with objective tests.

The essay examination also promotes a desirable type of study; since pupils preparing for this type of examination are inclined to outline the material, to draw cause and effect relationships, and to summarize the material. In contrast, pupils preparing for objective examinations tend to focus on specific points or details which might be asked as objective test items.

Three major disadvantages of the essay examination are (1) the difficulty of grading the examination and the consequent unreliability of the grade, (2) the limited sample of pupil learning which the examination permits, and (3) the marked advantage which it gives verbally inclined pupils.

Types of essay examinations. Essay questions can be classified in two categories: *restricted response,* or short-answer, and *extended response.* The restricted response includes questions which require pupils to outline, list, or define. Extended response includes questions which require discussion, evaluation, classification, or comparison.[3] Restricted response questions can be graded reliably. A number of such questions can be included on one test since pupils will spend but a few minutes answering each question. An essay examination, however, probably fails to achieve the major advantage which it potentially possesses if it is confined to restricted response items. The extended response items encourage a free range of expression, permitting pupils to express many facets of their experience and knowledge which the teacher would otherwise fail to perceive.

Teachers should be careful not to use too many extended response items on a single essay examination. This practice forces pupils to give cursory, poorly planned answers to questions which require treatment in depth. Teachers can get a more accurate estimate of the amount of time required to complete the examination if they themselves write complete answers to the questions which they have prepared.

Improving essay examinations. Several suggestions for improving the essay examination have already been implied in the foregoing discussion —specifically, the following: (1) The measurement sample can be broadened by increasing the number of items in each examination to include both restricted and extended response questions. (2) The reliability of grading can be improved if the teacher outlines the answers as he constructs the questions. If a definite number of points is to be assigned to each question, the points can then be equitably divided among the major topics included in the answers. (3) Pupils should be given practice in taking essay examinations in a nonpressure situation so that they learn to write well-organized essay examinations. This practice is particularly helpful to pupils in middle- and upper-elementary grades who have had little or no experience with such examinations. These practice examinations should have little grade weight; and at the beginning of the examination period, pupils should be given from ten to fifteen minutes to outline their answers, after which they are permitted to write the complete responses.

[3] For further discussion of the various types of essay questions see John A. Green, *Teacher-Made Tests* (New York: Harper & Row, 1963), pp. 63–66.

Essay examination grading can be improved by following one of two systematic procedures: (1) the rating or point-score method and (2) the sorting method. With the point-score method a specific number of points is assigned to each question, and the procedure outlined below is followed:

1. Read through the first question on all the papers and assign each paper a proportion of the total points which the quality of the answer justifies.
2. Repeat the process in step one for each subsequent question in the examination.
3. Total up the points for each pupil's examination paper.
4. The examination grade can then be assigned on one of several conventional bases: norms, percentages, curves.

The sorting method is probably a little easier to use and is about as reliable as the point-score method. The steps in this method are:

1. Read rapidly through all of the papers, sorting them into a predetermined number of letter-grade piles. For example, when a teacher wishes to give letter grades ranging from *A* to *F*, she will sort the papers as they are read into five piles (*A, B, C, D,* and *F*).
2. Identify with a question mark the papers which do not fall readily into any one pile; then place them in the pile which seems most appropriate. Reread for final sorting all papers which have been so identified.
3. Assign letter grades on the basis of the piles into which the papers have been sorted.

In grading essay examinations it is important that the teacher avoid being influenced by the "halo effect." Students who have performed well in previous class work are expected to do well on examinations and thus they may be graded higher than they deserve. If the teacher reads the papers without looking at pupils' names, he may avoid this problem. The legibility of pupils' handwriting is another factor which tends to bias essay grades. Although poor handwriting is distracting to the reader, it should not be permitted to adversely influence the examination grade.

An interesting recent development is the experimentation by the Educational Testing Service with grading essays by computer. Preliminary investigation of this method of grading indicates that it promises to give results at least as reliable as those of human judges.[4] Unfortunately the

[4] For a good preliminary review of "Project Essay Grade," see Ellis B. Page, "The Imminence of Grading Essays by Computer," *Phi Delta Kappan,* LXVIII (January 1966), 238–243.

reliability of teacher grades for essays is only about .43; [5] however the reliability of marking improves when the average of several teachers' judgments is used. The computer experiment is programmed to evaluate both the style and content of the essay and envisions the possibility of a computer print-out commentary as feedback to the student. Although it is unlikely that the teacher would be entirely replaced by the machine in performing this task, it is feasible that machine grading might in the future assume a good share of the burden, thus making it easier for teachers to use more essay examinations without unduly infringing on the instructional planning time.

ORAL EXAMINATIONS

The oral examination shares some of the advantages of the essay examination, and it merits more frequent use in the classroom. As a forerunner of written examinations, oral examinations were first supplemented by and then gradually replaced by written examinations during the latter half of the nineteenth century. The misuse and abuse which have virtually discredited this examination form are clearly evident in the situation in which the teacher successively questions each class member, asking one question of each and recording success or failure in the gradebook as he responds. Under such circumstances group pressure may prevent the pupil from performing well; furthermore the single question asked each pupil elicits too limited a sampling of his information to give reliable evidence of achievement.

The oral examination properly used as part of the planned program of measurement can be a valuable measuring technique. It permits an extended pupil response characteristic of the essay examination while lacking the essay disadvantage of difficult grading.

Types of oral examinations. Oral examinations can be roughly classified into three categories: (1) the oral performance examination, (2) the orally-administered, written-response type, and (3) the orally-administered, oral-response type. The oral performance examination is adapted to such subject areas as dramatics, public speaking, and foreign language. In these areas the quality of oral response is an essential learning outcome and must be measured. Dramatics and public speaking perform-

[5] Julian C. Stanley, *Measurement in Today's Schools,* 4th ed. (New York: Prentice Hall, 1964), p. 259, reports an average reliability of .43 on sets of examinations marked by the same teacher.

ances can be evaluated by an observation checklist or rating scale in which the desired elements of a good performance are checked or rated on a point-scale basis. The rating scale gives a numerical score which can be handled in the same manner as regular examination test scores.

The orally-administered, written-response question includes objective or short-answer examinations which are orally administered. The major purpose of such examinations is to check the auditory comprehension of pupils. When the examination is administered orally, questions should be enunciated clearly and read slowly; however no questions should be repeated. Thus the pupil is forced to concentrate in order to comprehend the questions. The true-false examination is most appropriate for oral administration. Multiple-choice items, with four to five choices, may be too complicated for pupils to comprehend in one oral reading.

A second type of orally-administered, written-response examination is that in which a series of 20–30 restricted response questions are asked, with each pupil answering one question orally. Before the examination is begun, pupils are asked to write on a blank sheet of paper the numbers from one to 20 (or 30); then as the questions are asked, they write "yes" or "no" following the appropriate question number to indicate whether they know the answer to the question. When all questions have been completed, the class results can be summarized on the chalkboard by a show-of-hands poll to determine pupils' scores. The resulting tabulated distribution of scores gives the teacher evidence of the range and level of class performance and at the same time shows the pupils their relative standing in class. When little grade weight is given the examination, pupils will generally report their scores honestly. Such an examination is valuable in summarizing and reviewing the content of a unit which has just been completed.

The orally-administered, oral-response examination can occasionally be substituted for an essay examination since the total time required for administering and grading the examination is approximately the same as that required for administering and grading the essay examination. With this type of examination, a series of essay-type questions are administered to each pupil in a one-to-one situation. Approximately five to ten minutes will be required to administer this examination to each pupil. As the examination is administered, the pupil who is taking it is segregated from the group so that the other pupils hear neither the questions nor the responses. The overall quality of a pupil's responses on this type of examination can be graded either on the basis of the number of correct responses or on the basis of a three-point quality scale such as that suggested below:

EXAMPLE: $\overset{-}{\sqrt{}}$ $\sqrt{}$ $\overset{+}{\sqrt{}}$

Below average   average   above average

Teachers should not overuse the oral examination, but some experience with the different types of this examination is valuable.

SUMMARY

The improvement and increasing use of standardized achievement batteries have relegated teacher-made tests to a backstage position in the school measurement program. With administrative attention and public concern focused on the achievement test results, teachers have frequently approached the task of constructing their own classroom tests reluctantly and unsystematically. Often, too, teachers have not developed the minimum skills necessary to utilize effectively the excellent variety of test forms available for measuring pupil achievement. When teacher-made tests are well planned and skillfully constructed, they give higher content validity than standardized instruments, which will at best only approximate the teacher's instructional emphases and coverage.

Measurement is an intrinsic part of the instructional process. The teacher who constructs poor tests or who tests subject matter other than that emphasized in the instruction is negligent in fulfilling his total responsibility and may be unaware of the relative achievement of his pupils. Measurement should be planned around the instructional objectives and main content topics. In fact, when these two elements of instruction form the test outline or test table of specifications, identity of measurement is virtually assured.

Selection of the appropriate test form is determined by the type of objectives which are to be measured. The objective test forms are useful for measuring knowledge and understanding, while the extended response essay examination gives a measure of pupils' ability to express themselves and to select and organize pertinent information in solving problems. In most classrooms the instructional objectives are so varied that it is unwise to rely upon one type of test form for measuring pupil achievement. Use of objective, oral, and essay examinations is necessary in most instances if the teacher wishes a comprehensive picture of pupil achievement.

DISCUSSION QUESTIONS AND PROBLEMS

1. Discuss the relative merits and limitations of the various test forms considered in this chapter.
2. Using *Bloom's Taxonomy of Educational Objectives: Cognitive Domain,* make a statement of educational objectives for your major field, classifying the objectives under Bloom's major categories.
3. Select the test form which is most appropriate for each category of objectives which you have stated above.
4. Formulate a measurement plan which you would recommend for use in a year-long field of study at the elementary or secondary level.
5. Make up the table of specifications for a multiple-choice unit or a semester examination for a course in your major field—e.g., American history, English literature, general science, etc.
6. Construct a multiple-choice examination using the table of specifications above as your guide.

SELECTED READINGS

Bean, Kenneth L. *Construction of Educational and Personnel Tests.* New York: McGraw-Hill Book Company, 1953. Chapter 2 is particularly pertinent.

Bloom, Benjamin S. (ed.). *Taxonomy of Educational Objectives, Handbook I: Cognitive Domain.* New York: David McKay Company, 1956. Part I of this book contains many helpful suggestions for formulating and classifying objectives in such a way that they are both teachable and measurable.

Furst, Edward J. *Constructing Evaluation Instruments.* New York: Longmans, Green and Company, 1958. Part I contains an excellent discussion of such basic problems of testing as determining what to evaluate and selecting appropriate test situations. In addition Chapter 7 deals specifically with planning the test.

Gerberich, J. Raymond. *Specimen Objective Test Items.* New York: Longmans, Green and Company, 1956. Part I contains a good short discussion of the construction of objective tests. Although the discussion is directed specifically to construction of objective tests, it also has some relevance to other test forms.

Green, John A. *Teacher-Made Tests.* New York: Harper & Row, 1963. Chapter 2 considers the planning of measurement instruments; and Chapters 3, 4, 5, and 6 are directed to the construction of the various test forms. Included in the discussion are illustrative test items to aid the test maker.

Krathwohl, David R., Benjamin S. Bloom, and Bertram B. Masia. *Taxonomy of Educational Objectives, Handbook II: Affective Domain.* New York:

David McKay Company, 1964. A discussion of an area of measurement often overlooked by teachers. The examples of instructional objectives and test items should be particularly useful in helping teachers construct items to measure such areas as interests, attitudes, and values.

Lindquist, E. F. (ed.). *Educational Measurement.* Washington, D. C.: American Council on Education, 1951. Part II deals with the construction of achievement tests. For those interested in item analysis, Chapter 9 is an excellent source.

Lindvall, C. M. *Measuring Pupil Achievement and Aptitude.* New York: Harcourt, Brace & World, 1967. Chapters 2, 3, and 4 consider planning and constructing various types of tests, as well as the selection of the appropriate type of test for various educational outcomes.

Magnusson, David. *Test Theory.* Reading, Massachusetts: Addison-Wesley Publishing Company, 1966. Item analysis is considered in Chapter 14. Of particular interest are pp. 207–214.

Remmers, H. H., N. L. Gage, and J. Francis Rummel. *A Practical Introduction to Measurement and Evaluation.* New York: Harper & Row, 1965. Chapter 8 gives a valuable overview of test construction. The chapter also includes many good examples of test items to illustrate the various rules of test construction.

Stanley, Julian C. *Measurement in Today's Schools.* 4th ed. New York: Prentice-Hall, 1964. Chapter 6 contains a good general discussion of the principles of test construction. Chapters 7 and 8 contain rules and examples to be followed in constructing objective and essay tests.

Travers, Robert M. W. *How to Make Achievement Tests.* New York: The Odyssey Press, 1950. This is a good reference for those who are primarily interested in the objective test forms.

Wood, Dorothy Adkins. *Test Construction.* Columbus, Ohio: Charles E. Merrill Books, 1960. A concise, practical manual for the test maker. It contains both rules for construction and concrete examples for the various test forms.

MEASURING LEARNING OUTCOMES— KNOWLEDGE AND UNDERSTANDING

INTRODUCTION

The educated person is an informed person; that is, he possesses knowledge and information not possessed by the uneducated. Furthermore, the highly educated person comprehends or understands the knowledge or information which he possesses. In these two terms—"informed" and "comprehends"—lies the blueprint for much of the teaching and measurement in schools. Both can be taught readily and measured effectively, yet the possession of knowledge does not guarantee the more important understanding; and instruction and measurement which stop at the first level—the level of recall—fail to achieve significant aims. Even the dull pupil can memorize and acquire knowledge, but understanding requires intelligence.

Knowledge is a tool for solving problems, it is rarely an end in itself. During men's historical development knowledge has been cumulative, a commodity which has been added to by each generation and which can be recorded, taught, and passed on from one generation to the next. Thus in a real sense the fund of knowledge has become a resource or wealth which the scholars of each generation use and add to. It is a resource which is not depleted by use but one which grows as those who use it add to the fund.

Preserving and passing on the fund of knowledge are an important aim of teaching. There was a time in the not too distant past when it was possible for one man to learn virtually all there was to know. Discovery, however, feeds on discovery, and the new knowledge has opened doors of inquiry heretofore unfathomed; so that for modern man yesterday's fantasy often becomes today's fact. This unprecedented expansion of knowledge has posed for schools the difficult task of selecting the most important areas to be included in the curriculum.

For pupils, knowledge serves the important function of opening up new vistas of understanding. In most fields, unless the learner possesses prerequisite knowledge, understanding of the concepts is limited. Understanding, in contrast to knowledge, depends upon individuals. Whereas knowledge can exist in a vacuum or be stored in computers, microfilm, tapes, or books, understanding can be stored or accumulated only in the minds of currently living men. As we have seen in modern society, it is quite possible for groups of uneducated people to live immersed in this prodigious fund of knowledge but be so enfettered by the intangible bonds of ignorance that the knowledge lies unused by them. Nations side by side geographically are often generations apart in understanding and ability to use knowledge. In a lesser sense what is true of the world is also true within the classroom; for two children sitting side by side, although exposed to the same knowledge, often have startlingly different levels of understanding. Even though both may be able to memorize the facts, one may use them understandingly; while the other, who lacks understanding, may consider them useless trivia. To reiterate, then, knowledge is necessary to understanding, but the possession of knowledge does not guarantee understanding; nor has it significant value to an individual unless he can use it.

TESTING KNOWLEDGE

Knowledge objectives are stated in terms of teaching pupils *to know*. In measuring the effectiveness of that teaching, the answers to two specific questions are sought: (1) what does the pupil know? and (2) how well does he know what has been taught? The answer to the first question requires an extensive inventory of the pupil's knowledge, and the manner in which that inventory is taken provides the basis for answering the second question. The knowledge which pupils possess is measurable on at least two levels: (a) the level of recognition, which is a level of tenuous retention, and (b) the level of recall, which is one of more stable retention. For example, the pupil who has an uncertain grasp of information may be able to recall or recognize from among a list of alternative answers the correct answer to a question, but only the pupil who retains or remembers the information can supply the answer without the aid of the list of choices. It follows, then, that the multiple-choice and matching-type test items measure only recognition; and the teacher is unable to determine from these tests whether the pupil who performs well on them has really learned the material well enough to go one step further and recall the information without being cued.

Pupil recall can, however, be measured by the supply-type or completion item, in which he must supply from memory the correct response. The difference in level of response required is illustrated in the examples below.

EXAMPLE A: Multiple-choice type item
_____ During what year did the Civil War begin?

a. 1841   d. 1871
b. 1851   e. 1881
c. 1861

EXAMPLE B: Supply-type item
_____ During what year did World War I begin?

The pupil who answers example A correctly may also have been able to recall the date correctly without the list to cue him, but the teacher cannot determine whether he answered on the basis of recognition or on the basis of recall. On the other hand, when the pupil answers example B correctly, the teacher knows assuredly that his basis for answering is recall. However, the teacher cannot then conclude that the information will be permanently recalled, and only by repeated measurement of the same information will he be able to draw any valid conclusion concerning the stability of recall.

Although the above examples point up the weakness of the multiple-choice item in measuring knowledge recall, it must be noted parenthetically that multiple-choice items can be designed to function well in measuring understanding. The multiple-choice test is discussed in the context of measuring understanding in the latter part of this chapter.

Kinds of knowledge. In the various subject areas there are numerous kinds of knowledge which should be taught and measured. The first step in teaching and measuring these knowledges is the statement of instructional objectives which are adaptable to instruction and measurement. It is in this first step that teachers often fail—either by failing to state the objectives or by stating the objectives in general terms that have little specific relation to actual classroom instruction. Fortunately, this need not be the case, since *Bloom's Taxonomy of Educational Objectives* is an invaluable resource which breaks down and classifies objectives in categories which relate specifically to the teaching-measurement program. For the knowledge category the following outline gives the suggested classifications for educational objectives:

1.00 Knowledge
    1.10 Knowledge of Specifics
    1.11 Knowledge of Terminology
    1.12 Knowledge of Specific Facts
    1.20 Knowledge of Ways and Means of Dealing with Specifics
        1.21 Knowledge of Conventions
        1.22 Knowledge of Trends and Sequences
        1.23 Knowledge of Classification and Categories
        1.24 Knowledge of Criteria
        1.25 Knowledge of Methodology
    1.30 Knowledge of the Universals and Abstractions in a Field
        1.31 Knowledge of Principles and Generalizations
        1.32 Knowledge of Theories and Structures [1]

In addition to the classification, the *Taxonomy* includes extensive explanation of each type of knowledge, examples of appropriate objectives, and sample test items for measurement. For example the condensed form of the *Taxonomy* gives the following explanation and examples of objectives for 1.21, *Knowledge of Conventions*.

> Knowledge of characteristic ways of treating and presenting ideas and phenomena. For purposes of communication and consistency, workers in a field employ usages, styles, practices, and forms which best suit their purposes and/or which appear to suit best the phenomena with which they deal. It should be recognized that although these forms and conventions are likely to be set up on arbitrary, accidental, or authoritative bases, they are retained because of the general agreement or concurrence of individuals concerned with the subject, phenomena, or problem.
>
> Familiarity with the forms and conventions of the major types of works; e.g., verse, plays, scientific papers, etc.
>
> To make pupils conscious of correct form and usage in speech and writing.[2]

Standardized tests. In preliminary discussion the concern has been with an analysis of measuring the levels of knowledge retention. While the test form is dictated by the level of measurement desired, the teacher has a choice between teacher-made tests and/or standardized

---

[1] Benjamin S. Bloom (ed.), *Taxonomy of Educational Objectives: The Classification of Educational Objectives, Handbook I: Cognitive Domain* (New York: David McKay Company, 1956), pp. 201–204.
[2] Bloom, p. 202.

achievement tests. Both have unique characteristics and advantages which call for specific consideration.

A test is properly a standardized achievement test only when it is characterized by (1) standardized content, (2) standardized administration, and (3) standardized norms. The content which such a test is designed to measure is most likely to be identified through a careful analysis of current published textbooks and school-system course of studies in the field.

To take a typical example, the *Metropolitan Achievement Test of Word Knowledge* for grades five and six is based on an analysis of the word content of thirteen reading series commonly used in those grades, and thus represents the common reading vocabulary required of pupils in those grades. From this analysis, the topics most frequently included in the texts and courses of study were selected as content to be measured. The test outline and test were then written to sample the content extensively enough to insure high content validity.

These test outlines or tables of specifications include both content and objectives and are similar in format to the example suggested for teacher-made tests in Chapter 9. In addition, however, the objectives are generally broken down into numerous specifics related to various items in the tests. For example, the *SRA Achievement Series Analysis of the Reading Skills Tests* list twenty-one specific abilities such as "ability to skim material rapidly to obtain the overall meaning of a selection"[3] on which measurement focuses.

The norms which are established for the test reflect the performance of the group of pupils selected as the standardization sample. In selecting the pupils an attempt is made to get a sample which truly reflects the salient characteristics of the total pupil population enrolled in that grade level or subject. The norms reported as age norms, grade norms, percentile norms, or standard scores then reflect the combined or average performance of pupils from good schools, poor schools, and typical schools. Thus in using the standardized test to measure achievement, the teacher must be aware of two problems: (1) the content measured may differ from that covered in his course; (2) the norms are not set up specifically for his class, and the performance of his class must be evaluated in terms of the local context.

---

[3] Louis P. Thorpe, *et al.*, *SRA Achievement Series, Manual for the School Administrator* (Chicago: Science Research Associates, 1956), p. 10.

Norms are rarely desirable goals. It would certainly be inappropriate for a teacher in a wealthy suburban school district with a sixth-grade class whose average IQ was 115 to aim to attain only the average sixth-grade norm on a standardized test. Higher achievement should be expected from this group unless the course content is markedly different from that covered in the test (low content validity) or unless the teaching is poor. The norms on the test do, however, provide an achievement scale against which the class and individual pupils within the class can be compared. A further use of the standardized test is that of measuring annual achievement gains of pupils. When the same test series is used in the school annually over a period of years, learning profiles can be charted for each pupil to help teachers evaluate pupil growth.

As an aid to teaching, standardized tests may also be used in an annual test-retest arrangement wherein a test is administered during the first month of school to determine the achievement status of the pupils and an alternate form of the same test is readministered in the late spring to ascertain the gain during the school year. This procedure provides teachers with a good basis of information for planning and evaluating the year's instruction, provided that they do not become so concerned about their pupils' doing well on the test that the program of instruction is essentially dictated by the test content.

When teachers begin to teach specifically for a given test or test program an invidious kind of curriculum control results. There is some evidence that this type of control has begun to have an impact on secondary schools as a result of the national merit scholarship examinations and the public esteem which the "merit schools" have received. When the test-retest procedure is used, any inclination of administrators to use the test results as a basis for comparative evaluation of teachers will also undoubtedly influence teachers to teach for the test. Such an administrative use of the test is poor practice and eventually defeats the main purpose of the testing program—that of improving instruction.

The teacher must keep in mind the fact that standardized achievement batteries vary greatly in coverage and emphases. For example, some, such as the *SRA Achievement* series, place a heavy emphasis upon the skills in each field. Some, such as the *Metropolitan Achievement Tests*, give about equal coverage to skills, concepts, and knowledges; and others, such as the *Essential High School Content Battery*, emphasize knowledge rather heavily. Furthermore, the teacher should be aware of the fact that many of the achievement batteries include specific tests designed to measure knowledge. Thus, the choice of test battery or specific test within a battery should be made by teachers only after they have determined by careful examination the coverage and emphasis of those available.

Several fields—particularly science, mathematics, and social sciences —require a great scope of factual knowledge which is prerequisite or concomitant to the required understandings and skills. In such instances the standardized test usually gives a considerably better survey of knowledge than the teacher-made test. Instruments such as Test 8—Social Studies Information—from the intermediate-level *Metropolitan Battery* focuses on knowledge in geography, history, and civics and could be given individually or as part of the battery. This test consists of four-choice multiple-choice items such as the following:

EXAMPLE: America's greatest inventor in the field of electricity was

a. Robert Fulton   c. Alexander Bell
b. Thomas Edison   d. Cyrus McCormick

The test provides a fairly adequate survey of intermediate-grade pupils' knowledge in social studies. Supplementary measurement with teacher-made tests could be used in addition to provide additional coverage or as a recheck of weak areas after further instruction.

In arithmetic a test such as the Arithmetic Concepts Test (Test 7) of the intermediate-level *Stanford Achievement Battery*, there are measures of both knowledge and understanding with items such as the following:

EXAMPLES:
Which has a 5 in the hundred's place?_____

a. 4615   c. 3526
b. 2154   d. 5842

Bob has more money than both Bill and Joe together. Bill has 20¢ and Joe has 15¢. Bob may have_____.

e. 50¢   g. 30¢
f. 17¢   h. 12¢

An example of a portion of a standardized test designed to measure knowledge retention taken from the *Essential High School Content Battery* is shown in Figure 10.1. In this more advanced test, items have five choices.

PART A. SCIENCE INFORMATION

Section I

1. Organisms take in oxygen and give off carbon dioxide by the process of —

    a. expiration.
    b. digestion.
    c. inspiration.
    d. respiration.
    e. inhalation.

2. Which of the following terms indicates the relative amount of water vapor in the air?

    f. condensation ratio
    g. evaporation
    h. humidity
    i. precipitation
    j. saturation

3. The science which deals with the action of different forms of energy and matter is called —

    a. archaeology.
    b. geology.
    c. paleontology.
    d. physics.
    e. biology.

4. The process by which a single organism becomes better suited to its environment is called —

    f. maturation.
    g. circulation.
    h. adaptation.
    i. osmosis.
    j. conformity.

5. The resistance offered by a body to a change of its state of rest or motion is known as —

    a. energy.
    b. momentum.
    c. velocity.
    d. acceleration.
    e. inertia.

Figure 10.1. EXAMPLES OF ITEMS USED TO MEASURE SCIENCE INFORMATION IN THE ESSENTIAL HIGH SCHOOL CONTENT BATTERY

From David P. Harry and Walter Durost, *Essential High School Content Battery* (New York: Harcourt, Brace & World, 1952). Reprinted by permission of the publisher.

Teacher-made tests. Teacher-made tests which are carefully planned and skillfully constructed can have higher content validity for measuring knowledge retention than standardized tests, even though they lack the advantage of comparability against a national norm. Obviously the teacher cannot afford to rely wholly on standardized tests for measurement in this area; but when he constructs his test ineptly, selects the areas to be measured haphazardly, and writes the items poorly, his tests provide little in the way of useful additional information. Measurement is a hoax when the teacher and pupils match wits—the teacher by devising a series of difficult puzzles to fool pupils, and the pupils by attempting to second-guess the teacher. Writing a specific outline for each test and selecting a test form appropriate to the objectives to be measured help solve this problem. When the objective is recognition of information, the appropriate forms are multiple-choice, matching, and identification. Recall of information is best measured by completion and short-answer forms, such as definition, outlining, or listing. Other suggestions for improving classroom testing include:

First, *construct the tests in such a manner that guessing is minimized.* This requires that the teacher avoid the common error in multiple-choice items of establishing a pattern of response for answers and of including nonplausible choices which encourage guessing. Using the correction formula $(score = rights = \frac{wrongs}{(N-1)})$ discourages guessing on multiple-choice tests; and the use of well-constructed completion items virtually eliminates successful guessing. (See p. 201 in the preceding chapter for a fuller discussion on minimizing guessing in tests.)

Second, *tests should be administered frequently to insure continuous evaluation of pupil achievement.* Once or twice a semester measurement gives insufficient evidence of achievement. Both teachers and pupils need more frequent assessment—teachers as a basis for planning further instruction and pupils as motivation for studying specific areas of weakness. Furthermore, pupils perform better on tests when they are accustomed to taking them as a normal part of the instructional routine. When tests are rare, psychological pressure may inhibit normal pupil performance.

Third, *pupils should be notified ahead of time of scheduled tests.* This notification encourages pupils to study and reorganize their learning, thus achieving some direct instructional benefit from the test.

Fourth, *as a rule tests should be scored and returned to the pupils as soon as possible*. Tests which are returned should also be discussed, and pupils should be allowed sufficient opportunity to ask questions concerning the test items. Thus further learning can be assured by the test experience.

Use of test forms. Since the construction of various test forms has already been specifically considered in Chapter 8, the discussion in this section is confined to the use of the various forms.

The *objective forms*—multiple-choice, matching, and completion—are appropriate for elementary as well as secondary school children. Multiple-choice and matching, which require only recognition of the correct response, can be handled most readily by lower elementary grade children. When these objective forms are used in the elementary school, it is particularly important that the directions to pupils be clearly stated and that the items be concise and to the point. For these pupils the completion and multiple-choice items should be written as questions. Pupils understand the question more readily than the incomplete statement. "When," "what," or "who" questions elicit knowledge-retention responses and are readily understood.

EXAMPLE:
Completion: In what year was Jamestown founded?_____
Multiple-choice: In what year was Jamestown founded?_____

a. 1609   d. 1639
b. 1619   e. 1949
c. 1629

A statement such as "Jamestown was founded in the year ———" is less likely than the questions above to be answered correctly by elementary school children.

Completion, multiple-choice, and matching tests are useful for measuring pupils' information in a variety of elementary and secondary fields. In science and history pupils are required to learn much specific background information; in such cases frequent testing with one or more of these forms is desirable.

The *short-answer question,* which requires the pupil to list, define, or outline can also be used to measure recall. The following are examples of such items.

EXAMPLE: List the three branches of the United States government.

1._____

2._____

3._____

EXAMPLE: Define a pronoun.

_____

_____

EXAMPLES:

1. Outline the steps which should be followed in making a devil's food cake.
2. Outline the procedure by which a bill becomes law in the United States Congress.

The outline item can give a measure of both knowledge and understanding of important concepts.

The *identification item*, which requires the pupil to identify and explain, gives the same dual measurement that the outline item does.

EXAMPLE: Identify the numbered parts of the flower in the drawing below and explain the reproductive function of each part.

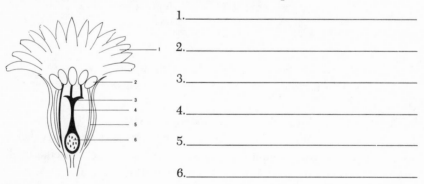

1._____

2._____

3._____

4._____

5._____

6._____

Map identification items can be used for measuring retention when pupils are being taught such information as place location, physical features of world areas, and climate characteristics of regions.

Table XV. TYPICAL INSTRUCTIONAL OBJECTIVES AND SAMPLE ITEMS
FOR MEASURING THEM

Objectives	*Sample Measurement Items*
1. Pupils should know the rules of punctuation.	1. State the punctuation rule which applies to introductory adverbial clauses.
2. Pupils should be able to recognize the difference between nouns and pronouns.	2. Draw two lines under the pronouns and one line under the nouns in the following sentence: You and your friends are invited to write the editor for our list of publications.
3. Pupils should know the characistics of a democratic form of government.	3. In a democratic form of government responsibility for administering the laws is delegated to the a. people b. courts c. legislators d. police e. executives
4. Pupils should know the important leaders of the American Revolutionary period.	4. Who wrote the Declaration of Independence?

In the foregoing discussion the use of several test forms was related to subject matter. However, since the objectives dictate the specific form which is used, an example of instructional objectives and related test items is shown in Table XV. These objectives are brief and specific, so that the relationship between objectives and items is evident. When objectives are stated in general terms, they are difficult to teach and to measure. All the objectives in Table XV require knowledge recall, and only the second objective calls for pupil "know-how." Although it is possible to measure know-how or procedure objectives with written items, performance tests, which require pupils to follow acceptable procedure in the laboratory, shop, etc., generally provide better measurement.

TESTING UNDERSTANDING

In most instances certain minimum background is prerequisite to understanding, but understanding is a higher level of learning than simple acquisition of knowledge Many pupils who *know* certain facts lack the insight to *know why* the factors are true or lack the understanding to *know how* they may be used to solve everyday problems. Certainly, too, there are numerous levels of understanding or insight. For example, pupils may learn multiplication as a rote process, in which case they *know how* to multiply by the first, second, and third digit and how to obtain the cumulative result; but few of them understand or *know why* the procedure is followed.

Understanding can be measured indirectly by measuring applications, since there is some logic in assuming that the person who uses abstractions—ideas, principles, etc.—in concrete situations has a good grasp of their meaning. Such measurement, however, is often difficult; and direct measurement of understanding is easier and more often the approach used in the classroom—even though we are aware of the failure of many who possess knowledge and abstract understanding to make the transfer from abstractions to use in concrete situations. The ensuing discussion is confined primarily to the measurement of abstract understanding. The discussion of application and performance is contained in Chapter 12.

Standardized tests. Because of the intimate tie between knowledge and understanding, conventional standardized and teacher-made achievement tests focus on both. However, the teacher-made tests frequently focus too heavily on the measurement of knowledge retention and only slightly on understanding of important concepts. The standardized achievement tests generally give good coverage of knowledge, understanding, and skills in specific subject areas; although there is variation among the different test batteries in the number and scope of subject areas covered.

A brief comparative analysis of subject areas covered by three good achievement batteries is shown in Table XVI. Only in arithmetic, reading, and spelling do these three test batteries cover the same subject areas. Since test content obviously differs in coverage, just as do the numerous textbooks in each subject, the teacher must select the standardized test which most nearly approximates the areas of instruction which have been emphasized in class. Only by a careful item-by-item examination of the test can teachers adequately evaluate the extent of coverage of each test battery.

Table XVI. SUBJECT AREAS COVERED IN THREE SELECTED JUNIOR HIGH SCHOOL STANDARDIZED TEST BATTERIES

Subject Area	Metropolitan Tests	SRA Achievement Series	Stanford Achievement Test
Word Knowledge	x	x	
Word Discrimination	x		
Reading	x	x	x
Spelling	x	x	x
Arithmetic			
Concepts and skills	x	x	x
Problem solving	x	x	x
Computation	x	x	x
Language:			
Usage	x	x	x
Punctuation and			
Capitalization	x	x	x
Parts of speech	x		
Kinds of sentences	x		x
Dictionary skills			x
Language Study Skills	x		
Social Studies Information	x		x
Social Studies Study Skills	x		x
Science	x		x
References		x	
Charts		x	

Teacher-made tests. Bloom classifies the levels of understanding as:

2.00 Comprehension
2.10 Translation
2.20 Interpretation
2.30 Extrapolation [4]

Comprehension, the lowest level of understanding, refers to the ability of the individual to grasp an idea or communication. This level of understanding is easily measured by both objective and essay examinations. Bloom suggests the following as an item appropriate to the measurement of this level of understanding:

[4] Benjamin S. Bloom (ed.), *op. cit* (above, n. 1), pp. 204–205.

EXAMPLE: Which of the following represents the best definition of the term "protoplasm"?

    a. A complex colloidal system made up of water, proteins, and fats.
    b. Anything capable of growth by a regular progressive series of changes into a more complex unit.
    c. A complex mixture of proteins, fats, and carbohydrates, capable of responding to changes in its environment.
    d. A complex colloidal system of proteins, fats, carbohydrates, inorganic salts, and enzymes which manifests life.[5]

Translation refers to the ability to convert information or communications from one medium to another, as in converting a passage from one language to another or, in mathematics, change from number to letter symbols. The item below illustrates measurement of translation ability from one number base to another:

EXAMPLE: How many X's are there if counted in a base of eight instead of ten?

XXX XXX XXX XXX XXX XXX XXX XXX
    a. 25 eight   c. 26 eight
    b. 21 eight   d. 168 eight [6]

Interpretation refers to the ability to explain such material as literary passages, charts and graphs, scientific theories. A typical method of measurement used is to quote a literary passage, then require the pupil to write an essay interpreting the meaning of the passage.

Extrapolation refers to the pupils' ability to predict from a given set of facts or data, or to project trends—as population projections, business and economic trends, etc.

The teacher-made tests for measuring comprehension or understanding include various types of true-false, multiple-choice, and essay tests and can be used to measure each of these levels of understanding.

While the true-false test has the advantage of being relatively easy to construct, guessing may be a significant factor in the pupils' scores; and the teacher is thus unable to determine what proportion of the items the pupils actually know and what proportion they guessed correctly.

It is also true that many problem situations which call for understanding are not readily adaptable to the true-false form since the solutions are difficult to dichotomize into simple either/or choices; often there are

[5] Bloom, p. 100.
[6] Item taken from Test 5, Intermediate Battery, of the *Stanford Achievement Test.*

numerous alternatives which would provide logical, workable solutions to such situations. The absurdity of the either/or choice is apparent in the following true-false statement: "Slavery was the cause of the Civil War." Although slavery was a major issue which led to the Civil War, other factors—such as geographic, economic, cultural, religious, and philosophical differences—were also so significant that the above statement is neither wholly true nor wholly false. When teachers present pupils such confusing alternatives on true-false tests, pupils are apt to write in qualifications before answering the items and argue vigorously in support of their responses. Such tests cause both pupils and teachers to lose confidence in the value of the true-false form.

This criticism of the true-false form when used to measure understanding can be avoided by using the multiple-true-false form in those subject areas which permit several correct alternatives.

> EXAMPLE: Notable educational trends during the Early National Period of American history were:
>
> T F 1. the development of state responsibility for education
> T F 2. an expansion in philanthropic provisions for education
> T F 3. an increase in the number of private educational institutions
> T F 4. a diversification of the content of education

Another variation in the true-false form which reduces guessing and which can be used to measure understanding is the test in which an underlined portion of each statement must be corrected by the pupil if the statement is false. When the statement is true, no correction is made; but when the pupil decides that the item is false, he must also know why it is false in order to correct it.

> EXAMPLE:
>
> T F 1. When the volume of a gas is reduced the temperature decreases.

In the above false statement the word "decreases" should be changed by the pupil to "increases." With such statements it is also feasible to require the pupil to justify his change in the item, thus demonstrating the extent of his understanding.

Multiple-choice tests. The multiple-choice test is the best objective test form for measuring understanding. In addition to the conventional multiple-choice item, several variations are useful for this purpose. These include (1) items with several correct answers, (2) most correct answer items, and (3) analogies.

With items which contain more than one correct choice, the pupil must identify all correct answers. Such items are both difficult to write and difficult for the respondent who is accustomed to one correct response. However, such items may actually present a more realistic test parallel of actual practical problems than do items with only one correct choice.

EXAMPLE: Every man is in certain respects like

    a. no other man
    b. all other men
    c. some other man
    d. some other men
    e. all of the above

In the item above a strong, rational argument supports the correctness of each choice. When the item appears as a four-choice item, all four choices are correct; but when the fifth choice, "all of the above," is added, it becomes the *most correct* choice. Thus the item can be presented as one with several correct answers or as a best-answer type. The best-answer type item requires the pupil to exercise judgment and discrimination in selecting a best answer from among several correct solutions or answers to the problem or premise proposed. Although the best-answer item is not easy to construct, it does measure more complex understanding than the item with a single correct response.

Multiple-choice items written as analogies can also be used to measure understanding and mathematical or verbal reasoning.

EXAMPLE: Metal is to iron as automobile is to

    a. trip   d. car
    b. Buick   e. bicycle
    c. train

In order to answer the above item correctly, the pupil must understand that *metal* is the general classification and *iron* the specific within that classification. It would then follow that *automobile* is the second general classification to which *Buick* relates as a specific. Standardized tests often contain both word analogies and picture analogies to measure understanding and reasoning. For example, the *Terman-McNemar Test of Mental Ability* includes a complete sub-test of analogies.

Essay tests. Essay questions provide another excellent means for assessing understanding. Questions which require an analysis of cause and effect relationships or which require the pupil to explain a concept or literary passage can be used. If pupils understand the concepts and possess adequate verbal ability, they can answer such questions satisfactorily.

Table XVII. INSTRUCTIONAL OBJECTIVES AND TEST FORMS APPROPRIATE FOR THEIR MEASUREMENT

Instructional Objectives	*Test Form*
1. Pupils should understand the concept of democracy.	Essay Best-answer multiple-choice True–false
2. Pupils should understand the role of science in everyday living.	Essay Multiple-choice
3. Pupils should demonstrate an understanding of the decimal number system and systems such as the binary, the duo-decimal, etc.	Multiple-choice analogies Multiple-choice number-conversion problems

Since pupil understanding can be measured by several test forms, the choice of form is often difficult. In many cases, in fact, several test forms would give more adequate measurement than one. In any case, a statement of the various objectives to be measured simplifies the choice of measuring instrument. Table XVII presents such a statement followed by several test forms which could be used to measure each objective. The first two objectives are general and could be evaluated by other techniques, but the suggested test forms are appropriate and will give considerable evidence of pupil achievement.

SUMMARY

Knowledge is the commodity which underlies the entire school curriculum. The acquisition of a fund of knowledge is a prerequisite step in learning upon which further, more complex learning is predicated. Pupils must possess certain information in each field before they develop the understandings which permit them to use the information in solving problems.

The mastery of knowledge is measurable at several levels of retention: (1) the recognition level, (2) the immediate recall level, and (3) the extended recall level. Multiple-choice and matching items measure recognition. Immediate recall can be measured by completion and short-answer items such as listing and outlining. Extended recall can be determined only by repeated measurement over an extended period of time.

The measurement of understanding is more difficult than the measurement of knowledge retention. However, several test forms are useful for this purpose—notably, multiple-choice, true-false, and essay. Because of the complexity of understanding, the use of several test forms often gives a more complete picture of the level of understanding which the pupil has attained.

Standardized achievement tests provide an excellent means for supplementing the measurement of pupils' level of knowledge retention and of understanding, provided that the content of instruction and of the test are comparable.

REPRESENTATIVE ACHIEVEMENT BATTERIES

The American College Testing Program Examination. Science Research Associates.
California Achievement Tests, 1957 Edition. California Test Bureau.
Cooperative General Achievement Tests. Cooperative Test Division.
Coordinated Scales of Attainment. Educational Test Bureau.
Essential High School Content Battery. Harcourt, Brace & World.
Iowa Tests of Basic Skills. Houghton Mifflin Company.
Metropolitan Achievement Tests, 1960 Edition. Harcourt Brace & World.
National Merit Scholarship Qualifying Test. Science Research Associates.
SRA Achievement Series. Science Research Associates.
Sequential Tests of Educational Progress. Cooperative Test Division.
Stanford Achievement Test, 1953 Revision. Harcourt, Brace & World.

DISCUSSION QUESTIONS AND PROBLEMS

1. State fifteen to twenty specific knowledge and understanding objectives for a subject which you plan to teach. Classify these objectives using Bloom's *Taxonomy.*
2. Examine several of the standardized tests for the subject which you have selected to determine how closely they coincide with the objectives which you have stated above.
3. Select one standardized achievement test, read through the test, and tabulate the number of items which measure each of the above objectives.
4. Develop an item file for a subject in your teaching field. Write each item on a 3″ x 5″ card and file it according to the objective and content area which it measures.

5. Evaluate the usefulness of objective test forms in measuring pupil understandings.
6. Is high pupil performance on a knowledge test good assurance of long-term retention?
7. How does the pupil's retention of understanding compare to his knowledge retention?

SELECTED READINGS

Ahmann, J. Stanley and Marvin D. Glock. *Evaluating Pupil Growth.* 3rd ed. Boston: Allyn and Bacon, 1967. Chapters 3 and 4 contain very good discussion of the use of objective tests to measure knowledge and understanding.

Buros, Oscar Krisen. *Tests in Print: A Comprehensive Bibliography of Tests for Use in Education, Psychology, and Industry.* Highland Park, N. J.: Gryphon Press, 1962. This is the most complete listing of in-print tests.

———. *The Sixth Mental Measurements Yearbook.* Highland Park, N. J.: Gryphon Press, 1965. This is the best source for reviews of most of the tests currently published. The reviews are authoritative and relatively complete.

Ebel, Robert L. *Measuring Educational Achievement.* Englewood Cliffs, N. J.: Prentice-Hall, 1965. Chapters 4, 5, and 6 are replete with suggestions for constructing and using essay and objective tests.

Garrett, Henry E. *Testing for Teachers.* New York: American Book Company, 1965. Chapter 5 presents a concise evaluation of several of the better-known standardized achievement tests.

Gerberich, J. Raymond. *Specimen Objective Test Items.* New York: Longmans, Green and Company, 1956. Chapters 4 and 6 include numerous examples from standardized tests of test items for measuring knowledge and understanding.

Henry, Nelson B. (ed.). *The Measurement of Understanding.* Forty-fifth Yearbook of the National Society for the Study of Education, Part I. Chicago: The University of Chicago Press, 1946. Chapters 3 and 4 are of particular interest. Section II also has separate chapters devoted to the measurement of understanding in the subject fields.

Jordan, A. M. *Measurement in Education.* New York: McGraw-Hill Book Company, 1953. Chapters 5 through 13 give separate consideration to each of the major subject divisions of the elementary and secondary schools.

Lindvall, C. M. *Testing and Evaluation: An Introduction.* New York: Harcourt, Brace & World, 1961. Chapter 12 has a brief, but valuable, discussion of standardized achievement tests. The method of standardization is described, and there are suggestions for using the tests.

Smith, Fred M. and Sam Adams. *Educational Measurement for the Classroom Teacher.* New York: Harper & Row, 1966. Construction of tests to measure knowledge and understanding is discussed in Chapters 7 and 8.

MEASURING LEARNING OUTCOMES—
REFLECTIVE THINKING AND
PROBLEM SOLVING

INTRODUCTION

It is an enigma in schools that those objectives which we profess to value most highly—reflective thinking and problem solving—are probably most poorly taught and certainly most poorly measured. The reasons for this failure are many, but at least several stand out. First, since many of the significant problems of our society are unsolved, teachers neither feel able to teach about them nor willing to permit pupils to wrestle with them. Second, teaching and measuring reflective thinking and problem solving are much more difficult than teaching and measuring knowledge and understanding. Finally, there is an unexpressed, but nonetheless implicit, faith that those who know and understand will apply their knowledge and understanding in the solution of society's problems—a faith which is as yet unconfirmed in the experience of other generations of learners.

Although no startling innovations are presented here for revolutionizing this area of measurement and evaluation, there *are* some useful techniques and instruments to consider; and the clear need for improvement is ample incentive for an examination of the area.

"It has often been said that democracy requires teaching pupils, not *what* to think, but how to think." [1] However, many American teachers do teach children *what* to think; and even though they may be unaware of the hazard which attends their failure to teach pupils *how* to think, they

_____

[1] Ernest E. Bayles, *Democratic Educational Theory* (New York: Harper & Brothers, 1960), p. 188.

are seldom unaware of the inconsistency of the approach with our democratic philosophy. In a world embroiled in an ideological struggle which periodically erupts into heated conflict, the advantage of initiative often falls to the dedicated, single-minded countries which can move with dispatch and firm purpose to thwart and repel the democracies. For the past generation this threat has proved to be an enticing invitation for indoctrination to strengthen the resolve and eradicate the differences within our democracy. As inviting as this approach may at first seem, it is likely to be fraught with increasing erosion of personal freedoms, perhaps leading ultimately to dominance by the state and subservience of individual citizens. One need not, however, look beyond our country's borders to discover unsolved social, political, and economic problems urgently awaiting solution. The problems of riot, increasing crime, minority groups, and poverty are examples of the most critical. Without experience and training in problem solving during their school years, pupils will be ill-prepared to contribute significantly to the solution of such problems. The future payoff for this in-school experience could well be in better investigation and resolution of the then current social, economic, and political problems—both domestic and international.

Before discussing specific means of evaluating and measuring this important learning outcome, we will examine the nature of thought and some of the common errors in thinking and problem solving which the teacher should be aware of to assess the status and growth of pupils.

NATURE OF THOUGHT

What is thought? [2] It is a timeworn cliché that man's superiority is a result of his superior intellect, his rational intelligence as it were. That he possesses this attribute there can be no doubt, and it follows as a natural consequence that he uses it—that he thinks. However, granting that he does think still leaves unanswered the crucial questions, "What is thought?" and "How does he think?" Synonyms for "thought" are such words as "cogitation," "reflection," and "meditation"; and the process itself is described as "mental activity." But one's own experience with the process of mental activity suggests that it occurs on numerous levels. All of us have experienced the *random thought* process of association, for instance, in which impressions, fragmented memories, and half-formu-

---

[2] For a good discussion of this question, see John Dewey, *How We Think* (Boston: D. C. Heath & Company, 1910), Chapters 1, 6, 7, 8, 9, 10, and 11.

lated ideas cascade through the spotlight of attention in a kaleidoscopic array of entertaining but profitless activity. For most this effortless mental activity is but the by-product of a restless, searching mind, filling the intervals between sessions of purposeful thought. Such activity when overindulged becomes a psychological mechanism for escaping from reality into the fantasy world of daydreams.

A step removed from this level is *impulsive thought,* which often arises from the need for immediate decisions or solutions to problem situations. Such thought is appropriate for noncrucial problems, such as the selection of a tie, choice of food from a menu, or decision to get a haircut; but it is not an appropriate means for answering such questions as "Whom shall I marry?" "Shall I purchase an automobile, and what type of automobile?" "Which teacher should be employed in the position?" "What course mark should the pupil receive?" It must be granted, however, that too many persons resolve such problems through impulsive thought, unhampered by relevant facts or tentative hypotheses which would—in most instances—lead to a sounder resolution. These crucial individual problems and the complex problems of society deserve the more intelligent and considered approach of *reflective thought.* Dewey believed that there are five distinct steps in the process of reflective thought:

1. A felt difficulty or problem
2. Definition of problem
3. Suggestion of possible solution or hypothesis
4. Development by reasoning of the bearings of the suggestions (implications)
5. Further observance and experimental verification or corroboration leading to acceptance or rejection of the suggested solution [3]

The entire process need not be as formidable as it first appears as one examines the steps; and the process should not take more time than the nature and seriousness of the problem warrants, lest we become caught up in the maze of scholastic dalliance with a myriad of lesser problems while we procrastinate the solution of the most important. With most problems the first two steps fuse as the awareness of the problem blends into its definition. Likewise steps 3 and 4 intertwine as one reasons or thinks out a plausible hypothesis and searches its implications as a possi-

[3] *Ibid.,* p. 72. These steps are not original with Dewey. In the sixteenth century Sir Francis Bacon was an early proponent of the scientific problem-solving approach.

ble solution. Finally, the nature of the problem determines the extent of observation, experimentation, and data gathering required before one verifies or rejects the hypothesis as the correct solution.

Thinking abilities. J. P. Guilford has theorized that there may be as many as 120 thinking abilities, which can be classed in five major groups: (1) cognition, (2) memory, (3) convergent production, (4) divergent production, and (5) evaluation.

The first of these, the cognitive abilities, are used in recognition and discovery of facts. The second, memory, is used in retaining what has been learned or discovered. The third, convergent thinking, is the process of seeking the best conventional answer to a problem. The fourth, divergent thinking, is the process leading to new and creative solutions. Finally, evaluation is the process of determining the goodness or suitability of solutions. The first two types are essentially nonproductive, while both convergent and divergent avenues are productive in that they result in either conventional or creative problem solutions. Conventional achievement and intelligence tests are used to measure the first three, but divergent thinking and evaluation are not measured by conventional instruments.[4]

Some elements of thinking. The previous discussion of thought is primarily descriptive of the process. In addition thought or thinking may be classified into several specific elements according to the nature of the thought-objective or thought-problem. Included among these elements are:

1. Observation
2. Meaning
3. Analysis
4. Synthesis
5. Judgment

The last four of these are classified in the *Taxonomy of Educational Objectives: Cognitive Domain* as:

2:00 Comprehension
4:00 Analysis
5:00 Synthesis
6:00 Evaluation

[4] The reader is referred back to the discussion of measurement of creativity in Chapter 5, pp. 111–115.

The measurement of the various levels of comprehension was discussed in Chapter 10; and the other three are also measurable as we shall see in subsequent discussion.

In numerous contexts throughout the book we have suggested *observation* as one of the valuable techniques in measurement and evaluation. In each instance observation was suggested in relationship to a problem or purpose which gave reason and direction to the observation—e.g., observation of pupils' social adjustment, observation of pupils' physical handicaps, etc. Observation in itself has little value without some controlling purpose which orders the impressions, permitting them to become a meaningful, cogent whole. Haphazard observation of the world, of people, of natural phenomena—while they may be interesting and increase the fund of information—have little real value without some ordering concept or purpose which gives them meaning and usefulness. Without this organization, when the need to use one or several of the specific impressions arises, it is apt to be learned and lost in a cluttered mass of disorganized impressions.

Observations, then, begin to assume meaning as they are organized around the ordering concept of a purpose. If we wish to determine why a child has no friends, we may observe his specific behavior and note that he is aggressive, that he is tactless, that he rejects friendly overtures. Thus with purpose and thought we bridge the gap from observation to meaning and can answer *why*.

Meaning corresponds to *comprehension* in Bloom's *Taxonomy*. Although a specific concept—such as number—can have several meanings, the individual may have but limited comprehension of the meanings.

Analysis is the process of breaking down a complex problem or concept into its specific parts. Such a breakdown or analysis may be performed to facilitate working toward a satisfactory solution, or it may be necessary when the problem is too complex to be understood or attacked *in toto*. The antithesis of analysis is *synthesis*, in which the specific elements are combined into a meaningful whole. Both are necessary elements in thinking, and as such they are germane to the teaching and evaluating processes.[5]

In measurement and evaluation *judgment* is akin to evaluation, for it

[5] The synthetic function and the analytic function are discussed extensively in H. Gordon Hullfish and Philip G. Smith, *Reflective Thinking* (New York: Dodd, Mead & Company, 1961), Chapters 5 and 6.

requires that the individual exercise reason in assessing the worth, pertinence, and validity of the data gained through measurement and the information collected by observation. The data and information may be judged to be relevant or irrelevant as they bear upon the problem or purpose for which they were collected, and judgment is again required as the data and information are put to use in curricular changes or new instructional approaches.

Modes of thinking. All thinking can be roughly divided into two modes: the concrete and the abstract. Dewey suggests that abstract thinking is theoretical and not closely associated with practical concerns. He distinguishes between the two modes in the following manner: "When thinking is used as a means to some end, good, or value beyond itself, it is concrete; when it is employed simply as means to more thinking, it is abstract." [6] Abstract thinking can also ultimately be practical when the theoretical concept which is formulated becomes widely adopted as a working concept. For example, in government the original, theoretical works of Marx and Engels became practical working concepts when implemented by Stalin and his predecessors. Both modes of thought are necessary, and the person who has facility with both can cope with a greater variety of problems than the person who uses only one or the other.

Systematic modes of thought can be employed for both concrete and abstract thinking. Three applicable systems are (1) inductive-deductive reasoning, (2) empirical thinking, and (3) scientific thinking.

1. *Inductive-deductive reasoning.* Many of the problems which stimulate men to think have numerous plausible solutions, but some are better than others. Thus the intelligent approach is to withhold judgment and to look beyond the first plausible solution for others which can be tested and critically examined in the search for a *best solution.* The first solution, while it may answer the problem, may be a poor answer which could readily be improved on by further reflection and investigation.

Inductive-deductive reasoning is a means through which problems can be systematically attacked and logically solved. Inductive reasoning is used in the first phase of problem solving as one examines the facts; recalls previous experience bearing on the problem; makes pertinent observations; and then inductively formulates the general principles, ideas,

[6] Dewey, *op. cit.* (above, n. 2), pp. 137–138. Chapter 10 contains a thorough discussion of concrete-abstract thinking.

or hypothesis which the specific bits of information suggest. Induction thus moves from the specifics to the general principle which ties them together. In the second phase, deductive reasoning is used to test the principle, idea, or hypothesis in specific instances to determine whether it can be verified, rejected, or modified. Deduction thus moves from the general to the specific.

In the school situation a teacher using inductive-deductive reasoning and faced with the problem of determining why a pupil is a low achiever would withhold judgment while he systematically observes the child in a variety of school situations and as he collects various test scores, records of physical well-being, and evidence of social and emotional adjustment. He might then inductively hypothesize that poor emotional adjustment accounted for the underachievement. To test this hypothesis he could interview parents, administer personality inventories, talk with other teachers, collect information concerning the child's out-of-school behavior, etc. Thus he might arrive deductively at a tentative verification of the hypothesis, leading possibly to such actions as modification of the child's program and work load, transfer to another classroom, or referral to the school psychologist.

2. *Empirical thinking.* Empirical thinking is a type of thought in which conclusions based on observations and previous experience are arrived at inductively. Since the observations and experience are not apt to be extensive, they may lead to a biased conclusion—a conclusion which is not usually deductively tested to verify it. Men observed, for instance, that certain meteorological circumstances preceded a storm and concluded that the two phenomena were related long before they understood the actual reasons for weather changes. Similarly the changes in season were observed before they were understood, with the understanding in each example coming through a process of scientific experimentation.

Since numerous traits of human beings seem to be related, it appears logical to assume that there is a causal relationship between them. For example, intelligence and physical coordination are positively correlated; therefore, it might empirically be concluded that one causes the other or that they are both caused by a common factor. Actually on the basis of this statistical relationship a conclusion as to the cause is not justified; however, a hypothesis concerning the cause could be formulated for further testing.

Dewey notes the following weaknesses in empirical thinking:

1. It is apt to lead to false beliefs.
2. It encourages the fallacy that because a thing comes *after* another, it comes *because* of the other.
3. It leads to laziness and presumption.
4. It leads to dogmatism and reliance on previous "laws" and authorities.[7]

3. *Scientific thinking.* The scientific method of problem solving, in contrast to the empirical, uses controlled experimentation to produce a large number of cases and to vary systematically the conditions surrounding the cases so that the specific conditions which cause the phenomenon may be identified. The problem may be formulated and hypotheses for its solution based upon empirical observation and experiences, but the hypotheses are then tested experimentally. Since the scientific method follows a prescribed approach which can be described and repeated, the conclusions or problem solutions can be verified by other experimenters who follow the same steps. Dewey contrasts the empirical and scientific methods in the following ways:

> The empirical method inevitably magnifies the influences of the past; the experimental method throws into relief the possibilities of the future. The empirical method says, "*Wait* till there is a sufficient number of cases"; the experimental method says, "Produce the cases." The former depends upon nature's accidentally happening to present us with certain conjunctions of circumstances; the latter deliberately and intentionally endeavors to bring about the conjunction.[8]

Improper modes of thought.[9] There are at least three modes of thought which are either inefficient or erroneous for problem solving. These are (1) trial and error, (2) rationalization, and (3) impulsive thinking. The first of these—seeking problem solutions through pure *trial and error* without a controlling hypothesis or without benefit of previous experiences—is obviously unintelligent and inefficient problem solving.

Rationalization, unfortunately, is a rather common pattern of thought, particularly in problem areas where emotional bias is involved. In such cases—e.g., political choices—one may make a preconceived choice and then rationalize his choice with a logical set of arguments. Although the arguments may be good ones, they are of little value since the decision was made before the supporting case was formulated. The real error in this mode of thought is that it prevents the individual from seriously con-

---

[7] Dewey, *op. cit.* (above, n. 2), pp. 147–149.
[8] Dewey, *op. cit.* (above, n. 2), p. 154.
[9] See Hullfish and Smith, Chapter 8, "Inference and Fallacy."

sidering any of the numerous alternatives other than that which was selected.

Impulsive thinking is, in most instances, an improper mode of thought for solving complex problems. The "snap decision" precludes the possibility of properly examining the alternatives and testing their consequences. However, in an emergency or crisis situation when an immediate decision is required, such a decision based upon the immediate facts and experiences which one can quickly marshal may be necessary. When one is faced with an impending automobile accident, the decision must be made quickly. Even though the various alternatives may all be fraught with serious consequences, one alternative is probably less hazardous; and failure to make a decision will inevitably result in the accident.

MEASUREMENT OF THINKING

Actually two approaches may be taken in the assessment of thinking: one is the *gestalt* approach, with evaluation of the entire reflective thinking or problem solving process; the other is the analytic approach, in which the process is broken down into specific measurable elements. The latter of these is the easier, although not necessarily the better, approach. It is more readily adapted to the classroom situation and to conventional measurement forms.

Measurement of analysis and synthesis. Two elements of thought which are relatively easy to measure are *analysis* and *synthesis*. In the *Taxonomy of Educational Objectives* these are broken down into the following subheadings for measurement:

4:00 Analysis
    4:10 Analysis of Elements
    4:20 Analysis of Relationships
    4:30 Analysis of Organizational Principles
5:00 Synthesis
    5:10 Production of a Unique Communication
    5:20 Production of a Plan, or Proposed Set of Operations
    5:30 Derivation of a Set of Abstract Relationships [10]

Tests of reading comprehension generally require the pupil both to comprehend and analyze passages as a basis for answering a series of questions. Examples of this approach may be found in the reading section of the *California Achievement Tests*. In literature classes pupils are

[10] Benjamin S. Bloom (ed.), *Taxonomy of Educational Objectives: The Classification of Educational Objectives, Handbook I; Cognitive Domain* (New York: David McKay Co., Inc., 1956), pp. 205–207.

also required to develop the ability to analyze literary passages, and the measure of their ability can be taken by presenting the passage together with a series of related questions which must be answered, provided that the questions focus upon analytical meaning rather than fact.

Another approach to the measurement of analytical ability is to use a scrambled outline—e.g., in geography, science or history—and ask pupils to analyze it and reorganize it into a logical sequence with appropriate topics, subtopics, sub-subtopics, etc.

The following example includes scrambled topics for a high school unit in geography or earth science:

> *Directions*: In the scrambled unit outline which follows pick the topical heading and arrange the main topics, subtopics and sub-subtopics in proper order.

1. Chemical weathering	10. Climate
2. Soil formation	11. Topographic conditions
3. Carbonation	12. Oxidation
4. Shale formation	13. Frost wedging
5. Speed of weathering	14. Hydration
6. Nature of rock	15. Types of weathering
7. Exfoliation	16. Mechanical weathering
8. Weathering of rocks	17. Talus formation
9. Results of weathering	

Before the pupil can arrange the outline correctly he must have some knowledge of the general topic, but further than this he must also possess considerable analytical ability before he can correctly arrange the topics. Before referring to the correct version of the outline the reader may wish to arrange the topics as a self-check on the analytical process which is involved in the problem.

Such outlines may be used in several fields and they may be ordered by chronological, logical, or psychological arrangement. The above example is logically arranged. Chronological arrangement is easiest for the pupil and psychological, the most difficult. A variation which makes this exercise even more difficult is to include several irrelevant topics so that the pupil must arrange the outline and identify the irrelevant topics.

CORRECT OUTLINE:

Unit Topic: Weathering of Rocks

> I. Types of Weathering
>   A. Mechanical weathering
>   1. Frost wedging

        2. Exfoliation
    B. Chemical weathering
        1. Carbonation
        2. Oxidation
        3. Hydration
  II. Results of Weathering
    A. Shale formation
    B. Talus formation
    C. Soil formation
 III. Speed of weathering
    A. Nature of rock
    B. Climate
    C. Topographic conditions

Synthesis requires some creative response from the pupil. It ranges from the relatively simple process of drawing inferences and formulating a hypothesis to explaining a phenomenon or tentatively solving a problem to the complex processes of invention and creative writing. The ability to synthesize is frequently required in the science laboratory, and the pupil who formulates a plausible hypothesis to explain a given set of scientific phenomena displays this ability (this is true even though the hypothesis may have been proposed before, as long as the pupil is not aware of the previous proposal). In measuring this ability the instructor can present a series of items each of which contains a list of facts and data for which the pupil must propose a feasible explanatory hypothesis. In composition classes an assignment requiring pupils to write a creative work in poetry or prose gives a measure of this ability, although the evaluation of the quality of the work will be subjective. Similarly in music composition the same procedure provides a subjective measure of the pupils' abilities.

Other measurable aspects of thinking. Both concrete and abstract modes of thinking can be measured with the standardized tests which are currently available. The primary mental abilities intelligence tests and aptitude tests, such as the *Differential Aptitude Tests*, include tests or sub-tests for measuring abstract and verbal reasoning; and the verbal reasoning tests include both concrete and abstract measurement items. Since these tests were discussed in Chapter 5, the reader is referred back to that chapter for further discussion of these tests.

Ingenuity or inventiveness, the ability to formulate a unique solution to a problem, can be measured by standardized tests. The Ingenuity Test in the *Flanagan Aptitude Classification Tests* battery is an example of an instrument which appears to be quite valid for measuring this ability.

Another aspect of thinking which is measurable is the ability to determine whether adequate or appropriate data is available to solve a problem. It is possible to measure this ability with teacher-made items. Such multiple-choice and true-false items as the following measure pupils' ability to make a logical choice without being influenced by irrational bias or extraneous information.

EXAMPLES:

1. In the United States the mean IQ of native-born Negroes as measured by group tests such as the *Kuhlmann-Anderson* and the *Otis* is lower than that of native-born whites. On the basis of this evidence which of the following is a legitimate conclusion concerning the two groups?

   a. Negroes are innately less intelligent than whites.
   b. The tests are not culture-fair for Negroes.
   c. The evidence is inconclusive.
   d. There is no innate difference in intelligence.
   e. Whites perform better on the group tests than Negroes.

2. Why do men in the United States wear trousers and women dresses?

   a. It is appropriate.
   b. It is physically fitting.
   c. It is morally correct.
   d. It is customary.
   e. It is a mark of male dominance.

T   F   3. The physical differences between men and women make it desirable for men to wear trousers and women dresses.

Mathematical and abstract problems can also be set in the multiple-choice form with the problem stated in the premise and the solution given as one of the choices. In mathematics the problems should be analyzed ahead of time to determine the common errors so that these erroneous solutions can be included among the choices as plausible detractors. In abstract reasoning, the most-correct-choice form and the form in which several choices are correct are useful.

An interesting method of measuring pupils' observation and judgment is suggested by Wilson in the following passage:

Everyone will have an opportunity to go to the window and look outside for a few minutes. When you come back to your seats, you will write down all the things you saw that you would not have seen on a rainy winter day. If you write something that no one else noticed, your score on that word will be *ten*. If only two or three people in the room noticed it, your score on that idea will be *five*. If four or five people put down the same idea, the score on that item will be *three*. If more than five noticed it, just take the score of *one*. You will see that the closer you observe and the more uncommon are your responses, the higher your score will be. We'll take four minutes to look out the window and six minutes to write our list of things seen that you would not have seen on a rainy winter day.[11]

A test of this kind can be followed up with a discussion which will help all pupils understand what is logical and illogical and also how observant they are. In this area of measurement the teacher must be constantly alert to any new tests or techniques which offer promise; and he must continually seek to identify novel problem situations or formulate novel questions which cannot be answered by the student by rote or by an "off-the-cuff" snap decision. Building a card file of such problems or items will facilitate test construction, since the experienced teacher will have an extensive list from which to select and will have to spend less time constructing new items for each test.

EVALUATION OF THINKING

If teachers are to be successful in evaluating pupils' modes of thinking and problem solving, they must be "thinking teachers" who are aware of the pitfalls in erroneous modes of thinking and who habitually use systematic thinking in solving their own problems. The questions which must be answered in evaluating this area of pupils' learning are:

1. What thought process did the pupils use?
2. Was the process appropriate to the problem situation?
3. Were the data, observations, and facts valid and representative?
4. Were there errors in the pupils' thinking?
5. Were the conclusions consistent with the evidence?
6. Were the problem solutions effective?

It is further evident that attempts to evaluate pupils' thinking and problem solving will be fruitless unless the curriculum includes numerous

[11] Robert C. Wilson, "Creativity," in Nelson B. Henry (ed.), *Education for the Gifted*, Fifty-Seventh Yearbook of the National Society for the Study of Education, Part II (Chicago: The Society, 1958), p. 122.

opportunities for pupils to do independent thinking in search of solutions to problems which have no ready-made solutions. Many of these problems will be socially important and controversial in nature; and the teacher cannot, as he has traditionally done in knowledge and information areas, evaluate against a single, correct answer or solution. As the questions above imply, skill in the use of appropriate processes; ability to collect valid data to test hypotheses; ability to determine which data is valid and which invalid; as well as the final problem solution are all important and must be evaluated. Skillful use of the steps which precede the solution is the best assurance that pupils can cope successfully with other novel problems which they will face.

Since the evaluator will appraise both the thought process and the solution, it is necessary that he have some evidence of the process which was used. In *problem solving* this requires that the pupil describe, orally or in writing, the steps which he followed; the hypotheses which he used; the data which he collected; and his methods for testing the hypotheses. In *decision-making* it requires that the pupil set down all plausible alternatives, that he list the foreseeable consequences of each, and that he select the best alternative. In *research* it requires that the pupil write a report which clearly delineates the problem, describes the method of procedure, analyzes the data, and reports the conclusions.

From these descriptive reports the evaluator has the basis for appraising the quality of the pupils' thinking and answering the questions which were noted earlier. These descriptive evidences of the pupils' thought processes together with their conclusions permit the teacher to determine whether all the steps were followed in proper sequence so that a grade can be given which is based on the quality and correctness of the procedure as well as on the appropriateness of the conclusion or solution. The grade should be assigned on much the same basis as that used in grading written compositions and essay examinations, although less attention should be paid to the mechanics of expression than to the correctness of the thought process. In assigning the grade it may be helpful to use the six questions cited on p. 230 as a checklist to insure adequate attention to each aspect of the pupil's thought process.

One pitfall which the evaluator may have difficulty avoiding is that of distinguishing between rationalization or preconceived bias and true reflective thinking, in which judgment is withheld until all the evidence is in and the alternate solutions or hypotheses have been properly tested and verified or rejected. The pupil who sets out to prove a given hypothesis rather than objectively test the alternative hypotheses may note the alternatives and even cite some evidence in their support but present overwhelming evidence in support of the one which he first selected. Since his case may be quite logical, the evaluator must determine whether he purposely overlooked important evidence supporting other alternatives and opposing the chosen solution. It is important also that the evaluator be aware of his own biases and prejudices and that he not reject pupils' problem solutions on the basis of his bias without first examining the hypotheses and supporting evidence which they have presented.

A type of essay examination which can be used to evaluate pupils' ability to solve problems systematically is one in which a complex social problem is described and the pupils are asked to write a systematic solution to the problem following as nearly as they can in the test situation the five steps of systematic thinking. In such an examination they should be required to (1) state the problem precisely; (2) list previous experiences, observations, and sources of data which bear on the problem; (3) list the plausible solutions to the problem; (4) note the consequences and various ways in which the solutions can be tested; and (5) recommend one solution which appears to be best. The evaluation of such an examination can be made on a comparative basis in which the papers are judged against one another: (1) on the basis of the thoroughness with which each step was completed (number and plausibility of suggested solutions, extent of evidence, understanding of problems); (2) on the basis of logical consistency between evidence and the chosen solution. After the teacher has graded the examination, a follow-up discussion of the problem and the various solutions should lead to pupil self-evaluation and growth.

On some occasions an essay examination such as that suggested above might be administered by the teacher and then evaluated by the pupils themselves. Such self-evaluation, however, should not be attempted until the pupils have considerable facility with the problem-solving process and have had experience with such teacher-evaluated examinations. When pupils do the self-evaluation of their papers, the teacher provides each with a checklist like that which he uses and with a model which includes the various steps, plausible alternatives, etc. The pupils will thus have a sound basis for comparison. Such an experiment may be both an interesting and a disconcerting experience for the teacher; for he may find that some pupils in the class have formulated a number of plausible alternatives not on his list, and some may have arrived at a better solution. This should not cause "face loss" for the emotionally secure teacher; since it indicates growing competence of his pupils, and it provides an opportunity for an object lesson in the fallibility of authority as a basis for solving problems.

Errors in thinking. Following acceptable modes of thought does not protect against faulty conclusions when one makes one or more of the following errors:

1. Use of biased data
2. Generalization from limited data
3. Substitution of authority (opinion) for facts
4. Failure to observe inconsistencies in the data or facts
5. Selection of a solution which is illogical on the basis of the data

When one sets out to prove a hypothesis or contention, rather than to test its validity, he is apt to resort to the use of biased data and ignore or play down the data which discredits the hypothesis. This is actually a form of rationalization, and in education it accounts for many of the contradictory "research" conclusions relating to such matters as the effect of class size on pupil learning. The fallacy of generalization from limited data is related to the use of biased data since a limited sample of data may reflect extreme bias unless carefully selected to give an unbiased sample. Although in this case the bias may be unintentional, it is nonetheless real and may lead to capricious and contradictory conclusions when the investigation is repeated with another limited sample.

Since men are fallible in their thinking, even the opinions of authorities in a field must be critically evaluated against the facts before they are accepted as correct. Substitution of authoritative opinion for facts is sloppy, lazy thinking which bases conclusions on a foundation of sand that may disintegrate when the opinions are incorrect. Children who are taught to accept textbook opinion as fact are prone to fall into the deplorable habit of uncritically relying on "the book says" or "Dr. Blank says" as the ultimate authority for their conclusions.

Failure to see inconsistencies in the data and formulating conclusions or problem solutions which do not logically follow from the data may result when one neglects a thorough analysis and testing of the data or lacks the perceptiveness to see the nature of the inconsistency.

SUMMARY

It is unquestionably true that pupils need a certain backlog of knowledge and understanding, but teachers are negligent of their responsibility if they fail to go one step further and teach the pupils how to think so that they can use their fund of knowledge in solving problems. In a democracy such as ours it is particularly important that the citizens make decisions rationally instead of emotionally. School children who learn to practice reflective thinking and systematic problem solving, and to recognize and avoid the common errors in thinking are apt to continue to use correct modes of thought in adult life.

Teaching and evaluating reflective thinking are difficult. Such teaching must deal with problems without "pat answers"; it cannot avoid controversial issues; it will invade areas in which the teacher is not the authority; and it must focus on *how* to think, not *what* to think.

Thinking occurs on numerous levels—for example, *random thought,* which proceeds with little pattern; *impulsive thought,* which is often used in making immediate decisions; or *reflective thought,* which may be used to generate solutions to complex problems.

Thought is a complex act which can be broken into at least five elements: (1) observation, (2) meaning, (3) analysis, (4) synthesis, and (5) judgment. The last four of these elements correspond to comprehension, analysis, synthesis, and evaluation in Bloom's *Taxonomy of Educational Objectives.*

All thinking can be roughly classified as either concrete or abstract. Concrete thinking is that used as a means to some practical end, while abstract thinking is theoretical, with no immediate practical concern. Both concrete and abstract thinking, however, can be systematic—utilizing inductive-deductive, empirical, and/or scientific approaches. There are at least three modes of thought which are either inefficient or erroneous for problem solving. These are (1) trial and error, (2) rationalization, and (3) impulsive thinking. The first of these is inefficient; the second is biased; and the third is inappropriate for complex problems.

The methods for measuring and evaluating pupils' modes of thinking which have been discussed in this chapter give the teacher a reasonable repertoire of evaluative techniques, but the ingenious teacher will use not only these but will also devise others to improve the validity of his evaluations.

DISCUSSION QUESTIONS AND PROBLEMS

1. Select an aspect of thinking and construct ten or twelve multiple-choice items which could be used in measuring it.
2. Select a controversial social or political problem; write an analysis of the problem; and formulate the solution which seems most feasible. Then go back and evaluate your analysis and solution on the basis of the six questions on p. 230.
3. Make a list of some of the problems and issues in which your opinion and/or decision has been influenced by emotional bias.
4. Select one problem which you resolved by a snap decision and subsequently justified by rationalization. Then make an attempt to examine thoroughly and in an unbiased way other plausible alternatives. After such examination, do you still feel that your original decision was the correct one?
5. From your personal experience or from the literature suggest ways, other than those mentioned in the chapter, of evaluating critical thinking.
6. Examine as many standardized achievement tests as you have ready access to in order to determine the relative emphasis that they give to measurement of critical thinking and problem solving.

SELECTED READINGS

Burton, William H., Roland B. Kimball, and Richard L. Wing. *Education for Effective Thinking.* New York: Appleton-Century-Crofts, 1960. Of particular interest are Chapters 2, 11, and 21. Chapter 2 describes the thinking process. Pages 212–223 contain a comprehensive classification of errors and fallacies in thinking. Chapter 21 suggests numerous techniques and instruments for evaluating critical thinking.

Dewey, John. *How We Think.* Boston: D. C. Heath & Company, 1910 (rev. ed., 1953). Chapters 1, 6, and 7 are particularly pertinent. The chapters define thought, analyze the complete act of thought, and describe the inductive-deductive processes.

Hullfish, H. Gordon, and Philip G. Smith. *Reflective Thinking: The Method of Education.* New York: Dodd, Mead & Company, 1961. Chapter 1 presents an interesting, provocative rationale for a major emphasis on critical thinking throughout the school program. Part II contains five chapters devoted to the analysis of different aspects of thought.

Sherwood, John C. *Discourse of Reason.* New York: Harper & Brothers, 1960. This book includes good discussions of inductive and deductive logic, with specific examples and exercises in logic.

Smith, Eugene R., and Ralph W. Tyler. *Appraising and Recording Student Progress.* New York: Harper & Brothers, 1942. Chapter 2 is one of the early efforts toward evaluation of the various aspects of thinking. Several instruments and techniques to be used in evaluation are also suggested.

Wellington, C. Burleigh, and Jean Wellington. *Teaching for Critical Thinking.* New York: McGraw-Hill Book Company, 1960. Chapter 14 offers some help with several types of formal and informal evaluation instruments and techniques.

Wrightstone, J. Wayne, Joseph Justman, and Irving Robbins. *Evaluation in Modern Education.* New York: American Book Company, 1956. Chapter 20 contains several very good suggestions and illustrations for evaluation.

Chapter 12

EVALUATING LEARNING PRODUCTS AND PROCEDURES

INTRODUCTION

Education is ultimately concerned with the improvement of pupil performance in life situations; but the knowledge, understanding, and skills which pupils acquire in school are not always applicable to life problems. In the previous chapter our concern was focused on one specific aspect of pupil performance, that of reflective thinking and problem solving. In this chapter the concern is with general performance in a variety of subjects and with aspects of learning in the school curriculum. If the reader would take some time to review the worthwhile objectives of education reflectively, he would quickly find that one large segment of them is concerned with some aspect of preparing pupils for future occupations or activities: preparing them to be good teachers, doctors, carpenters, homemakers, citizens. In each instance the ultimate concern is with improving their performance; yet in too many instances the teaching focuses primarily on the knowledge and concepts which are the prerequisites to successful performance, with but slight attention to the actual performance itself. The evaluation of the teaching in these areas, too, tends to follow this same pattern of emphasis, utilizing paper-and-pencil measures of knowledge and understanding, with apparent confidence that pupils will make the difficult transition from the acquisition of knowledge to the application of that knowledge in performance and problem solving— a faith that the pupil who *knows* the functions of government and the relationship between citizen and state will *perform* as a good citizen. This faith that pupils will make the transition from knowledge to application is too scantily substantiated by fact to justify a teaching-evaluation approach which does not vigorously and directly attack the problem of improving pupils' performance whenever and wherever possible.

SPECIAL VALUES OF PERFORMANCE EVALUATION

Performance evaluation is not a panacea to be used to the exclusion of other measurement approaches, but it is an approach which has been slighted and which deserves a place in measurement where it fits the teacher's instructional objectives. Obviously teachers must continue to use conventional means of measurement to assess pupil growth, particularly in the acquisition of knowledge and understanding. However, when the instructional objectives stress performance, appropriate performance tests should be selected for measurement.

The major values of performance-type measurements are:

1. The tests measure pupils' ability to apply knowledge in typical life situations.
2. The tests have higher predictive validity than most forms for predicting successful job performance of the examinees.
3. The tests provide a supplement to other useful measures of ability and achievement.
4. Several of the instruments provide a combined quantitative and qualitative score.

Valid measurement of the ability to apply knowledge, although important, is not always easily achievable in the simulated conditions of the classroom. One cannot build a house, cure a sick patient, or vote for a president or senator in the classroom, but elements or approximations of these tasks can be simulated in the classroom. On the other hand, in such fields as music, art, and vocational education, in which performance is what is taught, it is not so difficult to bridge the gap between the classroom and life situations.

While the performance measures have higher predictive validity for determining successful job performance than most conventional measures, the multiplicity of jobs for which pupils are preparing precludes the practical possibility of either providing specific preparation for all of them or for constructing specific measures of them. Thus a practical compromise is to attempt to measure those jobs for which the majority of pupils are preparing or to measure the most common skill elements which appear in numerous jobs. The latter approach is that which was taken in constructing the *Flanagan Aptitude Classification Tests,* which were reviewed in Chapter 5.

The need for supplementary information other than that provided by conventional measures of achievement concerning pupils' performance abilities varies according to the teacher's instructional objectives and according to the subject field. In some fields the dependence should be almost wholly on the performance measures—e.g., physical education and music—and at the other extreme there are fields, such as history, in which conventional measures of achievement are entirely adequate.

The combined quantitative-qualitative score provided by such instruments as rating scales can be a mixed blessing; while they provide room for the exercise of judgment in assessing intangible qualities, they are also fraught with the hazard of unreliability when poor judgment is used. With tests such as typing speed tests, however, the score may provide a reliable index of the quantity-quality as it represents the speed and accuracy of pupils' performance.

OVERVIEW OF PERFORMANCE MEASUREMENT

Pupil performance consists of two elements which can be measured: (1) the procedure, skill, or technique; and (2) the product or result. For example, in home economics the cake which a pupil bakes is a product. The quality of the cake can also be evaluated as another element of performance. Obviously, however, the evaluation of both elements, product and procedure, is usually desirable because a pupil could conceivably produce a good product without following the correct procedure, in which case it would be highly unlikely that he could duplicate the result in subsequent efforts.

Measurable performance aspects of learning. Much instruction in schools is aimed at developing certain specific skills which lend themselves to performance-type measurement. Examples of these are (1) laboratory technique, (2) handwriting, (3) physical skills, (4) speaking skills, (5) artistic skills, (6) musical skills, (7) social skills, (8) creative writing skills, and (9) vocational skills. From the variety of these skills it is apparent that they cut across most of the areas of instruction in the school curriculum; furthermore, in the majority of the instances both the tangible product of pupils' achievement and the skills can be measured. While conventional measurement may give some indication of pupils' skills in some areas—e.g., music—the ultimate measure is in performance. The pupil who understands the intellectual basis of music and reads music well, scoring well on conventional tests, may actually sing or play an instrument poorly; however, lacking performance measurement, the teacher has a distorted picture of his achievement.

Fields of application. The variety of skills which can be assessed by performance instruments gives an indication of the fields in which this approach is applicable. The subject fields in which performance measurement should be used either as the principal or a supplementary approach include:

1. Speech
2. Drama
3. Music
4. Art
5. Foreign languages
6. Journalism
7. Vocational education—including home economics, business education, vocational agriculture, industrial arts, distributive education, and trade and industrial education
8. Physical education
9. Science

In some fields—e.g., science—the performance measurement will merely supplement conventional measures of achievement; and the laboratory procedure is the important area in which this approach is essential. In contrast, the fields of vocational education should rely heavily on performance measures; and good tests of performance are relatively easy to construct in these fields.

Evaluative methods and instruments. Performance instruments and techniques can be classified into three general types: (1) standardized tests, (2) teacher-made tests, and (3) observer-evaluator methods. Another way of classifying them is as (1) object tests, (2) procedure evaluation methods, and (3) project evaluation methods. In this chapter the first method of classification seems most convenient, although the relationship to procedure and product evaluation of the various tests and evaluative methods will be pointed out throughout the discussion.

1. *Standardized tests.* Several of the standardized tests which have been discussed in other contexts can properly be classified as performance tests. In fact this is true of most of the tests of physical fitness

which were reviewed in Chapter 6. One of the best known and most widely used of these is the *American Association of Health, Physical Education, and Recreation Youth Fitness Test*. This test has been administered to a large number of junior high and high school pupils in this country and Europe and has established norms for several aspects of physical performance.

The *Wechsler Adult Intelligence Scale*, which was reviewed in Chapter 5, includes a group of sub-tests to measure intellectual performance on nonverbal tasks. Numerous other tests of intelligence and aptitude stress performance. These tests are available for measurement in the special fields of music, art, and business education. The *MacQuarrie Test for Mechanical Ability* measures certain elements of manual or mechanical performance, including tracing, tapping, dotting, and copying. This test is applicable from grade seven through adulthood and, in addition to its educational use, has been used in industry to select inspectors, assemblers, draftsmen, blueprint readers, machinists, etc.

Even more specialized tests are those which can be used as a screening device to identify persons who possess the requisite skills for successful performance in clerical positions. An example of such a test is the *Detroit Clerical Aptitudes Examination*. Taken with conventional measures of speed and accuracy in typing and shorthand, these tests have considerable predictive validity and have been used both in business and in the preparation programs to establish appropriate levels of competence.

An interesting performance scale is the *Zaner-Bloser Evaluative Scale for Handwriting*. Although this instrument is not standardized in the conventional sense, it consists of a quality scale of handwriting specimens which are the quality norms against which pupils' handwriting can be compared for evaluation.[1] Examples taken from the sixth grade are shown in Figure 12.1. The two specimens in the figure are the best and the poorest for that grade level. These scales are useful only to evaluate the product or specimen of writing and do not help the teacher evaluate the strengths and weaknesses in the process of writing which may account for the relative quality.

When using such a scale the evaluation is still a matter of the teacher's

[1] The Zaner-Bloser staff has also prepared a chart showing handwriting faults and how to correct them. The chart is available to aid teachers in instructing pupils in cursive handwriting.

Specimen I — High for Grade 6
Similar cursive handwriting may be marked 85, and writing better than
this may be evaluated accordingly.

*I pledge allegiance to the flag
of the United States of America
and to the republic for which it
stands, one nation under God, indivisible, with liberty and justice
for all.*

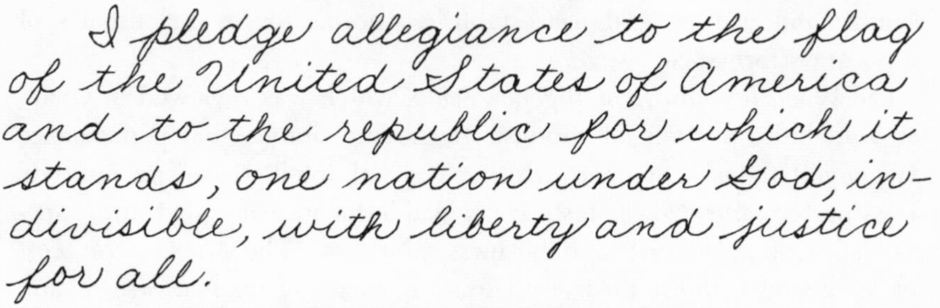

Specimen 5 — Poor for Grade 6
Similar cursive handwriting may be marked 65, and writing poorer than this
may be evaluated accordingly.

*I pledge allegiance to the flag of the
United States of America and to the republic
for which it stands, one nation under
God, indivisible, with liberty and justice
for all.*

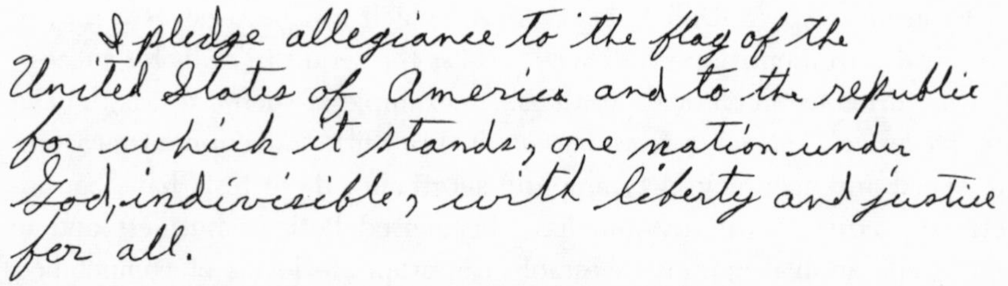

Figure 12.1. EXAMPLES FROM THE ZANER-BLOSER EVALUATIVE SCALE FOR HAND-
WRITING

From *Zaner-Bloser Evaluative Scale for Handwriting* (Columbus, Ohio: The Zaner-
Bloser Company, 1958). Reprinted by permission of the publisher.

personal judgment but with the obvious advantage of a concrete standard. The suggested procedure for using the scale includes the following
steps:

HOW TO EVALUATE WRITING WITH THIS SCALE

I. Procedure
   A. On the chalkboard teachers may write the sentence given in the
      scale.
   B. Pupils practice writing the example several times.

C. Pupils then may be asked to write the sentence carefully on other paper.
D. At the end of two minutes papers may be collected and graded.

II. Grading
A. Classify the papers roughly into three groups, calling them good, medium, and poor.
B. Beginning with the "good" group, compare each paper individually with the specimens of the scale. If it is equal to any of the specimens, give it the grade assigned to that specimen. If it is better than the specimen, give it a grade of 90 or 95. If it is poorer than the bottom specimen, give it a grade of 60 or lower.[2]

In several of the vocational fields, a teacher-constructed quality scale similar to that above is appropriate for use in evaluating the products which pupils construct. For example, a scale could be developed for evaluating the quality of hand-sewn buttonholes by collecting a half dozen samples which represent a continuum of quality from very poor to excellent. The work of pupils could then be compared against the quality scale and assigned a grade. Leather work, wood work, and metal work are also subject to the same evaluative approach.

2. *Teacher-made tests.* The teacher-made tests of performance include (1) object or identification tests, (2) work-sample tests, and (3) simulated conditions tests.

The *object tests* require the pupil to identify parts of a drawing or object—e.g., a flower in botany, an insect in zoology, a sewing machine in homemaking, a power saw in shop. As identification requires only pupil recognition or recall, the test can be improved by asking pupils to explain the function of the parts as well as identify them, thus measuring understanding as well as recall. Whenever practical it is probably best to use the actual object and ask pupils to write their identifications and explanations of the numbered parts on an answer sheet. However, since this is not always possible in the classroom, the drawing—with dittoed copies for each pupil—is frequently substituted for the actual object. The combined drawing and answer sheet in Figure 12.2 is an example of such an identification test for botany. In this case pupils must identify and explain the reproductive function of each numbered part of the flower which is depicted in the drawing. This test is scored by allowing

[2] *Zaner-Bloser Evaluative Scale for Handwriting* (Columbus, Ohio: Zaner-Bloser Company, 1958).

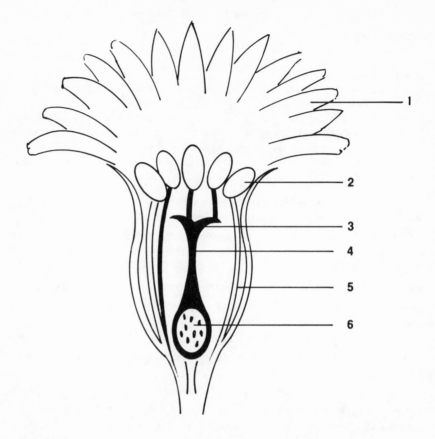

Figure 12.2. EXAMPLE OF AN IDENTIFICATION TEST FOR BOTANY

one point for each part correctly identified and one point for each correct explanation.

Work sample is the second type of teacher-made performance test. This test is based on a job analysis which lists the specific aspects of the job for which the pupil is being trained. From this job analysis a sample of the essential elements is taken and included on the test. This type of test is excellent in cases where pupils are being trained for specific jobs—e.g., carpenter, auto mechanic, or stenographer. The test has validity only for the specific job from which the work-sample elements are taken, unless these elements are common to numerous occupations. Thus the test does not have general application but must be constructed for each

Figure 12.2. CONTINUED.

Directions: In the blanks below identify and explain the reproductive functions of each of the numbered parts of the flower which is shown in the drawing.

1. _____

2. _____

3. _____

4. _____

5. _____

6. _____

specific job situation. A test of this kind in auto mechanics would include problem situations which are most commonly encountered in the repair shop, with pupils being asked to diagnose the trouble and repair the malfunction. In the work-sample test a series of such problems are set up, and the pupils move from one work station to another in a timed sequence.

The *simulated conditions test* is one which has limited application but is quite valuable in the instances in which it can be used. With this test the teacher tries to simulate in the classroom the actual conditions which the real job situation includes. The best example of this type of test is that which is used in teaching and measuring the field of driver education. In this case automobile mock-ups are used both as instructional aids and as checkup devices to determine when the pupils are ready to move out of the classroom and actually begin driving. Such a simulated approach has the advantage of permitting pupils to gain some skill in manipulating the automobile controls in a situation where errors have no serious consequences.

3. *Observer-evaluator methods.* The observer-evaluator methods are those in which primary reliance is placed upon observation of the subjects, although—as an aid to the evaluator—the observations are often structured through use of such instruments as the rating scale. These methods are discussed in some detail on pp. 272–277.

PLANNING FOR EVALUATION

Performance evaluation, like conventional types of evaluation, requires several steps in planning before actual construction of the instrument is undertaken. In fields where performance evaluative techniques are to be used, a course evaluation plan based on instructional objectives and content areas is valuable. This plan gives a general outline of the techniques and instruments which will be used in the total evaluation program for the course. Such an evaluation plan is as essential in measurement as the course outline is in instruction, and basing the evaluation plan on course content and instructional objectives assures close correlation throughout the course between instruction and evaluation.

Evaluation outline. An evaluation plan for the field of industrial arts is shown in Figure 12.3. Included in the evaluation plan are the following instructional objectives:

1. To equip pupils with the skills needed for home repairs and to stimulate them to make common repairs in their own homes.
2. To develop skillful use of the common hand and power tools.
3. To insure the observance of safety procedures in using these tools.
4. To interest pupils in the industrial-arts field through the construction of wood and metal projects.
5. To develop the skills and interests which will lead some pupils to the industrial-arts field as their vocational choice.[3]

The content areas included are:

1. Common hand tools and their use
2. Common power tools and their use
3. Qualities of various types of hard and soft wood
4. Safety rules
5. Joints: butt, miter, doweled, and mortise
6. Fasteners: screws, nails, staples, corrugated fasteners and glue
7. Finishes: oil, wax, paint, varnish, shellac, lacquer, glass, and plastics
8. Project selection and construction [4]

It is notable in this example that both conventional measurement instruments and performance measurements and techniques are used in a combined approach to give total evaluation of pupil achievement. Also it is to be noted that the choice of instrument or technique is determined by

[3] John A. Green, *Teacher-Made Tests* (New York: Harper & Row, 1963), p. 45.
[4] Green, p. 45.

the type of instruction objective which is being evaluated. The nature of the objectives also determines where the emphasis in evaluation will be placed—on product, procedure, or both.

Figure 12.3. TABLE OF SPECIFICATIONS FOR MEASUREMENT OF PERFORMANCE IN INDUSTRIAL ARTS

Behavior Objectives	*Content Areas*	
	1 2 3 4	5 6 7 8
1. To equip pupils with the skills needed for home repairs and to stimulate them to make common repairs in their own homes.	Objective test	Work-sample test
2. To develop skillful use of the common hand and power tools	Objective test Identification test Rating scale	Work-sample test
3. To insure the observance of safety procedures in using these tools	Objective test Observation checklist	Work-sample test
4. To interest pupils in the industrial-arts field through the construction of wood and metal projects	Project construction (Rating scale)	
5. To develop the skills and interests which will lead some pupils to the industrial-arts field as their vocational choice	Interest checklist Essay examination Interview	

John A. Green, *Teacher-Made Tests* (New York: Harper & Row, 1963), p. 46. Copyright © 1963 by John A. Green.

In addition to listing in the outline the instruments and techniques to be used, the instructor will have to decide when each will be used. He should space the evaluation throughout the instructional period so that it is a burden neither to himself nor to the pupils and so that there will be sequential evaluation to show the continuity of pupil progress throughout the entire period.

Planning the specific measurement. While the evaluation outline provides a general plan to be followed throughout the year, each test or evaluation included in the outline must also be planned carefully if pupils'

progress is to be accurately assessed. *The first and most important step in this pre-planning is analysis of the desired performance.* The analysis may be in the form of a specific job analysis, a list of the measurable elements of the performance or procedure, or a list of the measurable aspects of the product.

When pupils are being prepared for specific jobs, such as secretarial positions, a job analysis which includes the numerous duties and responsibilities of the secretary is a desirable base for evaluation. However in instances when the preparation is more general and may apply to several jobs, a list of the performance elements common to all is useful. Measurable elements of pupil performance include:

1. Speed of performance
2. Accuracy of performance
3. Number and seriousness of procedural errors
4. Errors in following instructions
5. Discrimination in selecting appropriate tools or equipment
6. Economy of effort (amount of "lost motion")
7. Timing as it is involved in the use of machinery or in physical performance, such as gymnastics
8. Intensity or force as it is involved in sports
9. Coherency related to the appropriateness of the sequence of steps followed [5]

When pupils are required to produce a product—a piece of furniture, a dress or a painting—the measurable aspects of the products may be the base for evaluation. Examples of these are:

1. The quality of finish for furniture
2. The quality of the seams for a dress
3. The harmony of color for a painting

The second step in planning is to select the approach which will be used. This selection is determined by the objective and by the aspect of performance to be measured: for a complex job, a work sample test; for a procedure such as diving, a checklist or rating scales; for a product, a quality scale or rating scale.

The third step is to select for evaluation the most representative elements of the task or product. This is a crucial step since poor selection invalidates the entire evaluation. When the elements selected are not

---

[5] James M. Bradfield and H. Stewart Moredock, *Measurement and Evaluation in Education* (New York: The Macmillan Company, 1957), pp. 330–331.

representative of the total performance, the evaluation lacks validity even though those elements selected are carefully evaluated.

The fourth step is the planning of a series of tasks which incorporate the elements which were selected for evaluation.

The fifth step is the selection of the tools and materials needed by the pupils.

The sixth and last step is the preparation of directions and an appropriate answer sheet.

CONSTRUCTION AND USE OF MEASUREMENT INSTRUMENTS

Test construction. The three types of performance tests—identification, work sample, and simulated conditions—were referred to briefly earlier in the chapter.

1. *Identification tests.* The identification test is easily constructed and can be used in a great variety of subjects, but it fails to measure complex elements of performance and is actually closely related to the conventional objective tests. This type of test may be used in a shop class to determine whether pupils are familiar with and understand the equipment, in which case pupils will be asked to identify and explain various parts of the machines. (See the example of an identification botany test using a drawing in Figure 12.2.) Suggested rules for the construction and use of these tests are:

1. Adequate directions should be given so that pupils clearly understand the type of response called for.
2. When drawings are used, they should be carefully reproduced and clearly labeled.
3. Pupils should be asked to identify only significant parts of the product or drawing.
4. Whenever feasible, pupils should be required to explain the function as well as to identify the item.
5. The blanks for the responses should be uniform in length and should be conveniently arranged to facilitate scoring.
6. The test should be scored by allowing one point for each response.[6]

This test should not be the sole measure of performance but is useful to give supplementary measurement when used with other conventional and performance instruments.

2. *Work-sample tests.* When properly constructed, work-sample tests

[6] John A. Green, pp. 48–50.

are probably the most valuable and versatile of the performance tests. These tests should measure the most important elements from the job analysis, although the finished product as well as the procedure can be measured. The test may be set up either as a series of tasks which are described, as in secretarial practice; or a series of work stations, as in industrial arts. In the first case, using the descriptive approach, each pupil should receive an instruction sheet describing the specific tasks which he is to complete.

The following two work samples could be used in an advanced typing class.

WORK SAMPLE 1

Directions:
Type the following letter in an acceptable style. Indent paragraphs 5 spaces. You will have to determine the paragraphing and decide upon complete sentences, in addition to supplying all punctuation and apostrophes. Make a carbon copy of the letter.

mr john e williams 72 east washington street portland 16 oregon dear mr williams we have received your letter of may 10 and appreciate your interest in our proposal your many years experience in business will be a definite asset to us if it would be convenient to you we would like to arrange a meeting in vice president henry a adams office at 2 p m on thursday june 10 to negotiate a long term contract we are looking forward to a pleasant and profitable partnership with you. very truly yours james j bradford president

WORK SAMPLE 2

Directions:
Type the following table, centering it vertically and horizontally. Leave 10 spaces between each of the columns. Use double spacing but triple space after the title.

Total Sales by Department for 1964 and 1965　　　(title)

Department	1964	1965
Clothing	$75,291.12	$80,460.01
Cosmetics	$ 3,496.10	$ 3,847.16
Draperies	$10,609.42	$11,775.40
Dry Goods	$48,246.53	$50,117.66
Furniture	$ 6,128.95	$65,123.07
Kitchenware	$ 5,047.23	$ 5,935.53

Two problems which face the teacher in using this type of test are (1) determining the proper length of the test and (2) assigning an appropriate score value to each item. The teacher's best method of estimating the time which it will take pupils to complete the test is to take the test himself, noting the time required and then allowing some additional time for pupils who will be less adept. The assignment of score weight to the items will be subjective as it is in essay examinations and will probably vary according to the difficulty level and time required by each item. If the items are approximately equal in these respects, they may be assigned equal weight. If unequal score value is assigned the items, pupils should be made aware of the values so that they may budget their time accordingly.

In the second kind of work-sample test, in which the test is set up as a series of work stations, one task is normally located at each station, although the stations are sometimes set up to require the use of multiple skills, materials, or projects. In a laboratory or shop it is convenient to set up fifteen to thirty stations, with pupils required to use one or two skills or materials at each station. Each pupil can then be moved sequentially around the stations, with one to two minutes allowed at each. This permits the test to be completed within the class period if the class is not too large.

EXAMPLES OF TYPICAL WORK-STATION PROBLEMS:

1. Make a simple metal weld.
2. Sew a fell seam.
3. Alphabetize a series of cards.
4. Complete a simple electrical circuit.

Administration and scoring of the test can be facilitated by adhering to the following suggestions.

1. The directions should indicate clearly both how the pupils are expected to respond and the sequence of the various stations.
2. The stations should be separated to prevent cheating.
3. The stations should be numbered, and all objects at each station should be lettered.
4. Time limits should be observed, with all pupils advancing from station to station when the signal to move is given.
5. All stations should be set up with independent problems which give no clue to the solution of problems at other stations.
6. To aid scoring, an answer sheet with written instructions and numbered

and/or lettered spaces should be provided for the problem at each station.

7. Equal scoring weight should be allowed for each station.

8. A key providing all acceptable responses and procedures should be prepared as the stations are set up.[7]

3. *Simulated conditions tests.* Simulated conditions tests are not tests in the conventional sense, and they have limited applicability because of the difficulties which are encountered in setting up a reasonable facsimile of the job situation in the typical classroom. Nevertheless these tests have high validity for measuring the few job situations to which they are adaptable, notably the vocational fields and such areas as driver training and science laboratory procedure. Since the test usually consists of a total procedure rather than a series of tasks, as does the work-sample test, the results are difficult to evaluate. Either a checklist or rating scale which includes the essential elements of the procedure is helpful in focusing the attention of the evaluator on the most important points, as well as providing a means for getting a comparative score for pupils' performances.

Observer-evaluator methods. Some aspects of pupil performance are poorly measured by tests and are best evaluated through one or more of the following methods: (1) checklists, (2) rating scales, (3) quality scales, (4) consensus rating, (5) rank ordering, and (6) paired comparison.

1. *Checklists.* It is common practice in evaluating pupils' use of power machinery to use a checklist based on the principles or rules for proper handling of the machinery to avoid damage to the equipment and physical injury to the user. In such classes the pupils are taught the rules, then are systematically observed with the aid of a checklist to determine whether they observe them in practice. Thus improper procedures can be effectively pinpointed, and careless pupils identified before serious injury results. Although the checklist does not, as it is sometimes claimed, objectify the evaluation, it does focus the attention of the observer-evaluator on the most important points which must be judged.

A checklist can be constructed by the teacher simply by listing the most important rules or principles which constitute acceptable procedure. Following the instruction in use of the equipment, each pupil should then be observed and evaluated with the checklist.

[7] Green, *op. cit.* (above, n. 3), pp. 51–52.

Use of the checklist is not confined to shop instruction. It is also readily adaptable to science laboratory procedure or the area of secretarial studies. In a typing class a checklist might include items referring to pupils' care of the machine and their typing procedure.

EXAMPLES OF SAMPLE TYPING CHECKLIST ITEMS:

1. *Care of machine*
   _____ moves machine carefully and only when necessary
   _____ pushes carriage to one side when erasing
   _____ keeps keys clean
   _____ types only with paper in machine
   _____ turns off switch when machine is not in use (electric)
   _____ covers machine when not in use
   _____ changes ribbon before it is worn
   _____ returns carriage positively without force
2. *Typing procedure*
   _____ has correct posture
   _____ uses correct fingering and hand position
   _____ uses firm, even touch
   _____ has smooth, rhythmical speed
   _____ uses tabulator stops for indented spacings
   _____ inserts and removes paper correctly

2. *Rating scales.* Rating scales are essentially checklists with the added dimension of a numerical scale for evaluating pupils' performance on each item. They are constructed in the same manner as checklists but have the advantage that they permit pupils to be given a numerical score which typifies the quality of their individual performances. These scores can also be handled in much the same way as typical test scores, and thus are easily translated into a grade. Many types of performance are adaptable to rating scale evaluation—e.g., teaching, public speaking, dramatic performance, athletic performance, and numerous types of vocational performance.

There is some danger when using rating scales of being lulled into the belief that the numerical scores which pupils are assigned are as reliable and objective as conventional test scores. Therefore, the evaluator must keep in mind the fact that the scores are subjectively assigned and are no better than the extent of care and judgment exercised in assigning them. It should also be remembered that various evaluators assign scores differently when judging the same performance. Some may be lenient and assign high scores while others who are less generous assign low scores. Also the same person making evaluations on different days may find, if he does not guard against it, that he is being influenced by extraneous factors and has changed from a lenient to a harsh evaluator or vice versa.

In several areas of physical education the rating scale is a valuable aid in helping the instructor judge the comparative performance of pupils, therefore an example of a rating scale for evaluating diving performance is shown in Table XVIII, as a model for those who wish to adapt rating scales to this or other areas of instruction.

Table XVIII. EXAMPLE OF A TEACHER-MADE SCALE FOR RATING DIVING PERFORMANCE

Directions: In evaluating the performance, circle the appropriate number on each criterion. 4 stands for excellent; 3, good; 2, fair; 1, poor; 0, unacceptable.

1. Erect, balanced stance on the board	0	1	2	3	4
2. Smooth approach to the takeoff	0	1	2	3	4
3. Proper timing of jump with springboard	0	1	2	3	4
4. Graceful arm and leg movements during takeoff	0	1	2	3	4
5. Sufficient height for dive requirements	0	1	2	3	4
6. Graceful flight through the air	0	1	2	3	4
7. Correct body movements for specified dive	0	1	2	3	4
8. Straight entry into the water	0	1	2	3	4
9. Minimum splash at entry into the water	0	1	2	3	4
Total rating of the dive					

3. *Quality scales.* Quality scales are used to rate products which pupils construct. Some quality scales—e.g., that shown in Figure 12.1—are available in published form; however, in most instances it is more feasible to construct the scale than to purchase one. Examples of some instructional areas which lend themselves to quality-scale evaluation include map work, woodworking, metal work, leather work, and sewing.

Perhaps the easiest way to construct the scale is to collect samples of pupils' work representing a continuum of quality from poor to excellent. Thus samples of wood finishing, leather tooling, welding, or sewing might be collected for a scale which would be used for evaluation in those classes. For example, in leather tooling a quality scale should include eight to ten work samples of the same design. Next the samples should be arranged and mounted in order from the poorest to the best product. Then evaluation of pupils' completed leather tooling projects is made by comparing them against the quality scale to determine which sample they most nearly approximate. With ten samples letter grades ranging from *F* to *A* could be assigned by allotting a two-sample range to each letter grade.

EXAMPLE:

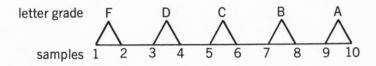

4. *Consensus rating.* Because some raters are more lenient than others, consensus rating rather than single rating is sometimes used to offset the individual errors. This method employs several raters, and an average of all ratings is taken as the final score. If the ratings are numerically scored by totalling the number of points which each rater assigns, it is a simple matter to compute a mean rating merely by totalling the scores assigned by each rater and dividing the total by the number of ratings.

Consensus rating is useful in public speaking classes. The teacher can construct a simple rating scale similar to that in Table XIX and ask pupils to rate the performance of each speaker. Ratings can then be averaged to get a reliable score. When unsophisticated raters—i.e., pupils—are used, it is desirable to keep the scale brief and the items simple to minimize errors.

5. *Rank ordering.* Rank ordering offers another means of comparatively evaluating products. This method requires that the products be arranged in order of quality from the poorest to the best. A variety of pupils' work—including themes, handwriting, map work, wood work, art work, and sewing projects—can be evaluated by rank ordering. Ranking the few best and poorest products is usually not difficult; ranking the large number of those which are mediocre is extremely difficult since there is so little difference in their quality. Rank ordering of the best and

Table XIX. SCALE FOR EVALUATING A SPEAKING PERFORMANCE *
Directions: Evaluate the speaker by circling the number which most

nearly represents his performance on each of the specific aspects listed below. For superior performance circle 4, above-average performance 3, average performance 2, below-average performance 1, and unsatisfactory performance 0.

Item		*Rating*			
1. Rapport with audience	4	3	2	1	0
2. Enthusiastic, interesting presentation	4	3	2	1	0
3. Effective organization of material	4	3	2	1	0
4. Clarity of presentation	4	3	2	1	0
5. Correct grammar usage	4	3	2	1	0
6. Good word choice	4	3	2	1	0
7. Adequate knowledge of subject	4	3	2	1	0
8. Significance of material presented	4	3	2	1	0
9. Good stage presence	4	3	2	1	0
10. Appropriate gestures	4	3	2	1	0

Total effectiveness of presentation

* John A. Green, *Teacher-Made Tests* (New York: Harper & Row, 1963), p. 79. Copyright © 1963 by John A. Green.

poorest samples of work, therefore, is fairly reliable, but it is considerably less reliable with the larger number of medium quality samples. A disadvantage of ranking is that the ranks apply only within the group. For example, the best product in one class might be no better than average if it were ranked among those of another class.

6. *Paired comparisons.* The paired comparisons method is adaptable to the evaluation of the same types of products as rank ordering; and it is a more reliable, but considerably more sophisticated, method. This method, however, is rarely used by teachers because it requires too much time and computation. In using this method to evaluate products—e.g., paintings in an art class—the observer must evaluate all possible pairs, deciding which of each pair is better. Thus with nine paintings the first would be compared against each of the remaining eight, then the second would be compared against each, etc., until the total of 36 possible paired comparisons had been made. As each paired comparison is made, the decision is recorded so that a tabulated summary would show the preference rank of all nine paintings.

PROBLEMS OF PERFORMANCE EVALUATION

Although the advantages of performance measurement are significant, the approach is not without problems. Notable among these are:

1. It is difficult to plan and construct performance examinations.
2. The complexity of many types of performance makes it impractical to break them down into measurable specifics.
3. Use of the examinations is limited to certain subject fields in which the instructional stress is on actual performance skills.
4. Administration of the examinations is often more difficult and time-consuming than conventional examinations.
5. It is difficult to validate the examinations since in most instances the validation would require extended follow-up studies of the on-the-job performance of the examinees.

Although performance examinations are difficult to plan and construct, they are not more so than the carefully constructed multiple-choice examination. Familiarity with the task of constructing the multiple-choice examination has made the task for most teachers seem relatively easy compared to the apparently formidable task of constructing the performance test. Increased use of this form would help teachers view the task in proper perspective.

While the use of performance evaluation is limited to those fields which stress performance as an educational outcome, the spectrum of such fields is considerably broader than the limited group of vocational fields in which this type of evaluation has traditionally been stressed. Even such professional fields as medicine, law, and teaching are basically performance oriented, albeit the desired performances are complex and difficult to analyze and evaluate. Nevertheless, it would be profitable to adopt further performance approaches to evaluation in such fields.

To the uninitiated, the administration of performance examinations may seem difficult and time-consuming; however, as one gains skill as a result of repeated use of the form, the problem of scheduling the tasks within the allocated class-period time becomes a routine one which is easily solved. The total time required for administration and scoring of performance examinations is comparable to that required for such other forms as objective and essay examinations. Both performance and objective examinations require a considerable amount of time in preparation, a nominal amount in administration, and a small amount in scoring. In contrast the essay examination requires a shorter preparation period, but the larger amount of time required for grading causes the time investment of the teacher to approximate that of the other two forms. Adequate evaluation with any of the forms requires a reasonable investment of time; slighting this investment can but lead to haphazard, invalid evaluation.

The final problem, the difficulty of validating the performance examination, is shared to some extent by all other examination forms. However, the follow-ups of graduates to determine on-the-job performance of examinees is even more essential with performance examinations than with most other forms, particularly in the vocational areas in which pupils terminate their education during or immediately following high school. Such follow-up is costly, but it would be valuable to most curricula both as a basis for evaluating the preparation programs and for determining predictive validity of pupil evaluations.

SUMMARY

Much of the instruction in school is ultimately concerned with teaching pupils to apply knowledge. If pupils eventually become good teachers, physicians, carpenters, citizens, it is both because they know how and because they perform appropriately and skillfully. They *know* and they *apply*. Measurement and evaluation which focus only on the "know" level of learning has left unassessed the most important half—application. Performance evaluation focuses on that remaining half to round out the picture.

In spite of the limited use of performance measures, they actually are adaptable to numerous fields besides the vocational areas, where their essential usefulness is obvious. Science, art, music, physical education, and speech stress performance; and failure to measure that performance is teaching negligence.

The two major elements of performance which are measurable are the procedure and the product. The instruments and methods available for the measurement of these two elements include: (1) standardized tests, (2) teacher-made tests, and (3) observer-evaluator methods, notably checklists and rating scales. While the tests tend to stress the measurement of pupil procedure in completing work samples, the observer-evaluator methods often stress the evaluation of the learning product—painting, wood project, sewing project, etc.

The effectiveness of measurement and evaluation of pupil performance is closely related to the care with which the instruments were planned and the validity of the evaluator's judgment. An essential prerequisite to measurement is the preparation of a detailed job analysis, followed by careful selection of the most important measurable elements. Without this step, evaluation is apt to focus on the wrong aspects of performance and consequently be invalid.

In the final analysis, although conventional paper-and-pencil tests of achievement are necessary, in most fields of teaching at least supplemental performance measurement is also required if the teacher is to get a total picture of pupils' achievement.

DISCUSSION QUESTIONS AND PROBLEMS

1. Construct a checklist to be used in evaluating a specific type of performance —e.g., swimming, a dramatic performance, a musical performance.
2. Select one field in which performance is stressed and make a list of the specific performance skills which should be taught and evaluated.
3. Discuss the relative merits of conventional paper-and-pencil examinations and performance-type examinations for evaluating pupil achievement in mathematics; in history; in home economics.
4. Select an occupation and do a job analysis of tasks which a worker in the occupation might be expected to perform.
5. Suggest ways in which performance tests can be used to measure achievement in fields for which paper-and-pencil tests have been the major means of measurement.

SELECTED READINGS

Ahman, J. Stanley, Marvin D. Glock, and Helen L. Wardeberg. *Evaluating Elementary School Pupils.* Boston: Allyn and Bacon, 1960. Chapter 11 provides a good background concerning the problems involved in performance testing, although it includes but few practical illustrations.

Bradfield, James M. and H. Stewart Moredock. *Measurement and Evaluation in Education.* New York: The Macmillan Company, 1957. Chapters 6 and 13. Chapter 13 is particularly pertinent for those who wish to construct their own performance examinations.

Green, John A. *Teacher-Made Tests.* New York: Harper & Row, 1963. The construction and use of performance tests are discussed in Chapter 4. Both principles for planning performance tests and concrete illustrations are included.

Micheels, William J., and M. Ray Karnes. *Measuring Educational Achievement.* New York: McGraw-Hill Book Company, 1950. Chapters 11–14 contain a thorough discussion of various types of instruments for measuring perfor-

mance. There are numerous helpful suggestions and illustrations of performance items.

Simpson, Elizabeth Jane. *The Classification of Educational Objectives, Psy-
chomotor Domain.* Project Report based on Vocational and Technical Educational Contract No. OE 5–85–104, May 31, 1966. Washington, D. C.:
U. S. Department of Health, Education, and Welfare, Office of Education.
Chapter 4 contains the proposed classification of objectives, together with
examples from several subject fields.

Wandt, Edwin, and Gerald W. Brown. *Essentials of Educational Evaluation.*
New York: Holt, Rinehart and Winston, 1957. Rating scales and checklists
are discussed in Chapter 4. This is a brief but informative book.

Chapter 13

ATTITUDE AND OPINION MEASUREMENT

INTRODUCTION

In 1958 when the federal troops were called to Little Rock, Arkansas, to enforce the integration of a handful of Negro pupils in the public schools, Little Rock became the symbol and rallying point for both those in favor of and those against racial integration. In this incident it is significant to note that the majority of people involved acted not on the basis of rational decision but on the basis of their feelings, their emotional bias, or their *attitude*. There were, of course, lengthy logical arguments supporting those attitudes; but frequently both the pro and con groups had rationalized their choice on the basis of personal attitude. So it is with many of the personal-social choices which men are constantly making at all levels of living from the community to the international scene. Attitude conditions the decision-making and opinion-forming process.

Attitudes hinder or facilitate human relationships. A perfectly agreeable and likeable chap may suddenly assume an aura of distastefulness if we are informed that he is a communist. Or we may wish to get acquainted with another person simply because his clothing and customs are strikingly like our own. The new teacher says of her principal, "I don't like his nasty little mustache. I'm sure that he is a regular Hitler." Each of these snap judgments based on attitude conditions the future behavior of the persons involved.

Since attitudes are so obviously important in determining behavior, in channeling thinking, and in conditioning applications of knowledges and understandings, they must indeed be important in teaching and the related evaluative process. Nevertheless such attitudes as those cited above have been acquired in acculturation and are thus largely dependent upon the group into which the individual happens to be born, certainly a chance circumstance over which he has no control. It is rare indeed that a concerted, well-planned program for developing certain attitudes is undertaken in the home, the school, or the national scene. But in those rare instances in which such a program is undertaken, striking results may be expected—witness Hitler's program for fostering and developing hatred of the Jews, which resulted in the calculated extermination of several million human beings.

It is the aim in this chapter to help teachers gain an understanding of the nature and importance of attitudes and to aid them in developing more effective programs for evaluating the attitude changes which they seek in their teaching. To this end the following topics are discussed in the chapter: (1) the nature of attitudes and opinions, (2) the functions of attitudes and opinions in personality adjustment and human relations, (3) sampling of attitudes and opinions, (4) scaling techniques for measuring attitudes, (5) other methods of measuring attitudes, and (6) application in the educational program.

THE NATURE OF ATTITUDES AND OPINIONS

The teacher who says of a pupil, "John has a bad attitude toward school" expresses a common concept of the meaning of attitude. This concept is indeed important since such an attitude will condition the effectiveness of the child's learning and progress in school as well as affect the teacher's attitude and mode of behavior toward that child.

The term "attitude" originally meant a body position which prepared for a certain physical action. The boxer assumed a physical attitude appropriate to his action; the fencer had a certain attitude; the diver, another, etc. In psychology and education this older meaning is replaced by a wide variety of meanings. Among them, the commonest and the broadest is a "feeling for" or a "feeling against" something. This value judgment or feeling may have been rationally worked out or may have been acquired through acculturation, but it is probably the result of the entire psychological background of the person. It will therefore influence the usual ways of thinking, acting, and feeling.

Attitudes possess several attributes. First, attitudes vary in complexity, from the relatively simple attitude toward a new style of dress to the complex attitude toward a religious group. Second, attitudes are usually learned within a group and are conditioned by the typical group mores, customs, and folkways. Third, although attitudes are relatively stable, they can be changed, even though the direction of change may be difficult to direct. Fourth, behavior attitudes are difficult to verbalize and may, in fact, be somewhat different from the verbal representation of the attitude. Attitudes also show individuality since any two individuals may profess the same verbal attitudes but behave quite differently in situations affected by those attitudes. Fifth, attitudes imply a subject-object relationship of the person holding the attitude toward some attitude-object.

Opinions are related to attitudes since they are often the verbal expression of one or several attitudes. Opinions are also related to beliefs. Beliefs are those things which we *know* to be true, whereas opinions are those things which we *think* to be true—frequently with regard to a controversial issue. The opinion is an expression of attitudes logically or emotionally arrived at. Habits and attitudes also have something in common. Habits are usual ways of acting, and attitudes are usual ways of thinking and feeling.

The failure to teach or to measure attitudes effectively often results from the teacher's failure to understand the nature of attitudes and from consequent failure to plan an instructional and measurement program. Teachers more often concern themselves with the measurement of opinion than of attitude. But the only type of opinion measurement which most teachers employ is a verbal poll of pupils concerning school or community issues, and the results of such measurement are seldom used as the basis for any further actions unless they constitute a vote on some school issue which must be decided. The failure to measure attitudes and to plan an instructional program to develop desirable ones often leaves the teacher ignorant even of pupil attitude toward her and the subject which she is teaching. Poor instruction without concern for the resultant pupil attitudes can lead pupils to develop a lifelong antipathy toward a subject field which will more than offset the slight gains in subject matter knowledge in the course. The pupils' attitude toward one teacher or course may significantly redirect the whole course of their lives. Interesting teaching attracts pupils into the field, while poor teaching may drive away even the pupils who are most talented in the field.

Dimensions of attitudes. When we speak of attitudes, most frequently we speak of whether the attitudes are favorable or unfavorable. Although this aspect of attitudes is certainly important, it is only one of the dimensions of attitudes; and the other dimensions may be equally important to the teacher whose aim is to make significant change in attitudes. The most important dimensions of attitudes include: (1) favorableness, (2) intensity, (3) salience, and (4) generality.[1] Perhaps an example might serve best to illustrate two of the above dimensions. In the typical school district the parents are favorable toward the public school which the district operates, thus pointing up the first dimension. The fact that they are favorable does not, however, tell us how intensely they are favorable; nor would a poll of the parents which gave the percent of those who are favorable and the percent who are unfavorable give us any evidence of the intensity of the pro and con feeling. Hypothetically, the attitudes in this instance might be represented by a continuum such as that in Figure 13.1

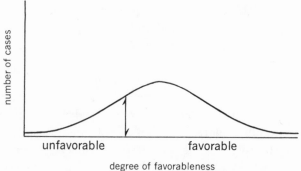

Figure 13.1. ATTITUDE OF THE PARENTS TOWARD THEIR SCHOOLS IN A TYPICAL SCHOOL DISTRICT

This representation of parents' attitude toward their school exhibits several of the characteristics of the normal distribution. The majority of parents cluster near the center of the curve, holding neither intensely favorable nor intensely unfavorable attitudes, although there are more persons who are favorable than unfavorable. Only small minorities lie at either end of the scale, and these are the persons whose attitudes are intensely favorable or unfavorable. It is probable that low intensity of favorable or unfavorable attitude of the majority is the reason why a

[1] These dimensions are suggested by H. H. Remmers. For further discussion, see H. H. Remmers and N. L. Gage, *Educational Measurement and Evaluation* (New York: Harper and Brothers, 1955), Chapter 23.

vocal, organized minority of unfavorable citizens can occasionally, as in the Pasadena school system a few years ago, influence many of the weakly favorable to adopt a temporarily unfavorable attitude and thus disrupt the school system. Well-organized school bond election campaigns often achieve the opposite result by influencing many whose attitudes have low intensity to vote favorably on the issue.

When attitudes are not intense, teaching directed at changing attitudes is quite effective. In such areas as race problems and school integration in the southern states, the curve in Figure 13.1 probably does not apply; and the bimodal curve in Figure 13.2 probably gives a better pic-

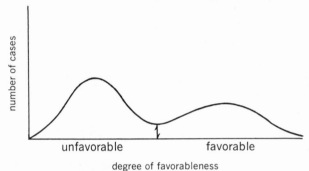

Figure 13.2. BIMODAL CURVE SHOWING HIGH INTENSITY OF FAVORABLENESS AND UN-FAVORABLENESS

ture, showing the majority unfavorable but the clustering of attitude on both sides of the scale at the extremes representing high intensity. In such cases it is difficult to change the attitudes of enough people to swing the balance.

Salience of attitudes is related to their intensity. Salience is how close to the surface or how easily aroused the attitude is. Attitudes toward emotionally charged objects such as war, religion, and politics generally have a high degree of salience and are easily aroused. There is, therefore, probably an element of truth in the old adage, "Never argue about religion and politics."

The last dimension, *generality*, refers to the total attitude concept of an individual or a group. We say of an individual, "He has a liberal viewpoint," or of a group, "That is a conservative group of people." In both cases the implication is that the liberality or conservatism applies to the total attitude outlook. It is, of course, true that there are marked individual variations concerning the generality of attitudes. One individual may be liberal in his politics but conservative in his economic activities, whereas another shows a reversal of the pattern. It is probably true, though, that most individuals tend to have a fairly consistent pattern or a generality in their attitude outlook. The young person is popularly believed to favor change and to hold liberal viewpoints and attitudes, while the older person is believed to incline to the conservative view.

In addition to the four dimensions, there are differences between many persons' public and private attitudes and between attitudes which they hold as part of a group and those which they hold as individuals. It is also true that people may have different attitudes toward public and private property. The automobile from the state motor pool may be driven less carefully than one's own automobile or the automobile borrowed from a friend. School-purchased textbooks are frequently less well cared for than those purchased by the individual pupil. Public buildings may be almost maliciously treated by those who would never think of defacing private property.

In our group-oriented society it has been said that man's opinions are those of the organizations to which he belongs and, further, that he assumes many different attitudes and personality roles as he moves from one group to another. Even teachers who have had many years of experience in directing the learning of others slip very readily into the pupil role when they go back to college in the summer; and they are loath to accept the responsibility, even in a limited way, of planning and directing their own classroom learning in the few classes in which the instructor is willing to call on them for their ideas.

SAMPLING METHODS

In recent years the sampling techniques used by pollsters to measure public opinion have proved so effective that the politician and the businessman, who are both ultimately practical, have awaited anxiously the results of the polls before planning a campaign, proposing new legislation, or introducing new products to the market. Although the polls are not infallible, they have become reliable enough that they can be used profitably as the basis of action. Much has been learned about sampling and prediction since the fiasco of the *Literary Digest* Presidential Poll. Furthermore the development of efficient electronic computers has made it possible to handle large amounts of data quickly and efficiently, thus permitting the selection of larger, more representative samples than heretofore.

All sampling techniques for assessing attitudes and opinions are based on the rationale that a limited representative sample of the total population will reflect accurately the attitude or opinion of the entire group. The sampling techniques which are most frequently used include (1) random sampling, (2) stratified-random sampling, (3) area sampling, (4) quota sampling, (5) spot-check sampling, and (6) opinion panels.

Random sampling is in many ways an ideal method since it is an accurate and an unbiased procedure. The sample can be drawn from any population by following a table of random numbers which can be found in most textbooks on statistical methods. Thus if one desired to sample the opinion of all the teachers in a state concerning an issue such as merit rating, it would be possible to select a random sample of 500 from the state teachers' directory by using the table of random numbers. In fact, either smaller or larger samples could be selected the same way; however if too small a sample were selected, the hazard of poor representation of the total population by the sample would be magnified.

Stratified-random sampling is a variation of the random sampling technique which is useful when there are obvious differences or subgroups among the population to be sampled. To take educators again as an illustration, superintendents, principals, and teachers are obvious subgroups which may show fairly marked divergence of opinion on such an issue as merit rating of teachers. When such subgroups do exist, each group is referred to as a *stratum,* and random samples should be drawn from each stratum. The number of persons chosen from each stratum should be proportionate to the representation of the stratum in the total population. Such stratified samples, in addition to giving better representation of the total population, also make it possible to compare any differences of opinion of one subgroup with those of another.

When random sampling or stratified-random sampling is too time-consuming or expensive to undertake, as in the case of statewide or national polls, a fairly accurate sample can be obtained by using the *area sample.* With area sampling the towns, cities, and rural areas to be sampled are laid out in a series of squares. The squares are then selected at random, and the addresses to be included in the sample are randomly chosen from within these squares. Each of the residences will then be contacted for interview; but as all the residences may not be occupied or the residents may not be at home when the contact is made, some will escape the interview. Such a procedure gives a reasonable facsimile of the opinion of the total population.

In such large area polling as the National Presidential Election Polls, for example the Fortune Poll by Roper or the American Institute of Public Opinion Polls by Gallup, random sampling is not feasible; therefore the *quota sample* is used. Quota sampling requires that the total population be analyzed according to its demographic features and the sample quotas allotted on the basis of these features. The demographic features most commonly used for allotting quotas are geographic region, age, sex, race, income, urban, and rural. The interviewers, who are located in various parts of the country, are then given a quota of interviews for each of the above categories.

Spot-check samples may be resorted to when extensive sampling is too expensive and time-consuming. The spot-check sample generally consists of a locally chosen group which gives proportionate representation of the demographic features of the total population. Because the sample is local, the interviews are easily and quickly made. Such spot-check samples give a fairly accurate reflection of the opinion of the total population when they are polled on national issues; however they tend to reflect the common local biases and prejudices on local issues or on national issues which affect them directly and about which there is a strong community feeling. It would be possible to select from among the citizens of most average-size school districts a small spot-check sample giving a reasonable facsimile of the total population. The use of polling to obtain opinions from such a sample might prove both useful and interesting to a high school social science class, particularly a senior class in American Problems.

Opinion panels are used for the same reason as spot-check samples. They can be contacted readily and inexpensively. The opinion panel consists of a group of people so chosen as to give a representative sample. In contrast to the other sampling techniques, the opinion panel is generally contacted through the mail by questionnaire rather than by personal interview, and the panel which is selected is stable so that questionnaires concerning a variety of issues can be referred to it periodically. There are obvious advantages in such a technique; however, there is no assurance that such a panel retained over a period of time might not change in ways other than those of their counterparts in the total population—education or income changes, for example, might shift some members of the panel to categories other than those which they were chosen to represent. Further, continued experience with the questionnaire may make some panel members "questionnaire-wise," as the pupil becomes "test-wise," with the result that they begin to anticipate in their answers the opinions which they feel they *should* hold rather than those they actually *do* hold.

Importance of opinion measurement. The teaching realm is an opinion realm. Few other factors are more influential in determining pupil learning than the opinions which they hold concerning the problems and issues being studied. It is virtually impossible to study the atomic bomb without an opinion-expressing and opinion-forming discussion of the why's and how's of its use. In fact, in dealing with such a controversial issue as birth control and the world population explosion, the entire rationale for one's position may well be based upon one's attitude toward birth control, so that all subsequent research or learning is bent toward an effort to support one's position pro or con; and all analyses of the problem, as well as suggested solutions, will be based only on the bias which one holds. For example, one who abhors birth control may reason from the thesis that other solutions to world population are possible, or may offer the substitute thesis that increased food production resulting from technological breakthrough will ultimately outstrip the population boom so that another equilibrium will be reached. The opponents, equally affected by their biased opinion, may also investigate only those theses supporting their opinion.

Frequently those students who are doing library research for graduate papers seek only the data and authoritative opinions which serve to reinforce their own opinions; thus it is that much educational research has come to contradictory conclusions through the fallacy of the half-blinded approach which frequently ignores other facets or other solutions to the problem under consideration. Classic examples are research studies concerning the effectiveness of large-group versus small-group instruction. Most teachers "know" that small groups are more effective, and research carried on by some investigators tends to favor their viewpoint slightly. On the other hand, there is equally good "controlled" research carried on by others which indicates that the large group may be as effective; and it certainly is much less expensive. Ability grouping is another educational issue which has encountered similarly conflicting research results.

Opinions of pupils can be influenced by teaching. But the teacher who would influence opinions and attitudes in desired ways must understand the basis for opinion formation, the function of opinions and attitudes in learning, and the difference between logical problem-solving research and rationalization. Such a teacher is in a much better position to utilize the effects of attitude and opinion in his instruction and to measure the pupil changes which may have resulted from the class experience.

SCALING METHODS

The polling methods, discussed in the first part of this chapter, are used primarily for the measurement of opinions. Scaling methods are used primarily in attitude measurement. Several of the methods discussed give relatively crude measurement with lower reliability and validity than might be desired, but they certainly can add immeasurably to our knowledge of the changes which take place in the children under our tutelage. These are the best instruments available for measuring attitudes, and teachers should use them in spite of their shortcomings. Even an ignorant man would not dig a hole with his hands if he had a shovel available. Attitude measurement is past the shovel stage of development, but it has not yet achieved the effectiveness of the power shovel.

One of the recent helpful developments is the *Taxonomy of Educational Objectives, Handbook II: Affective Domain*.[2] In the *Taxonomy* attitudes are classified for measurement under:

    3.0   Valuing
      3.1 Acceptance of a Value
      3.2 Preference for a Value
      3.3 Commitment

The *Taxonomy* provides examples of instructional objectives and measurement items related to each of the areas above.

The measurement of attitudes is not a new field, since such pioneers as H. H. Remmers and L. L. Thurstone have done work in the field for many years. One of the difficulties with the construction of attitude scales which these men and others have encountered is inherent in the

[2] David R. Krathwohl, *et al.*, *Taxonomy of Educational Objectives, Handbook II: Affective Domain* (New York: David McKay Company, Inc., 1964), pp. 139–153.

nature of attitudes themselves: attitudes consist both of the verbalized concept and of the behavior resulting from the attitude. The aspect of attitudes which is measured, however, is the verbalized concept, which is incompletely measured and which may well differ from resultant behavior. Another difficulty arises from the lack of any tangible criteria by which to measure change, as in the case of most other types of educational measurement—e.g., increased skill in spelling, reading, writing, etc. In spite of this difficulty there have been a number of good scales devised for measuring attitudes. Among the types of measurement Remmers lists the following:

1. The Interview.
2. The Priori Scales, or public opinion polls, which use the case method or ballot.
3. Psychophysical Scales, which are a series of opinions or attitude statements which are arranged in equally spaced units along a continuum.
4. Sigma Scales, which are a modification of the psychophysical scales. These are based on the assumption that attitudes are distributed normally and they use standard deviation units.
5. Master Scales, which are a modification of the psychophysical scales.
6. Behavior Scales, in which a situation is described and the subject asked to respond.
7. Analogous Measurements, in which attitudes are inferred through an interpretation of various types of stimuli or behavior situations. These are the projective techniques using such instruments as play therapy, pictures, music, and the Rorschach ink-blot test.[3]

Equal-appearing interval scales. The equal-appearing interval scale is a promising technique for attitude measurement devised by L. L. Thurstone. This scale is based on the assumption that a group of judges are able to arrange a series of attitude statements in order so that they range from the most favorable to the least favorable, with equal intervals of difference between each statement selected for the scale. The processes for judging and arranging the attitude statements for the scale are fairly complex. The first step requires that a large number of attitude statements referring specifically to the attitude object concerned be constructed. The second step is to have a group of thirty or more judges individually sort all the statements into eleven categories ranging from the one extreme of *most favorable* to the other extreme of *least favorable*. The judges must attempt to keep equal intervals of favorableness be-

[3] H. H. Remmers, *Introduction to Opinion and Attitude Measurement* (New York: Harper and Brothers, 1954), pp. 7–13.

tween each of the eleven categories. The third step is the calculation of the median value and the Q-range for each statement based on the category level into which the statement was placed by the various judges. For example, a statement might have a median value of 5.5, which would indicate that it should be placed at the middle of the scale if it is one of the eleven statements to be used in the final instrument. Only those statements which have a small quartile deviation, however, will be retained since they are the statements on which the judges showed relatively high agreement as to favorableness of the item. Ambiguity and relevance are also considered in selecting the final eleven statements which appear on the scale.

One such scale is that assigned to measure attitude toward war. In the scale the statements are arranged so that there are nearly equal intervals between each one. Such a scale represents a continuum of favorability toward a specific attitude object and can be used for measuring the favorableness of persons toward that object. The subject's score on the scale is the median value of the statements which he endorsed. Obviously such a scale could be constructed by teachers for classroom use. If statements were collected from the pupils, and the pupils were used as judges for categorizing the statements, a relatively good instrument of this type could be constructed. Such an instrument might well be used at the beginning and the end of a course to determine the attitude change which resulted in the interim.

The advantages of *Thurstone's Equal-Appearing Interval Scales* lie in the ease with which they can be administered and scored, in the fact that the scores are subject to conventional statistical computations, and in the fact that the scores obtained give a basis for comparisons between pupils. Too, the scales give quite reliable scores. The disadvantages include the following problems: (1) the fallibility of the judges may partially invalidate the completed scale; (2) the scales are not applicable to all groups—e.g., ethnic groups concerning racial problems; (3) the time and cost of construction may be excessive in view of the specificity of the scale—it applies to only one attitude object; (4) the scales measure only the verbalized concept of attitudes and not the actual behavior resulting from attitudes. Nevertheless the Thurstone scales are among the best of the attitude scales which have been developed up to this time.

Remmer's master scales. These scales are constructed in much the same manner as the Thurstone scales, that is the judges are used to determine the equal intervals of the statements which are included in the scales. The essential difference, however, lies in the more general application of the Remmer's scales. Remmer's scales are designed to apply to a class of attitude objects instead of one object and may include several vocations, several school subjects, or any other group of attitude objects which fall into the same classification. Thus it would be possible to determine a pupil's or a group of pupils' attitude toward each of four or five vocations by using one of Remmer's master scales which lists the four or five vocations about which the information was desired.

A scale of this type is the *Kelly-Remmer Scale* for measuring attitudes toward any institution. In this scale there are sixteen statements which range in order from the most favorable to the least favorable. It is worth noting that Remmer's scales simplify the scoring by arranging the statements in order of favorableness, whereas the *Thurstone Equal-Appearing Interval Scales* frequently present the statements in random order.

Likert scales. The Likert scales are used for determining the attitudes of people concerning a variety of issues, including such widely diverse areas as "internationalism" and "morale." An excerpt of a Likert scale is presented in Table XX. In this scale the subject is asked to choose one alternative on a five-point scale for each statement. The choices "strong approval," "approval," "undecided," "disapproval," and "strong disapproval" reveal the direction and the intensity of the individual's stand on the issue. The numbers shown in the example beneath each alternative give the score value for each alternative and do not appear in the original test. The higher values indicate a pro or favorable stand on the issue, and the lower values indicate a con or unfavorable stand.

Although the Likert scales can be quickly and easily constructed, the attitude statements which are included are not arranged on the basis of their favorableness toward the object under consideration. The statements are not submitted to a group of judges for scaling; thus their relevance, relative favorableness, and ambiguity are decided by the one person who constructs the scale. In spite of this weakness the Likert scales are quite comparable in validity and reliability to the scales devised by Thurstone and Remmers.

Bogardus social distance scales. These scales have been used to a limited extent for the last twenty-five to thirty years, the first of them devised by Bogardus in 1925. They are not, however, scales in the conventional sense (as are the Thurstone and Remmers scales) since no attempt

Table XX. LIKERT SCALE FOR MEASURING ATTITUDE TOWARD COMMUNISM

	Strong Approval	Approval	Undecided	Dis- approval	Strong Disapproval
Communism is the best form of government.	(5)	(4)	(3)	(2)	(1)
Communists in the United States should be guaranteed the same rights as members of the major political parties.	(5)	(4)	(3)	(2)	(1)
Communists should be allowed to recruit party members in our country.	(5)	(4)	(3)	(2)	(1)
Communists should be deported from this country.	(1)	(2)	(3)	(4)	(5)

is made to arrange the items from unfavorable to favorable on some type of interval basis. They also differ from the Likert scales, since they require only a positive or a negative response to each item. Furthermore, the social distance scales apply only to those aspects of attitudes dealing with social relationships or social acceptances between ethnic groups. The scales are unique in that they are mainly concerned with various levels of social acceptance which one group of people might have for another. The following categories of social distance may be employed in the scales as criteria for determining the extent of social acceptance which is accorded to the group toward whom the scale is directed:

1. Close kinship by marriage
2. Club membership as personal friends
3. Neighbors living on the same street
4. Employees in my occupation
5. Citizens of my country
6. Visitors in my country
7. Persons who should be excluded from my country

In either the Bogardus scales or the Guttman scale (discussed in the next section), there are few instances in which persons select items more favorable than any of those which they have rejected. For example, if a person were to reject items in the fourth category above (Employees in my occupation), he would not be likely to accept any of the items in categories one, two, or three. The Bogardus scales have the advantage over some of the other scales in that they measure projected behavior based on attitudes rather than the verbalized concepts of attitudes themselves. They give poor results, however, with individuals who either lack insight or who falsify their responses to make them conform to the socially acceptable attitudes of their group. If the person lacks insight, he will be uncertain of his reaction to a situation which he has never actually encountered in his own experience, e.g., "Would you accept a Negro as a co-worker in your profession?"

The Guttman scale. The Guttman scale is a unilateral approach to the measurement of attitudes based on the thesis that an individual who endorses an attitude statement will also endorse all the other related statements which are less extreme, whereas he will reject all statements more extreme than the first statement which he rejects. This thesis, of course, assumes that the statements are all clearly understood by the respondent and that his attitude pattern toward the object concerned is consistent. L. Guttman reasoned that there are no such accepted or easily verified standards for measuring attitudes as the yardstick for measuring physical size, the only yardstick being the variety of individuals' responses to establish the scalability of scale items. Figure 13.3 shows a perfect response pattern based on nine items and nine respondents. In the figure, subject A agrees with all nine of the items. At the other extreme, subject

item									
1	1	0	0	0	0	0	0	0	0
2	1	1	0	0	0	0	0	0	0
3	1	1	1	0	0	0	0	0	0
4	1	1	1	1	0	0	0	0	0
5	1	1	1	1	1	0	0	0	0
6	1	1	1	1	1	1	0	0	0
7	1	1	1	1	1	1	1	0	0
8	1	1	1	1	1	1	1	1	0
9	1	1	1	1	1	1	1	1	1
	A	B	C	D	E	F	G	H	I

person

Figure 13.3. RESPONSE PATTERN FOR A PERFECT GUTTMAN SCALE

I agrees only with item nine and rejects all other items since they are more favorable than item nine.

Although Guttman's thesis is intriguing, it has been difficult to construct actual scales which exhibit the perfect pattern of an unidimensional scale as illustrated in Figure 13.3. In fact, even close approximation of this perfect pattern is difficult. This difficulty need not, however, detract from the value of further investigation to find an approach which will give a rank-order measurement of the attitude of people. It would be valuable to know that one individual in a class had the most favorable attitude of all the pupils toward the course even when the extent of that favorableness was not indicated on a numerical scale. This would be analogous to the situation in which we know that a pupil ranked at the 90th percentile of his class on an achievement test administered to the group. The information has some value even though the teacher does not know the scores of the pupils or the relationship of a pupil's score to the scores of those in the standardizing sample.

OTHER METHODS OF MEASUREMENT

In addition to the polling and scaling methods of measuring attitudes, there are available to the teacher a variety of other methods. These include (1) observational methods, (2) questionnaire methods, (3) free-response methods, (4) error-choice method, and (5) multiple-attitude or crosscut method. Several of these methods are easily adapted to the classroom situation and have been used by some teachers for a number of years.

Observational methods. Observation of classroom or informal school behavior provides the teacher with the opportunity to gather pupil behavioral data from which attitudes may be inferred. Observation techniques are always subject to some serious limitations. The first of these limitations is that the observers may not be unbiased and objective. Second, observation is time-consuming since no worthwhile conclusions can be reached unless enough time has been spent to observe the subject in a variety of behavioral situations. Third, there is a low correlation between behavior and verbalized attitudes which is further aggravated by the error of the observer as he attempts to infer attitude from the observed behavior.

The *anecdotal record* and the *case study* have frequently been used by teachers as an aid in analyzing pupil behavior and identifying the underlying attitudes. Such records and studies are useful as aids to the teacher in helping pupils solve problems of adjustment or in helping them develop more desirable attitudes, providing that the data has been carefully collected and objectively recorded. Six principles which should be followed in recording observations for anecodotal records are suggested by Baron and Bernard.

1. Note the setting for the behavior—classroom, playground, etc.
2. Record the activity in progress at the time of the observation—study, free play, etc.
3. Note special circumstances—other persons involved, events leading up to the behavior.
4. Give a factual description of the behavior without any opinion or judgment concerning the behavior.
5. Sample the behavior over a period of time.
6. Interpret cautiously and be certain that the interpretation is based on observed data.[4]

Checklists of behavior may also aid the observer in limiting his observations to factual data. The checklist in Figure 13.4 is designed to aid the teacher in observing the behavioral attitudes cf nursery school pupils. This checklist gives three categories—"favorable," "indifferent," and "unfavorable"—for rating the attitude toward food, people, and games and activities. Similar checklists are easily constructed by teachers for observing pupil attitude at various grade levels toward a variety of attitude objects.

The *log* or time sample is another device which teachers find useful for giving a spot check of pupil behavioral patterns over a period of time. The log book can be used either for periodic entries of observations of a child's behavior or for recording a series of time samples of behavior. In the first instance, behavior incidents might be recorded at intervals of several weeks to show attitude changes.

With time sampling, behavior may be observed and recorded every day for a period of several weeks. Each day the pupil might be observed for a period of fifteen minutes, during which time all of his activities are noted and those which are pertinent recorded in the log. As aids to studying the attitudes of one or two children at a time these techniques are valuable, but it is obvious that they require so much time that the average classroom teacher is unable to use them for an entire class and must

[4] Dennis Baron and Harold A. Bernard, *Evaluation Techniques for Classroom Teachers* (New York: McGraw-Hill Company, 1958), pp. 172–173.

Susan Smith

Attitudes toward	Favorable				Indifferent				Unfavorable			
A. Food	Date				Date				Date			
1. Juices												
2. Soups												
3. Meats												
4. Fish												
5. Vegetables												
6. Desserts												
7. Milk												
B. People												
1. Teacher												
2. Parent												
3. Boys												
4. Girls												
5. Visitors												
C. Games and activities												
1. Sandbox												
2. Painting												
3. Playing House												
4. Workbench												
5. Blocks												
D. (Write in Others)												
1.												
2.												
3.												
4.												
5.												

* Insert date in box next to each item when observed.

Figure 13.4. NURSERY SCHOOL CHECKLIST

From J. Wayne Wrightstone, Joseph Justman, and Irving Robbins, *Evaluation in Modern Education* (New York: American Book Company, 1956), p. 368. Reprinted by permission of the publisher.

confine their use to the cases in which there is some urgent need to change attitudes or help the child solve some emotional adjustment problems.

The *sociodrama,* which is occasionally utilized by social science teachers as a means of helping pupils gain insight into the attitudes of others through assuming roles of behavior which are not customary, also provides an opportunity for the teacher to observe attitudes of several pupils as they interact in their assigned roles. A sociodrama in which pupils assume various roles in a racial conflict situation would certainly elicit expression of racial attitudes which could be observed. The difficulty with the sociodrama is that pupils are often reluctant to enact the various roles, or they may be inhibited in the portrayal so that the real attitudes are not apparent. Too, in the social situation persons are inclined to express attitudes which will be acceptable to the group rather than risk rejection by expressing variant attitudes. Such a situation may exist in many southern communities, in which strong vocal expression of attitudes opposing school integration deters those who favor integration from expressing their beliefs.

Questionnaire methods. The questionnaire or opinionnaire actually consists of a series of attitude questions such as those asked on the public opinion polls. The questionnaire, however, may be long and be designed to ascertain attitudes toward a variety of attitude objects. School administrators often find it useful to send out questionnaires to all parents in the community to determine their favorableness or unfavorableness toward certain aspects of the school program. Questionnaires to the pupils are also occasionally used as the basis of action programs for changing some aspects of the curriculum or the extracurriculum in ways which may better meet expressed needs or desires of the pupils. It is questionable whether the respondents should be required to put their names on the questionnaires. Further bias may also be introduced by the fact that questionnaires are returned on a voluntary basis, and those who do not return the questionnaires are not considered in the results. If the percent of returns is low, the results may not represent the attitude of the total population. In school questionnaires, percent of returns has been markedly improved by having the pupils distribute and collect the questionnaires.

Personal interviews, based upon a questionnaire, help to insure a high percent of participation; but even here some persons refuse to be interviewed, or their responses are biased by the presence of the person who is interviewing so that they will not voice any socially unacceptable attitudes.

Free-response methods. Free-response methods include either a series of general questions which will permit free response or unfinished stories related to the attitudes being measured. The subject may respond either verbally or in writing. If the response is verbal, it may be less restricted than if it is in writing; but there will be no record of the response for further analysis unless the response is tape recorded or written as the subject responds.

An example will serve to clarify the free-response method which utilizes questions. If attitude toward labor unions were to be measured, a series of questions such as the following could be used to stimulate an attitudinal response:

1. How have labor-management relations been affected by unions?
2. How have working conditions been affected by unions?
3. What means, if any, should be used to control unions?
4. What effects have unions had on the general economy of the country?

If the unfinished story method were used to measure attitudes toward unions, a story such as that which follows might be presented for completion by the subject.

> You are a skilled carpenter who has worked at the trade for a number of years in a small, nonunion town. You move to a large town in which you have had a job offer with a large construction company. When you arrive and apply for the job, you are informed that you will have to join the union before you can be employed, that you must be examined by union officials for competence, and that you may have to serve an apprenticeship as a carpenter's helper before you can take a job as a carpenter. Describe what you would do.

Both of these free-response methods have the disadvantage that they do not give any kind of a standard response pattern which would permit meaningful comparisons to be made between the attitudes of a group of persons. Likewise the analysis of the responses when a group such as a class is measured will be rather time-consuming and difficult since there are no norms or standards to help in the analysis.

The most notable advantage of the method is that questions or stories can be easily constructed and used by the classroom teacher, and they give the teacher a notion of the attitude climate of the class as well as some identification of those who are most favorable and those who are most unfavorable toward the object concerned.

Error-choice method. The error-choice method is a disguised technique of assessing attitudes. The method requires the construction of an achievement examination, usually with multiple-choice items having only two responses. About one-half of the items are actually conventional achievement test items, whereas the rest of the items have no correct response given so that the subject indicates the direction of his bias by the choice which he makes. With this method the choices on those items which have no correct answers must reflect divergent attitudes toward the object considered; thus one choice would be favorable and the othe unfavorable. An example of such an item which would reflect a favorable or unfavorable attitude toward recently constructed school buildings might read as follows:

> Two to three billion dollars' worth of school buildings have been constructed annually in the United States during the past three years. During that period how much higher has the average cost of school buildings per-square foot been than the cost per square foot for residential dwellings?
>
> A. $10
> B. $ 1

Actually the cost per-square-foot averages less for school buildings than for residential dwellings; and the person who selects $10 expresses disapproval of the expenditures, whereas the person who selects $1 has a more favorable attitude. This item along with a number of other similar items could give a good picture of the attitudes of a group of people toward school expenditures and might also reflect, incidentally, the attitude toward the public school in general. The error-choice technique is relatively new, but it seems to be a promising technique which may become more useful as it is improved.

Multiple-attitude method. The multiple-attitude method is an objective test which, with one test administration, provides much information about a person. It contains seventy-two items, each printed on a separate card, twelve of which are included to conceal the nature of the test. The items test attitude toward parents, siblings, preference for mother or father, preference for sister or brother, superiors, equals, and religious and political tolerance.

These cards are shuffled, and the subject sorts the cards to select those with which he agrees. These cards with which he agrees are then sorted again to find the ones with which he "completely agrees," and those which were discarded in the first sorting are sorted to find those with which he "completely disagrees." By charting the subject's classification of each item the trend and intensity of his attitudes can be interpreted.

CONSTRUCTING A CLASSROOM SCALE

Teachers do not always have access to the latest measuring devices; and frequently some of these devices, particularly in attitude measurement, are not readily adaptable to the classroom situation. In such instances it may best fit the teacher's purpose to construct his own scale for measuring attitudes. In constructing a scale the following steps should be followed:

1. Ask the pupils to hand in a series of statements indicating their feelings toward the attitude object in question.
2. Edit the statements eliminating the duplicates and those which are factual rather than attitudinal.
3. Duplicate the statements and ask the pupils to mark the statements which they consider favorable with a "+" and those which they consider unfavorable with a "—."
4. Examine the papers and select those statements which at least three-fourths of the pupils classified favorable or unfavorable.
5. Rank the statements in order as nearly as possible from those on which all agreed to those on which only 75 percent agreed. Do this with both the favorable and the unfavorable statements, placing the favorable statements at the top of the list.
6. Readminister the statements to the pupils asking them to number the statements in order from most favorable to least favorable.
7. Summarize the results of the rankings, using median rankings for each statement and quartile deviations. The average rank of each statement might be used here instead of median and Q; however it would probably be less defensible.
8. Select those fifteen to twenty statements with the smallest Q-range and rank them according to median value. The test can then be administered by having pupils circle those statements with which they agree.

Quantitative scores can be computed by assigning descending positive weights to the favorable statements and descending negative weights to the unfavorable statements. The pupil's score would then be a summation of the weighted values of those statements with which he agreed. Perhaps a concrete example might serve best to illustrate this scoring process. Figure 13.5 shows the arrangement of scale items and their score values. If pupil A circled statements one through seven, his score would be +28. If pupil B circled statements five through nine, his score would be +3. If pupil C circled statements six through ten, his score would be −3.

There are several problems with this teacher-made scale which should be noted. First, it takes time to construct (but it is available for use with several classes once it has been constructed). Second, arranging the statements in order of favorableness may have some tendency to bias results, thus indicating more favorable scores than true pupil attitudes would warrant. Shuffling the items would tend to avoid this difficulty. Third, a few pupils may indicate inconsistent patterns in their response —e.g., circling only statements four, six, nine, and eleven in the illustration above. For these pupils a quantitative score such as that suggested

Figure 13.5. SCORING ARRANGEMENT FOR TEACHER-CONSTRUCTED ATTITUDE TEST

Score Value	Item	Favorability
+7	1	Most favorable statement
+6	2	
+5	3	
+4	4	
+3	5	
+2	6	All statements ranked in order
+1	7	of median favorableness
−1	8	
−2	9	
−3	10	
−4	11	
−5	12	
−6	13	
−7	14	Least favorable statement

would be meaningless. If this pattern persists with many pupils, the teacher might ask pupils to give a Likert-type response based on the five-point scale: "strongly agree," "agree," "undecided," "disagree," and "strongly disagree." Likert gives favorable items values of 5, 4, 3, 2, and 1 ranging from "strongly agree" to "strongly disagree"; and unfavorable items have values of 1, 2, 3, 4, and 5 ranging from "strongly agree" to "strongly disagree." Pupils must respond to all items; and their scores are the sums of the numerical values which they checked, with high scores indicating favorable attitudes.

If the teacher decides to use the Likert-type response, it is not necessary in constructing the scale to have pupils rank the statements from most favorable to least favorable, thus eliminating scale construction steps five, six, seven, and eight. It is probably well for the teacher to experiment with both types of instruments to determine which best meets her classroom needs.

SUMMARY

Few factors are as influential in determining the direction and extent of learning in the classroom as the attitudes of pupils toward the school, the teacher, and the subject being taught. Not only will the attitudes learned in the home and the school environment influence the immediate life of the child, but they will also influence directly his future choice of friends, a wife, a vocation, education, religion, and politics. The very opinions which the child will hold as an adult concerning a myriad of controversial and problem areas may be more influenced by the attitudes which he has developed than by the facts, knowledges, and understandings which he has garnered. For few men are able to put aside emotional biases and intolerant attitudes in order to adhere to objective logic when faced with real life problems. Part of the responsibility for this tendency for men to solve problems emotionally rather than logically unquestionably rests with the teachers of those men, teachers who, either through lack of understanding of or concern for attitudes and consequent opinions, failed to concern themselves with the measurement and teaching of attitudes and the development of logical problem-solving techniques.

Attitudes and opinions are measurable, and they can be changed through skillful teaching. The means through which opinions have been most successfully measured include the various *sampling techniques* ranging from random sampling to opinion panels. The sampling techniques have made it possible to assess accurately the opinions of large groups of people by contacting, through interviews or questionnaires, relatively small groups which reflect the total group composition. Such techniques have been extremely useful for predicting group behavior in such instances as presidential elections, support or opposition to proposed legislation, and acceptance or rejection of new business products. Schools have done little to exploit the possibilities of sampling techniques in teaching, although the techniques are utilized occasionally in school public relations programs.

The measurement of attitudes has been experimented with for a number of years, and a variety of *scales for measuring attitudes* has been developed. The scales, however, are less valid and reliable than the instruments in areas such as achievement and intelligence testing; and public school teachers have used them infrequently. Among the most notable scales are *Thurstone's Equal-Appearing Interval Scales, Remmer's Master Scales, Likert Scales, Bogardus Social Distance Scales,* and *Guttman Scales.* In addition to these scales, there are available to the teacher a number of miscellaneous evaluative techniques ranging from observational methods to tests and behavioral checklists.

For the teacher whose special instructional objectives are not adaptable to measurement with the attitude scales or miscellaneous techniques discussed in the chapter, there is always the possibility of constructing a teacher-made attitude scale. Such a scale, if constructed by a teacher who is acquainted with the better attitude scales and familiar with the nature of attitudes, may well meet the needs for measurement in his classroom better than one of the published instruments.

DISCUSSION QUESTIONS AND PROBLEMS

1. Construct a Likert-type scale to be used in measuring the attitude of pupils toward a subject field of your choice.
2. Select a nationally important political issue and poll a small random sample of the student body. Compare the results of this poll against a national poll.
3. Write a series of free-response questions or stories which would be appropriate for class use.
4. Outline several situations which could be used as the basis of an attitude-related sociodrama for elementary or junior high school pupils.
5. Make a list of issues or problems in the high school curriculum for which attitude scales could be constructed.
6. Distinguish between the following terms: "attitude," "habit," "opinion," and "belief."

SELECTED READINGS

Allport, G. W., P. E. Vernon, and G. Lindzey. *A Study of Values.* Boston: Houghton Mifflin Company, 1952. This is an excellent reference.

Anastasi, Anne. *Psychological Testing.* 2nd ed. New York: The Macmillan Company, 1961. Chapter 19 is devoted to a discussion of interests and attitudes.

Edwards, A. L. *Techniques of Attitude Scale Construction.* New York: Appleton-Century-Crofts, 1957. This book is an excellent source for those who intend to develop their own attitude scales.

Freeman, Frank S. *Theory and Practice of Psychological Testing.* 3rd ed. New York: Holt, Rinehart, and Winston, 1962. Chapter 24 discusses the measurement of interests, attitudes, and opinions.

Jackson, Douglas N. and Samuel Messick (eds.). *Problems in Human Assessment.* New York: McGraw-Hill Book Company, 1967. Part 7 contains a series of articles related to attitudes and their measurement. Articles number 61 and number 63 apply specifically to measurement.

Krathwohl, David R., *et al. Taxonomy of Educational Objectives, Handbook II: Affective Domain.* New York: David McKay Company, 1964. This is an excellent job of classifying instructional objectives related to attitudes and values. It includes examples of objectives and measurement items.

Remmers, H. H. *Introduction to Opinion and Attitude Measurement*. New York: Harper & Row, 1954. This is a comprehensive consideration of the techniques and instruments for measuring attitudes and opinions.

Shaw, Marvin E. and Jack M. Wright. *Scales for the Measurement of Attitudes*. New York: McGraw-Hill Book Company, 1967. The nature of attitudes is discussed in Chapter 1, and construction of scales is considered in Chapter 2. The remaining chapters present a number of different scales for measuring attitudes toward numerous attitude objects. This is an excellent reference.

Sherif, Muzafer and Caroly W. Sherif. *An Outline of Social Psychology*. New York: Harper and Brothers, 1954. Chapters 15 and 16 deal with the measurement and change of attitudes. Several examples of the measurement instruments are included.

Wrightstone, J. Wayne, Joseph Justman, and Irving Robbins. *Evaluation in Modern Education*. New York: American Book Company, 1956. Chapter 19 is a brief, but good, overview of the techniques for evaluating attitudes and values.

Chapter 14

MARKING AND REPORTING
TO PARENTS

INTRODUCTION

An onerous task of teachers is that of grading pupils' work and assigning the course marks for the periodic reports to parents. Too few actually consider marking as an opportunnity for taking stock of their own instructional success and of the pupils' progress, yet this is a major justification for periodic marking. When the report card is viewed as a distracting interference in the instructional program, the final examinations are apt to be poorly planned and conceived; and the course marks may poorly reflect the extent and caliber of pupils' achievement.

The careless marking attitude of a few teachers can spread a pernicious distrust of the course-marking procedure, causing teachers and pupils to regard the process as a necessary but disagreeable hurdle. In such an atmosphere, some teachers may view tests as opportunities to match wits with pupils in a guessing game wherein the test items literally become a series of difficult, ambiguous puzzles with little relationship to the course content or instructional objectives. Pupils faced with such examination ordeals often retaliate by devising all sorts of ingenious methods for cheating on the examinations.

Fortunately such an attitude has not permeated our entire educational system, although it is widespread enough to be rather disturbing. On the other hand, the fact that the course marks given in high school constitute one of the most reliable factors for predicting the success of students in college is mute testimony to the conscientiousness of many teachers.

PURPOSES OF MARKING

As a rule, the course mark and the unit of credit are the only tangible evidence in the pupil's permanent record that he actually enrolled and completed the course. The course mark is generally accepted as *prima facie* evidence of the pupil's level of attainment when he transfers from school to school or seeks employment in post-school years. Most teachers, parents, and employers are convinced that they understand the meaning of a course mark such as "A." Yet, knowledge of the objectives and content of the course is necessary before one can really understand the meaning of a specific course mark. An *A* mark in a course with restricted objectives and limited content topics may actually represent a lower level of achievement than the *C* or *B* mark in a similar course which has broad objectives and numerous content topics.

When properly used, the course mark gives a valid indication of pupils' attainment of the content and objectives. Together with explicit objectives and a carefully prepared course outline the mark can provide a meaningful index of pupil achievement for parents, teachers, and pupils.

PROBLEMS OF MARKING

The problems of marking loom large in the minds of many, but they are by no means insurmountable. A brief look at some of the more persistent problems can allay some of the distrust of the marking process and serve as a basis of attack in solving the most serious problems:

1. There is widespread misunderstanding of the meaning of the terms "scoring," "grading," and "marking."
2. Course marks often fail to reflect the real course achievement of pupils.
3. Course marks are often based on insufficient evidence of pupil achievement.
4. Many teachers lack clearly defined criteria for assigning course marks, or assign them carelessly without serious effort to assess achievement.
5. Teachers often permit such extraneous factors as the halo effect, personality conflicts, class attendance, and discipline to influence pupils' course marks.
6. Teachers, parents, and pupils rarely share an understanding of the nature and extent of achievement represented by specific course marks.
7. Pupils frequently work for a specific course mark rather than to learn as much as possible in a course.

Differences in scores, grades, and marks. The terms "scoring," "grading," and "marking" are not interchangeable; and precise definition and correct use of the terms is a first essential step toward clearing up the misunderstanding.

Scoring refers to the process of correcting assignments or tests and calculating a numerical score for the papers. The scores may be either *raw scores,* which indicate the number of correct items on the papers; or they may be *derived scores,* in which case they are translated into a common numerical language which permits several sets of scores to be compared. Examples of derived scores are IQ scores, percentile scores, standard scores, and percent scores.

Grading is a more general term than scoring. While it may include scoring as a basis for the grade, it also requires the additional step of assigning a grade—usually a letter-grade—to the test or assignment which is being evaluated. The grade may be assigned on the basis of (1) fixed standards, (2) group standards, or (3) individual standards.

Marking refers to the process of assigning a composite course grade at the end of the marking period. This grade, or course mark as it is properly referred to, represents the total complex of the pupils' achievement in the course.

Basis for marks. Probably the most serious problem in the entire process of marking is the failure of teachers to give course marks which truly reflect the total complex of pupils' achievement. This problem arises when teachers (1) fail to base marks on sufficient evidence of achievement; (2) permit personal factors to influence pupils' marks; and (3) fail to define clearly the course objectives and criteria for assigning the mark. In most classes fairly frequent testing is required to provide an adequate measure of achievement; and in assigning the mark, the teacher should not permit personal impressions to become a significant factor. Marks are not a proper means of disciplining pupils or forcing class attendance. They are a measure of achievement. Numerous and varied types of tests together with frequent class assignments should provide the necessary information for proper assignment of the mark, provided that the tests and assignments are related to the course objectives.

Much of the problem of marking could be alleviated if teachers devoted sufficient attention to the preparation of a concise, definitive statement of course objectives as the basis for instruction and measurement. Such a statement is necessary if both the teacher and his pupils are to know what is most important in instruction and what will be emphasized as achievement is evaluated. When the pupil knows what will be emphasized, it matters little if his primary motivation is the course mark since a good mark will also represent high-level achievement of all the important course objectives. Thus, as the two blend, the pupils' attention is more apt to shift from the extrinsic motivation of the course mark to the intrinsic motivation of desire to achieve all the objectives which have been set.

Pupils may apprise parents of the course objectives and the criteria for marking, but the major responsibility for informing parents of these standards rests with school officials. This is an educational process which requires both individual and group conferences with parents. It is an essential aspect of the reporting process without which the marks on the report card will fail to convey the message concerning their children's achievement which the teacher intended them to convey. Lacking a common understanding of the nature of the mark, both teachers and parents will interpret it according to the variety of past experiences which they have had. This failure to educate the public at least partially accounts for the widespread misunderstanding of school marks.

GENERAL PRINCIPLES OF MARKING

In addition to the suggestions made in the previous section, these general principles provide a workable framework for the marking process:

First, *marks should reflect the child's learning and be based on his actual achievement in the class.* The teacher should take an inventory of the status of pupils at the beginning of the year so that their marks may reflect as nearly as possible learning within the class rather than that which preceded his present class enrollment.

Second, *all concerned* (pupils, parents, and teacher) *should be aware of the goals of achievement set for the class.* This shared understanding makes the mark more intelligible and tends to dispel some of the dissatisfaction which results from misunderstanding. It also permits pupils to concentrate their efforts on those aspects of learning which the teacher feels are most important and against which achievement will be assessed. It is most frustrating to the conscientious pupil to find that he has misdirected hours of study effort in the wrong areas because he did not know what the teacher believed to be most important. Eventually such continued frustration will lead most pupils to develop haphazard study habits, to fail to study at all, or to study only in "cram" sessions just before examinations. These poor study habits cause pupils to have poor test psychology and result in their performing at a subnormal level. Furthermore, cramming results in short-term learning which is quickly forgotten after the examination.

Third, *pupils should be aware of their grade progress throughout the term.* As a general rule corrected tests and class assignments should be returned to pupils and followed up with class discussion so that all may learn from their errors. Furthermore, it is helpful to post the grades periodically on a class chart so that pupils can follow the continuous progress of their achievement in the class. To protect his anonymity each pupil can be assigned a number which only he and the teacher know. This information is confidential, and pupils should not be encouraged to share it with their classmates; yet it is valuable for each to know his progress and his relative status in the class if he is to have a realistic picture of his progress.

Fourth, *marks should not be used to enforce attendance or correct disciplinary infractions.* Enforcing attendance is an administrative responsibility, and the teacher who penalizes pupils by lowering their course marks for disciplinary infractions misunderstands the purpose of marking, distorts the pupils' concept of the mark, and may actually provoke further discipline problems by becoming in the eyes of the pupil an unfair teacher. Both pupils and parents feel strongly that lowering the mark in such instances is stealing from the child what he has already earned.

Fifth, *pupils should know what grading method is used and what factors are weighed in the course mark.* It makes considerable difference to the pupil whether the teacher grades on the basis of fixed standards, a curve, or an individual basis. Also when the pupil knows what factors are weighed in the mark, he can work more effectively toward improvement. For example, if he knows that daily assignments are weighted heavily, he can devote a larger proportion of his study time to these assignments.

Sixth, *the teaching staff should formulate a grading policy which all teachers accept.* If grades and course marks are to be comparable within the school and among schools, such agreement is essential. The grading policy should not totally restrict individual variation, but it should include a number of guidelines relative to such matters as the method of assigning marks, the weight of final examinations, and the proportional distribution of course marks. Without this staff agreement there is apt to be considerable variation among teachers, with some teachers giving a large number of high marks and others giving very few. This inconsistency encourages dissatisfaction among parents and pupils and frequently causes them to make unfair comparisons of the quality of instruction of the teachers involved. The child who received *A* marks one year from a teacher whose standards are lax may, in a subsequent year when he receives lower grades, blame the second teacher for this apparent decline in his performance. Inconsistency of marking causes dissension among pupils and within the community and may eventually totally disrupt teacher morale.

Seventh, *the grade distribution within each class generally should not vary significantly from the normal-curve percentages.* This principle applies particularly to the elementary grades and those required secondary courses which include the entire range of intellectual ability. Obviously, in homogeneous groups and elective courses different grade distributions are justified. In any case, it is helpful to have periodic studies of the schoolwide distribution of marks to determine whether an excessive number of high or low marks is being assigned. High school grade point averages have always been important information to employers; and with burgeoning college enrollment, they will assume even greater importance than they have in the past as a factor in selective admission. Thus unrealistically high standards, particularly in a select homogeneous group, may prevent some very capable children from gaining an opportunity to enroll in college.

SCORING TESTS

Tests must be scored before a grade can be assigned, and the total number of correct items which a pupil obtains is referred to as his *raw score.* Grades may be assigned on the basis of the raw scores, but the raw score is often converted into some type of derived score to facilitate grade assignment—e.g., percent, percentile, *z*-score, *T*-score, stanine. Because the number of items and the difficulty level vary on different tests, raw scores cannot be compared in a meaningful way; but the derived scores provide a common language which permits comparison among test scores in several classes within a subject field or across subject fields.

Objective tests. Objective tests are the most easily scored of the various types of tests. They can be quickly and accurately scored, and the preparation of a punched-out scoring key facilitates the process. Such a key should be arranged so that the correct responses are punched out to fit over pupils' answer sheets, permitting errors to be marked through the punched-out holes. When the test is short, the teacher may memorize the answers and score the test, although this introduces the possibility of additional error when the teacher's memory is faulty. Scoring objective tests is essentially a clerical task; it is not difficult, but it requires careful attention to avoid errors which distort the pupils' scores.

Guessing correction. Since guessing is a factor on objective tests, the scoring formula is often used to correct for guessing. This formula is: $score = rights - \dfrac{wrongs}{(N-1)}$ (N in the formula refers to the number of choices within the item). For a 50-item multiple-choice test with four choices on each item, the pupil who answers 30 items correctly, misses 10, and leaves out 10 receives a score of 27 ($30 - \dfrac{10}{3} = 26\frac{2}{3}$ or 27). For a true-false test, since the number of choices equals two, the score is calculated by subtracting the number of incorrect responses from the number of correct responses. Thus, on a 50-item test, the pupil who answers 30 items correctly, leaves out 10, and misses 10 would receive a score of 20 ($30 - 10 = 20$). As the number of choices increases on a test, as in five-choice multiple-choice type the pupil has less chance to guess the correct choice and correcting for guessing is unnecessary. However, on the true-false test the pupil has one chance out of two to guess the correct response on each item and should be able to get half of the items correct by guessing. Therefore, use of the guessing formula for this type of test is desirable. When the guessing formula is used for scoring a test, pupils should be informed in the test directions so that they can leave blank those items which they do not know.

Essay tests. The grade on essay tests is often assigned directly on the basis of the teacher's evaluation of the quality of the examination. In this case no numerical score is given; however, when the point-score [1] method is used, each question is assigned a point value, and the papers are actually scored according to the evaluator's judgment of their quality. Thus, each examination has a total raw score which is then translated into a letter grade.

METHODS OF GRADING

Although numerous grading methods have been developed, teachers tend to rely on the method which their own instructors used. This section reviews the basic methods and their advantages and disadvantages

---

[1] The point-score method is outlined in Chapter 9, p. 212.

in an effort to point out the folly of exclusive reliance on one method. The three methods discussed include (1) individual standards, (2) fixed standards, and (3) group standards.

Individual standards. While many teachers are aware of the need for an instructional program designed to meet children's individual needs, interests, and abilities, few actually fully implement such a program. Nevertheless, these few should evaluate achievement on individual standards using comprehensive testing at the beginning of the term to determine pupils' status and at the end of the term to assess achievement in the interim.

When individual standards are applied, those whose intellectual capacity is lowest are not required to achieve as much for a given mark as those with higher capacity. Achievement which would earn an A grade for the dull child might, in fact, be considered failing level for the bright child. To some extent the individual standard concept is implemented in numerous schools in which children are grouped homogeneously according to ability level, since the slow groups are sometimes given A grades for performance which is often below the failure level for the accelerated groups. On the other hand, the accelerated-group pupil who competes with his intellectual peers must perform at a very high level of competence to achieve an A grade. However, use of this variable standard often causes some dissatisfaction, particularly among the bright pupils who think it unfair to require a greater quantity and a higher quality of work of them than of the slower pupils.

Whenever individual standards are used, it is absolutely essential that the method be understood and accepted by pupils and their parents. Otherwise opposition to the method may cause school and community conflict detrimental to the entire school system.

Fixed standards. Traditionally teachers have graded on the basis of fixed standards which had as their referent levels of subject-matter competence. Such standards are easily understood when a minimum level of competence within a field or grade level is defined and agreed on. In such skill areas as the "three R's" in the elementary school, these levels have been established with some degree of confidence, although critics have frequently asserted that the levels are unrealistically low, offering too little challenge, particularly to bright children. However, the problem of establishing fixed standards which insure minimum levels of competence is more difficult in the comprehensive secondary school, which includes general education requirements, a college preparatory curriculum, and a vocational curriculum.

Historically, when the secondary population was relatively select, a college preparatory curriculum with rigid standards could be established and adhered to. But in recent years the secondary population has become almost as intellectually diverse as that in elementary schools, so that teachers have the alternatives of either changing their standards or failing an excessive proportion of pupils.

When grades are assigned on a fixed standard, the level of subject-matter competence is established by the teacher and represents his judgment of an appropriate level for acceptable achievement. With this method the raw scores are generally converted into percent scores and then assigned letter-grade equivalents. For example the pupil who answers correctly 40 of the 50 items on a test receives a raw score of 40, a percent score of 90, and a letter grade of *B*. Seventy percent is the generally accepted level for a minimum passing grade; and although it appears to be fixed, is actually easily manipulated by changing the difficulty level of the test. As a result, the fixed standard is actually an illusion and may be changed at the personal whim of a teacher. Teachers have no consensus on the difficulty level of the fixed standard; consequently, some set low standards and give an excessive number of high grades, while others set excessively high standards and fail too great a proportion of pupils.

A final problem with the fixed-standard grading method is that it fails to take into account the year-to-year changes in the caliber of a teacher's classes. While there are those who believe that the standard should be inviolate as a hurdle of achievement to be attained by each class, most would argue that the capacity of individual class members is a primary consideration. This argument is particularly valid when the standard is set by the teacher without an outside validating criterion such as follow-up of pupils to determine the effects of the standard on their future performance.

Norms and percent grades. With these comments concerning the problems of the fixed-standard basis for grading in mind, we can examine two fixed-standard methods frequently used for assigning the grade. These are the system of norms and the percent system. In order for a teacher to establish reasonable norms it is necessary that he have records of the performance of several hundred pupils, otherwise his sample is apt to be biased so that it gives a distorted picture of the performance which should be expected of a normal sample of pupils in the class. To collect this data the teacher may either keep records over a period of years; or he may, if he has four or five sections of the same class, base his norms on the performance records of all his sections for a one- or two-year period. Norms established in this manner are based on pupils' relative achievement of the total course content, with an *A* grade representing the mastery of 90 to 95 percent of the course content, a *B* grade a smaller proportion of the total, etc. This method assumes that there is a relatively fixed body of subject matter and skills which are to be taught in each course, and the grading standards can be changed either by varying difficulty of content or by raising or lowering the proportion of the total content which pupils must achieve for the various letter grades. If the content difficulty is decreased, more pupils will master it and receive high grades. Likewise, if the content remains unchanged but pupils must master only three-fourths of the content instead of nine-tenths for a grade of *A*, more pupils will receive high grades. Thus the content of the course as well as the standards of achievement for each letter grade must be empirically based on the performance of a large number of students if the grading system is to be defensible.

The *percent system* of grading is similar to the system of norms since it utilizes subject-matter standards. The difference is that instead of using the record of performance of a number of pupils in setting the standards, the teacher uses his judgment to determine the course content and the test difficulty, and each pupil is assigned his grade on the basis of the percent of the test items which he can answer correctly. Seventy percent is generally set as the passing mark, and the upper 30 percentage points of the scale are used to show the level of pupil performance.

With this system grades can be reported either numerically according to the percent each pupil achieved, or they can be translated into a letter grade based on a scale similar to the following:

$$A = 94 - 100\%$$
$$B = 86 - 93\%$$
$$C = 78 - 85\%$$
$$D = 70 - 77\%$$
$$F = 69\% \text{ and below}$$

Even though grades are calculated on the percentage basis, they are almost always reported as letter grades; however many teachers fallaciously hoping to increase the precision of their scale add "plus" and "minus" letter grades and thus increase the number of possible grades to 15 by reporting $A+$, A, $A-$, etc. The obvious fallacy here is that the scale is no more precise as a measure of pupil achievement than the subjective judgment of the teacher as he established the level of difficulty for the course content and for the tests. Some unethical teachers have, in fact, claimed to raise their standards by raising the failure mark from 70 percent to 75 or 80 percent, while still continuing to fail about the same number of pupils by the simple device of making their test easier.

Group standard. While the fixed standard may be appropriate in courses or curricula which pupils elect, the group standard permits a desirable flexibility for general education areas required of all pupils. This method relies on either the rank order or the curve as the basis for assigning grades. It emphasizes competition among class members, but permits the standard to be varied according to the intellectual level of the group.

The *ranking methods* include rank order and percentile rank. The rank-order method requires that the teacher rank the pupils' scores from the highest to the lowest and assign the marks on the basis of rank, the "A's" to those who rank highest, etc. This is a poor grading method since the differences between the ranks are not the same; for example, the first and second pupil may have scores of 91 and 90 respectively, while the third pupil's score is 85. Furthermore, the teacher may use no basis other than his judgment to determine the proportion of the class who shall receive each mark.

The method of percentile ranks is a better system, particularly when applied to a large group. A pupil's percentile rank in the group indicates the percent of pupils whose scores were below his. A percentile rank of 75th percentile on a test indicates that 75 percent of the pupils received scores below that point. Calculation of percentile rank from the frequency distribution and the ogive curve is illustrated in Chapter 3. However, for a small group of pupils the calculation is simply made by arranging the scores in rank order and dividing each pupil's rank by the total number of scores in the group. A pupil who ranked 20th in a group of 30 would have a percentile rank of $20 \div 30 = 67$th percentile. Sixty-seven percent of the class ranked below this pupil. For small groups the percentile rank is little more useful than rank order; however when the records are kept for several classes the percentile ranking method can be useful in establishing norms against which each class can be compared.

Curve grading is based on the rationale that unselected, heterogeneous groups, particularly in the elementary and early secondary school years, tend to approximate normality in intellectual ability; and each class, if it is an unbiased sample, should have about the same percent of outstanding, average, and slow pupils as that in the normal distribution curve. It is then assumed that the grade distribution should be normal, as shown in Figure 14.1 with the following grade assignments:

7 percent *A*
24 percent *B*
38 percent *C*
24 percent *D*
7 percent *F*

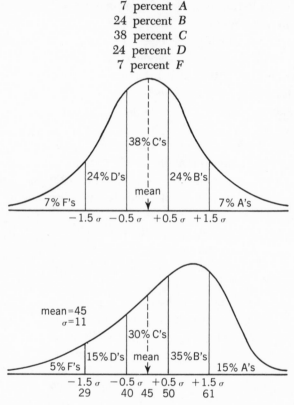

Figure 14.1. GRADE DISTRIBUTION BASED ON MEAN AND STANDARD DEVIATION FOR A NORMAL CURVE AND FOR A SKEWED CURVE.

This method works well as long as the group intellectual distribution approximates a normal curve but leads to serious injustices in classes which are homogeneous or badly skewed. Such atypical classes may be skewed —either bright or dull—or they may be bimodal, with a few average and an abnormally high proportion of dull and bright pupils. In these cases the normal curve does not apply, but the fixed standard also fails to fit the situation. For a homogeneous group, appropriate fixed standards provide a better grading basis. And rather than force a skewed group, which contains a disproportionate number of bright or dull pupils, into a normal-curve pattern, the calculated mean and standard deviation [2] may be applied to distribute the grades, as in the second example shown in Figure 14.1. This is probably the best system of curve grading for the classroom teacher. In using this method these steps should be followed:

1. The mean and standard deviation should be calculated.
2. One-half standard deviation should be added to the mean and subtracted from the mean to get the range of *C* grades.
3. One standard deviation should be added to the top of *C* grade-range to determine the range of the *B* grades, and one standard deviation should be subtracted from the bottom of the *C* grade-range to get the *D* grades.
4. All grades which fall one and one-half standard deviation above the mean are *A* grades, and all grades which fall one and one-half standard deviation below the mean are *F* grades.

In the case shown in Figure 14.1 the calculated mean is a raw score of 45, and the standard deviation is 11 raw-score points. Thus when the curve is divided off, those above 61 receive *A*'s; those in the range from 51 to 61 receive *B*'s; those in the range from 40 through 50 receive *C*'s; those in the range from 29 through 39 receive *D*'s; and those below 29 receive *F*'s.

The major advantage of calculating the standard deviation rather than using the normal distribution for assigning test grades is that the calculated grade assignment takes advantage of the skewness of a group and permits a greater proportion of high grades to be given when the class performance is outstanding as well as giving a greater proportion of low grades when the class performance is low.

Figure 14.2 gives examples of a negatively skewed grade distribution in which the class performance is high, a positively skewed distribution in which the performance is low, and a class in which performance follows a normal curve. In examining this figure it is evident that approximately half of the students in the bright group receive *A*'s and *B*'s, whereas almost half of the students in the low group receive *D*'s and *F*'s. However, a word of caution is in order here since skewness may result

---

[2] See the method of calculation of these statistics in Chapter 3.

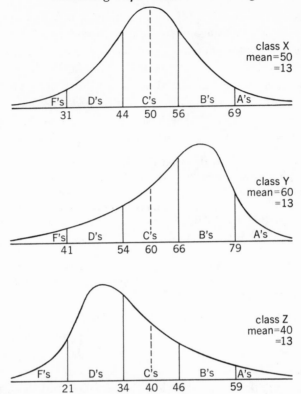

Figure 14.2. A COMPARISON OF THE GRADE DISTRIBUTIONS OF HYPOTHETICAL BRIGHT, NORMAL, AND DULL CLASSES USING THE CALCULATED MEAN AND STANDARD DEVIATION TO DETERMINE THE RANGE OF GRADES

either from improper test difficulty (too easy or too difficult) or skewed class performance. Thus, it may be that the level of test difficulty should be increased or decreased; and before awarding too high a proportion of either high or low grades throughout the year, the teacher should examine the class intelligence test scores as an aid in determining the intellectual level of the group.

Fixed versus group standards. There are a few instances when either the fixed standard or group standards should be used exclusively. The absurdity of selecting either standard for all types of groups is clearly depicted in Figure 14.3, which presents a graphic comparison of the results when each is applied to bright, average, and dull classes. When classes are homogeneously grouped, standards may be fixed at different levels for the bright and the dull, while the calculated curve would be quite

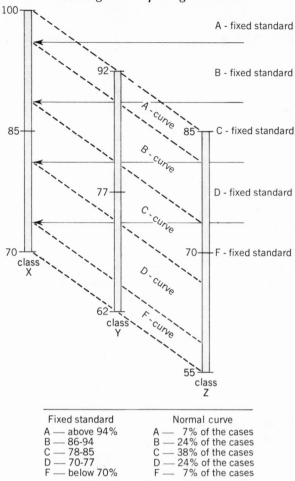

Figure 14.3. COMPARISON OF GRADE DISTRIBUTION FOR THREE CLASSES ON A DIFFICULT 100-ITEM OBJECTIVE TEST, USING FIXED STANDARDS AND CURVES

From John A. Green, *Teacher-Made Tests* (New York: Harper & Row, 1963), p. 112. Copyright © 1963 by John A. Green.

appropriate for the average group. With heterogeneous groups the normal curve could be applied.

The type of subject matter should also be taken into consideration. For instance, elective subjects in a specified college preparatory or vocational curriculum should probably have standards fixed according to the competence required for continuation in the program and subsequently the occupation or profession. On the other hand, in required general education courses, which include all pupils, the group standard would undoubtedly be the better basis. Much of the misunderstanding and criticism of grades results from haphazard or indiscriminate use of one or the other standards without explanation of the basis used and without general faculty agreement concerning the criteria for choice.

ASSIGNING COURSE MARKS

For the conscientious teacher the course mark represents the composite picture of a number of grades which pupils received during the term. However, when too little evidence concerning pupils' achievement is collected or when the grades have been improperly assigned, teachers understandably face the task of assigning course marks with considerable reluctance. They figuratively shudder at the prospect of facing the inevitable stream of querulous pupils and dissatisfied parents, since the task of attempting to justify unjustifiable marks can never be a pleasant or satisfying one.

There are a number of good methods of assigning course marks, but these methods will not measurably improve the validity of the marks if the teacher collects insufficient pupil achievement data, grades tests and assignments carelessly, or constructs poor measurement tests. Three acceptable methods of assigning course marks are (1) the simple average, (2) the cumulative point score, and (3) the grade-point average.

Simple averages. Most teachers use the arithmetic mean to establish the pupil's course mark. This method can be used with raw scores or percent scores. In calculating the mean, daily assignments and tests are averaged together with important tests, such as the final examination, which are weighted more heavily than the other assignments or tests. This method works well as long as pupils conscientiously turn in all assignments and miss none of the tests. However, the pupil who has an occasional lapse of memory, misses school when a test is given, or receives an uncharacteristically low grade on one assignment is unduly penalized because the mean is heavily influenced by a deviant score. For example, the pupil whose mark is based on the following seven percent scores— 100, 98, 95, 92, 90, 85, and 0—would have a mean score of 80 percent ($560 \div 7 = 80$). All work on which he was graded was of high caliber, but the one missing assignment lowers his mark to a C. Based on the median or mid-score he would receive 92 percent or a mark of B. In the situation above, two reasonable alternatives are open to the teacher: he may either drop out the one deviant score and calculate the arithmetic mean on the remaining more typical scores, or he may use the mid-score as the marking basis.

Point-score method. In the majority of classrooms many different types of evaluations are necessary to get the entire picture of pupils' achievement. These may include informal and standardized tests, daily assignments, checklists, rating scales, attitude scales, and sociometric devices. When such a variety of evaluations is used, the obtained scores and grades are not readily translated into the same numerical or letter grade so that they can be averaged. Under these circumstances the point-score method of marking is useful. With the point-score method each test, rating, daily assignment, etc., is allotted a point-score weight, and together they constitute the maximum cumulative points which a pupil can earn.

For example, daily assignments and class work can be evaluated on a 3, 2, or 1-point basis using the symbols $\overset{+}{\sqrt{}}$ to represent a 3 and superior work; a $\sqrt{}$ to represent a 2 and satisfactory work; and a $\overline{\sqrt{}}$ to represent a 1 and unsatisfactory work. Oral performances can also be evaluated on this point basis or given a letter-grade equivalent from the average score obtained on a rating scale. Test scores may be translated into letter grades and given a grade-point equivalent, or the raw scores may be accumulated for a total score.

An example of the use of the cumulative-point-score method is shown in Table XXI. This example contains four grading factors: (1) daily assignments, (2) oral performances, (3) unit tests, and (4) final examination. Each of the factors has approximately the same point-score weight. The final examination is weighted four times to give it a weight equivalent to each of the other three factors because it is a comprehensive measurement of achievement for the entire term and, if carefully constructed, should give the most valid measure of total pupil achievement. The final examination should have a significant weight in the final course mark, as a rule about one-fourth of the total.

Pupils' cumulative-point scores should be posted throughout the marking period; then at the end of the term, when they are totalled, the course mark can be assigned on a calculated curve or set norm basis. This method is easily explained to pupils and parents, and there will be little argument over the marks which are given.

Grade-point average. The grade-point average method is the easiest to

Table XXI. EXAMPLE OF THE USE OF CUMULATIVE-POINT-SCORE METHOD AS A BASIS FOR ASSIGNING A PUPIL'S COURSE MARK

	Assignments	Oral Perform- ances	Tests	Final Exam	Total Point Score
Pupil's grades	√ √ √ ⁺√ √ √	B B B	B B C C	B	
Score weight	2 2 2 3 2 2	3 3 3	3 3 2 2	12	44
Maximum score	3 3 3 3 3 3	4 4 4	4 4 4 4	16	62

use. It takes less time to calculate than the point-score method, can be readily explained to pupils, and is very reliable. To use this method all assignments and examinations must be converted to letter grades; the letter grades are then averaged, using numerical equivalents such as the following: $A = 4$ points, $B = 3$ points, $C = 2$ points, $D = 1$ point, and $F = 0$ points. In a course in which four factors—daily grades, a written report, unit tests, and a final examination—are to be averaged, the pupils' course marks would be calculated as follows: A pupil receives B on daily work, C on the written report, B on the unit tests, and A on the final examination for a total of 12 points and a 3-point grade average $(3 + 2 + 3 + 4 = \dfrac{12}{4}$ or 3). His course mark would be B. Since final grade-point averages do not always come out even, the marking scale below is suggested.

$$A = 3.6 - 4.0$$
$$B = 2.6 - 3.5$$
$$C = 1.6 - 2.5$$
$$D = 0.6 - 1.5$$
$$F = 0.5 \text{ and below}$$

REPORTING TO PARENTS

Besides providing the permanent record of pupils' achievement, an important reason for giving course marks is to keep the parent apprised of his child's school progress. A variety of methods has been used, but the most frequently used and those discussed here are the parent conference, written reports, and report cards.

Parent conference. Parent conferences are used more in the primary grades than at any other grade level. In these grades instruction focuses on teaching children to read. Pupils are grouped into about three groups according to their reading readiness or reading level, and their individual progress and achievement are evaluated on an individual basis. For this reason the informal parent conference is appropriate and more informative to the parent than a formal report card. Some schools, however, still use report cards in these grades or follow a compromise policy using both conferences and formal reports in alternate reporting periods. This policy normally permits two conferences and two formal reports per year.

The conference has the advantage over other reporting methods of permitting a two-way exchange between teacher and parent. While it is primarily a reporting session in which the teacher analyzes the child's achievement, it also permits the parent to ask questions concerning his child's progress and the instructional program. It also provides the parent an opportunity to provide information to the teacher concerning the child's out-of-school behavior and activities.

In order for the conference to be successful, it must be carefully prepared by the teacher, and from a practical standpoint each conference must be held rigidly to the 15–20 minutes which are scheduled for it. Otherwise the conferences will fall behind schedule, and busy parents will be forced to wait unnecessarily for their conference. When there are problems which require a longer conference with the parents, arrangements can be made for another meeting at a later time.

Two methods of pre-planning which help the teacher hold successful, informative conferences are (1) preparation throughout the term of individual folders with samples of pupils' work to be reviewed at the conference and (2) preparation of an outline of the main points which are to be covered in the conference. The work samples in the child's folder give the parent tangible evidence of his child's progress and current status. It is also helpful to include some anecdotal records concerning the child's behavior together with a record of any unusual social problems, health problems, or academic problems. Special talents of the child should also be noted and discussed. As a means of giving the parent a realistic concept of the status of his child in the class some teachers lay out on a table in the conference room or post on the bulletin board the entire class's work on a specific written and/or an art assignment. In this case the comparison among children need not be a pointed one, but the parent will be interested and aware of his child's relative status.

One of the problems which teachers face with the conference is the difficulty of scheduling a time suitable for some parents who work or who are reluctant to attend. Also the conferences are almost inevitably held with the mother since the father works and is unable to attend. Some schools have, therefore, adopted the policy of holding at least one conference per year outside of school hours, after school or at night, to permit working parents to attend.

Written reports. The written report is a second method of informing the parent of his child's progress. While this method does not provide the two-way communication of the conference, it does give the teacher considerable leeway to report a variety of aspects of the child's achievement, school adjustment, personal problems, and special talents. The major disadvantage of the written report is the fact that it requires much time to prepare comprehensive, informative reports. Teachers, because they have limited time, often fall into the habit of preparing cursory, uninformative reports which follow the same pattern for each child each reporting period. The task of preparing 35 to 40 detailed reports in the elementary classroom is formidable even to the teacher who enjoys writing. For the secondary teacher, who teaches 100 to 150 pupils daily, the task is totally unmanageable unless his reporting task is confined to the 35 to 40 pupils in his home room.

Written reports can be improved by adhering to the following suggestions:

1. Reports should follow an outline which includes the most important aspects of pupils' progress—notably achievement, group status, social and emotional adjustment, interests, special aptitudes, school problems.
2. Reports should be concise, straightforward, and expressed in easily understood language—no educational "pedageese."
3. Reports should be factual, and opinion statements should be avoided.
4. Reports should be typed for easy legibility.
5. Teachers should be provided clerical assistance and given sufficient time free of instructional responsibilities to plan and write the reports.

Report cards. Report cards are the most widely used means of reporting pupils' progress. On the typical report card teachers record the course marks as letter grades. The report card generally includes a record of pupil attendance and some explanation of the meaning of the marks, giving either the percentage equivalents for each letter (e.g., $A = 94\%$ to 100%) or a verbal interpretation. An example of such a card, designed for use with the computer, is shown in Figure 14.4. While many

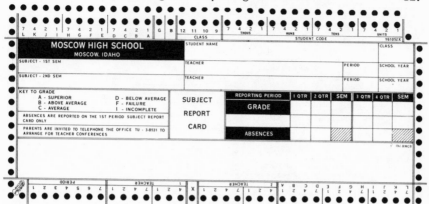

Figure 14.4. EXAMPLE OF HIGH SCHOOL REPORT CARD FOR USE WITH THE COMPUTER
Reprinted by permission of the Superintendent of Schools, Moscow, Idaho.

older teachers still use percentage equivalents, test authorities generally disapprove of their use. They are too easily manipulated to change grading standards, and they imply a precision in grading which is false.

The report cards vary from those which provide only a simple report of the course marks to rather complex cards which provide for evaluations of both citizenship and achievement, which include interpretive statements to help pinpoint pupil difficulties, and which permit brief teacher comments. An example of an elementary school card which includes all three of the provisions noted above is shown in Figure 14.5. While a card such as this can provide much information to the parent, it takes almost as much of the teacher's time to prepare as the written report; and some teachers will fill in only the course marks, ignoring the interpretations and comments.

SUMMARY

While teachers generally agree that measurement of pupil achievement is important, they are less than enthusiastic when it comes to the time-consuming tasks of scoring tests, grading class assignments, and assigning course marks. In fact, some look upon these latter tasks with such distaste that they hold their testing and assignments to the bare minimum which periodic marking at each reporting period necessitates. Such a course of action is not a feasible solution to the problem of course marking and may even compound the problem as the teacher is forced to defend his marks to disgruntled pupils and irate parents. There is no easy,

MOSCOW PUBLIC SCHOOLS

Moscow, Idaho

19_____-19_____

REPORT TO PARENTS

Name of Pupil _____

Grade _____

Teacher _____

Principal _____

Superintendent _____

ITEMS TO BE CONSIDERED BY PARENTS

1. Have remedial defects been considered?
2. Does your child have sufficient sleep?
3. Does your child have a quiet place for relaxation?
4. Does your child have sufficient time in the morning to prepare for school?
5. Is he prompt and regular in attendance?
6. Many health habits are more dependent upon the home than upon the school. A clean body and clean clothing aid the child socially.

INTERMEDIATE GRADES

EXPLANATION OF MARKS

A—Superior
B—Above Average
C—Average
D—Below Average
E—Working to limit of ability but below group standard
F—Below Passing

Under the subject analysis no mark indicates satisfactory attainment, a √ needs attention, and an I indicates improvement.

CITIZENSHIP	1	2	3	4
Work and Study Habits				
1. Is neat and orderly				
2. Tries to help self				
3. Begins work promptly				
4. Follows directions				
5. Pays attention				
6. Takes part in discussions				
7. Makes good use of time				
8. Works up to ability				
Social Habits				
1. Is courteous and considerate				
2. Uses self control				
3. Cooperates in group activity				
4. Obeys regulations				
5. Is careful of personal and school property				
6. Is friendly and fair in games				
Health Habits				
1. Is neat and clean in habits and dress				
2. Sits, talks, and stands correctly				

SCHOOL ACHIEVEMENT	1	2	3	4
Reading				
1. Reads with understanding				
2. Reads well to a group				
3. Reads varied material				
4. Remembers new words				
English				
1. Tries to speak correctly				
2. Expresses ideas well				
3. Uses good form in written work				
Spelling				
1. Spells well in written work				
2. Uses a dictionary				
3. Retains words learned				
Writing				
Arithmetic				
1. Works with accuracy				
2. Knows number facts				
3. Reasons well in thought problems				
Social Studies				
1. Takes part in discussions				
2. Brings outside information to class				
Vocal Music				
Art				
Science				
Instrumental Music				
Attendance				
Days of School				
Days Present				
Days Absent				
Times Tardy				

PARENT'S SIGNATURE

1st Quarter _____

2nd Quarter _____

3rd Quarter _____

REMARKS BY TEACHER

1st Quarter _____

2nd Quarter _____

3rd Quarter _____

4th Quarter _____

PROMOTION

Promoted to the _____ Grade _____ Date _____

Teacher _____

Figure 14.5. EXAMPLE OF ELEMENTARY REPORT CARD

Reprinted by permission of the Superintendent of Schools, Moscow, Idaho.

simple solution to the problem, but there are a number of suggestions and several methods of grading which make it easier to assign course marks which validly reflect pupils' achievement. Most important among the suggestions are (1) relate all tests and assignments on the stated objectives and topics of the course; (2) base the course mark on a sufficient variety and number of measurements to give an adequate sample of achievement; and (3) use the course mark only as an assessment of pupil achievement, not as a disciplinary measure or a reward for effort.

The methods of grading include (1) individual standards, (2) fixed standards, and (3) group standards. Unless instruction is highly individualized, the individual standard in which each child is graded according to how well he achieves his potential is inappropriate. The fixed standard is a method in which grades are assigned on the basis of levels of subject-matter competence. The method is a good one if appropriate levels are set, but there is rarely consensus in a field concerning the points at which acceptable levels should be set. Therefore, fixed standard is best adapted to elementary school skill subjects in which there is some agreement regarding appropriate competence levels and to elective secondary subjects in which there is the pragmatic base of competence prerequisite for follow-up courses—e.g., high school chemistry and college chemistry. When the fixed-standard method is used the teacher need not rely upon his own judgment as the sole means of establishing standards but can use the records from a large number of pupils from previous classes or current sections of the same class to establish standards empirically.

Group standards are established in terms of group performance and generally rely upon percentile rank or the curve methods of grade assignment. Either the normal curve or a calculated curve may be used; the normal curve when the class is heterogeneous and symmetrical in distribution, the calculated curve when the class is skewed. These methods are particularly useful in junior high school and in the high school required general education courses.

The recommended methods for assigning the final course mark are the *cumulative-point-score method* and the *grade-point-average method*. Both provide an objective, defensible means of assigning the mark, provided that test and class assignments which are averaged are valid measures. Since the course mark is the final record of pupil achievement, teacher, pupil, and parent should share an understanding of its meaning and a confidence in its validity and reliability.

DISCUSSION QUESTIONS AND PROBLEMS

1. Discuss the pro's and con's of the question: Is the course mark necessary?
2. Define the terms "score," "grade," and "mark."
3. Collect and discuss several different types of report cards.
4. What information should the course mark convey?
5. In recent years some school systems have used a computer printout of the pupils' cumulative record—courses completed, grades earned, test scores, etc.—as the reports to parents. What are the advantages and disadvantages of such a method?
6. In a high school which uses ability grouping of pupils, what problems do you foresee in using group standards of grading? Fixed standards?

SELECTED READINGS

Bradfield, James M. and H. Stewart Moredock. *Measurement and Evaluation in Education.* New York: The Macmillan Company, 1957. Chapter 9 contains a good discussion of marking and reporting. The criteria for a marking and reporting system, pp. 210–212, are particularly helpful.

Clark, Leonard H., and Irving S. Starr. *Secondary School Teaching Methods.* New York: The Macmillan Company, 1959. Chapter 12 provides a practical, easily understood discussion of marking and reporting to parents.

Durost, Walter N. and George A. Prescott. *Essentials of Measurement for Teachers.* New York: Harcourt, Brace, and World, 1962. Chapters 8 and 9. This is a brief, practical reference—see general specifications of a marking system, pp. 103–104.

Ebel, Robert L. *Measuring Educational Achievement.* Englewood Cliffs, N. J.: Prentice-Hall, 1965. Chapter 13 is one of the best brief discussions of marks and marking systems.

Green, John A. *Teacher-Made Tests.* New York: Harper & Row, 1963. Chapter 8 gives attention to scoring, grading, and marking; includes brief consideration of problems of marking and systems of marking.

Lien, Arnold J. *Measurement and Evaluation of Learning.* Dubuque, Iowa: Wm. C. Brown Company, 1967. Chapter 9 includes a brief, but helpful, discussion of marking and reporting practices. Several different practices are discussed and illustrated.

Lindvall, C. M. *Measuring Pupil Achievement and Aptitude.* New York: Harcourt, Brace & World, 1967. Chapter 9 discusses the use of measurement and evaluation in assigning grades and preparing reports.

Magnusson, David. *Test Theory.* Reading, Massachusetts: Addison-Wesley Publishing Company, 1966. Chapter 14 contains a good discussion of item analysis for those who wish to refine their tests and establish norms to permit meaningful comparisons among groups.

Smith, Fred M. and Sam Adam. *Educational Measurement for the Classroom Teacher.* New York: Harper & Row, 1966. The topic of assigning marks and reporting to parents is handled well in Chapter 13.

Strang, Ruth, *Reporting to Parents.* New York: Bureau of Publications, Teachers College, Columbia University, 1947. This is a comprehensive discussion of the methods of reporting to parents. It also includes some consideration of course mark assignment.

Thorndike, Robert L. and Elizabeth Hagen. *Measurement and Evaluation in Psychology and Education.* 2nd ed. New York: John Wiley and Sons, 1961. Chapter 17 discusses marking and reporting.

Wrinkle, William L. *Improving Marking and Reporting Practices.* New York: Rinehart, 1947. This is one of the most comprehensive discussions of the entire problem of marking and reporting.

Part IV

EVALUATING THE
EDUCATIONAL PROGRAM

In the first three parts of the book we have introduced some of the theoretical concepts which underlie testing and have examined the specialized measurement and evaluation instruments used for assessing various human characteristics and achievements. In a sense this is the "so what?" section, in which we will look at ways in which measurement data can be summarized and analyzed and at some appropriate uses of the data as they affect the instructional program, the curriculum, and the entire school system.

Standardized testing has become an intrinsic part of our instructional program, and with 50,000,000 pupils enrolled in the nation's schools we are administering an estimated 100 million tests at an annual cost of about $25,000,000. For a program which had its inception in the schools little more than twenty-five years ago, this is prodigious growth. During the same quarter of a century school enrollments have also grown spectacularly. In fact the recent growth, particularly in secondary schools, has been so dramatic that extraordinary effort has been required to maintain a high quality educational program and still accommodate the annual enrollment increases. Measurement has been a principal factor in the struggle to maintain educational quality and accommodate the large number of pupils. Decisions to introduce innovations in instruction or program, to add or delete courses, to group pupils on bases other than chronological age—all are made on the basis of measurement results or are directly affected by those results.

Furthermore, in the future educational problems will multiply and aggravate as the effects of accelerating social change, knowledge explosion, population growth, and competition for limited public funds complicate the already difficult task of providing each of millions of school children an education uniquely suited to him and to the general needs of the American social order.

At first glance measurement appears to impersonalize education; actually, however, it is the practical means through which it is possible to order and analyze information concerning the millions enrolled so that the educational program may be made responsive to the individual. Measurement is the essential handmaiden of program evaluation. Large-scale measurement provides the basis for continued improvement of education.

Chapter 15

PLANNING AND ADMINISTRATION OF THE MEASUREMENT PROGRAM

INTRODUCTION

As we have in turn examined the different phases of the educational measurement and evaluation program, we have frequently admonished the reader that the value of the program lies in the uses to which it is put. The specific classroom uses of the program have been elaborated upon in the previous chapters but the more general, administrative uses are pretty largely reserved to the discussion in this chapter. This division was made with no intent to slight the importance of administrative uses; rather it serves to highlight the importance of these general uses. In this broader realm we will be concerned with the testing program—its planning, administration, and use in instruction, in guidance, and in educational decision making.

PLANNING TESTING PROGRAMS

As there is no one best test for use in every classroom, so there is no one best testing program for use in each school system. A remarkable characteristic of the American school system is the tremendous diversity among school systems within the United States. The approximately 30,-000 school districts in the country range in size from a few square miles to almost 100,000 square miles, and from enrollments of fewer than ten to more than one million. In view of this great difference it would be foolhardy to suggest that an ideal testing program could be devised to fit the needs of all. Nevertheless, there are some principles and suggested programs which can serve as guides to school personnel concerned with planning a testing program which will fit the unique needs of their particular school system. As a general frame of reference Lennon's checklist, which appears as Figure 15.1, provides a good set of guidelines to those responsible for planning a testing program.

Principles of program planning. Beyond the guidelines referred to above, there are several principles which should be adhered to either in the planning of a new testing program for a school system or in the revision of an established program:

First, *the purposes of the program should be clearly formulated and written.* Without this preliminary step it is impossible to make an intelligent choice of tests or intelligent use of the test results. The general purposes of a testing program can be classified under (1) classroom uses, (2) guidance uses, and (3) administrative decision-making uses.

Second, *provisions should be made in the program to provide articulation and continuity throughout the elementary and secondary grades.* For maximum usefulness the testing program should be continuous so that it can show pupil growth and progress from year to year. The program should also be planned to provide articulation between elementary and secondary testing, eliminating unnecessary duplication and serious gaps in information. Such articulation is more difficult, but quite essential, when children from numerous elementary schools or districts are channeled into one central high school. Unless these pupils' previous testing records are sent to the high school, it is necessary to expend extra time and funds in testing to gain information which already has or should have been gathered earlier.

Third, *the program should be comprehensive.* Testing should cover all the areas that bear substantially on classroom instruction and pupils' future educational-vocational goals. A testing program confined only to achievement fails to provide sufficient information to permit intelligent pupil guidance, even in the educational realm, much less in the vocational and personal-social areas.

Fourth, *the testing program should be jointly planned* by those who will use the results. Teachers, guidance counselors, and principals should be represented on the planning committees. Each uses the results and each desires a core of common information; but, in addition, each desires specific kinds of information related to his special functions. This planning should also establish the annual test schedule, including the dates during which the tests will be administered.

Fifth, *trained personnel should administer and interpret the results.* This obviously means that teachers and test specialists in each school sys-

Figure 15.1. EXAMPLE OF TESTING PROGRAM CHECKLIST

A CHECKLIST OF FACTORS AFFECTING THE SUCCESS OF A TESTING PROGRAM

	CHECK
1 PURPOSES OF THE PROGRAM	
Clearly defined	_____
Understood by parties involved	_____
2 CHOICE OF TESTS	
Valid	_____
Reliable	_____
Appropriate difficulty level	_____
Adequate norms	_____
Easy to administer and score	_____
Economical	_____
Best available for purpose	_____
3 ADMINISTRATION AND SCORING	
Administrators well trained	_____
All necessary information provided	_____
Scorers adequately instructed	_____
Scoring carefully checked	_____
4 PHYSICAL CONDITIONS	
Sufficient space	_____
Sufficient time	_____
Conveniently scheduled	_____
5 UTILIZATION OF TEST RESULTS	
Definite plans for use of results	_____
Provision for giving teachers all necessary help in using scores . .	_____
Provision for systematic follow-up on use of results	_____
6 SYSTEM OF RECORDS	
Necessary for purpose	_____
Sufficient for purpose	_____
Convenient form for use	_____
7 PERSONNEL	
Adequately trained for the purpose	_____
8 AFFILIATED RESEARCH	
Full advantage taken of results	_____
Provision for special studies, analyses, etc.	_____

From Roger T. Lennon, "Planning a Testing Program," *Test Service Bulletin No. 55* (New York: Harcourt, Brace & World, n.d.), p. 3. Reprinted by permission of the publisher.

tem should have training in the measurement field. True, the level of training may differ, but teachers who lack training can neither help in the interpretation nor fully understand the interpretations made by others.[1]

Sixth, *testing should be part of the educational program,* not set aside as something to which time is begrudgingly allotted on certain "test days." When it is separate, it tends to be divorced from instruction, and few use the results in the classroom. On the other hand, when it is an intrinsic part of the instructional program, teachers can aid in administering the tests and are apt to be better motivated to use the results.

Seventh, *readily available aids, such as the test manuals and Buros' Mental Measurement Yearbooks, should be used in selecting the tests.*[2] While the use of the aids does not preclude the necessity for undertaking a thorough content examination of each test which is considered, it does help the committee screen out tests with questionable validity or reliability.

Eighth, *the results should be treated as confidential information, but should be easily accessible to professional school personnel.* This is vital personal information and pupils have a right to know that it will be kept in confidence. While parents have a right to the information, it is of little value to them without meaningful interpretation. Thus, when parents are given the test score information, it should be explained. Profile charts with scores reported as percentiles are probably most easily understood by parents and pupils.

Measurement purposes. The importance of a clear concept of purposes for the measurement program was noted earlier but merits further consideration. Appropriate general purposes can be classified as (1) instructional, (2) guidance, and (3) administrative decision-making. Katz suggests that the general purposes can be more clearly differentiated as placement, diagnosis, assessment, prediction, and evaluation.[3]

1. *Instructional purposes.* Perhaps the most important of the purposes are those relating directly to the instructional program; however, it

[1] A helpful test administrator's self-evaluation is Roger T. Lennon and Walter N. Durost, *Test-Giver's Self-Inventory,* Test Service Bulletin No. 85 (New York: Harcourt, Brace and World, 1956).

[2] For information on Buros' *Mental Measurement Yearbooks,* see p. 340.

[3] Martin Katz, *Selecting an Achievement Test,* Principles and Procedures Evaluation and Advisory Service Series No. 3 (Princeton, N. J.: Education Testing Service, 1958), p. 15.

should be noted categorically that it is a misuse of standardized tests to base course marks upon the results. Also, misconstruing the meaning of norms and taking them as instructional goals are generally improper. These two abuses, although uncommon, restrict the scope of instruction by confining it to the content of the test, thus setting too low achievement goals for all but slow classes. The test norms are valuable as a national reference point against which the individual teacher can compare his class performance, and they can help him assess the areas of major strength and serious weakness. Thus, for a class or a school system, diagnosis of the results may provide the basis for greater instructional emphasis of areas of weakness. Even though a class exceeds the national norms in overall performance, the fact that it is low in an area such as spelling may call for additional emphasis on spelling during the ensuing year. Or in another instance, a class which performs well might reasonably be expected to perform better if they are above average in intelligence.

Furthermore, children in selected urban centers and in certain sections of the country typically exceed the national norms, which reflect performance of a representative sample of all children in the country. For example, children in the northwest section of the country in statewide achievement testing programs typically exceed national norms by as much as ten percentile points; therefore comparisons within the state or section may be more meaningful than the national comparison. Comparisons for the purpose of instructional diagnosis is an appropriate use of standardized test results in contrast to their improper use as instructional goals or grading criteria.

In recent years another important purpose has been that of checking on the effectiveness of new methods and instructional media. Experimentation and innovation are becoming increasingly important aspects of instructional programs. However, change for change's sake is not desirable; and before new methods and media are introduced systemwide, they should be experimentally validated in a limited setting. In such experiments, suitable tests are among the best measures for assessing the value of the method or media in question.

2. *Guidance purposes.* Tests are essential in guidance; without them it would be virtually impossible to obtain sufficient information about the great mass of school children to provide intelligent guidance in the scho-

lastic realm, much less in the personal-social and vocational realms. Whether the guidance program in the school is comprehensive or limited to one or two areas—e.g., vocational—determines the type and number of tests which will be used.

3. *Administrative decision-making.* In administrative decision-making tests can also play a vital role—e.g., in (1) formulation of educational policy, (2) development and improvement of the curriculum, (3) grouping and placement of pupils, (4) selection of the instructional staff, (5) justification of the purchase of new instructional materials and equipment.

Although policy decisions must be made by people, the results of a testing program often give objective evidence upon which to base a decision. Policies concerning social promotion of pupils, length of the school day and school year, age of primary school enrollment are examples which certainly should be made with the testing results in mind. The whole area of curriculum planning and revision is another in which testing information is essential. Assessment of the educational effectiveness of existing curricular offerings, the need for new offerings, the need for additional emphasis in a field, the need to cull out nonessentials—all call for continuous scrutiny and periodic measurement.

Decisions concerning the grouping and placement of pupils for most effective, efficient instruction certainly must be made on the basis of testing. Many educational issues require the objective evidence from measurement and a knowledge of educational research before they can be intelligently answered within a given school system—e.g., large-group versus small-group instruction; homogeneous ability grouping vs. age-grade grouping; 8–4, 6–6, or 6–3–3 grade grouping.

DEVELOPING THE MASTER TESTING SCHEDULE

Were it not for the diversity in size and organization of school systems, a master testing schedule might be devised for all schools. However, such a suggested testing schedule is useful as an example from which the staff of a specific school system can begin work to develop their own unique schedule. Staff familiarity with measurement theory and the available tests is an important prerequisite to such planning. It is probably best to have the guidance director coordinate the planning and implementation of the testing program. His responsibilities in this realm include (1) developing a good test library; (2) conducting in-service training sessions for teachers who lack measurement background; (3) coordinating the planning of the program; and (4) aiding teachers or teacher committees in selecting the tests.

The decision concerning when the major portion of the annual testing program should be administered should be a faculty decision. There are advantages and disadvantages to either the fall or the spring administration of tests, but either is quite acceptable as long as the year-to-year records are kept up to date and easily accessible to the teaching staff. All things considered, it is probably better to schedule achievement tests during the fall in order to establish a reasonable beginning-of-the-year level from which instruction may begin. This permits time to modify the instructional program to meet the individual needs of pupils. On the other hand, spring administration provides the teacher with information concerning the year's terminal level of pupil attainment, information from which he can determine how well his instructional objectives were achieved. If scheduled for the fall, tests should be administered approximately one month after school starts so that pupils will be well adjusted to the school routine and will have had time to recoup the slight learning losses occurring during summer vacation. If scheduled for the spring, tests should be administered several weeks before the end of school to avoid conflict with the numerous spring school activities and the details of closing school before summer vacation.

The following principles summarize the guidelines which should govern the development of the master testing schedule:

1. A specific testing program should be designed to fit the unique needs of each school.
2. Expenditures in time and money for testing should be as large as, but no larger than, the expenditures for any other school service of equal merit.
3. Tests should be selected to measure teachers' specific instructional objectives as well as broader, generally recognized objectives.
4. Teachers should serve on the committees responsible for the development of a testing program.
5. A complete testing program should be articulated through all twelve grades.
6. The testing program adopted should make no unreasonable demands on the skills of teachers in administering, scoring, and interpretation of the tests.

7. The tests selected should provide comparability of results from one school to the other, and for each child from year to year.
8. In scheduling a testing program, care should be taken to avoid likely periods of emotional stress and excitement among children, interfering physical conditions within the school, seasons of the years when teachers have especially heavy activity loads, and a wide variability of testing dates from year to year.
9. Tests should be scheduled no more frequently than is necessary to provide adequate assessment of the objectives of the school.

Test selection. Tests which are directly related to the instructional program should be selected by teachers, not the guidance director or the administrator, although these latter persons may aid in the selection. The teacher obviously knows his own teaching aims and should know what type of information he needs concerning his pupils; however, he is frequently quite naive concerning the relative quality of different tests. He probably has little statistical background and very limited acquaintance with a few of the many standardized tests which are published. Therefore, he will need aid from someone competent in testing theory, someone who can help him interpret the technical manuals of the tests under consideration.

The importance of validity of evaluative devices has been stressed repeatedly throughout this book; test selection committees must be aware of the importance of this characteristic. No measurement instrument which lacks validity should ever be selected despite the fact that it might have a high degree of reliability and usability.

Sources of test information. Four of the best sources of test information are (1) measurement textbooks, (2) test catalogs and technical manuals of test publishers, (3) Buros' *Mental Measurements Yearbooks*,[4] and (4) test reviews in such journals as the *Journal of Educational Measurement.* Various textbooks review specific tests, while Buros gives excellent reviews of most of the available tests. The test catalogs generally do an excellent job of describing their tests. An example taken from such a catalog is shown on the following page in Figure 15.2. It is apparent from this example that the test catalog gives extensive information. This particular example, however, neglects to give information concerning the validity and reliability of the test. It is also impossible to get a very good

[4] O. K. Buros (ed.), *The Mental Measurements Yearbooks* (Highland Park, N. J.: Rutgers University Press and Gryphon Press, 1938, 1941, 1949, 1953, 1959, and 1965).

Mental Ability Tests

Pintner-Cunningham Primary Test, Revised   GRADES K-2

Rudolf Pintner, Bess V. Cunningham, Walter N. Durost © *1938, 1964, 1965*

The Pintner-Cunningham Primary Test, Revised, is a test measuring general mental ability of pupils from the second half of kindergarten to grade 2. It is entirely pictorial and administered orally. **Administration Time:** 25 minutes. **Scoring:** *Hand score* test booklets with appropriate Keys. **Norms:** Deviation IQs.

FORMS		
Pintner-Cunningham Primary Test (Revised)	A, B	**$6.70** pkg/35
Specimen Set		**1.25** each

Figure 15.2. EXAMPLE FROM TEST CATALOG

From *Catalog of Standardized Tests and Related Services,* 1969–70 (New York: Harcourt, Brace & World, 1969), p. 55. Reprinted by permission of the publisher.

comparison of several tests in a field from test catalog information because each company naturally presents only information concerning its own tests; therefore other sources should be used to supplement test catalogs. The bibliography at the end of this chapter lists several textbooks which also give useful information concerning specific tests.

Test selection checklists and rating scales. Sources such as those noted above can be very helpful in preparing the local school staff to make its final decision. A test selection checklist or rating scale is also useful in helping the group make its final choices. The group can either construct such a test selection checklist or use one of the published instruments. Table XXII contains an example of a simple rating scale constructed by students in one of the author's measurement classes. Since the selection committee may wish to include other criteria or change the point values, they should probably construct an instrument to fit their own unique needs. In assigning point values it would be well to weight validity heavily—as much as 50 points on a 100-point scale, say—since it is the most important single quality of a test. A rating scale which gives too little weight to validity might lead to the selection of an invalid test, on the basis of high scores in reliability, administration, scoring, and interpretation.

Master testing schedule. Setting up the master schedule or calendar of tests for a school system is in some ways like shopping for a new car. One may choose any from a Volkswagen to a Cadillac program, as it were—austere or embellished with numerous options to suit one's convenience and personal preference. However, in view of the financial limitations of many school districts, the austere program is likely to be most

Table XXII. STUDENT-CONSTRUCTED TEST SCORE CARD

Criterion	Possible Score	Test 1	Test 2	Test 3	Test 4
Validity					
A. Content	20				
B. Predictive	5				
C. Concurrent	15				
	Total 40				
Totals					
Reliability					
A. Length	5				
B. Objectivity	10				
C. Age Range	10				
D. Standard Error	5				
	Total 30				
Totals					
Usability					
A. Format	6				
B. Economy	6				
C. Administrability	6				
D. Comparable Norms	6				
E. Scorability	6				
	Total 30				
Totals					
Final Score	100				

realistic. Thus, committees charged with the responsibility of developing the master schedule of tests will probably be forced to work within a small budget, yet devise a program which meets the following specifications:

1. Costs less than 50 cents per year per student.
2. Relieves tedious hours of scoring.
3. Yields the most needed information about children at appropriate grade levels.
4. Yields accurate information regarding general development.
5. Provides the administrator with periodic surveys of the general excellence of his school.
6. Includes tests which can be given with a reasonable amount of in-service training.
7. Provides for choice among better tests while encouraging some uniformity of selection.

Actually a surprisingly broad testing program can be purchased for under 50 cents per pupil per year. Several test companies have programs which are useful for reference, but which will probably not be adopted *en toto* by a school system. The tests selected often come from several companies; thus, the minimum program suggested in Table XXIII is outlined without any specific test company in mind. This program includes only the general tests administered to all pupils and would be supplemented by such tests as individual intelligence tests for a small number of pupils and by the informal teacher-made tests. If the money is available to expand the program, it would also be desirable to do achievement testing each year.

It is very helpful to the selection committee if someone in the system prepares a list of the tests under consideration, including with the list an analysis of the salient features of each test. Some of the features which should be included are:

1. Grade or age range
2. Scoring procedure
3. Approximate time needed for administering
4. Score units used in reporting results
5. Areas or functions measured
6. Cost rating
7. Publisher

Table **XXIII**. SUGGESTED TESTING PROGRAM

Grade Level	Intelligence (Given in Fall)	Achievement & Diagnostic (Given in Fall or Spring)	Aptitude	Interest and Personality
K–First	Reading Readiness	Reading		
Second	Group Intelligence	Reading		
Third		Skills Battery		
Fourth	Group Intelligence	Achievement Battery Reading Diagnostic		
Fifth		Arithmetic Diagnostic		
Sixth	Group Intelligence	Achievement Battery		
Seventh		Study Skills		Problem Checklist
Eighth	Group Intelligence	Achievement Battery		
Ninth			Aptitude Battery	
Tenth	Group Intelligence *	Achievement Battery		Interest
Eleventh			Scholastic Aptitude	
Twelfth	Group Intelligence **	Achievement Battery		Interest

* Might be administered in the ninth grade if there is an 8–4 grade arrangement or if records of elementary testing are incomplete.

** For a minimum testing program, three group intelligence tests would be adequate—one in lower grades, one in intermediate grades, and one at secondary level. If the *Differential Aptitude Test* is used in the secondary school, it could be used to give both aptitude and intelligence scores.

Such an analysis for about thirty tests should take no more than one page if abbreviations are used. The analysis can be set up as that in the example below:

Test	Grades	Scoring	Time	Scores	Areas	Cost	Publisher
Otis Quick-Scoring	K-12-ad.	Hand, mach.	30 min.	MA, DIQ	General intell.	L	WBC

Regardless of the tests selected, particularly in achievement, it is desirable that the same test be used for several years to show the pattern of growth of pupils throughout those years. Since each test measures somewhat different objectives and content, changing the testing program frequently makes it difficult to get a continuous picture of pupils' growth.

ADMINISTERING AND SCORING THE TESTS

Administration. Achievement and group intelligence tests, particularly in the elementary grades, are typically administered by the homeroom teacher. As a result it is desirable both that the teacher have some skill in test administration and that the tests have simple directions for administration. Most of the tests for classroom use which are currently on the market provide simple directions in the test manual, directions which should be read verbatim without any deviation. Any change in administration—altered directions, changed time limits, extra instructions or help—abrogates the standardized procedure and invalidates the comparability of obtained scores with published norms.

It is usually desirable to hold in-service training sessions each year for those who will administer the tests. Such sessions should be conducted by the guidance director or a principal or supervisor who has adequate measurement preparation. Even though the teachers in some systems may have had previous preparation in measurement, the in-service sessions will serve to iron out problems which might otherwise arise; and such sessions will probably result in better administration, scoring, and interpretation of the tests than would otherwise result.[5] Such sessions might be organized around a series of topics similar to those in the checklist shown in Figure 15.1.

[5] Test administrators would profit from a review of Roger T. Lennon and Walter N. Durost, *Test-Giver's Self-Inventory*, Test Service Bulletin No. 85 (New York: Harcourt, Brace and World, 1956).

Scoring the tests. Hand scoring of tests by school personnel has both advantages and disadvantages. Its most important value is the fact that it requires the teacher's scrutiny of each pupil's test, permitting him to catch such problems as pupil failure to align the answer sheet properly, a mistake which can result in incorrect responses for an entire column. The major problem with hand scoring is the fact that it requires so much time, time which teachers can ill afford to spare from other classroom responsibilities. Also hand scoring is less accurate than machine scoring. The methods of scoring standardized tests include stencil scoring, carbon scoring, and machine scoring. The cheapest but most time-consuming method is stencil scoring, which uses the punch-out stencil which is placed over the answer sheet as the marking key. This method requires proper alignment of the key, care in marking all errors, and correct counting of errors.

The carbon-score method, although somewhat more expensive, is quick and less subject to error. Several instruments—e.g., the SRA *Primary Mental Abilities*—use carbon-score answer sheets. In this case, to determine the number of incorrect responses, the scorer merely has to open up the answer sheet and count the number of marks which do not fall in the boxes on the back of the sheet.

Most of the recently published group tests also provide machine-scoring service. Although relatively expensive, this service also includes some statistical summary and interpretation of the data for each class and for the entire school. The pupil's individual scores are reported on a small self-adhesive form which may be mounted in his cumulative folder. As more school systems in the country install computers for record keeping and research, it becomes feasible to utilize the local machines for test scoring and statistical analysis of the scores.

Recording test information. Individual pupil's test information is most easily used when recorded on profile sheets. Such a profile sheet should provide space for recording a graphic and numerical record of the achievement, intelligence, and aptitude tests. The test record should show both the child's current status and his long-term development or previous test scores. The recorded test scores should be placed in the child's cumulative folder along with other permanent records of his educational progress.

Cumulative folders should be stored in a fireproof vault. Since central storage of records tends to discourage teachers from examining the data as a basis for planning instruction, it is also desirable to have a duplicate set of the child's cumulative folder placed in a locked metal file in his homeroom. If this is not done, teachers should be encouraged to use central records and given some clerical assistance to help them record essential information for classroom use.

USING TEST INFORMATION

A testing program has little value unless it is properly used. Testing costs money and staff time; and if the results are to remain unused in the school vault, the money and time might better be spent on other aspects of the instructional program. The first step in optimum use of test results is that of summarizing and analyzing a large body of data. The statistical methods for carrying out this step are discussed in Chapter 3. Further than statistical analyses, however, there is a need to make a careful evaluation of the test results as they relate to the quality of the total educational program and to the effectiveness of instruction in each classroom. This recommendation is not intended to imply that teachers should be rated according to their pupils' performance on achievement tests. Such a misuse of test results is completely inappropriate, and it inevitably forces teachers to refocus instructional objectives and to "teach for the test." It is appropriate, however, to analyze and evaluate with the teaching staff the summarized results to identify areas of strength and weakness in the total educational program. This can be done without unethical, embarrassing comparisons of relative performance among various classrooms.

In analyzing test results we will make numerous comparisons. Katz summarizes the types of comparisons which may be made as follows:

1. We may compare a pupil's achievement test score with the scores of other pupils in his school (as we noted under placement).
2. We may compare a pupil's (or group's) score on a subtest with his (its) score on another subtest (as in diagnosis).
3. We may compare a pupil's (or group's) achievement test score with his (its) score on a previous testing (as in assessment).
4. We may compare a pupil's score on one achievement test with his score on another achievement test (as in prediction).
5. We may compare a school's achievement test scores with achievement test scores of a comparable group of schools (as in evaluation).

And let us add these:

6. We may compare a pupil's (or group's) achievement test score with some fixed standard of mastery.

7. We may compare a pupil's (or group's) achievement test score with his (its) scores on other kinds of tests (e.g., aptitude test, interest, personality, or attitude scales).

8. We may compare a pupil's achievement test score with other data about his achievement (e.g., school marks, ratings).[6]

In addition to making this overall analysis, it is the responsibility of instructional supervisors to help each teacher do strength and weakness analyses of his classes' performance, this information to be kept as confidential between supervisor and teacher. In both the overall evaluation and the individual analyses it should be kept in mind that standardized tests do not measure all the instructional objectives and content areas in each field. The objective instrument is not acceptable for measuring some important types of objectives, and the content reflects the coverage of basic texts in the field. Nevertheless some teachers will stress objectives and content not measured by the standardized instrument. In analyzing test results in such classes it is important to weigh these other objectives also and to encourage the teacher to supplement standardized measurement with teacher-made tests specifically designed to assess those objectives considered important but not included in the standardized batteries.

Earlier in the chapter it was suggested that the purposes for a testing program could be broadly classed under the categories of instructional purposes, guidance purposes, and administrative purposes (especially decision-making ones). The use of test scores obviously should correlate closely with these purposes, therefore we will examine the uses under each of these categories.

Instructional uses. A good portion of the previous chapters has been directed to a consideration of the various kinds of tests and their relation to some aspect of the instructional program, and it is not the intention to summarize these discussions in this section. Little previous consideration has been given, however, to four important uses of tests; namely their use (1) as the basis for interclass grouping, (2) to diagnose learning problems, (3) to identify pupils for enrichment and accelerated programs, and (4) to assess the relative success of experimental methods or learning approaches.

[6] Katz, *op. cit.* (above, n. 3), p. 16.

Within the domain of his classroom the American teacher is relatively free to determine the objectives, instructional methods, and standards so long as he does not infringe heavily upon subsequent grades or classes. He normally cannot prevent his pupils from taking the tests in the required schoolwide testing program, but he can, and sometimes does, refuse to use the results in his instructional program. The first use of tests suggested above, the use in interclass grouping, is a normal procedure for the primary grades, in which children are typically grouped for reading instruction and often for other areas of instruction as well. Likewise when the school is organized as a so-called ungraded primary school, the major criterion on which children are placed in slow, average, and accelerated instructional tracks is their performance on readiness and achievement tests. Beyond the primary level—in the intermediate grades, junior high school, and high school—interclass grouping is used less frequently, but the primary basis for grouping at these levels is also test performance. Most high schools today group pupils for instruction according to ability, normally in three homogeneous groups—slow, average, and accelerated. Whether interclass or homogeneous grouping is used, both the decision to group and the class assignment of pupils will depend heavily upon the pupils' achievement and intelligence test performance, although such other factors as grade-point average and teacher recommendations may legitimately be considered.

Regardless of whether classes are grouped, teachers should use tests diagnostically to help identify problem areas of the entire class and of individuals who need special help. This use of tests helps teachers concentrate their instruction on trouble spots rather than use the "shotgun"-review approach which some take in the hope that they will thus blanket the weak spots. Instructional time is too valuable to waste in this manner when there are so many new things to learn and too little time to teach.

Tests also have a useful function in identifying pupils who need, and can profit from, enrichment—particularly when school policy does not permit acceleration or homogeneous grouping for these bright children. At each level the scope of instruction can be broadened for such children to include topics and subject areas not required of the entire class.

Finally, since it is unlikely that we either have discovered—or will in the near future—the best way to teach, the best school curriculum, or the best school organization, each teacher has some obligation to experiment. He should attempt to discover new and better ways of teaching, to check and validate his findings—primarily through testing—so that they may be shared with others, subjected to the critical forum of professional criticism and subsequently to more sophisticated re-experimentation to corroborate or reject the findings.

Guidance uses. The guidance uses of tests are but briefly noted here— not because they are trivial or unimportant, but because there are numerous excellent texts devoted entirely to the topic. Teachers play an important guidance role in every school, whether or not there is an organized guidance program. At the lower grade levels, schools are often without the services of trained guidance personnel; and at the secondary level, particularly in small high schools, adequate services are also often lacking so that the major guidance burden falls on teachers.

Tests are of major importance in a guidance program, but test results are more fallible as predictive factors in guidance than they are as assessment factors in the instructional program. However, even in the areas where tests have the highest predictive validity—e.g., intelligence tests and future academic achievement—the results may be misleading. For instance, while the pupil who lacks the requisite ability is almost sure to fail, those who possess ample ability may also fail because they lack motivation, have personal problems, etc.

At best, the guidance person can merely help the pupil understand his chances for success in future education and in occupational choices. The decisions relative to such questions as which school? what level of education? what occupational choice? are personal ones which the pupil must ultimately make for himself. Guidance in the personal-social areas is unquestionably the most difficult of all, both because many of the measurement instruments have relatively low validity and because the future circumstances and environment of the individual are not foreseeable. Even an apparently well-adjusted person may disintegrate under the intolerable circumstances of war, poverty, or ill health, while the marginal person might maintain stability in a nonpressure environment. The guidance person, be he specialist or teacher, must see his function, then, not as one who makes the decisions for the counselee, but as one who interprets and informs so that the counselee *may make his own decisions.*

Administrative uses. It is an administrative responsibility to record testing information and maintain up-to-date cumulative records for each child. Administration can also facilitate the use of these records by placing duplicate records in the child's classroom or by storing them in a location which is readily accessible to the teacher. When the records are all located in a vault in the superintendent's office, they are rarely used by teachers.

The major administrative uses of measurement data center around (1) decision-making, (2) policy formulation, (3) program evaluation, and (4) educational change. As we indicated earlier, a decision to implement homogeneous grouping throughout a school might well be made on the basis of test results and certainly would be implemented by using test scores as at least one factor in the segregation of groups.

Numerous educational policies are at least partially based on the results of the testing program. Typical examples include the school promotion policy, the retention-acceleration policy, and the policy related to the school entrance age.

Program evaluation is a major topic in Chapter 16 and thus is not discussed in this context.

Change is a continuous feature of American education. In some schools it is stoutly resisted, in some it is welcomed indiscriminately, and in yet others it is planned and selectively implemented. For the first two categories of schools, the measurement results have little relevance since they will be largely unheeded; but in the last group, measurement is an intrinsic step in the entire evaluative process wherein alternative methods, different organizational patterns, new offerings, and new instructional media are experimented with, tested for effectiveness, and evaluated on the basis of their contribution to the school objectives and the improvement of instructional efficiency.

Finally, an administrative use not noted as of central importance to the school, but certainly of major importance to the pupil is the use of records in writing recommendations. After the pupil completes his education, the tangible record of his achievement is his permanent school record and, if he graduates, his diploma or degree. Beyond that, there is the tenuous impression which he left in the minds of his teachers and principals. During their post-high-school years pupils often request school officials to write letters of recommendation to college officials or prospective employers. In such cases the teacher not infrequently must refer to the pupil's record to recall him as an individual from a group of hundreds of former pupils.

SUMMARY

If the testing program is to serve its functions adequately in instruction, in guidance, and in administration, it must be planned according to the unique objectives and purposes of the specific school system. Also, in a very real sense, the testing program is a servant of the instructional program; therefore, the teaching staff should play a major role in the planning and selection of a testing schedule which will provide them with the kinds of information which they desire and which will give a valid measure of their pupils' achievement. As this statement implies, the testing schedule is best tailored to fit the needs of the individual school—not borrowed from another school or some test publisher. Furthermore, the testing program should be articulated through the grades, be comprehensive enough to include measures of the most important pupil characteristics and learning aspects, and be continuous over a period of years in order to give a longitudinal view of pupil changes.

Since teachers are not specialists in testing, they will need the aid of guidance specialists who can help interpret the technical manuals of the tests under consideration. Administrators should be represented on the test selection committee but should not direct it because instruction—not administration or guidance—is the primary function of the school. Three of the best sources of test information which the test selection committee can use to help them make the selection are (1) measurement textbooks, (2) technical test manuals and publishers' catalogs, and (3) Buros' *Mental Measurement Yearbooks*. Use of a published or teacher-constructed checklist or rating scale also improves the selection procedure by focusing attention on the essential characteristics of the measurement instrument: validity, reliability, and usability.

The administration of standardized tests should rigidly adhere to the standardized procedure in the test manual, otherwise the standardization is abrogated and scores are not truly comparable to those in the normative scale. Teachers who aid in the administration of the tests can usually profit from some in-service training sessions conducted by a testing specialist. After the tests are administered, particular care should be taken to see that they are accurately scored. With current tests machine scoring can be provided for a nominal cost. The machine-scoring service also usually provides some statistical analyses of the test results as an additional bonus.

The ultimate value of a testing program lies in the variety and extent of its uses. These uses should extend beyond the obvious use in assessing pupil changes to use in guidance, in prediction, in educational experimentation, in planning educational change, in formation of educational policy.

The scores which pupils obtain should be carefully recorded and filed in the cumulative record which, during their future years, is the permanent record of their growth and achievement.

DISCUSSION QUESTIONS AND PROBLEMS

1. On the basis of the qualities of measuring instruments, construct a checklist or rating scale which could be used for selecting an achievement test.
2. Suggest a minimum testing program for the elementary or secondary grades of a school system with which you are familiar.
3. Who should be represented on the committee which makes up the master testing calendar for the school?
4. Some feel that such national testing programs as the *National Merit Scholarship Test* constitute a strong and undesirable external control on the school curriculum. What are your reactions?
5. What is a desirable relationship between informal and standardized tests in measuring pupil achievement?
6. Which of the following do you consider to be legitimate uses of the standardized testing program? As a criterion in:
   a. ability grouping of pupils?
   b. determining pupils' educational curricula?
   c. denying college admission?
   d. assigning course marks?
   e. making modifications in instructional method and content?
7. Recently in some parts of the country parents have opposed the use of personality and intelligence tests on the grounds that they constitute an invasion of their children's privacy. Do you think this attitude justifiable?

SELECTED READINGS

Bauernfeind, Robert H. *Building a School Testing Program.* Boston: Houghton Mifflin Company, 1963. Chapter 14 includes consideration of the master testing program and methods of summarizing and recording test data.

Bradfield, James M. and H. Stewart Moredock. *Measurement and Evaluation in Education.* New York: The Macmillan Company, 1957. A brief, helpful discussion of the schoolwide testing program is included in Chapter 16.

Brueckner, Leo J. and Guy L. Bond. *The Diagnosis and Treatment of Learning Difficulties.* New York: Appleton-Century-Crofts, 1955. In Chapter 4 the authors give an excellent analysis of the techniques of diagnosing pupils' learning difficulties. Subsequent chapters relate to the diagnosis and treatment of difficulties in specific subject fields.

Buros, O. K. *Mental Measurement Yearbooks*. Highland Park, N. J.: Rutgers University Press and Gryphon Press, latest edition, 1965. There are six editions of this reference, published in the period between 1941 and 1965. These yearbooks provide the best reference on specific tests. Each of the tests included is reviewed by several reviewers, with comment on its strengths and weaknesses.

Findley, Warren G. *The Impact and Improvement of School Testing Programs*, Sixty-Second Yearbook of the National Society for the Study of Education. Chicago, Illinois: The University of Chicago Press, 1963. The entire book is excellent; however, Chapters 3, 7, and 10 are particularly pertinent since they relate to the selection and use of testing programs.

Flynn, John T. and Herbert Garber (eds.). *Assessing Behavior*. Reading, Massachusetts: Addison-Wesley Publishing Company, 1967. Chapter 9 includes three articles concerning testing programs. The first article is particularly well related to the problem of teacher use and misuse of tests.

Goldman, Leo. *Using Tests in Counseling*. New York: Appleton-Century-Crofts, 1961. Although this book is written primarily for the guidance counselor, Chapter 16 has a number of helpful suggestions for teacher-counselors. It also includes numerous examples of test-reporting methods.

Goslin, David A. *Teachers and Testing*. New York: Russell Sage Foundation, 1967. Chapter 5 is particularly informative and useful to the teacher who is seeking to improve his use of tests in the instructional program and in counseling pupils.

Lindquist, E. F. (ed.). *Educational Measurement*. Washington, D. C.: American Council on Education, 1951. The first four chapters give excellent delineations of the functions of measurement in instruction, counseling, and administration.

Lindvall, C. M. *Testing and Evaluation: An Introduction*. New York: Harcourt, Brace & World, 1961. Chapter 12, although brief, contains a number of helpful suggestions for planning and administering the testing program.

Smith, Fred M. and Sam Adams. *Educational Measurement for the Classroom Teacher*. New York: Harper & Row, 1966.

Stodola, Quentin and Kalmer Stordahl, *Basic Educational Tests and Measurement*. Chicago, Illinois: Science Research Associates, 1967. Chapter 10 includes an exceptionally fine treatment of the school testing program, giving attention both to selection and use of tests.

Thorndike, Robert L. and Elizabeth Hagen. *Measurement and Evaluation in Psychology and Education*. 2nd ed. New York: John Wiley & Sons, 1961. Chapter 16 is a particularly good statement of the ways in which the testing program should be planned, carried out, and implemented in the instructional program.

--------- *Chapter 16* ---------

EVALUATION OF EDUCATIONAL PROGRAM AND FACILITIES

INTRODUCTION

Schools in America are a complex of the desires of the people; the plans of the teaching and administrative personnel; and an admixture of sociological, demographic, and political factors within which the school is set. Thus, schools are peculiarly susceptible to the pressures of constant change. It would not be possible, even if it were desirable, to promulgate a system of education independent of these influences. Anyone, therefore, who undertakes the task of evaluating American education—the program, the personnel, or the facilities—cannot help but fail in that task unless he is aware of these factors and understands their influence. It is this required breadth of understanding which makes the tasks of educational evaluation so difficult. It is perhaps the lack of awareness of this total complex within which the school functions that at least partially accounts for the diversity in the estimates of the quality of American education reported by those who undertake evaluation. Certainly those who are ethical and conscientious will not undertake evaluations until they have examined numerous schools and understand the school-culture interaction complex.

Traditional indices of quality in education have been the level of education of the staff, the condition of the facilities, the amount of money spent per pupil, and the level of pupil performance on standardized tests. Although all of these factors are important, total reliance upon them results in neglect of other important factors which are intangible and which require subjective evaluation, including such factors as what is the total school philosophy? what purposes has the school? are appropriate subjects included in the curriculum? is sufficient consideration

355

given to the individual pupil? As the numbers of pupils increase, additional reliance must be placed upon measurement and evaluative techniques; otherwise the concern with staffing and providing facilities to accommodate masses of pupils may relegate to a secondary position our concern for a high quality education fitted to the needs of the individual pupil and to the needs of a progressive democratic society.

General factors to consider in evaluations. The school and its program cannot be evaluated apart from its political, sociological, and economic setting. Among the general factors of which the evaluator must be aware are:

1. The changing role and interrelationship of such social institutions as the school, the family, and the church.
2. The great mobility of our population.
3. The trends toward centralization reflected in politics and population concentration.
4. The rapid increase in school enrollments.

Though the importance of these and other factors would warrant their further consideration, their diverse implications are beyond the scope of this chapter; but the reader is invited to follow them up in one of the several references in the chapter bibliography from the various foundations of education.

Specific local factors. Beyond such general factors as those referred to above, there are several specific factors which invest the local school system with a unique flavor and which cannot properly be ignored in the task of evaluation. Some of the most significant include:

1. The composition of the community—educational, occupational, demographic.
2. The intellectual and cultural composition of the student body.
3. The stability of the student body.
4. The nature and extent of job opportunities in the locality.
5. The proportion of collegebound pupils in the school.
6. The financial resources of the community.
7. The level of community aspirations and the supporting cultural and educational resources.
8. The articulation of the local system with the state and regional educational system.

Without further consideration of these factors, other than the admonition that they constitute the backdrop against which the evaluation must be made, we turn our attention to three essential elements which must be assessed in the school evaluation: (1) personnel, (2) program, and (3) facilities.

EVALUATION OF PERSONNEL

Quality instruction is the most important single ingredient in the educational program. Fine facilities, peerless instructional materials, excellent buildings, and thorough evaluation of pupil progress are certainly important elements in upgrading the quality of education; but without excellent teachers to breathe life into the program, education will not prosper.

Teachers universally evaluate the *product of instruction,* pupil achievement, but are reluctant to permit evaluation of the *process of instruction,* citing subjectivity of evaluations, lack of valid instruments, and complexity of the teaching task as reasons for their opposition. Yet teaching quality unquestionably varies greatly, ranging from very poor to the highest excellence. One has but to recall his own student days to verify this statement in fact, for it is likely that he will remember with distaste his poorest teachers, with pleasure and appreciation his best teachers. The best teachers mold significant changes in pupils' lives, but the saddest experience in a child's educational life is to be condemned to spend a year in the classroom of a poor teacher. From the excellent teacher's classroom flows the effervescence of enthusiasm and purposeful achievement; from the poor teacher's classroom the pall of frustration, rebellion, and disinterest. Failure to evaluate instruction protects the incompetent while failing to reward the competent.

The process of evaluation. In teacher evaluation "rating" and "evaluation" are two terms, often used interchangeably, which have quite different meanings. *Rating* refers to the process of assessing instructional performance through the use of a rating scale. Rating is subjective and requires the exercise of evaluating judgment but is less comprehensive than evaluation. On the other hand, *evaluation* refers to the total process of judging, assessing, and critically reviewing as the basis for improving the instructional process.

Evaluation of teaching goes on constantly in every school. It underlies every teacher promotion, parent's request for a specific teacher, pupil's statement concerning the quality of his instructor, and colleagues' estimate of one's capability. Unfortunately these evaluations are often based on hearsay evidence, infrequent observation, and unsubstantiated opinions. A more valid, and much more defensible, evaluation program can be built around the answers to three pertinent questions: (1) Who properly should evaluate teaching? (2) Who should be formally evaluated? (3) What principles should be followed in the evaluation program? To these three questions we now turn our attention.

1. *Who evaluates?* As a rule all evaluations should be made by those who are concerned with instruction—administrative staff, supervisors, teachers, and pupils. The program should be planned to include assessments by all concerned: reliance on evaluations by one of the groups is inadequate. However, the functions served by the evaluations of each are somewhat different. Administrators evaluate for the administrative purposes of personnel selection, promotion, and dismissal. Supervisors evaluate to help teachers improve their instruction. Teachers' self-evaluations also serve this latter function, while pupil evaluations serve to highlight the teacher's major instructional strengths and weaknesses. It is particularly important in the upper school levels that pupils' assessments be included in the evaluation program. Pupils in high school and college are certainly mature enough to make valid evaluations of instruction, particularly when they are cognizant of the instructional objectives. Pupils are also acutely aware of the effectiveness of a teacher's personal interclass relations and of the climate for learning which the teacher helps create within the classroom.

2. *Who is evaluated?* The quality of the instructional program is not determined solely by the teaching staff. Administrators and supervisors must provide leadership, help plan an effective program, and provide appropriate instructional materials and adequate instructional facilities. Administration exists as a service to the instructional program. When the administrator loads teachers with clerical details, assigns them too heavy a teaching load, or fails to coordinate the program, the inevitable result is deterioration in instructional quality and teacher morale. Therefore, a good evaluation program includes provisions for the evaluation of administrators and supervisors as well as teachers. Administrators and supervisors should be evaluated by teacher committees or the entire teaching staff to forestall any possible administrative reprisals against the teacher-evaluators. Such a safeguard is necessary if the evaluations are to be valid.

3. *What principles?* In the past the assessment of personnel quality stressed the rating approaches and often had a deleterious effect on

uct of his teaching can be evaluated. Evaluation of the teacher certainly should include an appraisal of his intelligence, his preparation, his personal attributes, his attitudes, his emotional stability, and his health.

Assessment of the process of teaching requires the evaluator to possess a thorough knowledge of the total process—planning, objectives, techniques, and execution. Detailed analysis of the total teaching task is certainly a prerequisite to evaluation of the teaching process.[1]

Classroom visitation is an essential part of the evaluation program, and the visits must be carefully planned and initiated. Whenever possible prior to the first visit, a friendly relationship should be established between the supervisor and the teacher so that the teacher doesn't feel that he is being spied upon. It is also best to announce the first visits. Visits should always be carried out courteously. They should be followed by individual conferences to promote a better understanding and rapport and to assist the teacher in understanding his specific problems, although ready-made solutions should be avoided.

Evaluation approaches. Some years ago Averil Barr set up the following categories for teacher evaluation:

1. *The mental-prerequisite approach,* wherein the efficiency of the teacher is inferred from measures of essential knowledges, skills, attitudes, appreciations, and so forth.
2. *The qualities approach,* wherein the teacher's efficiency is inferred from measures of personal, social, emotional, and moral qualities commonly associated with teaching success.
3. *The performance approach,* wherein the efficiency of the teacher is inferred from observation of her behavior and instructional procedures in the classroom.
4. *The change-in-pupils' approach,* wherein the efficiency of the teacher is inferred from measures of changes in pupil growth and achievement.[2]

These four categories plus three additional ones which focus on the learning environment and the instructional media form the basis for Table XXIV. The figure also includes the instruments and techniques suggested for each category.

Teachers are responsible for the selection of instructional materials (category 7), but the evaluator can judge whether the text is being used

[1] Poor teaching is easily described, and excellent teaching takes a variety of forms; however, the list of factors at the end of the chapter sketches the most important characteristics of the excellent teacher.

[2] Averil S. Barr, *et al., Supervision, Democratic Leadership in the Improvement of Learning* (New York: D. Appleton-Century Company, 1957), pp. 371–373.

Table XXIV. APPROACHES TO TEACHER EVALUATION

Approaches	Evaluators	Instruments and Techniques
1. Intellectual-attributes approach	Administrator and preparation institution	1. College transcripts 2. Intelligence tests 3. Achievement tests 4. Personality tests
2. Teacher-quality approach	Administrator, supervisors, pupils, colleagues, or teacher	1. Checklists 2. Rating scales 3. Questionnaires 4. Observation
3. Teacher-performance approach	Administrator, supervisors, colleagues, and teacher	1. Observation guide sheets 2. Pupil participation charts 3. Checklists 4. Rating scales
4. Pupil-change approach	Administrator, supervisor, teacher	1. Achievement batteries 2. Follow-up studies 3. Pupil-parent questionnaires
5. Social climate	Administrator, supervisor, teacher	1. Classroom observation 2. Sociometry
6. Physical environment	Administrator, supervisor	1. Classroom observation 2. *Evaluative Criteria*
7. Instructional media and methods	Administrator, supervisor	1. Classroom observation

to achieve the teacher's stated objectives and whether the teacher is taking advantage of the great variety of instructional materials which are available.

Appraisal of the physical environment (category 6) is discussed in the latter part of this chapter. This evaluation should be made with the aid of such instruments as the *Evaluative Criteria* [3] or Odell's *Standards for the Evaluation of Secondary School Buildings*. These sets of criteria include minimal acceptable standards for such factors as lighting, heating, decor, space, and furnishings.[4]

[3] See "Selected Readings," p. 379.

[4] The reader is referred back to Chapter 8 for a discussion of evaluation of the social climate for learning and to the chapters in Part III for the evaluation of pupil change.

The remaining approaches focus specifically on the teacher. Evaluation of the intellectual attributes of each teacher is a necessary prerequisite to his employment. College transcripts are helpful in this appraisal, but there are some 1400 teacher preparation institutions in the United States with a wide range of entrance requirements and academic standards, and it is folly to accept the bachelor's or master's degree as *prima facie* evidence of a given level of academic achievement and intellectual status. One of the most promising instruments for the appraisal of teachers' achievement and intellectual status is the *National Teachers' Examination* published by Educational Testing Service. This instrument is used in pre-selection in such school districts as San Francisco and as a part of the in-service evaluation program in the state of Florida.

In some fields—e.g., foreign language, art, and music—additional evidence beyond the number of college credits and the grade-point average is desirable. A person may speak and write a foreign language fluently and have but a few college credits while, conversely, one who has amassed numerous credits may lack comparable fluency. In music and art, creativity and skillful, imaginative performance are essential and may not be evident from the record of the transcript.

Rating devices. Instruments for rating teacher's performance fall generally into the following six categories:

1. *Point scales,* which ordinarily consist of a list of qualities commonly associated with good teaching to which point scores have been assigned according to the supposed contributions of each to quality of teaching success.
2. *Graphic scales,* which are similar to point scales except that the degree of control exercised over each item is portrayed graphically.
3. *Diagnostic scales,* which are point scales organized around the different aspects of teaching in such a manner as to reveal levels of attainment with reference to the different characteristics ordinarily associated with teaching success.
4. *Quality scales* are scales in which the different degrees of teaching merit, each described in terms of its characteristic aims, methods, and procedures, are arranged at equal intervals according to a system of scale values from zero merit to perfection.
5. *Man-to-man comparison scales,* on which the judgments about the degree of control exercised by the teacher over the different qualities selected for consideration are derived by comparisons between the teachers rated and named individuals previously judged by the raters to be average, inferior, superior, or what not.

6. *Conduct or performance scales,* in which teaching is measured in terms of results only.[5]

There are literally hundreds of teacher checklists and rating scales in print, but it is probably desirable for each school system to develop its own instruments after examining a representative sample of those available. This approach is suggested for two reasons: (1) it insures widespread staff interest and support and (2) it permits adaptation to the local purposes and unique staff situation. The examples shown in the following pages are not necessarily the best. Rather, they are examples of good instruments which represent several different approaches.

The rating devices are generally based on an analysis of the teaching job. A typical analysis—that of the Summit, New Jersey, staff—includes the duties and responsibilities of the teacher, classified in the following ten categories:

1. Classroom management
2. Character development
3. Curriculum development
4. Daily preparation
5. Knowledge of subject matter
6. Public relations
7. Pupil-teacher relationships
8. School and system-wide effectiveness
9. Techniques of instruction
10. Pupil evaluation [6]

Example 1. The *University of Idaho Student Teacher Rating Scale* is based on analysis of the characteristics of teachers and responsibilities of teaching. It requires the evaluator to rate each characteristic on a five-category scale ranging from "excellent" to "poor." The scale includes the major qualities in four areas: (1) personal qualities, (2) professional and social qualities, (3) classroom management, and (4) techniques of teaching. See Table XXV.

Example 2. An interesting and promising approach is the forced-choice rating scale exemplified by the *Purdue Instructor Performance Indicator* shown in Table XXVI. The forced-choice rating scale is a psychologically scaled instrument requiring considerable experimental work for its

[5] William H. Burton and Leo J. Brueckner, *Supervision a Social Process* (New York: Appleton-Century-Crofts, 1957), p. 344.
[6] "Teacher Merit Plans that Work," *American School Board Journal,* CXXXVI (April 1958), 38.

Table XXV. UNIVERSITY OF IDAHO STUDENT TEACHER RATING SCALE *

E = Excellent G = Good A = Average F = Fair P = Poor

Qualities	E	G	A	F	P
I. *Personal Qualities*					
1. Dress and general neatness	...	...	...	...	...
2. Health and enthusiasm	...	...	...	...	...
3. Poise	...	...	...	...	...
4. Sense of humor	...	...	...	...	...
5. Voice	...	...	...	...	...
6. Attitude toward work	...	...	...	...	...
7. Dependability	...	...	...	...	...
8. Initiative and self-reliance	...	...	...	...	...
9. Leadership	...	...	...	...	...
II. *Professional and Social Qualities*					
1. Social adaptability	...	...	...	...	...
2. Cooperation and loyalty	...	...	...	...	...
3. Enthusiasm	...	...	...	...	...
4. Professional interest and attitude	...	...	...	...	...
5. Educational background useful in teaching	...	...	...	...	...
6. Use of English	...	...	...	...	...
7. Interest in room and school activities	...	...	...	...	...
8. Is interesting and interested	...	...	...	...	...
9. Accepts responsibility	...	...	...	...	...
III. *Classroom Management*					
1. Classroom control	...	...	...	...	...
2. Interest in pupils	...	...	...	...	...
3. Care of room and equipment	...	...	...	...	...
IV. *Technique of Teaching*					
1. Lesson plans and daily preparation	...	...	...	...	...
2. Ability to create and hold interest of pupil	...	...	...	...	...
3. Uses varied procedures	...	...	...	...	...
4. Skill in leading class discussion	...	...	...	...	...
5. Attention to individual needs	...	...	...	...	...
6. Good use of questioning	...	...	...	...	...
7. Skill in directing study periods	...	...	...	...	...
8. Scholarship	...	...	...	...	...
9. Economical use of time	...	...	...	...	...
10. Growth in teaching personality and technique	...	...	...	...	...

COOPERATING TEACHER_____

* Reprinted by permission of the University of Idaho, Moscow, Idaho.

construction since it is presented in a tetrad form with four statements in each category, two of which are normally valid and two invalid, although all must have face validity and appear to apply.

EVALUATION OF THE CURRICULUM

Nineteenth-century education is not suitable for the twentieth-century world, and it is much less suitable for the youth whose adult years will turn the corner from the twentieth to the twenty-first century. Prognostication and anticipation of the shape of things to come is a most neglected but a most important curricular concern of the educator. The *status quo* will not abide, and many skills suitable for the contemporary scene will be obsolete in the adult world of today's pupils. It is not too unrealistic to speculate on the possibility that electronic computers will alleviate the need for arithmetic skills; or that television will make reading skills obsolete; or that dictaphones and automatic typewriters will eliminate the need for handwriting skill; or that easy, rapid transportation will eliminate the language barriers and result in a universal polyglot language; or that total automation will void the need for many vocational skills.

The school curriculum must not continue to grow by the mere process of accretion until it becomes a patchwork quilt in which nothing is discarded, replaced, or changed except by the erosion of age. Each prospective new addition must be carefully evaluated in light of its contribution to the school philosophy and objectives and weighed against all the other courses in the curriculum to determine whether it should be added, rejected, or used to replace other less important courses. Educators must ask, and answer after careful consideration, such questions as the following: Are institutions other than the school better equipped to serve lunches? Who appropriately should handle the medical and dental problems of children? How far can the school go in insuring the mental health of children? What responsibility has the school in providing entertainment for parents and children? Who should instruct children in driver training? How much vocational training should be given? What social skills should schools teach? Are some of the academic areas obsolete for modern living? Should sex education be included in school programs? How much religious and ethical training should be given?

Schools can ill afford to undertake all the educational responsibilities traditionally handled by such social institutions as the family, the

Table XXVI. THE PURDUE INSTRUCTOR PERFORMANCE INDICATOR

Directions:

This rating scale consists of twelve groups or blocks containing four statements each. The statements are descriptive of instructors and their teaching behavior or activities. From each group or block of four statements you are to CHOOSE TWO statements that best describe or apply to the instructor being rated.

Indicate the two statements chosen from each group or block by filling in the pairs of vertical lines to the right of each group.

Samples:	A	B	C	D
	| |	| |	| |	| |

1A Sincere
1B Speaks Well
1C Easy to Get Along With
1D Is Very Diligent

	A	B	C	D
	| |	| |	| |	| |

2A Is Interested in Subject Matter
   He (She) Teaches
2B Connects Lectures with Textbook Used
2C Willing to Help Those Slow to
   Learn
2D Uses a Variety of Teaching
   Techniques

From John H. Smedeker and H. H. Remmers, *Purdue Instructor Performance Indicator* (Lafayette, Ind.: Purdue University, 1960). Reprinted by permission of H. H. Remmers.

church, and the community. Indeed there is already so much proliferation of curricular offerings in many schools that it is impossible to stretch the financial and human resources enough to do an effective job in any area, conjuring up the ridiculous picture of the teacher as a Don Quixote galloping off in all directions and gallantly attacking the windmills of frustration and ineffectiveness.

Informal and formal evaluation. Informal evaluation of the school program is a constant concern of the staff and the patrons. The supervisory program is primarily concerned with evaluation and improvement of instruction; and most of the in-service committees of the staff deal with informal evaluations of the curriculum, the instructional materials, or the purposes of the school. Their informal evaluations, however, are not extensive; and evaluation is probably not the primary purpose of these groups. In fact the limited evaluation which is made is probably used to justify new plans or suggestions which the particular group hopes to implement. Such informal evaluation, even though it is often poorly planned and executed, has value; and every school system should have a continuous program of informal evaluation, with administrative coordination to insure adequate planning and to prevent the program from focusing on too limited an aspect of the total program. Such informal evaluation is obviously most valuable when the school staff has a well-formulated educational philosophy as the referent for program evaluation.

In contrast to informal evaluation, formal evaluation is often carried out by a visiting committee of experts or by a staff-lay committee specifically charged with the task. Such a committee is expected to spend considerable time in collecting data before completing the evaluation. Their evaluation report is presented in a written form which is frequently supplemented with an oral report or hearing. School accreditation surveys or school building surveys are typical examples of such formal evaluations. Formal evaluations generally focus on school facilities, school program, school personnel, or on all these aspects of the school system.

Evaluation of school programs. Those responsible for the evaluation of school programs should keep in mind the legal and extralegal pressures on the curriculum; as well as the sociological, demographic, and political pressures discussed earlier. In addition they must be aware of the vast areas of knowledge from which curricular selections must be made. It is also important that they keep in mind the nature of the locality in which the school operates.

An apt parallel can be drawn between the desirable procedure for constructing a good measurement test and constructing a good school program. The first step in each is careful planning. In test planning the content areas and the objectives to be measured are identified, whereas in curriculum planning the behavioral objectives and educational philosophy to be implemented are formulated. Without this step, measurement would be haphazard and the nature of the school curriculum might well be no more than the combined result of tradition, capricious whim, and the current qualifications of the staff. Failure to plan carefully and continuously is probably the greatest single weakness of American schools.

The second step in the process is the construction of the instrument, the test or program of studies designed to implement the plan represented in the objectives and philosophy. This is the tangible result of the plan drawn up in step one, for it is just as difficult to evaluate the curriculum without the objectives and philosophy which underlie it as it is to evaluate a test without examining the table of specifications and the instructional objectives. An instrument which is widely used in school accreditation to help in the evaluation of secondary school programs is the *Evaluative Criteria.* Some of the criteria used in the instrument to aid in evaluating the program of studies are shown in Figure 16.1.

The third step is that of evaluation; in addition to the test it may also include such procedures as item analysis, expert judgment, and statistical analyses. In curriculum evaluation it is essential that the evaluation be a continuous process. It is also extremely important in curricular evaluation that as much data as possible be collected to insure validity. This data may be collected through testing programs, classroom observations, follow-up studies of pupils, opinionnaires to parents and pupils, and perhaps independent school surveys. Evaluative validity in curriculum study is concerned with how effectively the philosophy or plan is implemented, and how well the plan fits the needs of the pupils in the environmental situations in which they live or to which they aspire.

Figure 16.1. GENERAL CRITERIA FOR EVALUATION OF THE PROGRAM OF STUDIES TAKEN FROM THE EVALUATIVE CRITERIA

I. GENERAL PRINCIPLES

CHECKLIST

The program of studies

( ) 1. Is based upon an analysis of the educational needs of youth.
( ) 2. Provides a wide variety of experiences to meet both the common and individual educational needs of youth.
( ) 3. Is planned to help meet both present and probable future needs of pupils.
( ) 4. Provides opportunities for pupils as well as staff members to participate in the planning and development of curricular activities.
( ) 5. Provides for relating subject-matter fields to life problems of pupils.
( ) 6. Emphasizes critical and thoughtful approaches to present-day problems.
( ) 7. Provides opportunities for experiences especially adapted to the superior or advanced pupils.

( ) 8. Provides opportunities for experiences especially adapted to slow-learning pupils.

( ) 9. Provides organized sequences of courses carrying on through several grades.

( ) 10. Provides for coordination of educational experiences within each grade.

( ) 11. Places emphasis upon broad concepts taught for transfer value.

( ) 12. Is flexible in time allotments to meet individual pupil requirements (e.g., variation in number of periods for elective subjects, periods allotted to special-help and remedial work, or time devoted to pupil-initiated course work).

( ) 13. Provides for the evaluation of pupil achievement in the program in terms of each individual's aptitudes and abilities.

( ) 14. Recognizes the contributions made by the pupil activity program.

( ) 15. Encourages enlargement and enrichment of the pupil's scope of interests.

( ) 16.

( ) 17.

EVALUATIONS

( ) *a. How effectively are these general principles practiced in meeting the needs of youth of the community?*

COMMENTS

From *Evaluative Criteria* (Washington, D. C.: National Study of Secondary School Standards, 1960). Reprinted by permission of the National Study of Secondary School Evaluation.

The school accreditation survey, mentioned earlier as an example of formal evaluation, is a good model to follow in evaluating a school program. The accreditation surveys utilize the *Evaluative Criteria* as the evaluative instrument. As a prerequisite to formal evaluation by the visiting accreditation committee, the school staff is asked to conduct a self-evaluation directing their consideration to all aspects of the school program, school staff, and school plant. When this self-evaluation is carefully done, it involves all the staff members on working committees and takes from six months to a year to complete. This self-evaluation should then be followed up with the evaluative survey by a visiting committee. Although a complete discussion of accreditation surveys is beyond the scope of this book, further discussion of the evaluative procedures can be read in the manual of the *Evaluative Criteria*. Similar criteria are also available for the junior high school, and the state education departments in states such as Texas have published elementary school criteria.

Since lay people in the community are most interested in schools, they can with professional help contribute significantly to school evaluation. The Parent-Teacher Association, the National Education Association, and the former National Citizens Council for Better Schools have numerous checklists and suggestions for school evaluation. In addition texts on public relations suggest ways of involving lay advisory committees in school evaluation.

Certainly insufficient use of testing programs has been made as a basis for evaluating the effectiveness of the total school program, as a basis for planning program changes, or as a basis for assessing the effectiveness of changes which have already been made.

School surveys. A resource which is often utilized in evaluating school plants and in helping plan building programs but one which has been frequently neglected in evaluating school programs is the school survey by educational specialists in state departments of education and colleges and universities throughout the country. The members of such survey teams are generally paid for their services, but the fees are nominal; and the evaluation and recommendations are objective and professional since the members are not directly connected with the school system being surveyed.

In such surveys one month to several months may be spent in collecting data from test programs, follow-up studies, financial records, spot maps for enrollment projections, opinionnaires, school plant evaluations, and community composition and growth studies. After such data have been collected, an evaluation of the quality of the program is made and a summary of the anticipated needs is prepared. Such evaluation teams generally present the evaluation and the recommendations in a detailed written report for consideration by the school staff, school board, and community members. The surveys are often culminated with a public presentation of the report or presentation at an open board meeting.

Surveys, whether made by the school staff or by a professional team, should follow the principles recommended by Herrick and his colleagues:

1. The study should be conducted and reported as an impartial overview of the needs of the entire school district.

2. The procedures used in the collection and analysis of data should be technically sound and accurately used.

3. The survey should be so conducted and reported as to be relatively easy to keep up to date.

4. The recommendations should be of such a nature that the resulting physical plant most effectively facilitates the desired school program.

5. The recommendations should provide adequate capacity for housing and anticipated future enrollments.

6. The recommendations should take into account any existing or projected plans for the future development of the community and region.

7. The recommendations should include or be based on a stated long-range plan, as well as plans for the immediate future, and should provide a reasonable degree of flexibility to meet unforeseen changes in the future.

8. The recommendations should be of such a nature as to provide the most value to the community for each dollar spent.

9. The recommendations should be straightforward and unequivocal and clearly supported by data.

10. The recommendations should propose improvements which have a reasonable chance of acceptance without sacrificing principles of good planning.[7]

EVALUATION OF SCHOOL PLANT

Good school buildings do not insure quality in education, but the rising tide of pupil enrollment must be accommodated in reasonably satisfactory facilities; or standards of quality will be inundated in the quest for makeshift, short-term solutions to immediate housing problems. The easiest aspect of a school system to evaluate is the school plant. This is perhaps the reason why so many school surveys are confined to an analysis of school plant needs. Nevertheless the process of evaluating school plant facilities is not so simple as it would appear at first glance. It must be remembered that the school plant is the physical embodiment of the educational program, the concrete essence as it were of the educational plan. Therefore, it is insufficient to judge merely whether the school buildings are good or bad, but rather the judgment must be whether the buildings are good or bad as facilities for housing the educational program which is being carried on.

There are a number of score cards which are useful in collecting data concerning the adequacy of school buildings as compared to generally

[7] Herrick, John H., Ralph D. McLeary, Wilfred F. Clapp, and Walter F. Bogner, *From School Program to School Plant* (New York: Henry Holt and Company, 1956), pp. 23–24.

accepted standards for school facilities. The use of these score cards in building surveys improves the objectivity in data collection and provides a standard against which the buildings can be compared. An example of such a score card is Odell's *Standards for the Evaluation of Secondary School Buildings.* The score card is based on a 1,000-point scale, and the adequacy of a building can be judged by the total number of points which it receives during a survey. For example, buildings which receive 850 to 1,000 points are considered to be in "excellent" condition. Those buildings which receive 700 to 849 points are in "good" condition, but certain desirable features are lacking or inadequate. Those buildings which receive 550 to 699 points are in "average" condition; and although the deficiencies are more numerous and usually more serious than in good buildings, many of them can be corrected with relative economy. Those buildings which receive 400 to 549 points are in poor condition, and continued use of the building is debatable if it receives fewer than 500 points. If the building receives fewer than 400 points, it is definitely unsatisfactory and should be abandoned at the earliest possible time.

The first page of this score card is reproduced in Figure 16.2. In this score card each aspect of the building and the site is assigned a specific number of points, and the evaluator must decide how adequately the facility meets each criterion and on that basis assign it a proportion or all of the possible points. Detailed discussion of the criteria to be met for each division of the score card is included in the handbook to aid the evaluator in assigning the rating. The following quotation from the handbook concerning the nature of soil and surface for the school grounds is an example of the information which the evaluator will use in assigning the score card rating for that aspect of the school site.

> *Nature of soil and surface.* No type of soil and surface appears to be completely satisfactory for a school site. Probably the best is sandy loam, which dries quickly, is not very muddy when wet, allows surface drainage without erosion, is not liable to injure pupils who fall upon it, and is sufficiently fertile for good turf, lawns, and shrubbery. If this is not available, oil treatment or stabilized soil is probably the best substitute. Rosin, cement, or asphalt may be used for stabilizing. Except for running tracks, drives, and other special areas, surfaces covered with cinders, gravel, and coarse crushed rock should be avoided. Limestone screenings, treated with calcium chloride, provide a fairly good surface for most games. Some paved area, preferably adjacent to the gymnasium, is a good feature. For many games, cork, rubber chip or asbestos paving is best, but for a few

						Subtotal	Total
I. Site							120
A. Location						44	
1. Accessibility	0	6	12	18	24		
2. Environment	0	5	10	15	20		
B. Physical features						48	
1. Size	0	6	12	18	24		
2. Form	0	3	6	9	12		
3. Nature of soil and surface	0	3	6	9	12		
C. Improvements						28	
1. Type, number, and arrangement	0	5	10	15	20		
2. Landscaping	0	2	4	6	8		
II. Gross structure							160
A. Orientation	0	4	8	12	16	16	
B. Architectural style	0	2	4	6	8	8	
C. Educational plan						36	
1. Flexibility	0	4	8	12	16		
2. Expansibility	0	3	6	9	12		
3. Economy	0	2	4	6	8		
D. External structure						48	
1. Foundations	0	2	4	6	8		
2. Walls	0	2	4	6	8		
3. Roof	0	2	4	6	8		
4. Chimney	0	1	2	3	4		
5. Height	0	1	2	3	4		
6. Entrances and exits	0	2	4	6	8		
7. Condition and appearance	0	2	4	6	8		
E. Internal structure						52	
1. Stairways	0	3	6	9	12		
2. Corridors	0	3	6	9	12		
3. Lobbies	0	1	2	3	4		
4. Vestibules	0	1	2	3	4		
5. Walls	0	2	4	6	8		
6. Basement	0	1	2	3	4		
7. Condition and appearance	0	2	4	6	8		
III. Academic classrooms							156
A. Construction						108	
1. Size	0	6	12	18	24		
2. Shape	0	3	6	9	12		
3. Windows	0	4	8	12	16		

Figure 16.2. SCORE CARD FOR SECONDARY SCHOOL BUILDINGS

From C. W. Odell, *Standards for the Evaluation of Secondary School Buildings* (Ann Arbor, Michigan: Edwards Brothers, Inc., 1950), p. 11. Reprinted by permission of Professor Odell.

unlikely to result in pupils falling concrete may be employed. Rock asphalt also has many desirable qualities. Such surfaces can be used more quickly after heavy rain than can soil and are excellent for some games. The best subsoil is sand or gravel. Clay should be avoided unless there is a thick layer of sand or gravel above it. Surface soil should be nonalkaline, non-erosive, and free of any considerable amount of decaying organic matter.[8]

The use of a score card for evaluating the school plant does not constitute an evaluation, since this is but one of the steps in collecting the data on which the evaluation is made. There must in addition be data collected concerning the effective use of buildings, the anticipated building need, and the financial ability of the district before evaluations and recommendations can be made.

The data for efficiency of building use can be collected through a pupil-station and a period-use study. Ideally all classrooms and all pupil stations would be used each period during the day; however, in practice, particularly in the secondary school, the rooms and pupil stations are rarely used more than 80 percent of the available time. This low usage is due to the nature of the program, which includes elective courses of varying sizes, as well as the inefficiency of class scheduling and class sectioning of some high school principals. It is not unusual for survey teams to find by such a study that a facility thought to be overcrowded could accommodate a greater number of pupils by more efficient class scheduling.

The anticipated building need can best be arrived at by projecting the school enrollment over a period of ten to fifteen years. Both the data for projecting school enrollment and those for assessing financial ability are readily available from the administrative records.

Briefly, then, the steps which should be followed in the school plant evaluation include the following:

1. Collection of data through score cards and examination of facilities, enrollment records, and financial records.
2. Survey of needs and evaluation of the plant—including the efficiency of use of buildings, the desirability of replacing or remodeling facilities, and the appropriateness of plant for the present and the future educational task.

[8] C. W. Odell, *Standards for the Evaluation of Secondary School Buildings* (Ann Arbor, Michigan: Edwards Brothers, Inc., 1950), p. 11. Reprinted by permission of Professor Odell.

3. Formulation of written proposals to meet the long-term educational needs of the school system.
4. Formal presentation of the proposals at an open board meeting or public hearing.

SPECULATION AND SUMMARY

It is apparent that many changes in our current educational system will continue as trends in the future. Such changes are necessary responses to the complexities of contemporary life. The school system in a dynamic society must itself be dynamic if it is to meet the multitude of needs of the new generations in a yet undefined future. At the risk of being wrong the author takes this opportunity to preview some of the future developments which seem imminent in education:

1. The school day will be lengthened to eight hours and the school year to 200 school days.
2. There will be a new type of summer school which is available to all pupils and which will offer additional subjects to enrich their programs.
3. There will be more provisions in the curriculum for the talented pupil which will permit him to complete an enriched program of elementary and secondary education more rapidly than the average pupil.
4. There will be higher educational standards required of teachers; the six-year college program will become the norm for teacher education.
5. The cost of education will continue to rise with a broadened program and with the general recognition of the value of education as a means of survival in a complex, competitive world.
6. Different organizational patterns will evolve for the elementary and the secondary school as they utilize such concepts as audio-visual teaching, machine teaching, and team teaching.
7. There will be many more junior colleges, which will help to take some of the educational burden off the colleges and universities as more and more youth elect to stay in school for a longer period of time.
8. The night school and postgraduate enrollment will increase as adults with more leisure time recognize their need for additional education.
9. There will be more concern in the school for the social, emotional, and physical development of the pupils without slighting their intellectual development.
10. There will be many specialists added to the teaching staffs of schools —doctors, psychologists, psychiatrists, guidance workers.

These are but a few of the changes which seem most imminent. There will be many other changes of which we presently have little inkling.

We have noted that improved transportation and communication have reduced psychocultural distance among peoples of the world without greatly increasing their understanding. Many of the real issues and problems of the present and future are psychological and cultural. It is apparent that social inventiveness must keep abreast of technological advance if such problems are to be solved. The nostalgic preoccupation in many classrooms with today's and yesterday's problems will not prepare pupils for tomorrow.

The educational changes which have been anticipated call for much critical evaluation—evaluation of course offerings and evaluation of the human resources, of the school, and of the teaching. Only thorough and continuous evaluation based always on as much objective data as can be collected offers an adequate basis for the prognostication and change characteristic of a dynamic, successful educational system. Without this evaluation, changes in the program will be haphazard and capricious, since they are based on no more than intuition or ignorance. In such a changing world as this the time is too short to procrastinate, for tomorrow is here before yesterday has caught up with today. The excuse that we know how to educate better than we do is poor condolence to those whose education is loaded with solutions to yesterday's issues when they must struggle to cope with tomorrow's problems. Honest, unemotional evaluation, though it takes more courage than many possess, is the only avenue which can bypass the detours and open the bottlenecks to desirable changes.

Good teaching is the essential ingredient in quality education. In the hands of the poor teacher newer teaching strategies and excellent instructional materials do little to improve the quality of education—a fact which is truly reflected by valid evaluation. Thus, it seems appropriate as a final word to review briefly the qualities of the best teacher.

CHARACTERISTICS OF THE BEST TEACHERS

1. *The best teachers get the best results.* The changes which they make in pupils are dramatic and lasting.
2. *The best teachers do effective planning.* They formulate specific, worthwhile teaching objectives and select appropriate instructional techniques and materials to achieve those objectives.
3. *The best teachers vary their methods and course content to suit individual differences within their classes.* The principle of discovering

the learning status of each pupil and proceeding with teaching from that point is frequently recommended, generally accepted, but rarely implemented. It is the best teacher who takes the additional time and trouble to make plans to implement the principle.

4. *The best teachers give consistent, reasonable, and justifiable class assignments which contribute to the attainment of school objectives.* Pupils need to work to learn efficiently; however busy work or repetitious drill over previously learned material is neither useful nor appreciated when its function in attaining goals is questionable.

5. *The best teachers are intelligent and have acquired subject matter competence and high level communication skills.* Teaching is a communicative art dependent upon skillful use of language as well as an adequate subject-matter background.

6. *The best teachers use frequent evaluation to help them ANALYZE the strengths and weaknesses of their pupils.* Furthermore, they keep adequate records of both informal and standardized test results. They are competent in statistically summarizing and analyzing test results as a basis for planning an instructional program which includes remedial and enrichment activities in appropriate situations.

7. *The best teachers are effective in human relations.* They are friendly, considerate, and impartial in the classroom, and they get along well with pupils, colleagues, and lay people. It is apparent that they understand and like people.

8. *The best teachers' classrooms show evidence of a comfortable physical, emotional, and social atmosphere.*

9. *The best teachers give pupils enough freedom to permit them to pursue their interests and to develop self-direction.* Pupils cannot achieve independent adulthood without practice in making their own decisions, and democracy in action in the classroom prepares the way for adult democratic citizenship.

10. *The best teachers manage their classrooms effectively.* Their classes are orderly and purposeful with efficient handling of such routine matters as passing out materials, collecting lunch money, and taking attendance.

11. *The best teachers are flexible enough to adapt to a variety of situations;* however, they conform to the necessary school policies and regulations without giving up their individuality.

12. *The best teachers are cooperative participants in the planning and direction of school activities.* The teacher cannot confine herself to the classroom job but must in addition contribute to the success of the school's nonclassroom activities.

13. *The best teachers understand their community, participate in its activities, and use its resources in instruction.* Each community has unique needs which call for adaptations in the school program. There

are also in each community a variety of resources which the capable instructor can use to enrich the classroom experiences of his pupils.

DISCUSSION QUESTIONS AND PROBLEMS

1. Suggest the criteria against which you feel teachers should be evaluated. Who should make the evaluations?
2. Construct a rating scale for use in evaluating teaching.
3. Visit a nearby school building and evaluate it, using a score card such as that suggested in this chapter.
4. Construct an opinionnaire which could be submitted to parents and/or pupils as part of an evaluation program.
5. Read several articles critical of American education—e.g., articles by Arthur Bestor, Hymen Rickover, or James B. Conant—and critically analyze the articles on the basis of adequacy of data, validity of the evaluation, and justification for the conclusions.
6. Identify weaknesses and strengths in the educational program of the school which you attended which could have been identified by a comprehensive evaluation program.
7. In a comprehensive school evaluation, what kinds of data should be collected? What type of instruments should be used? Who should do the evaluating?

SELECTED READINGS

Burton, William H. and Leo J. Brueckner. *Supervision: A Social Process.* 3rd ed. New York: Appleton-Century-Crofts, 1955. Chapter 11 deals with the evaluation of instruction and teaching effectiveness. This is a comprehensive coverage.

Dropkin, Stan, Harold Full, and Ernest Schwartz. *Contemporary American Education.* New York: The Macmillan Company, 1965. This book of readings includes numerous selections which can help give the reader insight into the total social context within which the school operates.

Evaluative Criteria. Washington, D. C.: Cooperative Study of Secondary School Standards, 1960. This is the complete manual and criteria used for the accreditation of secondary schools in this country.

Haan, Aubrey. *Education for the Open Society.* Boston: Allyn and Bacon, 1962. This is an able description of the development and fruition of education in our democratic, open society. The author aptly contrasts this system with that in the closed society.

Herrick, John H., Ralph D. McLeary, Wilfred F. Clapp, and Walter F. Bogner. *From School Program to School Plant.* New York: Henry Holt and Company, 1956. Chapters 2, 3, 4, and 5 provide a comprehensive coverage of the school facilities survey. Part II of the book discusses standards for classrooms, site, etc.

Kneller, George F. *Foundations of Education.* New York: John Wiley and Sons, 1963. Part II and Part IV give an excellent overview of American education, its problems, and its social setting.

Odell, C. W. *Standards for the Evaluation of Secondary School Buildings.* Ann Arbor, Michigan: Edwards Brothers, Inc., 1950. This is one of the several score cards and sets of standards which are useful in evaluating school buildings.

Appendix A

MAJOR PUBLISHERS AND DISTRIBUTORS OF STANDARDIZED TESTS

Acorn Publishing Company, Rockville Centre, Long Island, New York 11570

American Guidance Service, Inc., Publishers' Building, Circle Pines, Minnesota 55014

Bureau of Educational Research and Service, Extension Division, State University of Iowa, Iowa City, Iowa 52240

California Test Bureau, Del Monte Research Park, Monterey, California 93940

Consulting Psychologists Press, Inc., 270 Town and Country Village, Palo Alto, California 94301

Educational Test Bureau, 720 Washington Street, S. E., Minneapolis, Minnesota 55414

Educational Testing Service, 20 Nassau Street, Princeton, New Jersey 08540

C. A. Gregory Company, 345 Calhoun Street, Cincinnati, Ohio 45219

Harcourt, Brace & World, Inc., 757 Third Avenue, New York, New York 10017

Houghton Mifflin Company, 2 Park Street, Boston, Massachusetts 02107

The Psychological Corporation, 304 East 45th Street, New York, New York 10017

Public School Publishing Company, 345 Calhoun Street, Cincinnati, Ohio 45219

Purdue Measurement and Evaluation Instruments, University Bookstore, 360 State Street, West Lafayette, Indiana 47906

Science Research Associates, Inc., 259 East Erie Street, Chicago, Illinois 60611

Sheridan Supply Company, P. O. Box 837, Beverly Hills, California 90213

C. H. Stoelting Company, 424 North Homan Avenue, Chicago, Illinois 60624

Western Psychological Services, 10655 Santa Monica Boulevard, Los Angeles, California 90025

Appendix B

BOOKS ON EDUCATIONAL MEASUREMENT AND EVALUATION

There are literally hundreds of good books in the field of educational measurement and evaluation. And while the list suggested below leaves out the names of such prominent men as Cattell, Thurstone, Spearman, the books included do give a good coverage of the field and could well be the basis for a more complete professional library. In addition to these books it would also be desirable to subscribe to one or more of the journals in the field—e.g., the *Journal of Educational Measurement*.

Ahmann, J. Stanley, and Marvin D. Glock. *Evaluating Pupil Growth*. 3rd ed. Boston: Allyn and Bacon, 1967.

Ahmann, J. Stanley, Marvin D. Glock, and Helen L. Wardberg. *Evaluating Elementary School Pupils*. Boston: Allyn and Bacon, 1960.

Amos, Jimmy R., *et al. Statistical Concepts: A Basic Program*. New York: Harper & Row, 1965.

Anastasi, Anne. *Psychological Testing*. 2nd ed. New York: The Macmillan Company, 1961.

Bass, Bernard M., and Irwin A. Berg. *Objective Approaches to Personality Assessment*. New York: D. Van Nostrand Co., 1959.

Bloom, Benjamin S. (ed.). *Taxonomy of Educational Objectives, Handbook I: Cognitive Domain*. New York: David McKay Company, 1956.

Bradfield, James, and H. Stewart Moredock. *Measurement and Evaluation in Education*. New York: The Macmillan Company, 1957.

Brueckner, Leo J., and Guy L. Bond. *The Diagnosis and Treatment of Learning Difficulties*. New York: Appleton-Century-Crofts, 1955.

Cronbach, Lee J. *Essentials of Psychological Testing*. 2nd ed. New York: Harper & Row, 1960.

Ebel, Robert L. *Measuring Educational Achievement*. Englewood Cliffs, New Jersey: Prentice-Hall, 1965.

Findley, Warren G. (ed.). *The Impact and Improvement of School Testing Programs*, Sixty-Second Yearbook of the National Society for the Study of Education. Chicago: The University of Chicago Press, 1963.

Freeman, Frank S. *Theory and Practice of Psychological Testing.* 3rd ed. New York: Holt, Rinehart, and Winston, 1962.

Furst, Edward J. *Constructing Evaluation Instruments.* New York: Longmans, Green and Company, 1958.

Garrett, Henry E. *Testing for Teachers.* 2nd ed. New York: American Book Company, 1965.

Gerberich, J. Raymond. *Specimen Objective Test Items.* New York: Longmans, Green and Company, 1956.

Gerberich, J. Raymond, Harry A. Greene, and Albert W. Jorgensen. *Measurement and Evaluation in the Modern School.* New York: David McKay Company, 1962.

Goldman, Leo. *Using Tests in Counseling.* New York: Appleton-Century-Crofts, 1961.

Green, John A. *Teacher-Made Tests.* New York: Harper & Row, 1963.

Guilford, J. P. *Fundamental Statistics in Psychology and Education.* 3rd ed. New York: McGraw-Hill Book Company, 1956.

––––––. *The Nature of Human Intelligence.* New York: McGraw-Hill Book Company, 1967.

Henry, Nelson S. (ed.). *The Measurement of Understanding,* Forty-Fifth Yearbook of the National Society for the Study of Education. Chicago: The Society, 1946.

Jackson, Douglas N., and Samuel Messick (eds.). *Problems in Human Assessment.* New York: McGraw-Hill Book Company, 1967.

Krathwohl, David R., *et al. Taxonomy of Educational Objectives, Handbook II: Affective Domain.* New York: David McKay Company, 1964.

Lindquist, E. F. (ed.). *Educational Measurement.* Washington, D. C.: American Council on Education, 1951.

Lindvall, C. M. *Testing and Evaluation: An Introduction.* New York: Harcourt, Brace & World, 1961.

Lyman, Howard B. *Test Scores and What They Mean.* Englewood Cliffs, N. J.: Prentice-Hall, 1963.

Magnusson, David. *Test Theory.* Reading, Mass.: Addison-Wesley Publishing Company, 1966.

Manuel, Herschel T. *Elementary Statistics for Teachers.* New York: American Book Company, 1962.

Pettit, Lincoln. *How to Study and Take Exams.* New York: John F. Rider Publications, 1960.

Remmers, H. H., N. L. Gage, and J. Francis Rummel. *A Practical Introduction to Measurement and Evaluation.* New York: Harper & Row, 1965.

Shaw, Marvin E. and Jack M. Wright. *Scales for the Measurement of Attitudes.* New York: McGraw-Hill Book Company, 1967.

Smith, Eugene R. and Ralph W. Tyler. *Appraising and Recording Student Progress.* New York: Harper and Brothers, 1942.

Smith, Fred M. and Sam Adams. *Educational Measurement for the Classroom Teacher.* New York: Harper & Row, 1966.

Stanley, Julian C. *Measurement in Today's Schools.* 4th ed. Englewood Cliffs, N. J.: Prentice-Hall, 1964.

Stodola, Quentin and Kalmer Stordahl. *Basic Educational Tests and Measurement.* Chicago, Ill.: Science Research Associates, 1967.

Stern, George G., Morris I. Stein, and Benjamin S. Bloom. *Methods in Personality Assessment.* Glencoe, Ill.: The Free Press, 1956.

Thorndike, R. L. and Elizabeth Hagen. *Measurement and Evaluation in Psychology and Education.* 2nd ed. New York: John Wiley & Sons, 1961.

Travers, Robert M. W. *How to Make Achievement Tests.* New York: The Odyssey Press, 1950.

Tyler, Leona E. *The Psychology of Human Differences.* New York: Appleton-Century-Crofts, 1956.

————. *Tests and Measurements.* Englewood Cliffs, N. J.: Prentice-Hall, 1963.

Wallis, W. Allen and Harry V. Roberts. *The Nature of Statistics.* New York: Collier Books, 1962.

Wandt, Edwin and Gerald W. Brown. *Essentials of Educational Evaluation.* New York: Henry Holt & Company, 1957.

Willgoose, Carl E. *Evaluation in Health Education and Physical Education.* New York: McGraw-Hill Book Company, 1961.

Wood, Dorothy Adkins. *Test Construction Development and Interpretation of Achievement Tests.* Columbus, Ohio: Charles E. Merrill Books, 1960.

Wrightstone, J. Wayne, Joseph Justman, and Irving Robbins. *Evaluation in Modern Education.* New York: American Book Company, 1956.

Index